LEARNING IN CHAOS

IMPROVING HUMAN PERFORMANCE SERIES

Series Editor: Jack Phillips, Ph.D.

Accountability in Human Resource Management
Jack Phillips

The Adult Learner, 5th Edition
Malcolm Knowles, Elwood Holton, and Richard A. Swanson

Bottom-Line Training
Donald J. Ford

The Global Advantage
Michael J. Marquardt

Handbook of Training Evaluation and Measurement Methods
3rd Edition
Jack Phillips

HR to the Rescue
Edward M. Mone and Manuel London

HRD Survival Skills
Jessica Levant

HRD Trends Worldwide
Jack Phillips

Learning in Chaos
James Hite Jr.

The Power of 360° Feedback
David A. Waldman and Leanne E. Atwater

Return on Investment in Training and
Performance Improvement Programs
Jack Phillips

Technology-Based Training
Serge Ravet and Maureen Layte

Gulf Publishing Company
Houston, Texas

LEARNING

JAMES HITE JR.

IN CHAOS

Improving Human Performance in

Today's Fast-Changing,

Volatile Organizations

**IMPROVING
HUMAN
PERFORMANCE
SERIES**

LEARNING IN CHAOS

Gulf Publishing Company
Book Division
P.O. Box 2608 □ Houston, Texas 77252-2608

10 9 8 7 6 5 4 3 2 1

Library of Congress Cataloging-in-Publication Data
Hite, James Austin, 1946–
    Learning in chaos : improving human performance in today's fast-changing, volatile organizations / James Hite Jr.
        p.   cm.
    Includes index.
    ISBN 0-88415-427-0 (alk. paper)
    1. Organizational learning.   2. Organizational change.
3. Performance.   I. Title.
HD58.82.H527   1999
658.4´06—dc21   99-36243
                                                       CIP

Printed in the United States of America.
Printed on acid-free paper (∞).

In memory of
Pearle Wheeler Hite and
James Austin Hite

Contents

PART II: COMPLEXITY AND CHAOS

Chapter 4

Classical Chaos 54

What Is Chaos? 56. The Mythology of Chaos, 56.
Classical Chaos and Cosmology, 58. Classical Chaos and
Early Science, 62. Classical Chaos and the Collective
Unconscious, 66. Classical Chaos and Organizational
Systems, 73. References, 74.

Chapter 5

Technical Chaos 76

Introduction, 76. Significant Influences on NDS, 80.
Influences from Physics, 80. Influence of Mathematics, 83.
Influence from a Community of Learning, 85. Influences
from Biology, 86. Definitions, 86. Nonlinear Dynamical
Systems, 87. Chaos Theory, 88. Other Characteristics of
Chaos, 94. Phase Space, 95. Bifurcation, 96. Attractors, 99.
Fractals, 103. Complex Adaptive Systems, 105. Juxtaposition
of Classical and Technical Chaos, 111. References, 113.

Chapter 6

Extended Applications 115

Introduction, 115. Social Sciences, 116. Psychology, 123.
References, 129.

Chapter 7

Nonlinear Dynamical Organizational Systems 131

Introduction, 131. Organizational Chaos, 131. Networks and
Creativity, 134. Leadership and Human Behavior, 136.
Management, 141. Self-organization in Systems, 143.
A Loop Toward Reality, 146. References, 150.

PART III: OPEN LEARNING AND LEARNING SUPPORT

PART IV: NOVUS ORDO SECLORUM

Acknowledgments

My thanks to Neil Nadler, Pat Arnold, Claire Smrekar, and John Bransford for confirming some of my initial thoughts about the topics included here. Thanks to Jack Phillips for giving me the incentive to put something together on paper. My appreciation to Kelly Perkins, who edited the manuscript and gave me some valuable suggestions about how to express these ideas. Finally, but certainly not least, my grateful thanks to my wife, Ellen, who supported me while this was in the thinking and assembly process and who encourages me always.

Preface

This book came about as the result of three primary influences that I can recognize and remember. First, as I realized that organizations were never going to achieve stasis, I came to understand the virtues of change and dynamics in operating systems and organizations. At one time, as I experienced high levels of change and even upheaval in organizations, it seemed that such things occurred for immediate, short-term gains or for the immediate survival of the organization, but it also seemed that, inevitably, long-term survival lay in stability. Coming to terms with the rationale of constant change and the reality of dynamism in organizational systems was not easy, nor did I achieve it in a short time. I am, in fact, still more comfortable with stability than with systemic anarchy, but at least I am now more aware that anarchy and systemic change and volatility do not represent evils to be exorcised from the system.

Second, as a professional in human and organization development, I became heavily involved, during a period of years, in the development of self-instructional materials. As I did so, I moved naturally to the development and use of electronic performance support tools, courseware, and systems. It became evident to me that such systems were of benefit because they could be delivered to the learner as the learner needed them. They were easily modified and updated, they could be delivered using a variety of media, and they supported various flexible ways for learners and subject-matter experts to interact. Moreover, electronic performance support tools offered a way to enable high degrees of change to take place in organizations, during shorter time frames. This led to the recognition that, beyond some obvious economic benefits to organizations, such learning modes may be more likely to adapt and change with changes in the operating systems that they were designed to support. That is, the flexibility of electronic media seemed a good match for the flexibility, adaptability, and volatility to be recognized as integral parts of most organizational systems.

As electronic technologies offered more and more capability to simulate learner performance environments, it seemed that such electronic learning support methods offered a way to support both individual and organizational learning in ways that had not yet been available. In fact, this is proving to be the case in many organizations.

A third major influence, and the more direct stimulus for the book, was a conversation I had with Jack Phillips, the editor of the Improving Human Performance series of books into which this work fits. During lunch, we discussed the increase in open approaches to organization development, which brought with it increased needs to measure what happens when direct, on-site supervision is no longer a norm. The opening of organizations—and in fact the emergence of virtual organizations, which have a minimum physical presence anywhere—introduces the question of how such organizations will be managed. We are also concerned with how they maintain coherence of operations, how people interact with ever-changing equipment and networks, and how learning will be delivered to support such systems. How can traditional, school-model learning, prevalent in most organizations, be expected to satisfy people who live and work in virtual organizations?

Jack asked me what I would call a book about these issues and opportunities. I had a clear concept of the topics, but a title didn't immediately pop into mind. A few days later, he called me and suggested the title you see on the front cover. Bells went off, neurons fired, and the result is here.

The book will draw from four principal areas of thinking:

1. Chaos, including chaos theory. This area of consideration will include a review of complexity theory and will differentiate between classical chaos, which relies on the historical definitions and connotations of the term, and technical chaos, which refers to the application of chaos theory, now more fashionably known as nonlinear dynamical systems (NDS) theory. NDS is actually a body of theories that support the general ideas that nonlinearity is OK and that we may not be paranoid if we see two or more sides to every question. NDS, when applied to organizational thinking, offers some new ways to look at and measure the activity in the organizational systems.

2. Organizational theory and practice, including some key thinking about organizations as systems. How we put organizations together and how we maintain them are questions of significance when we consider the ramifications of chaos theory and the roles that learning and learning support play within these systems.

3. Learning theory and practice, including those theories and practices that will support learning in individual agents, as well as across the organization as a whole. Learning is a highly adaptive process. At its core, it is an individual matter. Where the emphasis, however, is currently on human learning and adaptation, we need to understand that this landscape is quickly changing to incorporate machines that can simulate thought and certainly memory. The advent of biotechnology, specifically the capabilities of cloning, means that bioengineering may replace many of the functions of silicon and electronic machinery. Such genetically engineered devices may learn at a scale that more closely approximates human thought, demanding new views of what learning support means and the audience it addresses.

Moreover, we have effectively moved, on a global scale, beyond the existence of stand-alone processors to a world in which learning strategies facilitate the integration of humans with machines through electronic and electronically mediated networks. In this new environment, learning is an open system, and informal and incidental learning take on increased significance within the organizational setting. Learning support is increasingly provided outside the walls of traditional classrooms and has increasingly come to encompass more than just formal training courses. The definition of organizational system interventions has changed to merge much that was once diversified as "training" and "organization development."

4. The general social environment, including such areas as family life, formal education in schools and universities, art and literature, and government, as events and thinking in these areas impact organizations, their dynamics, and their learning. The events occurring in social systems and governmental systems have a direct bearing on the attitudes, beliefs, and capabilities that are brought to bear in other organizational systems. As we shall see, the opening of governments, the globalization of economies, and increased sensitivity of once strongly bounded systems to external influences are all having notable impact on how people live, learn, and work.

THE AUDIENCE

The intended audience for this book will be managers and organizational leaders, as well as organization development practitioners, human performance technologists, human resource development executives and managers, and training and development professionals. These are the people who will need to refocus the directions of their organizations to realize the benefits of learning under changed environmental circumstances.

Senior management will need to address the changing ways in which work gets done. Mid-managers and supervisors will need to be concerned with the particular implications of increased use of technology, increasing presence of network-based working environments, and changes in which people, machines, and networks come together into meaningful organizational sets or units. Learning, as senior, middle, and supervisory management is finding, is more integral to the success of organizations than it once was. Yet the messages of the "learning organization," as this renaissance in learning has been called, do not necessarily make full use of some of the ideas arising from chaos and complexity theories. In fact, this group may need to rethink the mental models that underlie and form the foundations of the learning organization.

People who profess that their calling is human resource management and development, and in particular, the development and fine-tuning of systems that incorporate people, will be called upon to rethink the focus or the place people hold in evolving organizational systems. Moreover, persons who already profess an advanced view of human performance technology will need to rethink the concept of gap analysis, which has been a flag-bearer for that particular parade. The linear thinking and Cartesian logic that informs much of this construct may not be sufficient to understand organizations as they are being formed today and as they will be formed in the future. Dynamical systems cause a rethinking of the notion that a gap can be filled and then we can move on to some other need. Needs must be seen as highly interrelated and volatile. Interventions must become more fluid and dynamic themselves, with a new understanding that what were previously considered deviations, and therefore problems, may in fact constitute beneficial fires in the organizational forest.

Theories of how learning is supported will, I believe, depart radically from those theories that dominate today's organization. Current models no longer sufficiently address the dynamics of organizational forms that are now in the experimental or field trial stages.

KEY MESSAGES

For all these audiences, a number of key messages can be summarized at the outset:

1. Changes noted across organizational landscapes are temporal indicators of deeper, chaotic operations at work on a more elemental, permanent basis. Change is not temporary and won't go away. Further, change is a functional characteristic of organizational existence. There is no "right" time for change to occur, and often it will seem sudden and uncontrollable.

2. Many organizational changes will tend to release individual agents, regardless of value or organizational level, from controls, restrictions, and even from the fixed "organization" itself.

3. Organizations are now moving toward open structures, but this process of opening will continue toward virtual, non-permanent organizations. Organizations, as historical entities, will cease to exist. The value of an organization will be its value at the current instant, but that value will change quickly over time. There is no steady growth curve, and optimization of organization performance is instant. Linear metrics will be less important than nonlinear metrics. Organizational activity will respond in more sensitive ways to stimuli, and changes will be abrupt and often radical. Measurement of performance cannot assume a baseline, and goals are reset often and quickly.

4. Organizational success will depend on people, in close partnership with equipment, and the networks, both human and electronic, that enable activity. People will no longer be the sole determinants of system direction, focus, decision-making, power, or organization culture. This will result, in part, from increased emphasis on "knowledge work." It will also result from increasing capabilities in machine and network intelligence.

5. Organizational structures will be affected by socialism, as bureaucratic organizational regimes are replaced by more democratic ways of integrating people, machines, and networks to produce products or provide services. The associated dialectical nature of a democratic socialist organization model will be accepted as a norm, rather than as a delaying element in the system dynamics. Where representative substrata are now strongly entrenched in governments, as well as in other organizational governance structures, the increased accessibility and communication capabilities through electronic

networks will tend to bring more decision-making directly to the people. Representation may not disappear entirely in the short term, but it will be modified to incorporate increasingly complex input from the entities that are represented.

6. To be successful in open and virtual organizations, learning must operate effectively at individual, team, and organizational levels. It must, however, be focused at the individual level, because individual agents, in an open system, play key roles. They become more important as directive management behaviors are reduced.

7. Individual agents, not organizations, will energize learning. The concept of co-evolution, if encouraged and supported in organizations, will reduce the delays between learning and behavior modification, and will align behavior changes at individual, team, and organizational group levels. Emergent behavior will be encouraged, not discouraged or subordinated to power structures.

8. Learning will be done in different ways: There will be an increase in individualized and informal learning efforts, directed to particular ends or to wider, more strategic goals. Mass production of training will go away and will take with it curricula and classrooms. Like jugs of milk, learning events will be dated, and even refrigeration won't keep them fresh for long. Learning—and in fact other "performance" support—will be designed to be disposable because the systems they support are dynamic.

9. Sources of learning support will expand far beyond the traditional classroom and traditional teachers. Learning, however, will depart from the models of today, which tend to want to organize material into an assembly-line order, for efficient learning. We are already recognizing the value of struggle and failure in the learning process, and have adopted this philosophical model in concepts including lifelong learning, action learning, problem-based learning, and mastery learning. These forms of learning must be redefined to include non-human learning. This means that there must be greater acceptance of differences in learning strategies and that learning strategies are themselves dynamic. Learning strategies of machines and networks need to be accounted for in learning support. Where we have tried to build approaches based on average performance, an understanding of chaotic systems leads us to believe that averages may not sufficiently represent what is important in system dynamics or behavior.

10. Measuring and evaluating learning, either for efforts of individual agents or for assessing organizational capability, will require new tools and methods and will become a chief function in the larger community, not restricted to individual organizations. Evaluation will shift to the holistic system and away from human efforts alone. As organization structure becomes less important, community capabilities will become more important. Focus on capability will shift from micro- to macro-environment. Metrics will shift from those based on linear projections or histories to those based on multiple potentials and histories. Traditional business metrics, based on central ten-

dency, will be found to be less effective and accurate than nonlinear measures that account for differentials in system behavior and multiple variables. Nonlinear dynamical systems are not well represented by static averages or by independent measurement of variables.

11. As organizational work moves toward a community typology, so too will learning. Synergistic approaches to learning and performance have been demonstrated to be effective at a variety of levels, from young learners to older learners. Increased system complexity means that processes may be impacted by a number of humans, carrying out specialized but synchronized actions, as well as by actions from the electronic network and actions of machines that must be synchronized into the processes. The realization of organizational systems outcomes will depend less on the decisions and actions of single heroes than on the combined and aligned efforts of multiple contributors. Problems will best be solved by the amalgamation of varied perspectives, and not through directives concocted in some out-of-the-way boardroom or management decision-cave. Management, as the literature has already generously suggested, becomes a facilitative role, not a directive one, in the learning and doing community.

12. Electronic technology will play an unprecedented role in organizational activity and in learning. In fact, electronic technology will itself develop a learning capability amalgamated with the capabilities of other system agents. These changes, along with genetic engineering, will introduce new forms of technology that may integrate features of humans with features of machines and networks. Learning and learning support, therefore, will cease to be homocentric and will be more integrative.

When these factors are taken all together, it means, for managers and system performance specialists alike, that a number of paradigms need to be revisited and some radical rethinking of processes may be in order. The ways in which we measure and intervene in organizational systems today have more in common with mechanical, linear, and localized environments. The tools we use, as well as the methods we employ in the future, for managing and intervening in systems will need to reflect the realities of diversity, decentralization, disintermediation, and chaotic systems. What we must begin to learn is how to promote effective learning and how to develop effective learning support interventions in an environment with few certainties, constant change, and radical surprises.

STRUCTURE OF THE BOOK

I have created the book in four main sections, to reflect four key areas of knowledge and learning for those interested in this topic. First, I have reviewed some of the current observations and thinking about systems in general. We are beginning to see variety in the forms of organizational systems that are being put into play. It is important to understand at least three forms on this continuum: nuclear organizations, open organizations, and virtual organizations. Much of our need to understand the operation of chaos theory and chaotic learning is embedded in this form of system thinking. Second, I have provided a brief introduction to complex adaptive systems and to chaos theory. The second section integrates our traditional, or classical, concept of chaos with more recent, technically oriented viewpoints regarding chaotic systems activity. In this section, I have also expanded consideration of chaos and complexity theories to include research and thinking that begins to extend application of those theories into areas of particular interest for organizational leaders and human performance consultants.

The third section illustrates important changes in the way we view learning theory, learners, and learning support, which begin to address issues raised by open and virtual organizations. Some of the approaches and tools we need are in place. Others need to be rethought or developed to incorporate chaotic organizational systems into our models. In the last section, I have brought all these ideas together to develop some thoughts about learning in chaotic systems. Such learning, and the support we provide to learners, will make use of open and virtual system characteristics, will adopt principles of complex and chaotic systems, and will serve to enhance the effectiveness of chaotic organizational systems. To meet this goal, we will change our learning and learning support strategies to adopt a chaotic model.

James A. Hite, Jr.

Chapter 1

First Observations

Organizations are increasingly seen as chaotic, disturbed, volatile, and vulnerable to outside influences and forces over which they often have little control. John Kotter [1] notes some of the fallout of world events:

Increased global economic interdependence has disrupted systems of social welfare capitalism in the U.S. and Europe, shaken rigid structures of state ownership and family capitalism in the developing world, and helped destroy Communism in the Soviet Union and Eastern Europe. It has also had a devastating effect on the global market share of a number of U.S. industries.

This level of disruption continues. In early 1998, a report [2] about the economy observed that:

With the crisis in Asian economies, forecasters are paring earlier predictions of U.S. economic growth by as much as half a percentage point. That only increases the prospects for more consolidations, more downsizings, and other cost-cutting moves.

By the last quarter of that same year, analysts were calling for concentrated attention on the global economy [3]:

The fear now is that a series of defaults would cause an unraveling of the global financial system, bringing international lending and borrowing to a halt.

Much earlier, Donald Schön observed a direction toward general organizational instability:

In response to new technologies, industrial invasions and diversification away from saturated markets, *the firm has tended to evolve from a pyramid, built around a single relatively static product line, to a constellation of semi-autonomous divisions* [4, p. 66].

The "firm" itself, here, is not an autocratic structure that can claim a machine-like progress through its environment. Instead, it "defines itself through its engagement in entrepreneurship, the launching of new ventures, or in commercializing what comes out of development [4, p. 67]." The utility of the central organization lies in its ability to provide some high-level coordination to the efforts of the divisions.

1

Hamel and Prahalad carry this idea to the edge of chaos when they advise:

> Getting to the future first . . . requires that a company learn faster than its rivals about the precise dimensions of customer demand and required product performance. . . . If the goal is to accumulate market understanding as rapidly as possible, a series of low-cost, fast-paced market incursions, what we call expeditionary marketing, is imperative [5].

The role of learning becomes more significant in these organizational and economic circumstances. Learning is a means to bind such churning organizations together, establishing communication, information-sharing, and other links that act to transfer knowledge and ability from one part of the organization to another.

From this view, learning will occur most rapidly across an organizational system if the system is free to experiment with various options and possibilities [6]. In such a system, there is an advocacy of openness and free will, as opposed to a directive, over-organized march across the competitive landscape. Hamel and Prahalad, in fact, spend some time explaining the virtues of "unlearning." In their view, organizational systems that are able to move agilely through their environments are as good at unlearning old models and habits as they are at learning new ones.

This level of organizational freedom is characteristic of a complex adaptive system, a near-chaotic system. Organizations that move to this level of openness need an acceptance of near-chaotic systems that encompass a wider range of product, service, and market opportunities, created through rapid learning and unlearning. By extension, learning support must change as well.

This theme of freeing systems from hierarchical and linear domination recurs in recent literature. The idea of a constellation of inter-networked suborganizations has also been reflected in Charles Handy's idea of the "Shamrock" organization [7] and in Russell Ackoff's idea of the "Democratic Corporation" [8]. These thinkers and writers have recognized for some time, then, that dogmatic, hierarchical, and multi-layered organizational systems do not fit well in a systems environment that is open, fast-paced, and radically changing.

These, and other observations about the nature of organizations and the relationship between organizational behavior and learning, lead to two key questions that motivate this book:

1. How do learners learn and apply their learning, and how does individual learning relate to team and larger organizational learning in chaotic organizational systems?
2. How is learning support to be provided under these conditions of turbulence, change, and sharp shifts in organizational direction?

Learning, in many organizational instances, is viewed as something that is permanent and lasting and, in fact, capable of certification. This view suggests stability, retention, and certainty, not volatility. If volatility, however, is an accepted characteristic of organizations, then learning must share this characteristic if it is part of the same organizational system. The main issue to be confronted is that learning, as it is currently practiced by learners and supported in organizations, does not complement chaotic organizational systems. It complements and reinforces stable situations.

By looking at the impact of this idea on organizational behavior, three results are paramount:

1. Learners are not prepared, at present, to learn in volatile organizational climates;
2. The concept of "learning organizations," as described in theory and practice, does not go far enough to satisfy learning needs in chaotic organizational systems; and
3. The design and implementation methodologies associated with learning and performance support are locked into paradigms of stability, incompatible with chaotic organizational systems.

LEARNERS ARE NOT PREPARED

Regarding assertion No. 1, learners—whether individuals, teams, or organizations—are not prepared to learn under conditions of uncertainty. The opposite is true: Our usual paradigm for learning insists that students look to a master teacher in a passive way, to be given facts and historical interpretations that carry the authority of certainty. Old paradigms and mental models have informed existing learning strategies, and these strategies are based on models of imagined stability, not upheaval and volatility. In primary school, the first lesson many children have learned in the past is conformity. Teaching children where to sit, how to sit, how to respond to the teacher, and how to line up to go to the lunchroom or auditorium are all examples of programming people in structured ways. The learning strategies reinforced under such a constrained system are not those that will support learning in chaotic environments. Such strategies that are formed at these early ages, in most societies, are those that serve the societal norm, creating humans who know how to follow orders, toe the line, play the game, and thus survive as members of the mass society.

To ensure this outcome, students are tested using norm-referenced tests, which compare their knowledge and application ability with defined scales. Grading is a unique way of ensuring stability and conformity, and a way of ensuring that young people have met society's requirements before they are allowed to move from the micro-organization of the school into the macro-organization of society itself. This grading system is carried over into adult life in the form of supervisory or managerial assessments, which sometimes add peer reviews and subordinate reviews to the mix. This more elaborate form of business organization assessment, known as 360° feedback, is the continuation of a human performance grading system that begins in elementary schools. To complicate matters, in school or in adult organizations, grades are not allowed, in the best models, to be skewed toward either the acceptable end or the unacceptable end of the scale. In school, this paradigm is met by the bell curve, which allows some form of statistical distribution of grades, with the majority of them falling in the middle, with the exceptional performers falling at both ends of that middle bell, or bulge. This ensures that there are very few *summa cum laude* graduates and very few failures. In adult organizations, adoption of the bell curve in performance grading has the same effect and is used for the same purpose. In addition, such curve grading affects payroll, at least for non-exempt employees. The statistical distribution around a mean allows compensation managers to calculate incremental merit (or performance) pay, based on the bell curve.

At the culmination of the formal educational experience, young people generally go through a ceremony called a graduation. The graduation, whether at kindergarten or college level, conveys the same predominant message carried out by the system. Young people dress in the same garb, line up in alphabetical order, and march across a stage, to be handed a standard form certifying their acceptability according to the standards set by governmental bodies at various levels of authority. The diploma means that an individual satisfies standard and accepted curriculum and has demonstrated at least minimally acceptable performance in tests. Society is the one that has approved the curriculum and the grading standards. Therefore, completion of the curriculum means achieving acceptance by society. Again, this ritual suggests adherence to a structurally stable model. Certified learners who are allowed to enter society are those who have submitted to the control of the requisite societal systems.

When compared with descriptions of current organizational turmoil, change, and upheaval, it is no wonder that this learning model, which produces acceptable standard performers, seems inadequate. Yet we have reproduced and honored this same model as organizations beyond the formal societal education systems have taken up the task of molding people to fit organizational norms. Business training settings, such as those established in many "corporate universities," bear strong resemblance to the classrooms of the public and private school systems, and expected behavior and outcomes bear similar resemblance.

Actual evaluation of learning in adult organizations has remained something of a mystery. Courses often carry no grades and nearly as often have only tentative connections between job performance standards and learning events. The general systems results from such training events are difficult to observe, measure, and report. If learning is becoming of increasing interest in organizations that are becoming more open and volatile, this lack of ability or motivation to measure learning becomes a significant factor in organizational system success. In any event a creative, democratic, self-directed and inspired organization—business or otherwise—does not arise from organizational or individual learning support practices that are normative.

We can develop more dynamic organizations only if we help people learn in such a way as to develop learning strategies, and then performance strategies, which are matched with the reality of organizational life. Standard and traditional approaches to learning deny the growing reality, in the organizational universe, of open, networked organizational systems and of virtual organizations.

THE LEARNING ORGANIZATION

The second of the three assertions suggests that the concept of the "learning organization" does not go far enough to explain the current state of organizations, nor does it provide necessary guidance for learning in turbulent organizational situations. It is directed more toward evolutionary change and learning in relatively stable circumstances. As Peter Senge envisions the learning organization as one "that is continually expanding its capacity to create its future" [9, p. 14]. He stresses the point that such an organization cannot be satisfied with survival alone, in its marketplace or its service environment; it must go beyond survival. Senge distinguishes between survival learning, or adaptive learning, and generative learning. Generative learning, he believes, allows a more open exploration of alternatives and gets us to a point at which our participation in organizations and organizational environments is creative. In organizations that are fixed on short-term, fast results, this argument for creativity can quickly be lost. Managers, professionals, and technicians who are intent on simplification of work, on clear divisions of labor, on utilizing the learning curve are not looking for creativity, but for continuity. They are willing to be a part of what is going on around them, and so they surrender opportunities to innovate and to learn at the bleeding edge of system activity. In tradition lies safety.

A number of influencing forces operating inside and outside the organization seem to inspire such thinking. Market price for stock shares is one motivator that drives event thinking. Short-term business results drive events that are immediate reactions to those results. A strong culture exists, in public business corporations, that believes shareholder value is the primary business of the CEO and officers of the company and, moreover, that shareholders are the only significant stakeholders in the organization. Such thinking, though rarely understood outside corporate boardrooms, has a strong influence on direction setting among leaders of such organizations. In turn, this attitude influences learning in the organization.

The situation that developed in the Sunbeam Corp illustrates just how powerful, and often how destructive, event-driven thinking can be for an organization. In an effort to strengthen the corporation and renew its vitality in its various markets, the board of directors brought in a CEO whose philosophy and commitment was clearly short term. Yet, the board made its selection deliberately, hoping for a quick turnaround for corporate value, as well as sustained growth into the future. As things turned out, the directors only realized one of their wishes.

From a low in the range of $12 per share prior to the arrival of the new CEO, the stock began to climb immediately, based on his reputation for quick fixes. Within fifteen months, the stock was valued in the range of $48 per share, based chiefly on plant and product-line closures and shutdowns, with associated personnel layoffs. In an effort to sustain this level of performance, the CEO bought three other companies but also, apparently, began to book orders and sales for merchandise to be delivered later. To close such sales, it was necessary to offer discounts to retailers to encourage them, for example, to pay for inventory of gas grills in November rather than to purchase such items in the first quarter of the year. Sunbeam then arranged for storage of the finished inventory, with shipment to stores scheduled for spring sales promotions.

Booking orders this way makes early quarterly results look good but sacrifices results in the first and second quarters of the next year, when such merchandise would ordinarily be ordered and paid for by the retailers. As this action played itself out in the spring quarters, the company, as might be expected, reported poor earnings and earnings potential, and the stock quickly dropped within three months into a range below $10 per share [10].

In this example, although short-term thinking and leadership brought the value of the company up, from the day-to-day perspective of the stock market, the longer-term effect of simplistic, structurally focused changes did not lead to growth but to loss of value. A second weakness illustrated in this example rests in the detached decision-making on the part of the board of directors, which discovered the hole in the ship only after it not only had hit the iceberg but also had sunk from sight.

In such situations, the organization does not learn, nor does it take advantage of internal learning. Instead, a visceral survival spirit results in transactional, not sustained activity. No generative learning exists. In the Sunbeam example, the CEO relied on purchases of companies to enhance the earnings picture. The development of capability in the organization occurred through acquisition, not through any change or growth efforts internal to the core organization. Although acquiring skill is certainly a means of survival and a source of instant change, in this instance the organization as a whole did not measurably learn. It is possible, then, in public companies to survive in the short term but not learn. Further, no one can guarantee, in this approach, that any learning will be incorporated across and through the organization. Short-term solutions, especially when imposed from the outside, do not guarantee a learning organization.

The situation is no more optimistic in privately held organizations, including non-profit organizations. Here, the story of short-term thinking is repeated, though in a different structure: without shareholders and often without external boards of directors. Although advisory councils may exist that provide input to the organization's leaders, such input carries little or no weight in final decisions about investments, products, or services. Private organizations, driven by the need to attract donations, gifts, or other contributions, have both short-term cash flow and longer-term capital investment obligations that focus their attention on quarter-by-quarter results. The result is event-focused systems strategies, designed to bring the organization to the attention, on a continuing basis, of the giving public. Immediate financial results constitute a driving force for such organizations.

The implication, therefore, is that such organizations, given these interests in short-term and event-focused successes, may not be structurally suitable, at their core, to become learning organizations. It is difficult to conceive of a CEO or executive director opening an organization to generative learning and experimentation while at the same time satisfying stockholders or major contributors and the need for immediate cash flow. At this point, systems thinking, described by Senge and others as a vital main step in becoming a learning organization, becomes difficult to accomplish. Systems thinking, as Senge describes it, "is a framework for seeing interrelationships rather than things, for seeing patterns of change rather than static 'snapshots.'" It is an attitude toward a system that incorporates all that is a part of the system along with those other elements or systems that may not be a part of the system, but that touch on it and influence it. Yet, to be realized, systems thinking lies in direct contrast to the core structure of many organizations, both public and private.

Whereas the learning organization tries to emerge from such existing models and structures, it may be unable to struggle to the surface and breathe. The organization becomes, in such a case, an adaptive learning organization, which is tied genetically to its ancestors and to the economic systems that are its parents, instead of becoming a generative learning organization, which is free to recreate itself. Such a description suggests that learning organization concepts do not allow for operation in chaotic systems environments and are restricted to small-scale, limited deployment in divisions and subsets of organizations. If this proves to be the case over time, the learning organization model is not compatible with and cannot be implemented in macro-systems. In particular, organizations that are subjected, as was Sunbeam, to violent discontinuities must learn under chaotic conditions. Continuous learning is not sufficient, nor is systematic thinking, where such thinking merely adjusts current parameters.

Further, the learning organization, regardless of protests of wholeness, is presented as homocentric, with other key elements of the system presumed to be under the continuing control and dominance of humans. Systems analysts presume that all intelligence and decision-making resides in the human element in the system, nearly ignoring two other key elements: the machines and networks that are parts of the system. As Marsick and Watkins [11] summarize their study of learning organization implementation, they note strong emphasis across the organizations in use of interventions to change the ways in which people work and think about work. In various ways, the authors stress the importance of communication to the well-being of an active system. This includes the provision of computer systems, along with other means, which will store data and information, and act as organization-wide resources. They call for mechanisms and system tools that will support the collective learning in the organization, generating the fuel that powers a generative learning environment.

These summations encourage the conclusion that more than just human elements in an organizational system must be involved in the process of becoming a learning organization. Yet, as the case examples illustrate, such elements as equipment and networks are peripheral to the importance of human decision-making, attitudes, and interventions. The learning organization, conceptually, is shaped and controlled by people, who tangentially use electronic systems and networks to achieve human-based goals. Then the practice of learning organization formation is not yet holistic and systemic, nor, if these examples are representative of best efforts, does it reflect the importance of electronic systems in the overall generative success of organizations.

These elements, however, have become just as volatile and subject to change as the human element always has been. These mechanistic system agents increasingly strive for intelligence and currently have the power to generate knowledge. The future points to a time when science fiction will become science fact and subprocessors in organizational systems may include biological and biomechanical elements that have been derived from DNA manipulation. The "brains" of a machine may, in this future, actually be clones of brains, with similar functionality and capability to rationalize and understand and predict. Nowhere does a homocentric model of organizational learning take these new technologies into account, nor have the learning processes of such an organizational system been explored or projected.

A tendency exists in organizations to avoid "reinventing the wheel" and to avoid "upsetting the boat," but in so doing, creativity, innovation, and potential breakthroughs are stifled in favor of maintaining the system and tweaking it from time to time. The managerial ideal is stability, and most organizational systems are measured by their ability to make incremental, transparent changes that do not disrupt service or product delivery.

This attitude extends to customer relationships, or relationships with benefactors and service recipients. Because customers are so rarely fully involved in an organization's supply chain, they are held at arm's length, put on a pedestal, and considered more in the abstract than in the real world. They become immortalized as the Customer, with a capital, generic C. The great organizational game then becomes one of guessing what this great Customer wants or needs. By amalgamating customers into abstraction, managers generate service and product delivery models based on averages and assumptions, rather than on targeting specific customer idiosyncrasies. This model affects organizational learning by restricting the extent to which learning proceeds beyond incremental changes. Playing it safe in the marketplace means moving only so far as is necessary to adapt products and services in response to minimal changes in the market. Small changes leading to small, controlled effects do not encourage generative learning for the organization. This is not expeditionary marketing, as Hamel and Prahalad advocate. Small changes encourage only adaptive learning, which may not lead to long-range survivability and dominance. Such continuous change and continuous learning, perhaps through minor business process reengineering, may not be enough to satisfy clients and users in volatile environments.

Listening to the voice of the customer, if that voice is one of an individual customer, may demand that an organization accept radical change and tailoring of products and services as a goal. Such tailoring and customer-focused change will reach throughout the organizational system and is not confined to service representatives, sales staff, or manufacturing processes alone. If one part of the organization is prepared to be flexible and to respond flexibly to changes across the customer environment, then the whole organizational system must be prepared to do so. This model of radical change is not fully evident in the concept of the learning organization, nor in its execution. The learning organization concept, to be implemented in an environment of chaotic system behavior, must expand to include nonlinear change and learning, as well as the more conservative continuous learning philosophy.

METHODS FOR LEARNING SUPPORT

The final concern about learning and its occurrence in chaotic systems has to do with the creation and dissemination of learning and performance support. Learning support methods are locked into a stable paradigm dominated by the instructional systems development (ISD) model and by an organizational development paradigm. The ISD model, discussed in some detail later, is fully illustrated in Chapter 9. For this initial discussion, Figure 1-1 is a summary.

The model describes the way in which learning support is to be conceived, assembled, distributed, and measured. During the assessment (analysis) phase, a problem indicator is described, as it fits into its environment.

This initial information feeds a second stage, which includes the design of a learning support intervention appropriate to the needs discovered and described in

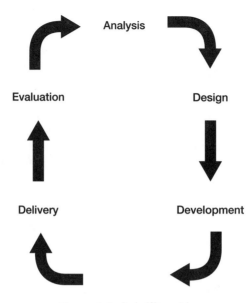

Figure 1-1. Basic ISD model.

the analysis stage. The design phase results in a full description of what the intervention will look like, including objectives for learning and for later job performance, instructional strategies to be used to ensure effective learning support for each objective, and a plan for use of media and delivery methods.

This high-level design is then translated into actual materials, exercises, tests, simulations, and discussion guides. In this development stage, the actual learning support materials are assembled into student kits and trainer guides, and the whole package is piloted to ensure that it does what it is supposed to do, in light of the objectives for learning and performance and in light of the original expressed needs.

At the implementation (delivery) stage, the materials are turned over to facilitators or, if self-instructional, are incorporated into some inventory management scheme. Electronic courseware is opened to production mode and is made available and accessible through appropriate media. Where classroom training is involved, scheduling and registration processes are activated, using methods and documentation and processes appropriate to the audience and circumstances.

Evaluation consists of both formative efforts during the production phases and summative evaluation after the intervention. The primary form for evaluation, however, is summative evaluation that most often takes place after course completion. Here, evaluation is directed at two simultaneous questions: Did the learners learn what they were supposed to learn, and how efficient is the learning support system that has been designed, developed, and implemented? The first question is tested through various means, including reaction questionnaires, tests and self-assessment instruments, and observation tools used by participants and instructors. The second question is generally checked through follow-up after the learners have returned to their workplaces and through the use of cost/benefit and ROI ratios.

Finally, because ISD is a system, it feeds back into itself. If the system has had the desired effect, the problems and performance needs identified at the analysis stage have been answered and resolved, and performance or productivity gaps have been closed. The target system—whether production, service, sales, or support—is now functioning within normal expectations. There is, then, a point at which the results of the intervention are compared at a macro-level with the needs as described during the analysis phase, to establish that learning has resulted in sustained changes in performance that resolve the original issues as described.

The ISD model has the advantage of being well recognized and well accepted by those in the training and development community. The model is, however, confined almost solely to that community and is not well known in other leadership, organization, or management disciplines. Because it is well known to those who profess training and employee development, or human resource development, its logic has been accepted for some time. Some issues, however, are arising from a closer view of the model.

First, the system, as depicted here and elsewhere in the literature, is depicted primarily as a sequential system, with one activity or stage flowing into the next. One recent notable exception to this depiction is a form of the process called the "Layers of Necessity" model [12]. Although the same five processes described above are seen as core to this process, they are viewed as modular, rather than linked. Some elements and activities of design are portrayed as variables that can be added or subtracted as needed to tailor the process model to a particular need or project scope. In general, however, the expected flow for the activities is sequential.

As noted in the description above, reality in practice does not match such a sequential representation of the system flow. ISD may happen, but rarely does it happen in neat piles of activity according to the stages and their sequence. It is, as most HRD professionals will verify, a messy process. Many clients who seek help with human performance issues believe they have a handle on both the problem and its solution, and so they leap to solutions before any sequential analysis work can be done. Some training specialists largely ignore summative evaluation and the feedback portion of the cycle, assuming their job complete when they turn over training materials to a client group. In other instances, design teams will be asked to integrate off-the-shelf courseware into an existing organizational curriculum, with little or no time or resources to validate the objectives or instructional strategies that were made in the generic creation of such products. There are as many ways to mess with the system as there are minds to think them up.

What remains, then, is frustration on the part of HRD specialists, who have been carefully trained in the logic of ISD and in its logical application. They become frustrated, in part, because they often do not know how to resolve the gaps in their own consciences between knowing what to do and having the time or resources in which to do it. Second, this frustration is exacerbated by the general ignorance of client populations, which choose to know as little as possible about the mysteries of human development. Although managers and leaders will often learn the basest details of financial and statistical analysis, believing this information to be the key knowledge for their organizational roles, they are willing to delegate or ignore the same level of knowledge about how people learn in their organizations. ISD, then, is a source of frustration because of the way it is taught, or not, and the way in which it is used, or not.

What is clear from experience with this systematic approach to performance improvement is that it tends to focus on linear processes. Moreover, rarely is the system finally closed in most applications. That is, evaluation that leads to reanalysis and recognition of progress is done in general ways but is not rigorous or methodical. One of the chief difficulties in the logic of this particular stage, of course, has to do with the fact that there is no stable state in organizations. If people are not changing, then markets, products, equipment, software, or networks are changing. Because there is some necessary time lag between analysis and evaluation in the implementation of ISD according to the model, there is the strong possibility that the situation so carefully described in the original analysis may not exist after the intervention has been carried out. Therefore, where some investment has been made to conduct a proper analysis, perhaps involving travel costs, interview time, and analyst time, the danger exists that the results of such analysis may be obsolete by the time training is completed and evaluation begins. In situations in which learning support is anticipated as an aid to organizational change, system modification is a given; everyone knows at the outset that the operating system at the back end of training will not be the same operating system that was analyzed at the front end of training.

This adds fuel to the frustration fire because analysis, design, development, and delivery are then predicated on a lot of "ifs" about what the final organization, or organizational processes and systems, might look like. HRD professionals are often in a position of developing learning support interventions when target performance is unknown and unknowable.

In some enlightened instances the ISD process is being brought toward stage front and is being integrated into the customer-focused areas of organizations. Analysis work leading to intervention development is being recognized as a normal part of business management assessment data, and the HRD process is being linked into organizational leadership thinking. In too many instances, however, learning support is event-driven and viewed as a temporary or peripheral activity, aside from the really important work of the organization. Such positioning leads to a lack of effectiveness of the ISD model.

The failure to use the tenets of ISD in nonlinear ways and the failure to link ISD to the pace, change, and dynamics of the organization have led to attempts to simplify ISD or abandon it altogether. Yet, across the HRD landscape, nothing new has come into general use to replace it. It is clear, however, that for ISD to continue to serve as a model for development and dissemination of learning support in chaotic organizational systems, it will need to be reconceived and repositioned as a nonlinear dynamic system, not as a linear, static, event-focused system.

Comparing the training process with organizational development (OD), a somewhat different situation unfolds. OD, after all, is based in change and so has no intent to serve stability. Beckhard [13] offers five key operational goals for organizational development:

1. To develop a self-renewing, *viable system* that can organize in a variety of ways depending on tasks
2. To optimize the effectiveness of both the stable and the temporary systems by built-in *continuous improvement mechanisms*
3. To move toward *high collaboration* and *low competition* between interdependent units
4. To create conditions in which conflict is brought out and managed
5. To reach the point at which decisions are made on the basis of information source rather than organizational role

The development of an organization calls for high emphasis on change management, with the expectation of complexity both in the change process and in the target systems themselves.

The ways in which we approach change in systems, however, often lead us to an assumption that stability is an end goal of the process. Managers often present change opportunities as challenges to be overcome and as temporary conditions from which the organization will recover and rebalance.

In presenting change in this light, although the end goals may be as Beckhard stated, the processes themselves are often geared to temporary interventions and approaches that reflect historical roots of OD. Kurt Lewin recognizes the variability of systems in his concept of field theory [14], and recognizes the importance of holistic interpretation of systems in the design of interventions and changes. Yet, the process that has been brought forward from Lewin is a relatively simplistic one of unfreezing the old system, making changes, and then refreezing the system, with the revisions now the building blocks for process behavior. In too many instances, people interpret *refreezing* to imply permanence, and their organizational changes reflect that attitude. Many OD practitioners use elaborate analysis methods to study jobs and tasks and then document those tasks in infinite process detail. Revised processes are treated in the same way. When participants in such systems observe and participate in such documentation and exquisite attention to detail, they begin to associate the elaborate process diagrams and charts with reality. They are too willing to refreeze their new behaviors, assuming that the changes, so difficult to accomplish, will now last awhile.

So, although OD professionals have said the right things at the theoretical level, their processes, like those of human resource development (HRD) professionals, often support *change* but not *changeability*. A new organization chart, after all, is merely a new chart with, perhaps, some new boxes and new names in it. Under many system circumstances, the essential nature of the chart itself has not changed to allow for high degrees of openness.

While HRD and OD offer some issues and challenges in the support of learning and human performance in volatile systems, another conceptual direction has attempted to expand the scope of both professional activities. The human performance technology (HPT) model offers an example of the confluence of training,

OD, and to a limited extent, other organizational disciplines. Human performance technology arose from the realization that training alone would not suffice to support organizational learning efforts and that there needed to be a better integration of training interventions with other organizational design and development activity. William Rothwell describes the resulting HPT model:

> It requires a systematic process of discovering and analyzing important human performance gaps, planning for future improvements in human performance, designing and developing cost-effective and ethically justifiable interventions to close performance gaps, implementing the interventions, and evaluating the financial and nonfinancial results [15].

Although the rhetoric here sounds like a description of ISD or OD, some significant differences exist in focus and in process. Human performance technology puts more emphasis, at the front end, on analyzing general organizational performance, reaching to the client or customer relationship. HPT depends on a clear understanding of the voice of the service recipient or customer to shape organizational changes and interventions, so analysis incorporates competitive and community environments in a more general way than does ISD. Whereas ISD tends to look for a particular problem to solve, HPT looks more widely at opportunities to enhance the organizational system and its place in its environmental landscape.

Moreover, HPT focuses on the proper definition of gaps between the vision and the actual existence of organizational performance. Gap analysis plays a key role in defining the direction for intervention and organizational change, and in measuring the impact of interventions and changes across the entire landscape. In this regard, HPT goes further than ISD and often further than OD in its description of gaps and in its dependence on gap analysis as a measurement baseline. In ISD, the emphasis is on the support of learning that will then be turned into productive activity. In OD, the emphasis is often on local change in a controlled environment, internal to the organization, with heavy guidance and influence from senior management. HPT wants to measure change at the organizational level, with individual performance changes only a part of the picture.

HPT opens the door, more so than does ISD, to changes that may involve processes, information systems, and other supportive elements within the target organization. To this extent, HPT offers more potential for including changes that are critical to performance but that are not human-centered, such as work redesign, environmental engineering, and information systems development.

Human performance technology, however, still tends to focus on humans in the enterprise and is, to this extent, homocentric. In the HPT model, as in other models, intelligence and thinking and problem solving are still human characteristics, and machines and networks exist to serve their human masters. The implicit impression left by the HPT model is that human performance depends on the existence of the right tools and circumstances in the environment, but it is finally humans who control the tools and who must remain in charge of the organizational system.

The HPT model, like other models, tends to prefer order over disorder and wants to resolve gaps between existing conditions and what is considered normal. This logic does not play well into a philosophy that accepts nonlinearity along with sudden change as a way of being and not a temporal anomaly. Fixing gaps regardless of the level, whether at individual or organizational, presumes that gaps are evil and need to be fixed. It assumes a norm that is artificially established by some human contingent, be it organizational leaders alone or in conference with other stakeholders in the organization. Norms become "stakes in the ground" and are often translated into policies and procedures by which the organization will live. The more that such entropic modeling is enabled and encouraged, the less open the organization is likely to be to change, to diversity, to exploration, and to acceptance of failure. The ethical message of the gap is that a gap between existing and desired organizational behavior is inherently bad and should be corrected.

Learning support, whether described as OD, HRD, or HPT, has focused on humans, creating a homocentric paradigm. David Hurst [16], for example, bases his consideration of crisis and renewal in organizations on five organizational elements: people, roles they play, organizing structures, information resources, and rewards.

Although these characteristics aptly capture the operations of humans in organizations, Hurst's list reinforces the homocentricity of much organizational thinking. It does not emphasize the key roles of technology. This tendency carries over into considerations of learning, learning support, and organization development. In fact, whether the emphasis is on technical or hard skills training or on leadership or soft skills training, emphasis is on ways to change human behavior as humans relate to each other and as they relate to their tools. Rarely has a learning needs analysis or a performance gap analysis gone beyond systemic changes that are human-oriented. Rarely has expertise from technical areas been used to describe learning issues encountered by equipment or networks in the organizational system. This is a new paradigm and way of thinking about organizational wholeness. As Shoshana Zuboff [17] notes in her intricate study of this integration of people with equipment, "Information technology not only produces action but also produces a voice that symbolically renders events, objects, and processes so that they become visible, knowable, and sharable in a new way." Organizations are not people, and people are no longer the sole source of organizational systems performance.

With increasing contributions to knowledge and systemic action and change from non-human players, including the machines and networks themselves that operate as part of the system, learning support begins to take on new audiences, as well as new delivery modes. In many instances, the best regime for such organizational systems may be a chaotic one, not a stable one. For humans, a chaotic system, whether defined mathematically or mythically, may be one thing. If viewed from the perspective of machine and network capabilities, however, the same system characteristics may not seem chaotic at all. Humans tend to define things from their capability matrix. They believe that system capability can be defined in terms of physical or mental abilities as defined for humans. It is difficult to get to the position in which people can accept that system capability may not be defined in terms of human limitations or capacities but instead must include a more holistic view of the players in the system.

To support learning activity in chaotic or near-chaotic (complex adaptive) organizational systems, people's thinking will need to expand beyond the limitations of ISD, the limitations of OD, the limitations of HPT, and the homocentric worldview of most organizational change and development processes. New models will be required that measure organizational systems activities in new ways, that account for nonlinearity, complex behavior, and chaotic behavior in these systems, and that are prepared to support the learner's dynamic learning strategies.

Existing models, which support Newtonian and stable organizational models, need to be replaced with a new focus on the dynamism and holistic nature of organizational systems. Learning support systems should share the characteristics of chaotic systems. The new models will help learners, whether human or non-human, understand ways in which their learning strategies can be effective in volatile circumstances.

REFERENCES

1. Kotter, J. P., *The New Rules: How to Succeed in Today's Post-corporate World,* New York: The Free Press, 1995, p. 42.
2. Greising, D., "It's the best of times—or is it?" *Business Week,* Jan. 12, 1998, pp. 36–38.
3. Mandel, M. J. and D. Foust., "How to reshape the world financial system," *Business Week,* Oct. 12, 1998, pp. 113–116.
4. Schön, D. *Beyond the Stable State,* New York: W. W. Norton, 1973, pp. 66, 67.
5. Hamel, G. and C. K. Prahalad., *Competing for the Future,* Boston: Harvard Business School Press, 1994, p. 262.
6. Esque, T. J., "Learning spurts," *Performance Improvement,* February 1997, pp. 40–42.
7. Handy, C., *The Age of Unreason,* Boston: Harvard Business School Press, 1989.
8. Ackoff, R. L., *The Democratic Corporation,* New York: Oxford, 1994, pp. 18–21.
9. Senge, P. M. *The Fifth Discipline: The Art and Practice of the Learning Organization,* New York: Doubleday Currency, 1990, pp. 14, 68.
10. Byrne, J. A. "How Al Dunlap self-destructed." *Business Week,* July 6, 1998, pp. 58–65.
11. Watkins, K. E. and V. J. Marsick. (Eds.) *Creating the Learning Organization,* Vol. 1. In Action Series, J. J. Phillips (Ed.), Alexandria, Va.: American Society for Training and Development, 1996.
12. Wedman, J. F. and M. Tessmer. "A layers-of-necessity instructional development model." *Performance & Instruction,* April 1990, pp. 1–7.
13. Beckhard, R., "What is organization development?" *Organization Development and Transformation,* W. L. French, C. H. Bell, Jr., and R. A. Zawacki (Eds.), Boston: Irwin, 1994, pp. 21–24, pp. 23–24 (orig. pub. in: Beckhard, R., *Organization Development: Strategies and Models.* Reading, Mass.: Addison-Wesley, 1969).

14. Lewin, K. "The field approach: Culture and group life as quasi-stationary process-es," in *Organization Development and Transformation,* W. L. French, C. H. Bell, Jr., and R. A. Zawacki (Eds.), Boston: Irwin, 1994, pp. 133–134 (orig. pub. in: Lewin, K., *Field Theory in Social Science,* New York: Harper & Row, 1951).
15. Rothwell, W. J. *ASTD Models for Human Performance Improvement,* Alexan-dria, Va.: American Society for Training and Development, 1996, p. 3.
16. Hurst, D. K. *Crisis & Renewal: Meeting the Challenge of Organizational Change.* The Management of Innovation and Change Series, M. L. Tushman and A. H. Van de Ven (Eds.), Boston, MA: Harvard Business School Press, 1995, p. 34.
17. Zuboff, S. *In the Age of the Smart Machine,* New York: Basic Books, 1988, p. 9.

Chapter 2

A Drive-Through System

THE LUNCHTIME BURGER BREAK

On a Thursday in late June, on his lunch break from his job with an insurance firm in a small city in Canada, John Frederickson walked to the parking lot, got into his late-model automobile, and drove to the fast-food hamburger restaurant about three blocks from his office tower. There, he pulled into the drive-through line behind three other cars and waited, with the auto's engine running, as the restaurant's slow order-and-delivery process took place. When his turn finally came, he pulled up to the large menu board and the box containing the communication device.

A metallic and barely recognizable voice came from the device: "Welcome to Happy Harold's Hamburger World. What can I get for you today?"

John shouted into the communication box from his car, "I want a Number One, with a medium diet." Although unintelligible in plain English, the code indicated that John was ordering a prepared combination meal, including a large cheeseburger, an order of french fries, and a medium diet soda to drink. Six such combinations were listed on the big menu board, offering various combinations of hamburgers, hot dogs, french fries, and fried onion rings.

The disembodied, metallic voice came back, after a short pause: "That'll be five sixty-seven. Drive around please." Having entered the order into an electronic point-of-sale (POS) workstation, the voice was announcing that the total cost of John's order was $5.67.

John pulled around the hamburger driveway, from the order point to the window on the side of the building from which food was to be dispensed. Again, he sat patiently behind two other cars waiting to offer their money and receive their food through the window. A few minutes later, John pulled up to the window in his auto, handed the clerk at the window a $5 bill and a $1 coin, and received his change, which he thrust into his shirt pocket without checking for accuracy. Immediately thereafter, a hand reached out the window holding a bag of food and a soft drink in a paper cup. John took the trophies, placed the soft drink into a plastic cupholder built into his automobile, and pulled away from the window. As he passed the front of the store, he noticed a sign in the large front window advertising "Help Wanted, Day Shift, Apply Within."

John returned to his building about thirty minutes after leaving, carried his food prizes upstairs via the elevator, and sat down in his cubicle to eat his meal and ponder the e-mail that had accumulated in his computer during his short trip for his lunch.

John represents many people who are caught up in daily affairs that grow increasingly more involved. The trip to the hamburger store relied upon an intricate set of interactions among human endeavor, technological appliances, and electronic networks. For it to occur within a thirty-minute period called for most, if not all, of the systems involved to work with high levels of accuracy. John, had he been distracted by business concerns while driving, could have had an accident with the automobile. The status of the automobile itself could have created delay in the overall process. The mechanical voicebox installed at the hamburger store could have failed, as could the cash register or any of the various cooking appliances in the store. Because such stores are small and generally rely on frequent shipments of meat, bread, and condiments, any event that could have delayed the shipment of material from a warehouse to the hamburger store could have created a delay in John's lunch plan. The automobiles in line ahead of John also had to be in reliable operating condition, or one of them might have stalled, forcing a delay in the processing of customers past the pickup window. Another driver could have caused a delay as the line moved forward. Finally, back at the office building, John depended twice on the capability of an electric elevator to carry him easily from his office to the ground floor and back. As suggested in the story, his work, too, depends on the correct operation of a computer and the e-mail network with which it is connected.

Although you may think of other systems involved in John's successful hamburger foray, the point is easily made. The life in which John participates, and in which many of us participate, calls for a successful interaction among subsystems. The systems involved today include some that are human, some that are machine-based, and some that rely on electronic networks to operate. Further, many of these systems and subsystems operate independently. The cash register in the hamburger store, for example, is independent of the actual making of the hamburgers and french fries. It is there to record financial transactions and may be linked to its own electronic network, into which it feeds revenue data and from which it retrieves pricing data. The making of hamburgers could go on all day without the existence of an operating cash register. In a similar way, John's presence is not necessary to the operation of the remainder of the processes described in the story. John could have decided to have spaghetti that day and therefore would not have visited the hamburger store. Yet, the operation of the hamburger store, and of the other people in the other automobiles, would have gone on without the presence of John.

These many independent systems, operating distinctly, introduce some interesting possibilities into our lives. Each system, including the human systems involved, operates independently and can exist without the presence of the other systems. The co-existence, that is the instances in which these subsystems come together and touch each other as a master system, causes each independent system to form itself in preparation for such interactions. Each system must plan to accommodate other systems that may come to it for service or support, or that may come to it to provide service, support, or materials. The ways in which these systems form and reform themselves as part of such virtual networks are at the heart of this discussion. As systems become subsystems in larger networks, their characters change. The squawk box at the drive-through, for example, may be a sufficient interface between human systems, in their automobile systems, and the hamburger systems only so long as the communicating systems have the same characteristics.

If, for example, a hearing-impaired person drove up to the order point at the hamburger store, she would not be able to interface with the hamburger store drive-through ordering system. This system depends on audio communication between two humans, one of whom is in the automobile and one of whom is in the hamburger store. There is an assumption, then, that a squawk box interface is sufficient for the two systems to work in an integrated way. The squawk box has been engineered to be positioned at the proper height from the ground to accommodate drivers in automobiles. Its gain control has been adjusted to eliminate at least some extraneous noise, and both its input and output channels are tuned to human hearing frequencies.

In some system interfaces, however, the tuning and adjustment is not so simple, nor is it fixed. Whereas the squawk box has been built to accommodate most humans who do not have serious hearing or speech disabilities, and has been situated where the majority of drivers can speak into it comfortably and clearly, it does not satisfy 100 percent of its users. Variations in hearing and speech abilities, coupled with differences in native languages, coupled with variations in size and height of vehicles may introduce complications. In such instances, the systems cannot work well together and often leave patrons frustrated or with the wrong food order at the end of the line. The squawk box is an example of a stable system, engineered to interface with average human users. Increasingly, however, systems are less stable than this, and successful operation and interfaces among different systems become a difficult and demanding activity.

By their very nature, systems are complex. Russell Ackoff [1] describes a system in this way:

A system is a whole that contains two or more parts that satisfy the following five conditions:

1. The whole has one or more defining functions.
2. Each part in the set can affect the behavior or properties of the whole.
3. There is a subset of parts that is sufficient in one or more environments for carrying out the defining function of the whole; each of these parts is separately necessary but insufficient for carrying out this defining function.
4. The way that the behavior or properties of each part of a system affects its behavior or properties depends on the behavior or properties of at least one other part of the system.
5. The effect of any subset of parts on the system as a whole depends on the behavior of at least one other subset.

A system, then, is not necessarily a simple thing composed of a single element. It may have, in fact, more than one defining function. The key implication of this definition is that the emphasis is on a whole, and not on the activity or operation of individual parts. It is a mistake to consider a subsystem without considering the other systems that may be operating with it. The successful visit to the hamburger store, therefore, cannot be considered John Frederickson's success alone. Although he is a part of the system, he is not all of the system, and parts of the system are beyond his control. Furthermore, some parts of that larger system are human, and some are not.

The hamburger store example illustrates a complex system operating in harmony. Real systems sometimes fall short of such harmony. For example, in a recent study, Canadian banks found that they can increase their profit margins to rates near 50 percent through use of electronic technologies [2]. Electronic customer interfaces allow these banks to reduce real customer transactions with real tellers, moving the customers toward use of electronic interfaces instead. In 1996, such electronic commerce was only some 3 percent of deposit-taking institutions in the country.

The attractiveness of such an opportunity is not difficult to understand. Branch banking requires real estate, which is sometimes expensive and hard to find in larger cities or even in suburbs. Zoning restrictions sometimes add to the cost of building such facilities. Branches require elaborate security measures. The personal interface represented in branch banking also requires staffing, a major cost factor in any financial institution. Transportation and communication costs between a central servicing facility and the branches add to the cost structure. To understand these costs, versus the hefty profit margins available from the use of automated teller machines, is to understand much of the banks' motivation toward electronic commerce.

Yet, the drawbacks of such a move are evident as well. Consumers do the work once done by tellers, and systemic processes are shifted toward the user of the convenience. Teller staff becomes less necessary, and so it can be reduced. Such cuts in service may affect customers who need to complete transactions such as opening or closing accounts, which are difficult to do through a machine. The banks run the risk of antagonizing customers if automation leads to curtailment of services or complicated processes.

The decision, on the part of customers, has to do with the extent to which they will accept a world without live tellers and without access to live, face-to-face transactions. The system, because the financial institutions control it, may tend toward increased use of automated devices, thereby increasing profit margin. So when making a decision, the banks themselves will have to consider potential customer dissatisfaction with a move to automation. If loss of service is an outcome, then the system will have failed to consider one of its key elements—the customer.

Automated banking in the United States went through a similar struggle regarding the relative merits of electronic banking versus branch banks. To date, the compromise seems to be that automated services will co-exist with human services. Consumers, aware of it or not, simply pay more per transaction in service fees. This is the general way in which many complex systems adapt in capitalistic markets. Increased convenience and service means increased prices.

The banking example provides a view of an unstable system operating as a part of a larger unstable system. The financial marketplace, if considered the larger environment in which this scenario works itself out, is unstable because of the general instability of monetary value and the general availability of money as a product. Both the supply of and the demand for money shift constantly and determine the transactions of the marketplace. The individual financial institution must, therefore, balance inside this larger system and consider other volatile factors. One of those factors is what it charges consumers for its services related to money, and the other factor is what services it provides. Obviously, the market is driven toward most service for least cost. In certain economic situations, however, consumers may be willing to accept higher costs for the same services, if the cost brings with it added convenience or features.

As Figure 2-1 illustrates, a close integration exists among the three elements—people, machines, and networks—and that integration creates a form of system that is increasingly prevalent.

THE INCREASING VALUE OF CHANGE

Given the variety of ways in which machines, humans, and electronic networks can interact, as systems or parts of systems, there is a strong suggestion that the interactions can occur in a wide variety of ways. In fact, systems and organizations of systems interact dynamically. There is constant change within the parts of a system, and there is similar change in the environment within which such systems operate, meaning that no two situations are alike. Time moves on, and as it moves, so do the circumstances within which activity or action takes place. In some systems, change may appear to occur slowly. In other systems, it may occur rapidly. Whether slow or rapid, the changes mean that if the system is measured at any two instances, the situation will have changed from the first instance to the second instance, and it may have changed enough to impact the measurement.

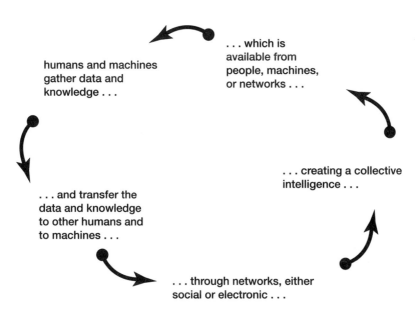

humans and machines gather data and knowledge . . .

. . . which is available from people, machines, or networks . . .

. . . creating a collective intelligence . . .

. . . and transfer the data and knowledge to other humans and to machines . . .

. . . through networks, either social or electronic . . .

Figure 2-1. The integration of human, machine, and network systems.

The recognition of change in systems has brought with it an attitude that change is good and proper, cannot be avoided, and in fact should be encouraged. Change and the speed with which systems change have been topics of increasing interest in views of systems and organization operations. The infancy and maturation of electronic technologies in the latter half of the twentieth century provided some of the background and have acted as one driving force for such thinking. The increasing diversity that has occurred in systems and in organizations, in part supported and reinforced by technologies, has been another driving force that has placed emphasis on change. As systems have moved away from purely mechanical equipment, such as the hamburger squawk box, to more versatile operants, systems themselves have acquired a volatility not previously available.

Aside from these influences, however, there have been some undercurrents and eddies in the philosophical and scientific underpinnings of Western thought that have also influenced an acceptance and recognition, and even celebration, of change in systems and organizations. Beginning in the 1960s, with a generation in Western culture that looked for alternatives to the hard realities and vicissitudes of life as it was accepted in the West, the interest in Eastern philosophies gained ground. Eastern philosophies and religions, suppressed in the West in part because of harsh memories of World War II, were revisited by a maturing generation that had not experienced firsthand the war between Western and Eastern nations. A growing cynicism regarding Western cultures and philosophies led to explorations of alternatives and to more liberal acceptance of other cultural knowledge.

Aside from the increasing interest in philosophies, discoveries in areas of physical science came hard on the heels of computer processing capabilities. Scientists working in mathematics, physics, and biology, in particular, became interested in the fact that increasing proofs were available that what were once dismissed as statistical anomalies were, in fact, evidence of new forms of order. Many such discoveries came with the introduction of available computer power and with increased attention to phenomena occurring across disciplines.

The discovery that systemic irregularities may point to a different form of measurable behavior led to the development of what was termed *chaos theory*. Scientists came to find that some forms of order existed in systems that had heretofore been regarded as disorderly. In these instances, chaos was not all it was cracked up to be, and it offered tantalizing evidence that system activity might follow a strange, though definable, pattern. Computers contributed heavily to these discoveries because they were able to simulate some events that otherwise might have taken years to observe and because they had no qualms about calculations beyond three or four decimal places. Accuracy and completeness of measurement were two keys to the new understanding of how things work. The veils of mystery were lifted, in part, because of increased ability to measure, define, and then predict. This understanding has now been applied not only in the physical sciences but also in other sciences as well, and has influenced the way in which business and other predominately social systems are interpreted.

Along with the understanding of how some chaotic systems operated came a simultaneous realization that systems change because they learn. Learning leads to adaptation, and co-evolution, as systems integrate new knowledge, apply it internally, and respond to similar changes and adaptations in other systems with which they are integrated, or which play a part in their environment. Business competition is a form of such co-evolutionary behavior, and business systems were included as complex adaptive systems. The similarities between the behavior of a biological entity and the behavior of a social business system were unmistakable. Social business organizations survive in their competitive environments in the same way biological life forms have survived—through a constant collective wariness, by keeping an eye on the overall *fitness landscape,* or fluctuating environment in which they operate, and by changing as often as necessary to ensure the capability to operate in changing surroundings. The recognition and acceptance of organizational systems as complex adaptive systems have brought with them a concomitant acceptance of change as a norm and an acceptance of learning as a mode of organizational survival. Learning is now a matter of enterprise success, and not a schoolroom somewhere at the back of the assembly line. It is a function that is effective when it propitiates change in the enterprise, which then allows the enterprise to remold itself to the ever-changing competitive environment. The total enterprise—humans, machines, and networks—must learn, change, and evolve, or evolution will not be successful.

This leads to a new view of how learning should be approached in organizations and how it should be encouraged and supported. Organizations are gradually moving to a focus on the support of learning, replacing a strong emphasis on directive education and training. This shift means that the business of learning support—which has grown up under the names training, education, organization development, human performance technology, human resource development, and even management—must rethink its own philosophies and processes. The schoolhouse model must be relegated to history, and along with it such recent iterations as the corporate university. The people engineering model must be put away because complex and chaotic systems are no more subject to engineering or process definition than are the learning activities and events that occur in such systems. Such models constitute a drag on the holistic and volatile learning environment that best represents the learning in complex and chaotic systems. Learning must co-evolve with the systems it has grown up to support and must adapt to a changing fitness landscape, with new responses, theories, models, and products and services.

Even more important is a stage of being that is beyond co-evolution and adaptation. The concept of a complex adaptive system, while recognizing and accepting volatility and change as necessary elements in continuing survival on the fitness landscape, or in the corporate business environment, does not recognize or address technical chaos. Beyond complexity and complex adaptive organizational systems lie chaotic systems. The two concepts, though related, are not the same. Learning in the two environments, one complex, and one chaotic, will not be the same.

Learning support functions will differ, as well, as organizations move from complexity to chaos and back. Parts of organizational systems may be in one regime—chaos or complexity—while others operate in another regime. Some parts of the organization may, in fact, show high indications of stability. Because an organization is a system and because a system may be made up of numerous subsystems, an organization is likely to be operating with a number of different dynamics at the same time. This form of diversity, too, is one that needs to be recognized, as learning flourishes in such an organization. The learning should fit the situation and the context, and should itself be adaptable on its own fitness landscape or within its own chaotic regime.

As organizational systems change, open, and recognize increasing needs for learning, they increasingly recognize that chaos is not simply disorder in their systems, but a profound part of the order. Organizations, like physical systems, are highly volatile and must open themselves even more to the environment to co-evolve with partners and competitors alike. As they do so, they depend not on managerial priests and priestesses, but on those who are experts at making products and delivering services to customers.

High levels of change speed in organizational processes means an acceptance of technical chaos. Although speed alone may not produce chaos, it increases the dynamics within a system. In turn, a system may begin to lose its coherence to strong attractors, which maintain consistency and easy predictability, and move toward a state in which activity becomes less predictable, less organized and perhaps, in terms of products and services, less accurate.

Such systemic chaos may be embraced to free the system for higher levels of performance. A child's helium balloon is only as tall as its string until the string is released and the balloon is allowed to pursue an unknown and unknowable path. Yet the balloon accomplishes more by potentially entertaining more people at thirty feet off the ground than at six feet. Loss of human control means a gain in productivity, if balloon productivity is measured in units of viewing public.

In a similar way, organizations must open in order to optimize. Such openness, whether achieved through diversity or some other means, leads to a sense of loss of control on the part of the humans involved in the organizational system. It leads to an attitude across the organization that allows things to happen, allows change to take place, and allows new experiences to be accepted, valued, and fostered. This is not pandemonium, nor is it classical chaos in any other sense. Opening organizations, on the contrary, gives them the freedoms they need to remain viable. Such openness calls for an understanding of chaos theory and of how technical chaos may be operating in the organization or may be introduced successfully into the organization. It may not be enough to adapt or to change continuously. It may be necessary to master and accept chaotic behavior in order to grow and prevail.

Outcomes and behaviors may be measured not only in human performance but also in the joint performance of the entire organizational *presence,* as it allows and supports and participates in the performance or behavior. The basis for the behavior may not be directly traceable to a time, place, training event, or particular action by a person, a machine, or one or more nodes in the network. Some events, significant in the behavioral change, may be unmeasurable using existing definitions and parameters for measurement. Events influencing learning may not happen sequentially and may not be traceable through linear time tracks. Finally, the observed behavioral change will depend on the place and viewpoint and constructs of the observer.

Given a radical rethinking of what learning is and how it happens, learning in chaos calls for different forms of learning support and different attitudes in the organization concerning what learning is, how it operates, and how it is to be supported. Learning support is not confined, and never has been, to the training department or the organization development department, nor is it, in fact, a major responsibility of the traditional human resources or staff management function. Learning is integral with the systems that compose an organization, and therefore is of concern to all entities in the organization, human, machine, or network. Learning in chaos, in fact, may be addressed not simply as a necessity in chaotic systems but as a desirable end in systems that may benefit from being urged into a chaotic regime to grow and develop. The support of learning may therefore be support of dissonance and disorder, not support for constancy, unity, and control.

REFERENCES

1. Ackoff, R. L. *The democratic corporation,* New York: Oxford, 1994, pp. 18–21.
2. Beauchesne, E. "Is customer service dead at big banks?" *The Ottawa Citizen,* Ottawa, July 9, 1998, pp. C-1, C-2.

Chapter 3

Turning and Churning: Organizational Change

INTRODUCTION

We cannot heartily proclaim what societies or economies will look like far in the future. Given our collective world history, it would have taken superhuman accuracy to have predicted, in the 1890s, what has transpired between then and now. In fact, when leaders and spokespeople from that era were asked to predict what the 1990s would be like, some of the answers came close to the mark, but many did not. In considering the future of the then-new technology of telephony, for example, John J. Ingalls, a Kansas politician, had this to say:

Telephone instruments, located in every house and office, will permit the communication of business and society to be conducted by the voice at will from Boston to Moscow and from Denver to Hangchow—just as readily as now occurs between neighboring villages [1].

This foresight, of course, proved more true than Mr. Ingalls could have imagined, with not only voice, but data and video available globally. On the other hand, Hempstead Washburne, a politician, recognized the near futility of predicting the future:

It is as useless to attempt to foretell the century-hence improvements in mechanics, in industrial arts, and in modes of travel as it would have been 40 years ago for any one to have anticipated the telephone and its now-universal use.

In fact, our ability to predict the future has not improved in the intervening one hundred years. Even so, the attempt to extrapolate next events from past and present environment is tempting and useful. Even visionaries must have some form of clay from which to form the future scenes, and to some extent our reality is an attempt to match the pictures drawn for us by these visionaries. So, although no picture of the future can claim 100 percent accuracy, the picture has at least some chance of presenting a kernel of truth. The question of how organizational thinking will evolve into the future is of paramount interest here.

AN ORGANIZATIONAL CHANGE CONTINUUM

Three identifiable organizational forms represent various mixtures of open systems thinking, diversity, and electronic technologies. The forms do not exist in three separate vacuum packs, however; they constitute representative entities along a continuum. The continuum, illustrated in Figure 3-1, shows these organizational entities arranged along a scale that suggests a range from tightly controlled organizational presence to more loosely arranged organizational presence. The process of change within these systems is a key ingredient to their operation and is an important factor in understanding how systems range across this continuum. To consider each of these primary forms—nuclear, open, and virtual—in some organized way, the discussion below has been based on the organizational frames proposed by Lee Bolman and Terrence Deal [2]. Their frames of reference include political, structural, human resources, and symbolic. These classifications offer a convenient way to consider characteristics and differences of the three primary forms. The continuum, like the organizational systems themselves, is a dynamic environment, with multiple, complex interactions.

Nuclear Organizational Systems

The nuclear form of an organization refers to an organizational system built on internal, vertical lines of control. Although ostensibly these lines could be referred to as a network, the realization of the network concept in this form is highly restricted. The lines of communication, for example, run from top to bottom, as do the lines of power and the lines of decision-making. Upper levels expect to be able to tell lower levels what is good for them and what to do, along with how to do it.

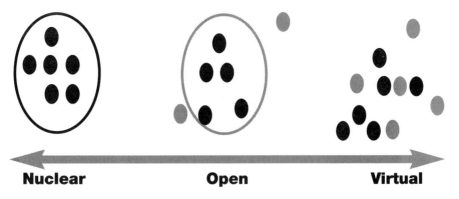

Nuclear   **Open**   **Virtual**

Figure 3-1. Organizational continuum.

Regardless of the creativity or innovative energy that may exist below each layer, the executive control function is specific in its role of containing such creativity and maintaining the parameters within which a system or subsystem operates. The executive control function is clearly divided and is distinguished vertically, as well as horizontally, in this structure [3].

In this model, machines are capital assets assigned to a particular task. Machines, in this form of organizational presence, form another layer in the hierarchy, below the human layer. Humans are expected to take output from such machines and make judgments about it, act on it, or otherwise use it.

Electronic networks are likewise seen as basic necessities for carrying out the intent of the organization but are not themselves included in the decision-making or control processes of the organization. Again, they are viewed as tools, and their role is relegated to maintaining communication within the organization, or between the organization and various elements in the outside world. In the nuclear organization, the emphasis on human control and power structures is uppermost.

Politics plays a significant role in the ways people interact and in the tightness of the system's presence. Position power determines which decisions will be considered and how those decisions will be made, as well as when they will be made. There is less emphasis on consensus than on compliance. The game is played out according to a specific understanding of a set of rules, set up as policies and procedures, and strictly monitored. Allegiance to policy and procedure is considered a valuable trait in such organizational systems.

Perhaps one of the best examples of this form of hierarchical system is the flight crew on a small- to medium-sized commercial aircraft that is making a trip of approximately one hour. The captain of the aircraft is in command and has general responsibility for all subsystems, including the aircraft itself, its crew, and passenger service. A portion of the command is specifically delegated to the role of co-pilot, chiefly in the areas of aircraft control and safety. Another portion of the command is delegated down to the senior flight attendant, who has chief responsibility for passenger safety and satisfaction during the flight. Each role is bounded by rules and regulations, some of which are derived from some national air travel authority, and others that have been created within the airline organization itself. Unions representing pilots and flight attendants influence some of the rules. The net result is a strict set of policies, procedures, and processes that must be followed from the time the crew members report to the aircraft at the departure gate to the time they arrive at the destination and park the plane at the arrival gate. Because time plays a significant factor in customer satisfaction, as well as in disposition of hardware, station staff, and the crew assignments themselves, schedules are strictly monitored. The two factors in the success of the flight, aside from the capability of the aircraft and the cooperation of the passengers, are control of time and control of process. Checklists ensure that all processes are carried out in preparation for departure, as well as during the flight and landing. Standard procedures govern the timing of announcements by flight attendants and the captain or co-pilot, and many of these announcements are under the control of regulations. Some things must be said in a certain way and are repeated in practically the same way on every flight. On a short flight, the necessity of maintaining control over the two key factors—time and process—become essential. In part, this is because of the need to maintain time position in airport schedules. To maintain a flight plan, and to attempt to ensure that passengers actually experience the schedules for which they contracted when they purchased their tickets, the aircraft must push back from the gate on time. This puts it in line for takeoff, and standards exist to allow for a certain amount of ramp hold time at a certain time of day at a given airport. If the pushback is within specs, a better-than-average chance exists that the flight will lift off on time and arrive at its destination airport on time. If pushback is out of spec, then anything can happen, such as takeoff delay, different routing once in the air, or a different hold, landing, or taxi pattern at the destination area.

A short flight also dictates that cabin service processes must adhere to a strict timetable. At a certain point in the flight, attendants are allowed to unpack equipment and prepare for cabin service, and at another point in the flight, all equipment must be restored and secured. On short flights with full cabins, service is thus based on established procedures that, if adhered to, will complete the full cabin service in the time allotted.

In this example, it becomes clear that to achieve success in this short-flight system, the people in the system are in command, and the equipment, as vital as it is, largely plays a supporting role. Final decisions rest in the hands of the crew. Passengers rarely, if ever, play a role in the operation of the aircraft, other than to fund it. Once on board, from at least one perspective, they are at the bottom of the hierarchy and are expected to take instruction from the flight crew. This clarity in rank, role, procedure, and timing is strong indication of the influence of a nuclear system.

Structurally, such organizations tend to be large, with the primary organization divided into product lines or geographic areas, and with further breakouts into divisions, which constitute large areas of work, and then to departments, which constitute still further subdivisions of the work processes. Below department level, work teams or project teams are formed to perform related collections of tasks associated with a sub-unit of a work process. Budgets are subject to the same power hierarchies that influence the human resources of the organization. Capital equipment budgets and major facilities acquisition budgets are often handled apart from expense budgets because such money is acquired and managed differently and because capital is often considered a general common resource, and not related to a specific product or geography. Capital acquisitions and investments are made, ostensibly, for the greater good of the entire organization. In practice, of course, political and other influences can affect capital allocation decisions.

The nuclear organization relies on position power more than referential power, or influence. Direct power structures are created from the top of the organization down, and little gets done without the approval of higher levels. The tiering that appears horizontally, evidenced by job grades, job titles, office size, and access to the corporate jet, is reproduced vertically. Power silos are created when separate but equal powers are allocated to product line executives or geographical executives and when separate but equal divisions, departments, and even projects are set up. The mapping of the power structure from the top is replicated at every subdivision of the organization.

Power and influence generally, however, work in only one direction. Those who are not invited into the halls of power, regardless of which upper floor of the building may be so designated, have no insight into the logic that lies behind such high-level decisions. Decision-making—especially if it concerns such heavy topics as organization mission, vision, and values—is reserved for discussions in the inner sanctum, under the assumption that power includes the license to make such decisions alone. "My people" is a commonly heard phrase, as are "my team," "I own that process," and "he is on my chart" (referring to placement on an organizational chart).

Politics and structure, of course, influence the human resources picture in a nuclear organization. Closely influenced by the structural picture, the management of human resources occurs largely through the implementation of comprehensive policies and procedures to cover almost every exigency. Hiring quotas are established based on forecasts of product line development, of service line development, and of actual revenue or contributions. These hiring quotas are set according to the skills that are required or forecast. The intent, as in the rest of the operation, is to minimize selection and recruiting expenses. Selection is intended to provide career employees. That is, the search criteria will attempt to find stable people who appear to be willing to commit to the organization for a period of years. This, of course, is a fantasy in most cases. Because of an environment in which downsizing and outplacement are at least as busy as recruiting and hiring, neither employers nor job candidates are under any real illusions. Yet the tapestry of commitment is woven on both sides, with both the candidate and employer pledging at least some modicum of loyalty. In fact, at this point the human resource management of hierarchical nuclear organizations shows its weakness. To maintain closed and tightly controlled boundaries, and to ensure some level of cooperation across internal silos, it is advantageous to have a stable and willing population. Stable members who are committed to the organization, perhaps even literally indebted to it, mean a population that will be compliant. It is the fertile ground for followers.

From a human resource management perspective, then, it is better to support high levels of member security, which will make membership and tenure attractive options to recruits. At the same time, a nuclear organization must keep its leadership options free and have the capability to dump large numbers of people on the streets at a moment's notice. This will maintain the flexibility in the organization's human resource management template. It will put people in the same category as the capital equipment and facilities that can be abandoned or subleased on short notice, whenever those in the power chain believe their own existences to be threatened by poor organizational financial results.

Human resource management in a nuclear organization is also characterized by its approach to human learning and development. In the nuclear organization, emphasis is on high control of expenditures in this area. The hierarchy will easily recognize the need to train and develop members. This development, however, is chiefly geared to skill training that is chiefly tailored to the specific processes, equipment, and products or services associated with this particular organization. Transfer of skills to other organizations, and sometimes within the nuclear organization itself, proves difficult because of over-specialization. "Here's how XZ Corp prepares its budgets and processes invoices" is a sentence indicative of the approach to employee development at XZ Corp. The nuclear message is this: "Things are done differently around here, regardless of what you might have learned at the last place you worked. We think our process gives us a strategic advantage over our competitors, so fall in line and do it our way, and don't tell anyone outside this department how you are learning to do it."

Clearly, this focus does little for the long-term growth of the organization member, nor does it prepare him or her for the inevitable layoff scenario. Either as one laid off or as one who remains, the employee has little of the big process picture and often finds it difficult or impossible to adjust to new roles or responsibilities. Rarely, in a layoff situation, are funds allocated to support retraining, either for those departing or for those remaining.

The nuclear organization assumes that progression through the hierarchy will be through a combination of technical skills and political skills. More general development of the individual is left to the individual himself. In its purest form, the nuclear organization is egocentric, and its structural boundaries do not admit others into its learning circles, nor does it encourage extension of members' learning activities beyond the local border.

Such organizations offer a symbolic touchstone for vendors, members, and customers. The organization, in this role, becomes a sovereign authority figure. Flag bearers for the organization are expected to make its symbols, images, products, and services known throughout the world. Not only is such name or brand recognition good for sales, it is also a source of pride for employees. Association with a powerful and profitable organization is, surprisingly, not enough for some people. They also want to be associated with a *well-known* organization.

People are hired into a corporate image and receive direction, either formally or informally, about how to fit into the organizational structure and power scheme. This involves compliance of dress, grooming, attitude, and general behavior. Uniforms play a large role in hierarchical organizations because they symbolize the illusion of oneness and unity. Because unity relates to stability, the symbols of the organization are carefully designed to yield a high comfort level, both in customers and in employees. Corporate logos are common in the nuclear environment. Symbolic statements are screened at the highest levels before being released for publication or promotion. All things must be coordinated, down to the font sizes, typefaces, and formatting allowed on internal or external documents. Even internal memos, a popular way for the levels to communicate downward, are subject to considered layout and control. Only certain people are allowed to send e-mail messages to the entire organization. Such communications are subject to proofreading and at least one level of approval.

The nuclear organization, with its tight and heavy outer boundary, exists largely within itself, holding the outside environment at arm's length. Internally it is composed of small or large islands of activity, each bounded by the restrictions imposed within its own hierarchy.

Open Organizational Systems

Open organizations approach all aspects of organizational presence from far different perspectives. The ultimate reality in the open organization [4] has to do with removing many of the boundaries, or at least reducing their influence, outside and inside the kernel organization. The immediate result is that activity, movement, and communication occur at an increased pace, and range across wider areas of the organization than in a closely bounded system.

The framework for such an organizational presence depends on integration of operations so that no one part of the system is viewed as standing apart from the others. Ackoff's concept of the democratic corporation [5] serves this structural end, as does the similar description of organizational characteristics by Charles Handy [6]. Integration of functions, so that functions and processes are interdependent, is necessary to remove the silos that tend to build up when structure allows separation of the parts of the system. Integration does not mean the organization conducts all its business around one big table, but that a given area of work, for example customer service, is closely linked with finance, product or service design, and materials shipping and handling. Customer service, as an organizational function in this instance, would not be structured to make its own decisions based solely on input from within or from the top of the organization. "The top" begins to be difficult to define in an open organization, with much more emphasis on lateral connectivity than on vertical, top-down flow. The structure of an open organization begins to recognize the legitimate claims for input from a number of other sources.

The open organization becomes more dynamic than its nuclear counterpart. Dynamics come in the form of increased lateral communication within the organization, increased communication with vendors and customers, and increased functional communication among members of the organization. The dynamics also include increased capabilities to support such communication, including electronic networks that support various forms of media. The nuclear organization is, for example, more likely to require on-site presence of its members, in order to reinforce the power structure and to oversee, visually and aurally, the work of employees. The open organization begins to remove the necessity for on-site overseers and workers. An open organization is more likely to include telecommuters and people who have primary work sites in places other than a central facility or campus. As this physical "opening" occurs, the physical structures to support the organizational system change, along with the makeup of the human elements of the open organization.

One of the recent concepts to be reinforced as organizations open is that of the supply chain. A supply chain, put simply, is the close alignment and linkages of internal processes to external processes. That is, the supply chain is a dynamic concept relying on a clear understanding of distributor (or intermediary) and end-user needs and on the actual internal operation of these organizations. A form of supply chain is illustrated in Figure 3-2.

There is a noticeable shift, in open organizations, toward a different kind of power than is exercised in nuclear organizations. Because the organization is now shifted to lateral focus, position power begins to be replaced by influential or refer-

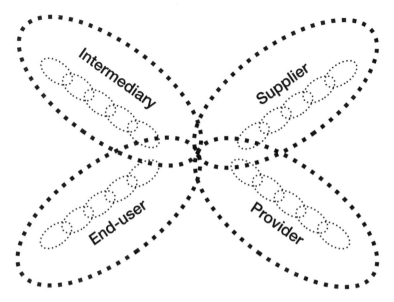

Figure 3-2. A supply chain.

ential power. Trust begins to enter the organizational power picture as an important factor in the success of the open architecture. In an interdependent and often networked structure, the ability and the willingness to trust others are vital. For example, in an open system a provider organization might have a customer representative in a room during a heated discussion about priorities. In closed, secretive, nuclear systems, the customer would be nowhere near the premises when such discussions are conducted. In an open system, the success of the enterprise is no longer entrusted simply to the hierarchy of priests and priestesses who manage the downward power flow within a single organization. These overseers disappear in open organizations, to be replaced by a wider representation of those involved in any given supply chain, who then become the decision-makers and process drivers. Such constituency is more representative and democratic, and includes suppliers, intermediaries, and end-users in the mix.

The role of the overseer is replaced by the role of the facilitator. The facilitator now provides a service to those being facilitated and is viewed as an integrated member of the organization, rather than as an artificial headmaster or -mistress, sitting apart from the real functionality of the system. Power begins to be apparent at lower levels of the open organization and begins to play a role in shaping the direction of the organization, as well as ensuring its arrival at its intended destination. In much of the literature about learning organizations, this shift is noted as a journey [7] in which the leader may be a pathfinder or guide, but who depends more on input and opinions from others during the journey. The organizational system, when this occurs, has begun to experience double-loop learning [8], which is to say that a feedback loop has been installed replacing the single-channel downward control prevalent in the nuclear model. The feedback loop allows increased input from all members of the organization, and the vitality and dynamics of the organization are now powered not by artificial management systems but internally from within the system as a whole.

Moreover, because the outer membrane of the open organization accepts external influences, the power model for the system begins to incorporate those influences traditionally excluded from the organizational presence. Consultants, contractors, vendors, suppliers, customers, and clients all constitute categories of contributors to organizational success. In education, parents, school board members, and students offer parallel groups. In the nuclear organization, these people are generally frozen out of the key decision-making processes of the organization. They may be heard but carry little power over organizational decisions that involve how things are to be done. In the open structure, however, these people begin to integrate themselves more fully into the life of the organization, and their participation becomes continuous, not sporadic. The occasional visit to a customer changes into a customer who has a representative on-site in the open organization. The opening of boundaries, obviously, must be something that both organizations must agree to. If schools, for example, invite parents to participate in the operations of the schools, then both parent and school must agree that this is a good thing and that both parties benefit. Power, in such a situation, can become a tricky and elusive thing. It is now shared and must be exercised by both groups or representatives of the shared systems. Unilateral decision-making is no longer an option in open organizations, and this characteristic alone may introduce instability into such systems.

While the actual structuring of an open organization is relatively easy to see on paper, and while the value of concepts such as supply chain management make good sense in theory, the working out of power dynamics is far from easy. Power is shared and interpersonal, much more flexible and volatile a concept than in the fixed power structures in nuclear systems.

The role of humans in such a system also changes dramatically, along with changes in structure and power from the nuclear model. Here, the human resources clearly view themselves as integral to the success of a process but not necessarily to the success of a given organization. Their emphasis shifts from a need for security to a need to be relevant contributors to one, two, or more process venues. Role flexibility increases, as does skill flexibility. Position becomes less important than involvement in meaningful projects or processes. The successful individual in an open system is one who holds some nominal position in the organization but is connected into a variety of contributory roles. These roles may range across both internal and external organizational structures, with considerable borrowing of staff from one activity to another, depending on current needs and the skills required for the activity. In the open system, employees or organizational members themselves may easily initiate such changes in venue and involvement, with some coordination with process facilitators. In this environment, it is not the overseers who take responsibility for good use of individual time, but the individuals themselves. Motivation is thus self-generated, as people are more able to work on those things that interest them intrinsically, rather than on those things that are simply dictated by a stable job position and description. Rules, regulations, process descriptions, and procedures begin to play a lesser role in the open system. Ways of getting things done are not preordained by the executive control function that existed with a heavy hand in the nuclear world. How things get done becomes a dynamic concept, with skills being pulled into a given process or project.

The influence on the development of employees is immediately obvious. In the open organization framework, development responsibility shifts from managers and overseers to individuals. As the dynamics of supplier, intermediary, and end-user begin to be felt with more intensity and immediacy, the pressure to provide goods and services in the shortest time possible increases. This pressure translates into an increased need to have available, within the provider organization, those skills and capabilities that may cover a variety of situations not yet introduced by the end-user. Another dimension of supplier relations becomes the supply of skills and capabilities from the outside of the traditional organization. Facilitators must now balance the need for internal skill capability with the supply of needed skills from outside sources. The feedback loops now developing in the open architecture become more complex in relation to human resources, since such resources may no longer be fully integrated into the organization itself.

Hiring and selection and outplacement processes add the new dimension of people who are in non-permanent categories. They are contractors or independent contributors who are incorporated with clear contractual limitations on time and function and pay. There is no mention of loyalty on either side, other than the provision of service as defined in these contracts. Loyalty, ethics, and trust—vital elements in an open organization—must be redefined across the entire enterprise. Those who are parts of the kernel organization must have a different model for interpersonal relationships, based on the acceptance of external contributors. Trust must be established across the entire supply chain, and in particular at individual levels, in ways that are not necessary in closed organizations. Ethical expectations change, as the mix of staff includes those without an intrinsic loyalty to an organizational flag. Ethics, loyalty, and trust, in the open world, cannot be legislated. Because power is now shared, some higher authority with the power to police and enforce can no longer mandate definition of these three characteristics. In fact, these characteristics must be defined and supported by the people who are engaged in what are now highly integrated and widely diversified activities.

In this regard, the corporate flag and other symbols under which nuclear employees marched become less significant. As the kernel organization grows smaller and begins to lose its identity in the amalgamation represented by the supply chain, the rites and rituals of the organization lose their influence. As people lose the sense of familial relationship with the organization and begin to view themselves as necessary only to the activity as it is currently defined, their attendance to symbolism and ritual grows more impatient. They generate other ties and loyalties, outside the open organization, that provide a sense of basic security and stability, which are natural needs.

As the schematic of the organizational continuum illustrates (Figure 3-1), elements of the open system that lie outside the permeable boundary are connected to the system through mutual interests in the activities of the organization. Outside elements are connected not by any understanding of lifelong employment opportunity, or by provision of benefits and member services, but almost exclusively by the economic bond. The organization that is an open system is, in its treatment of suppliers and contractors, highly pragmatic, providing benefits and human resource support chiefly to those who remain inside the kernel, and inside the organizational boundary.

Such organizations can move more quickly into a need area, collaborate more closely with those who have the need, and thus produce a more effective intervention or product than can highly separated nuclear systems. An open organization retains a core functionality that resembles the functions in a nuclear organization, but attempts to confine commitments to those system elements essential for the operation of the infrastructure.

The advantages, however, come at the cost of certainty and control, requiring increased reliance on a cooperative community. Rewards and recognition systems must change to recognize contributions from a variety of sources toward the accomplishment of goals, with less focus on individual achievement. An open system, unless fully implemented, does not co-exist well with closed, bounded systems. The permeable system is vulnerable to power struggles and to the influence from more concentrated elements of power. If vertical power structures are maintained and supported from executive level down through a fixed hierarchy, the concept of open systems will not work. It is tempting to believe that both a managerial structure and an open systems approach are mutually beneficial. An open system, however, is not managed. It is self-managed, and control is vested in the many, not the few. Getting to this paradigm shift is a painful part of the journey and one avoided by many organizations as they try to introduce learning organization concepts. The only way an organization can learn is if it is free to learn, without learning being imposed from leadership priests and priestesses.

Virtual Organizational Systems

A virtual organizational system is built on temporary associations of talent, capabilities, and purpose. It is *virtual* in the sense that a large percentage of the parts and pieces that constitute the whole system are defined solely by a particular point in time, a place in the environment, and the purpose of the system at those points. At its most extreme, such a system can be compared with a gas that is contained in the same shape as its environment—a spherical chamber means the gas conforms to a spherical shape—a box means the gas takes the shape of the inside of the box. The highly networked system is weighted more heavily toward execution than planning and control, since the virtual nature of the system makes it highly pragmatic and practical. Of all organizational system types, it is the one most likely to be a learner as it derives its purpose and thus functionality directly from the events and phenomena that surround it at any given time in any given place.

The virtual system is a highly generative system, as it seeks to discover its purpose and contributions in a highly dynamic way. It is the system form that is most sensitive to small changes in its environment, and so it is more likely than other forms to shift direction suddenly. It is often a leader system as it predicts what may happen to larger, slower, less volatile systems that may be interconnected and affected by it. These systems are open to reengineering, they are volatile and highly charged, they exhibit a tendency to welcome discontinuous change, and they invite innovation.

Note that in Figure 3-1, showing the organizational continuum, the virtual system has an undefinable boundary. The structure of this system depends on the tenuous interrelationship of various nodes, including people, machines, and electronic networks. The virtual system is the fullest expression of network, in which a node or a connector is of use only when the node is contacted by some other node, or when the given node has the need to contact other nodes.

Otherwise, while some potential connector interface may exist, it remains unused potential. That is, connections among nodes are not controlled continuously by an executive control function, and lines are not kept open at all times. The network is, therefore, not managed so much as it is facilitated, with nodes brought on-line when needed and left unconnected when not needed. The total energy of the system, then, is focused on the active nodes at any given time, and the place, size, and composition of the network depends on its definition at a single point in time. Nodes exist as a part of the network only when they are actively contributing to the purpose of the network. At a point where the network changes its purpose—and that may happen quite frequently—nodes that are not necessary to the new functionality are discarded. Other more-relevant nodes are added. In its most excitable structure, there is no extraneous node, and there are no extraneous connectors. Size, as a general variable, is irrelevant as a determiner of effectiveness, reach, or efficiency of such an organization. It is always big enough to accomplish its current purpose.

Politically, of course, such a network at the extreme end of the spectrum is difficult to imagine, if it involves humans. While an electronic network can approach the level of structural volatility described above, a network involving human elements begins to be less than a model for extreme virtuality. What would be required in the virtual organization would be a very low political impact on the decision-making of the entity as a whole. That means that power—as defined as human control over network elements—would have to be fully set aside in favor of self-generating power emergent from the collective nature of the network at any given time. We do not know how to do that.

The human concept of networking includes power as a requisite, and in fact, the current belief is that networking will increase referential power. Power, from the human view of politics, is therefore inextricably linked with control, and control with individual survival and dominance. While humans, generally, support independence, innovation, and freedoms, that support does not extend to organizational life. It is confined almost solely to some ethic of personal freedom and dignity that suggests that certain individual rights are inalienable.

These approaches to political engagement within the organization, however, lead to difficulties when trying to move along the path from semi-bounded organizational structures to boundaryless organizations. Ashkenas et al. describe some of the

history [9]: "While vertical boundaries derived from parent-child authority relationships, horizontal boundaries emerged from task differentiations in primitive societies, as leaders divided work between categories of clan and family members,
sometimes based on skills and sometimes based on social definitions."

As these historical organizational precedents have found their way into what we
now call organizations, their influence is still strongly perceived: "Once horizontal
boundaries become ensconced, people vie to protect their department's power and
resources. Any change in process is viewed as antagonistic to the status quo rather
than useful to the organization, and departments end up spending more time pro-
tecting turf than securing or satisfying customers."

The political positions occupied by human elements in an organization, then,
become anchors to the flexibility that defines the virtual organization. This is as
evident in a group of neighborhood kids gathering in a vacant lot to choose up sides
for a football game as it is in the political maneuverings and defenses evident in the
largest of business corporations. Who stays, who goes, who controls the biggest
group, who plays quarterback, and who stands on the sidelines are organizational
questions answered by human power and influence, with the overall goal of winning the game or gaining sustainable market share easing into second place.

Such political realities have stifled many attempts to open organizations and to
make them more self-generative. The alternative recommendation, as explained by
Deal and Kennedy, is an atomized organization: "Motivation will come from the
opportunity to accomplish complex tasks in an intimate, relatively simple work
environment. We won't waste time and energy worrying about how to climb the
corporate ladder because there won't be one. Most middle-management rungs will
be replaced by mechanisms of social influence—by emphasis on culture. We see it
as a no-boss business" [10].

James Champy [11], in assessing the leadership necessary to support a reengineering environment, echoes these ideas and reinforces the notion that political
power is an obstacle to opening the organization. He puts emphasis on the relationships that leaders must establish with the world outside the organization, as well as
inside it. Davidow and Malone [12] report one notable instance in which an organizational leader removed layers of power structures embedded in middle management, opened the organization, and created a computer program that provided a
place for employees and teams to record their activities and objectives. With this
form of alignment available across the organization, the emphasis shifted from
"what *I* am doing" to "what *we* are doing." In such an empowered environment, the
role of the overseer—as presented to us in traditional management roles—is obsolete. The emphasis now shifts toward alignment activities, including learning, that
support the collected objectives and activities.

The human resources play a much more important role in this organizational system than in others to the left of it in the continuum. Through learning, individuals
introduce knowledge into the network. The network collects a sense of the environment's needs, and learning about the environment is thus distributed across the
nodes. As the network becomes increasingly dependent—for its shape and capabilities—on its interaction with the environment, its sensitivity to new intelligence

leads to an increased dependence on synthesis of facts and insights. Through the connectors among nodes, information and insight flows in all directions since the nodes are essentially equal. They are defined in the network by their applicability to the current reality, and not by some political history. The nodes are therefore free to share, to give to each other and take from each other without the restraints of political or artificial boundaries.

Self-determination is an important but difficult step in achieving open or virtual organizations. The agents in the organization must be empowered, and that empowerment must permeate all the characteristics of the organization. The network must, in some sense, be able to exercise free will.

If this looks like the nuclear or open organization, it is. The difference lies in the percentage of people who are permanently linked into the network, and the ease with which these links can be terminated. The dialectical nature of the relationships has, so far, eluded simple answers. On the one hand, people who are fully dedicated to a network feel strong needs to be recognized and embraced by the organizational system. Their individual wholeness comes, in part, from a feeling of togetherness fostered by their connections with other people and systems across the organization. This sense of wholeness is, of course, a sense of stability that contributes to the individual's ability to concentrate and focus on his or her functionality in the network. From this perspective, the good of the network depends on the sense of ownership and connectivity enabled in the individual as a node. This is constructive, as long as the node contributes to the purpose of the system.

However, given that virtual organizations make radical shifts and turns relatively often, the likelihood that an individual human contributor will remain part of the network for a long period of time is reduced. The other side of the permanence coin, then, is that people who attach themselves to such a network understand the volatile nature of such a network. They know they must be prepared to disconnect from the network if and when their contribution becomes less important to the system's current definition of purpose. Supporting people in this atmosphere is not yet a well-defined art on the part of such networks and organizations.

Not only outplacement but also benefits, compensation, rewards, and recognition are different. These compensation systems are currently set to support long-term membership in the network, not shorter-term contributions. Bonus plans generally apply to those who have achieved a certain level within the organization or who have managed to remain with the organization for a minimum period of time. Tenure thus becomes a personal goal that is rewarded and reinforced by the network itself. Compensation plans for permanent people reflect pay increases set on an annual review of performance. Again, timelines and time structures are set to reward those who can stick around, and not those who can come in, make a well-defined and useful contribution to the system, and then move on. Versatility, while practiced from a hard-core "managed headcount" status in the system, is not a part of the reward and incentive systems, and permanent connectivity to the network is therefore preferable, from the individual's point of view, to a more flexible association.

The existence of the virtual organization, as it creates distinctive differences in the facilitation of humans into, through, and out of the system, also means a revision in thinking about the culture and symbols associated with the organization. The organizational presence of a virtual system may well include a sense of culture, even though the processes of the system dictate an underlying temporality of network existence. There is no kernel and no core in a virtual organization. So the culture of the organization must be established and expressed through the connectivity of the nodes. As connections are established in an electronic network, for instance, a framing bit may be sent to alert the receiving equipment that a transaction is about to take place. Additional information about the transaction itself (not content) may be sent in initial sets of digital information. This protocol and framing information serves to establish the nature of the sender and receiver, as well as the nature of the transaction, and therefore establishes the culture within which the transaction will take place.

We smoke the peace pipe before we begin trading, thus establishing a cultural frame within which the trading relationship will be built. We frame almost all our relationships in the network, regardless of whether human or electronic, with some form of handshake or establishment of protocol. It is within this transaction that culture and symbology are conveyed. A virtual organization will build its cultural image around service and flexibility, as does Amazon.com. This "bookstore," along with other such "stores," exists in physical reality chiefly as a collection of supplier warehouses scattered in various geographies. It is an example of a growing segment of business that has been called *e-commerce,* or electronic commerce. In this instance, the customer interface consists of a website, and not physical stores with salespeople and shelves full of books.

Instead, the warehouses act as shipping nodes for books. The public knows Amazon.com not by its 27-story office towers in major cities but by its ubiquitous accessibility through the Internet. It has established its reputation in some small part through print advertising and reportage but more through on-line advertising and access. Its culture is dependent on its presence on the Internet. It can compete with the ages-old bookstore down the street because it offers ease, convenience, and a range of products that cannot reasonably be offered from the shelves of a physical bookstore. Its service and availability define, in part, its culture. It is not dependent on bricks and mortar, typeface and standard color chart, or the personalities of its sales staff. The cultural shift is toward the non-physical attributes that can be conveyed through the network existence of the organization, and this is the defining culture shift from other forms of organization toward virtuality.

The growth of electronic commerce is just beginning [13], but like the emergence of the Internet itself, its impact on all organizational characteristics will be profound. We have only seen a fraction of the impact such capability will have for us.

The Internet, in fact, is only one enabling electronic technology that has allowed electronic business to thrive, either as another marketing channel for businesses using physical locations and sites, or as a primary marketing channel for businesses that depend on the Internet for their chief means of doing business. Such recent electronic network capabilities as improved bandwidth availability, improved high-speed digital switching capability, and increased focus on data-specific network products and services have contributed to ease of use and reliability. The advent, for example, of higher speed modems, supported by more bandwidth capacity in the network, has meant faster access times into networks and faster transaction times for sending and receiving data once connected. Moreover, the process for securing customer information, especially credit card charge information, is recent and is a major tool for e-commerce.

It is not accurate to say that virtual organizations could not exist without the more recent advances in electronics. In fact, before the general availability of reliable telephone service, people used an old-fashioned device known as the letter to establish connections and to communicate within networks. Before children had opportunities to participate in chat sessions with each other over continents, they had pen pals with whom they corresponded and exchanged thoughts, news, and information. Ecclesiastical organizations corresponded through letters or other written documents. Customers sent orders to suppliers by letter and received goods through the mail or courier services. So, while much has changed, much has not.

The advantage that the virtual organization has now, given these latest tools, lies chiefly in speed, but also in service. Obviously, electronic mail is faster than surface mail or shipping, and when the electronic variety can handle documents of some length and complexity (including photographs and detailed images), this is an obvious advantage over the speed available earlier. The fact that service can be provided directly through the network—as in help desks and information kiosks—means that end-users, whether customers, clients, or others, are better-served. In fact, it may be possible for some organizations to provide more service with Internet-based capabilities than through the traditional means. E-commerce and other electronic services have contributed to the disintermediation of many processes. Through electronic communications, that is, we have been able to eliminate the middleman and accompanying incremental costs.

CHANGE IN ACTION

Change in organizations has not only been tolerated and accepted, it has been embraced as a mantra. For a number of reasons, not merely change but *radical* change is a gleam in every organizational leader's eye, and along with change, the tempting chalice of speed. Where once stability was the desired goal, the latest thinking places emphasis on volatile, time-sensitive markets, which calls for volatile, time-sensitive production and service schedules. To realize these goals, change is an absolute characteristic now being accepted by most organizations.

For example, convenience stores have replaced the familiar corner drugstores, and they offer far more than medicine and ice-cream sodas. Where once the pharmacist leased a building, set up shop in 5,000 square feet, and closed the shop at 5 p.m. on Friday, to reopen at 8 a.m. Monday morning, such buildings are now owned or leased by conglomerates or drug chains. The buildings are precisely planned and often built to specifications provided by the chain's real estate group. When completed, they largely look the same and incorporate far more than just drugs and a soda counter in what may be a stand-alone unit with parking lot and 25,000 to 30,000 square feet in the store itself.

Such units are designed to produce revenue from prescription drugs, but they also depend heavily on sales of snacks, soft drinks, and many other such sundry items. These stores do not depend upon a boutique, single-product, or single-market approach to revenue generation. They take no chances with customer access and maintain long hours of operation, even through the weekends. Some even offer 24-hour access. These stores compete in the same category as the food warehouse down the street that is also open all day and night, often with pharmacy service, as well as with the gasoline/convenience store that occupies a corner not far away.

The Walgreen Company is an example of a drugstore chain that is taking advantage of changes in the market and is responding with changes in its sales and marketing methods. The company has more than 2,400 stores, and more than half of those are freestanding, on real estate that is not a part of a larger mall or other facility. In many of these locations, Walgreen has recently installed drive-through windows, to provide faster and more convenient service to customers who do not want to go into the store. In product mix, more than 45 percent of sales come from prescription drugs, with the other 55 percent distributed among over-the-counter medical products, cosmetics, toiletries, liquor, other beverages, tobacco, and general merchandise. For the 1997 fiscal year, the second highest revenue contributor, behind prescription drugs, was general merchandise.

In response to various market drivers, the company invested nearly $850 million in property and equipment during the year, opening or relocating 251 stores. Target for expansion is 3,000 stores by the year 2000. To increase market penetration, the company has introduced mail-order service for prescription drugs, a service that has helped reduce selling, occupancy, and administrative costs associated with the business. This move, along with the increased availability of store sites and the use of drive-through windows, is expected to appeal to consumers. From this evidence, the emphasis—in the corporate tactics and strategy—is clearly on maintaining flexibility, access, and variety in a changing marketplace. This is not retailing for the contemplative.

This same attitude toward creating versatile, fast-changing organizations is evident in most industrial and commercial segments, as well as in school systems and governments. The increases in speed, volatility, and radical change in organizations has led to an increase in uncertainty among people who participate in these organizations. Even in good economies, layoffs dominate the news, as organizations change and merge, or disappear. Old stability that is tied to national boundaries is being challenged by global competition. Products and even services such as higher education can now be provided economically from various global sources. The firm confidence we once had in local economies is now shaken by intrusion from far distant economies.

At the sociopolitical level, much has happened in the United States to spark disillusionment with current systems and to suggest the need for deep changes in the way things are done [14]. The story in the United States is not much different from the story in other countries. There is little stability, as the economies of Asia and the Pacific Rim suffer setbacks, as the governments of eastern Europe attempt to rebuild following the dissolution of the Soviet Union, and as the governments of western Europe grapple with the formation of a consolidated state, the European Union. Nowhere can we avoid change in these national organizational systems, and nowhere is it limited in its effect to a single nation's boundaries. The world is moving away from the essential stabilities once provided by national boundaries and is becoming inextricably tied together by trade, but also by social concerns and interests and the realization that there is no going back.

THE REPUTATION OF ORGANIZATIONAL CHANGE

Change, however, has not always had such a high reputation. In fact, it was the machine age that quickened the pace of change, with both positive and negative impact on organizations and systems. From the invention of the steam-driven engine, through the invention of devices that use electricity, through the invention of devices that use jet propulsion and nuclear power, machines have increasingly provided humans with ways to distance themselves from the effects of natural forces. People have continuously sought ways in which to channel the energies of the natural world into reliable, predictable structures that produce reliable, predictable results. The Chinese, who irrigated rice paddies using human-powered waterwheels and pumping devices, increased the predictability of the rice crop. The British, who built steam locomotives and ran them on metal tracks from town to town, increased the predictability of transportation and were proud to publish printed schedules that nearly, if not always, guaranteed results for the traveler. U.S. and Soviet inventors, working from baseline experiments and designs from German engineers, increased the reliability of rocket engines, which could lift satellites, monkeys, and even people into orbit or beyond.

In increased predictability and reliability lay safety, security, and profitability. A company intending to provide satellite-based telephone services, for example, would have difficulty finding capital funding, much less customers, if launching and placement of transmission satellites could not be predicted and guaranteed with some accuracy. Predictability and reliability lie at the heart of most business enterprises. Just as Abraham Maslow surmised that security was essential to the individual, so security is viewed as essential for organizations.

PREDICTABILITY, CONSISTENCY, AND RELIABILITY

Organizations do a number of things to ensure predictability, consistency, and reliability. First, they create vision and mission statements intended to focus the attention of the members, as well as non-members, on the chief rationale and purposes of the organization. Such statements are often enshrined on walls, included prominently on websites, and published in the first few pages of annual reports. These are symbolic statements that serve as touchstones for organizational communicants, be they partners, employees, representatives, vendors, or customers.

Second, organizations measure against standards that are most often derived from averages. In most organizations, performance relies heavily on means derived from surveys, from observations of performance, or from other measurement activity. Target goals are then set somewhere above or below the mean, depending on the type of measurement and type of activity. Measurements, moreover, are largely linear. Projections are made from extrapolations based on historical data, assuming that success lies in a growth curve. The mental model says that everything must get better, and go toward positive numbers, to claim success. Accountants go to great lengths to discount phenomena such as unusual purchases or investments, or one-time costs, that may appear to drive the graph downward. Such events are carefully documented and presented in such a way that the organization's business will be perceived to be healthy and growing, despite such special costs. Measurements are intended to preserve the idea that the activity of the system is stable and steady and is in an upward, growth mode.

Third, the structure of the organization is arranged and presented in such a way that order and unity of purpose are carried out. This supports, in particular, the nuclear form of organizational structure, in which everything—and everyone—has its place, and that place is clearly delineated in a vertical line of sight from top to bottom. Ambiguity is the enemy of the nuclear organization, and as ambiguity is reduced through policy, procedures, and policing, it is much easier for an organization to present a unified front to clients and users of its products and services. As organizations become more open, this unity is much more difficult to maintain, as energy is diverted into multiple concerns and channels within the organization, as well as between the organization and its suppliers and end-users.

Fourth, selection and treatment of personnel is based on policies and procedures. This time-proven method for creating stability is still widely supported [15]. The existence of procedures, as we have always known, is no guarantee that work will be done efficiently. In fact, in some work processes, strict adherence to procedures is neither possible nor desirable. For many knowledge workers, caught up in a never-ending sea of change, procedures are often outdated by the time they are published.

Fifth, the values of the organization, and its culture, are oriented toward stability. When Frank Phillips ran the Phillips Petroleum Company as a family business, the focal point for decisions regarding the company was the Phillips family. Decisions were made in Bartlesville, Oklahoma, where Frank lived and had his headquarters. At that time, as the stories go, the culture and entire presence of the organization took its shape from the values of the family. Frank is remembered as much for the money he gave to children in the streets of Bartlesville as for the exploration decisions he made for the company. Family values were translated into the company, and it became an extension of the family. To many company employees, regardless of level or rank, Phillips was known as Uncle Frank. While he was probably not addressed as such, the familial title hints at the extent to which his personal values, and those of his family, influenced the larger organization of which he was the head.

Sixth, the political and power structures are closely related to maintenance of stability. Position power is a significant factor in the hierarchical model, while referential power becomes more important as the organization opens. Stability lies in the understanding of where power lies, who has it, and who doesn't, and the extent to which power is shared or delegated. Stability equally lies in the extent to which politics dominate the organization's structuring, its decision-making, its personnel selection, its learning, and its relationships with those who are outside the boundaries. If product or process decisions depend less on inputs and the thinking of those skilled in the particular areas than on the political acceptability of certain alternatives, then the organization might just as well be run by the politicians and not by subject-matter experts.

THE SNAKE IN THE GARDEN

At the same time that organizations seek stability and a predictable center of being, they are also highly aware that change and adaptation are absolute necessities. The garden would be incomplete without the snake. What we are faced with is a situation that often frightens us with its uncertainty [16]. The dialectical nature of organizational cohesion is evident in the existence of both extremes in organizational reality. Whereas, on the one hand, control ensures mission and efficiency and profitability, deregulation helps ensure adaptation to quirks and anomalies in the environment, which may threaten stability. There is no tenable neutral ground. What is further unsettling to organizational thinkers and participants is the realization that change may be radical and deep, thereby changing the essential nature of the garden and of the snake. Today, organizational planners may recognize the organization and characterize it in one way; tomorrow, these characteristics may have mutated so thoroughly that the organizational entity may be totally redefined.

The ability to mutate quickly is at once an obsession and a nightmare. Given that constancy has been achieved through considerable expense and effort, rapid mutation, if achievable, provides comfort that speed of change in the organization can match speed of change in the marketplace, or among priorities of end-users. Customers can continue to rest assured that, even though they are changing, this provider organization is changing just as quickly. In fact, what a provider organization wants its customers or end-users to understand is that its change trajectory is actually a few degrees inside the trajectory pursued in the customer organization, and then it extends out ahead of the customer's changes. In Figure 3-3, this *inside-outside change-up* phenomenon is shown as the customer pursues change to increase and improve the customer's own position relative to the market and its volatility. At the same time, the provider organization's mutation occurs in relation to both the marketscape and the customer organization. The provider organization wants a position on the inside of the customer's track to maintain its current profitable relationship with the customer. This is sheer practicality since no relationship would exist unless the provider had goods and services of present interest to the customer's organization.

Within the dynamics of the provider organization, however, is the more complex attempt to change *before* the customer organization shifts forward and upward in its marketscape, and to move strategically in a pioneering relationship with the customer. The provider is the scout, and it prepares the way for its customers. The black arrow shows this inside-outside direction pursued by the provider organiza-

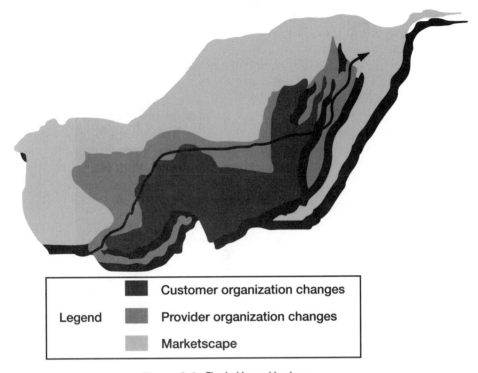

	Customer organization changes
Legend	Provider organization changes
	Marketscape

Figure 3-3. The inside-outside change-up.

tion, in relation to the marketscape and the customer. The limitations of the figure, however, lie in its inability to represent a true three-dimensional and dynamic interplay among the customer, provider, and market entities.

MAINTAINING THE GARDEN

There are clear advantages to maintaining stability. The open delegation of responsibility for the welfare of the entire organization is a risk of a high order. To enable work teams at the production or service level to make decisions that might impact the entire operation of the enterprise is not a naturally attractive option to those who style themselves as organizational leaders. The dissemination of power and authority is never as convenient as the accumulation of it. To take command, one only has to step in front of the troops and begin issuing orders. People, for the most part, will follow such an order-giver, as long as their own personal stability is not threatened. There is comfort in being part of a mob, as long as there appears to be someone at the front of it, organizing it and taking responsibility for it. The rest is mere participation. In an organizational fortress, participants can passively accept orders, carry out well-defined tasks, and go home with pay and benefits fairly guaranteed. Suppliers and customers alike are cared for, but controlled, with little integration or access into the central organization that is not orchestrated.

A stable organization also has the advantage of offering the illusion of upward mobility to those who wish it. The promise in the garden is that leadership at one level can lead to leadership at successively higher levels, and that power and control will be increased as one goes up the management career ladder. In the stable world, management and leadership are reserved and not distributed. Those who are not selected to lead will follow instead, with the implication, in this form of governance, that they will carry out the wishes of their superiors. Their reactions are thus stabilized and channeled into those avenues and tasks determined to be of value by the executive control function represented by management.

An emphasis on the development of leaders in an organization, then, is a sure sign that it is searching for stability through uniformity of thought and control over subordinates. There are no leaders without followers, and followers are there to be controlled. If this is considered the natural state of the organizational culture, then followers will not be challenged to think, decide, innovate, or realign the activities of the organization. While their opinions may occasionally be sought, their power will be limited, yielding stability and predictability. Compliance under these conditions is ensured, and the organization automatically gains a reputation as a rock-solid contributor to its environment.

INTRODUCING THE SNAKE

While stability yields many advantages for an organization in speed and efficiency and management, there are also advantages in instability. While it is not unheard of to "shake things up" in a nuclear organization, introducing change is generally a considered and agonizing affair. The actual change decision itself, however, is relatively easy, since it will be made, in proper order, down through the hierarchy. The focus is on the physical change or process change, and not on changes required in the human elements of the system. This is because the humans are followers and are therefore expected to be compliant with such changes as may be needed by the masters. While the cognitive domains are addressed in such change processes, the affective domain will receive less attention.

Susceptibility to change and to the impacts of change is different in a more open organizational atmosphere. Where boundaries have been opened, changes may impact not a single entity but several, including those residing outside the permeable boundaries of the larger organization itself. At this point on the organizational continuum, apparently small changes may blossom into larger changes or set off a chain of changes that reach beyond the immediate vicinity of the original change decision. Impact of change decisions becomes less certain and less predictable.

The role of change manager can be viewed as transitional between hierarchical organizations and open organizations. If placed in a hierarchical organization, the change manager may be the equivalent of a project manager, with direct reports and other resources devoted to planning, implementing, and ensuring the changes. If placed in an open organization, the role may act in a more consultative, facilitative fashion, working along with other organizational leaders to effect change.

By extension, this version of the role may exist as a node in a networked organization, becoming connected when change efforts need to involve several parts of the net and then being disconnected when unnecessary. In the virtual organization, change is integrated in the system and comes naturally as a part of networked operations.

The introduction of change can be aperiodic or periodic and can be minor or radical. Continuous improvement, a concept supported most visibly in Deming's Total Quality Management concept [17], is the foundation for an approach to change that is periodic and generally minor. The underlying philosophy suggests that through continuous monitoring of key activities within the organizational systems, changes can be introduced gradually so that, through a process of successive approximation, desired goals are reached without aperiodic disruptions to the system. This approach has taken on biblical proportions, as managers have attempted to introduce measurement methods that generate baseline and benchmark data within various functions of the organization.

While continuous improvement serves for applications where some stability exists, systems that operate with less stability do not yield good measures of linear progression. Change in such systems tends to be aperiodic and radical, and may involve greater scope within the larger organization than those changes managed under continuous improvement plans. The introduction of a new line of business, for example, offers opportunities for change that cut across most if not all subsystems. Such a change cannot be handled through continuous improvement and is often handled through processes that have come to be referred to as *reengineering*.

The term came into popular use in organizational change circles with the publication, by Michael Hammer and James Champy, of their book *Reengineering the Corporation: A Manifesto for Business Revolution* [18]. The direction taken by the authors was contrary to the ideas of incremental change and surgical changes that had previously dominated the literature and thinking. As noted in the earlier discussion of OD, the benchmark work by Lewin and others on change processes suggested caution, care, and focus in change efforts. They addressed much attention to the reactions of the people included in and affected by change. It was, in fact, Lewin's work that introduced a more participative role for those affected by change, in making the change successful [19].

Building on the ideas of organizational change already in place, Hammer and Champy raised the stakes for change, recommending wide-ranging radical changes in place of the more controlled and limited change efforts.

Reengineering creates a permanently generative function that removes barriers and controls on information and thus facilitates productivity. It tends to flatten and integrate the organization by radically altering the processes to eliminate unneeded management and control functions. This form of change may result in the total transformation of a function or an organization and how it accomplishes its goals.

SNAKE CHARMERS

In the late 1970s, the desirable characteristics and attributes of middle managers were summed up this way in a management-training course. Middle managers should:

1. Set realistic goals for themselves and their departments.
2. Not deny or excuse waste, inefficiency, or lost time.
3. Follow up on work assignments to assure adequate performance.
4. See the future as something they make happen, not something that happens to them.
5. Confront the people they supervise when work does not meet their standards.
6. See the whole of their departments in relation to the larger organization.
7. Assign work with due regard for worker capability.
8. Delegate jobs and responsibilities to those under their supervision.
9. Serve as organizers and conduits of information: upward, downward, and laterally.
10. View people as the primary resource they use to accomplish their goals.
11. Understand and assure compliance with company procedures, and recommend changes where necessary.
12. Take responsibility for the training and development of their subordinates.
13. Be physically accessible to their subordinates in modeling appropriate behavior.
14. Recognize the tools of control in their operation and be willing to use them.
15. Recognize that people do their best work when they feel a sense of involvement.

These guidelines and suggestions for mid-management behavior were based, of course, on a hierarchical model, with power flowing down from the top and being incrementally allocated to layers below the top. Mid-managers were the points of control where realistic goals were set. The role was confrontational, with the admonition to avoid excusing waste, inefficiency, or lost time. Mid-managers made the future happen, and subordinates were tools of the trade.

A major role of this manager was to "assure adequate performance." In practice, this meant using control, not influence, to accomplish work. While the manager was encouraged to "delegate jobs," this meant delegating tasks, with tactical responsibility. People were a "primary resource" mid-managers used to accomplish *their* (management's) goals. Managers were to train and develop subordinates and assign them work with "due regard" for worker capability. Compliance was important, and management had the responsibility to ensure compliance. These managers were also responsible for "modeling appropriate behavior" in the same way that a parent models appropriate behavior for a child.

The manager, moreover, was the special emissary in a chain of command. She was an "organizer and conduit of information" in all directions. Upward-bound information passed through her hands, as well as downward information. Impressions along with information from lower ranks, then, were filtered and interpreted as the mid-manager saw fit and presented to upper ranks when and where the manager felt appropriate. While she was expected to cooperate with her "peers," there was no such admonition regarding subordinates. Management, in this era, was the art of getting work done through other people.

In this atmosphere, the management of change was embedded in this whole view of the organization as something to be tamed. Supervisors and managers were *change agents* who were, consistent with the rest of their power, responsible for making change happen as they were directed to do so.

Emphasis on control of people and on getting work done through people meant less emphasis on technology. While electronic technologies and computer equipment was just beginning to make its presence felt, these technologies were regarded with the same attitude as were the hammers and tongs on the workbenches. It was people who made things happen, not machines, and what could not be accomplished with electricity and hydraulics could be accomplished through sheer human muscle and brains.

The guidelines for managers planning change are particularly revealing, as they illustrate the way in which change was viewed in organizations:

1. Planning is used in the solution or avoidance of problems.
2. Plans should be logically based on the *in-fact* operating realities rather than on an ideal of what *ought to be*.
3. Plans should be flexible to accommodate variances within the system.
4. Workers should be familiar with those parts of the plan that concern them.
5. Planning facilitates achievement of production goals.
6. Work should not only be planned, but planned in detail, taking into consideration likely slippages and devising methods of coping with problems and exceptions.
7. Planning is an approximation based on the facts we have at hand; it can be wrong.

Change had to do with those things that were wrong or might go wrong in the operating realities, or current set of organizational parameters (strategic planning was reserved for executives). The idea of flexibility is introduced, but note that it is intended only to "accommodate variances within the system," and not to take into account influences from outside the system. In a closed and closely bounded nuclear system, it was unnecessary to consider the potential impact of external variables in operational planning.

The intent of such planning was to achieve production goals and therefore had to do with very narrow and specific tasks and processes. In such a confined planning mode, it was more possible to apply logical tools, including contingency and preventive action planning, in some level of detail. Chances were good that in a microsetting, the whole system would not change so radically or quickly that detailed contingency or problem prevention plans would be rendered useless.

The last item in the list is important because it points the way toward current understandings of system behavior. Systems have come to be recognized, especially as they approach open and virtual behaviors, as more difficult to forecast. That planning for change is now an approximation is a given, and the notation that "it can be wrong" is more appropriate than ever. The change leader in the late 1970s was challenged to eliminate as much variability as possible from his change plan. Variance from plan, from spec, or from standards, even when making changes happen in the organization, was to be avoided. The full realization that change and volatility themselves must be factored into any plan for change did not fully arrive until the 1990s. It was only with a new understanding of the nature of the system, and an acknowledgment of the volatility and dynamics of an organizational system, that new views on change management began to take hold.

In 1995, Peter Drucker [20] observed that:

> Uncertainty—in the economy, society, politics—has become so great as to render futile, if not counterproductive, the kind of planning most companies still practice: forecasting based on probabilities.

The organization, then, is no longer a fixed planet in a predictable solar system. It is capable of influence from a number of things around it, and the effect of influence will be felt throughout the organization and not just at its periphery. Even the core must yield as changes are influenced from external forces, events, and philosophies. This approach to organizational systems is in high contrast to the approach taken by the planners and managers of the 1970s. To plan and manage change in a set of circumstances with high variability is a different set of challenges than those faced by change managers who still felt some solid basis underneath their organizational feet.

John Kotter [21] proposed an eight-step process to accomplishing change in such a volatile organizational environment. Chief ingredients in his prescription include "creating the guiding coalition" and "empowering broad-based actions." This framework for change management offers a different perspective from the legacy management approaches of the 1970s. The more recent thinking clearly incorporates the idea that change is a given and not an exception in organizational behavior, and that systems are dynamic by their nature.

The introduction of the idea of coalition results in a team-focused change effort from the outset. Vision and strategy are outputs of the coalition, as is communication. What is incongruous here is the suggestion that, like the 1970s model, there is a special group of leaders who will act as models for employees. This may be a holdover from hierarchical models and the nuclear organization, in which such superior-subordinate relationships depended on modeling of proper behavior by superiors, to be imitated by the childlike employees. In 1995, there appeared to be some elements of 1975 thinking. Those who studied leadership roles were still influenced by what they saw in the practice, and the practice of management and leadership was still very much hierarchical.

What is clearly a departure from earlier thinking, however, is the idea that communication should be continuous and not constitute a one-time pronouncement of change policy from the top. The possibility exists for true communication, including dialogue and empowerment, if the process is maintained and encouraged throughout the change effort and beyond. Risk-taking, not something that was featured in the 1970s view, was encouraged in 1996. This offset the earlier tendency toward stability and the assumption that a high percentage of potential problems could be anticipated and eliminated through contingency and preventive planning.

The management and control of change is a philosophy that is deeply embedded in organizational systems theory and practice. There are still some underlying assumptions that change is top-driven, that significant change should be managed by a few leading visionaries, and that the role of employees is passive. Change, moreover, is largely something that is handled by humans, and not by any other elements or agents operating in the system. Change processes still rely on human intelligence as the key factor, and tend to dismiss the role of equipment and networks. Finally, the picture of change management seems to rely on a before-and-after approach that takes an organization from one form of being and leaves it at another form of being. The danger in such approaches is that organizations are now exploring the boundaries of stability. The more activities that take organizations toward open and virtual behavior, the more likely it is that the organization as a whole will be a constantly changing environment. In open and virtual systems, the management of change is more likely to be an everyday activity that is pervasive throughout the organization, rather than a special, management-driven event. In such systems, the challenge becomes to allow changes to happen that may not fit a mold or picture of how management might view the future of the organization.

Introducing this level of spontaneity into systems thinking is a major challenge confronting all agents in the organization, not just the traditional leadership. To allow for complex or chaotic behavior in the system, which brings with it innovation and competitiveness, is to allow the system to be changeable. Our notions of chaotic systems as being out of control will change as we come to understand the elements of order that underlie what we often fear to be erratic system activity. With a deeper understanding of chaos in our organizational systems will come a deeper understanding of how we can measure and take advantage of the turbulence that brings with it a renewal of organizational energy.

REFERENCES

1. Walter, D. (Ed.) *Will Man Fly? And Other Strange & Wonderful Predictions from the 1890s,* Helena, Mont.: American and World Geographic Publishing, 1993, pp. 51, 90.
2. Bolman, L. G. and T. E. Deal. *Reframing Organizations,* San Francisco: Jossey-Bass, 1991.
3. Mintzberg, H. "The five basic parts of the organization," in *Classics of Organization Theory,* J. M. Shafritz and J. Steven Ott (Eds.), Belmont, Calif.: Wadsworth, 1991, pp. 243–254.
4. Mink, O. G., et al., *Open Organizations: A Model for Effectiveness, Renewal, and Intelligent Change,* San Francisco: Jossey-Bass, 1994.
5. Ackoff, R. L., *The Democratic Corporation,* New York: Oxford, 1994, pp. 18–21.
6. Handy, C., *The Age of Unreason,* Boston: Harvard Business School Press, 1989.
7. Belasco, J. A. and R. C. Stayer, *Flight of the Buffalo,* New York: Warner Books, 1993.
8. Argyris, C., *Knowledge for action,* The Jossey-Bass Management Series, San Francisco: Jossey-Bass, 1993.
9. Ashkenas, R., et al., *The Boundaryless Organization,* The Jossey-Bass Management Series, San Francisco: Jossey-Bass, 1995, pp. 112, 117.
10. Deal, T. E. and A. A. Kennedy, *Corporate Cultures,* New York: Addison-Wesley Publishing Company, 1982, p. 177.

11. Champy, J., *Reengineering Management,* New York: HarperBusiness, 1995, p. 27.

12. Davidow, W. H. and M. S. Malone, *The Virtual Corporation,* New York: HarperCollins, 1992.

13. Tapscott, D. and D. Ticoll. "E-businesses break the mold." *InternetWeek,* September 14, 1998, p. 80.

14. Castells, M. *The Power of Identity.* The information age: Economy, society, and culture series, Vol. II, Malden, Mass.: Blackwell, 1997.

15. Tracey, W. R., "Procedures: Indispensable productivity tools," in *Performance in Practice* (ASTD newsletter), Summer 1998, pp. 12–13.

16. DeBerry, S. T. *Quantum Psychology: Steps to a Postmodern Ecology of Being,* Westport, Conn.: Praeger, 1993, pp. 1, 7.

17. Walton, M. *The Deming Management Method,* New York: The Putnam Publishing Group, 1986.

18. Hammer, M. and J. Champy, *Reengineeering the Corporation,* New York: HarperBusiness, 1993.

19. Weisbord, M. R., *Productive Workplaces.* The Jossey-Bass Management Series, W. Bennis, R. O. Mason, and I. I. Mitroff (Eds.), San Francisco: Jossey-Bass, 1987, p. 72.

20. Drucker, P. F., *Managing in a Time of Great Change,* New York: The Penguin Group, 1995, p. 39.

21. Kotter, J. P., *Leading Change,* Boston: Harvard Business School, 1996, p. 21.

Chapter 4

Classical Chaos

Before moving too deeply into a consideration of learning and how it may operate in chaotic organizational situations, it is important to understand that the concept of *chaos* and the concept of *chaos theory* are not one and the same. What this book will refer to as *classical chaos* has a different set of definitions and connotative meanings from the more recent ideas of mathematical or *technical chaos,* which are bound up with chaos theory. While there is a relationship between the two applications of the term *chaos,* the relationship is one that needs to be thoroughly understood. One cannot be satisfied to understand the changes in organizations, and the uncertainties surrounding school, work, and home life, as the influence of classical chaos alone. It is important to go beyond that concept and view the changes themselves as a part of the systems in which we live and participate. As such, it is important to understand how technical chaos manifests itself within our organizational systems. We need to see how we can recognize it and how we might manipulate it to the greater success of the systems. We need to understand the role that learning might play in helping us, our machines, and our networks participate more effectively in a technically chaotic system.

To accept chaos as a given in systems, whether we are looking at the people, the equipment, or the network operations, is to lean toward an acceptance of classical chaos in operation. There is a fatal attraction to the dark side that tempts us to accept chaos as the other side of order and "goodness" and to go our way with the feeling that we are powerless. However, if we adopt a more measured view of chaos as a firm and measurable reality in these systems in which all of us participate, then it may be possible to identify, and even predict, behavior and changes in the systems, based on an understanding of how chaos operates. To move from a passive to an active view of chaos in organizational dynamics is a significant change in worldview. Yet this change will explain much that happens in life systems that are becoming, apparently, more complicated and less explainable.

I remember sitting on the front porch of the wood-frame house built by my grandfather on his farm. The farm itself, some 200 acres, lies in a slight valley, formed by low hills. As I think back to the view of the farm, and the barn, and the storage buildings, there is a sense that life was simpler back then. He did not have to deal with massive amounts of traffic or the noise, confusion, and frustration of air travel. He did not have to worry about whether a power outage might shut down his computer and Internet connection. He had little concern about the noises coming from the neighbors' house. There was no light pollution and very little water pollution in the creek behind the house, and even the U.S. Environmental Protection Agency would have approved the levels of particulate matter in the air he and his family breathed. When he hitched up his mule and went out to plow the cotton or corn or beans, he did not worry about the price of diesel fuel, nor did he have to worry about the electrical subsystems that controlled the power takeoff drive on his equipment. In short, it was a largely biological world, consisting of him; the wooden house; his family; his mules, cows, hogs, and chickens; the grain, corn, and cotton he grew; the manure he used for fertilizer; and the weather, which either supported the crop or not. Energy sources were largely wood, water, kerosene, and muscle.

In this idyllic picture, could there have been chaos? The answer, of course, is yes. From his perspective, my grandfather watched hail damage ready-to-harvest oats, a supply that would have fed the mules and cows for much of the winter. He saw dry weather turn the sand and clay soil into dry sand that would not support a corn crop, important for sale, as well as for the family and for the animals. He saw the dirt roads become clogged with deep puddles after a heavy rain, rendering the roads impassable in a four-wheeled wagon because of the mud. On market days, it was important that he get his crop—perishable vegetables and eggs, as well as less perishable items—into town for sale and trade. He and his family depended on this form of regular income to buy the things they could not make for themselves on the farm.

All these things, not to mention the potential for death or injuries of people and animals, could upset what we might see, from our perspective, as a more peaceful form of existence in a natural world. People in that time, from their perspective, saw disaster in as many changes as we see in our time and from our perspective. The world of nature offers many potential threats, and living in it is as challenging as living in an era when technology has surrounded humans with more complicated devices than nature alone could devise.

Chaos, to some extent, is a matter of perception and viewpoint. Moreover, chaos, in their time and ours, consists largely of those changes that happen to us, that happen without warning, and that bring about profound and often complicated changes in our lives, our systems, and our organizations. A recent perspective on the telecommunication industry, for example, opened with this thought: "In an industry that's been rocked by chaos repeatedly over the past year, AT&T really did it this time. By announcing it will merge with Tele-Communications Inc. (TCI), the second-largest cable provider in the country, AT&T chairman Michael Armstrong may succeed in breaking into local markets where other long distance companies have been struggling. He wants a local pipe into customers' homes—and he'll do anything to get it" [1]. This idea correctly reflects one definition of chaos—that which has to do with apparent randomness and radical change. It is the same feeling that might have been expressed by my grandparents, had hurricane-force winds and rain wreaked sudden havoc on their crops in the coastal sandhills.

The concept of chaos—present in philosophy, theology, and literature since the time of the Greeks, if not before—should be seen as an archetypal pattern in human thought and conceptualization, separate from chaos theory. Understood in this light, chaos theory may emerge as another manifestation of chaos, with similarities that link its various facets and beliefs to the larger construct that is chaos.

WHAT IS CHAOS?

In its classical tradition, the term itself goes back to the Greeks and was transferred through Latin to Middle English, and thus into the English vocabulary. Its definitions [2] center around the notion of confusion and disarray:

> (1) a state of utter confusion or disorder; a total lack of organization or order; (2) any confused, disorderly mass; (3) the infinity of space or formless matter supposed to have preceded the existence of the ordered universe; (4) the personification of disorder in any of several ancient Greek myths; (5) a chasm or abyss

Because the word has been used in so many kinds of situations, it is important to make some distinctions among these applications. By doing so, it will be easier to understand that not every reference to chaos is a reference to the particular connotations the term has in relation to scientific theory. At the same time, however, it will be easier to see links and connections between the historical uses of the term and the scientific or technical uses. This understanding may suggest some reasons for the tendency of researchers outside the physical sciences to show a strong interest in chaos theory.

THE MYTHOLOGY OF CHAOS

In Greek and Latin literature, both Hesiod and Ovid used the term in what might be described as a cosmological sense. Hesiod (c. 700 B.C.) anthropomorphized Chaos, as one of the first three powers that came to be at the creation. The other two powers were Earth and Eros, but "the very first of all Chaos came into being" [3]. It is possible to speculate that the Earth might represent the physical inorganic universe as the Greeks saw it, Eros nature, and Chaos the chasm, abyss, and seeming emptiness that is neither solid earth nor biological nature. If so, then Hesiod was attempting to describe, in his first three powers, all the basics that would explain what was observable.

Later, the Latin poet Ovid would again see Chaos as a starting point for the *Metamorphoses* (c. 2 A.D.) of life on earth and in the universe. In Ovid's cosmology, there was an initial metamorphosis from Chaos to Cosmos, the latter state representing order in the universe. Ovid further laid out relationships among the elements of universal structure:

> *Nor can these elements stand at a stay,*
> *But by exchanging alter every day.*
> *Th' eternal world four bodies comprehends*
> *Ingend'ring all. The heavy earth discends,*
> *So water, clogg'd with weight; two, light, aspire,*

Depresst by none, pure air and purer fire.
And, though they have their several seats, yet all
Of these are made, to these again they fall.
Resolved earth to water rarifies;
To air extenuated waters rise;
The air, when it itself again refines,
To elemental fire extracted shines.
They in like order back again repair;
The grosser fire condenseth into air;
Air into water; water, thick'ning, then
Grows solid and converts to earth again.
None holds his own: for nature ever joys
In change and with new forms the old supplies.
In all the world not any perish quite,
But only are in various habits dight:
For, to begin to be what we before
Were not, is to be born; to die, no more
Then ceasing to be such. Although the frame
Be changeable, the substance is the same [4].

In this view of relationships, then, there is order within disorder and change: the four elements—earth, air, water, and fire—are constants that operate in predictable ways yet change within ranges of predictability.

Scholars thus linked chaos with creation myths, and chaos is a primary concept in a number of them. Joseph Campbell, for example, describes an Eddic account of creation that begins with the "*Ginnungagap,* the void, the abyss of chaos into which all devolves at the end of the cycle and out of which then all appears again after a timeless age of reincubation" [5]. In this Eddic example, the conversion from Chaos is not without pain:

> after the "yawning gap" had given forth in the north a mist-world of cold and in the south a region of fire, and after the heat from the south had played on the rivers of ice that crowded down from the north, a yeasty venom began to be exuded. From this a drizzle arose, that, in turn, congealed to rime. The rime melted and dripped; life was quickened from the drippings in the form of a torpid, gigantic, hermaphroditic, horizontal figure named Ymir. The giant slept, and as it slept it sweated; one of its feet begat with the other a son, while under its left hand germinated a man and wife.

Campbell also recounts a Babylonian myth of a hero named Marduk, the sun-god; the victim is Tiamat, a dragon-creature, "attended by swarms of demons—a female personification of the original abyss itself: chaos as the mother of the gods, but now the menace of the world." In brief, Marduk overcomes Tiamat, as her will to fight apparently wanes, cuts her in half, and from her parts creates the physical and natural world.

One of the key points Campbell makes, in summarizing this stage in the cosmogonic cycle, is that there is a basic paradox in a number of mythologies, which he calls the paradox of the dual focus. "Just as at the opening of the cosmogonic cycle it was possible to say 'God is not involved,' but at the same time 'God is creator-preserver-destroyer,' so now at this critical juncture, where the One breaks into the many, destiny 'happens,' but at the same time 'is brought about.'" In creation from chaos, the universe as we know it is, largely, one with a central construct and architecture that is constantly "pouring into being, exploding, and dissolving," but the main construct remains as a peaceful center of stability.

CLASSICAL CHAOS AND COSMOLOGY

A significant starting point in understanding how the meanings of chaos have evolved is an understanding of the *Almagest* of Ptolemy, written about 140 A.D. This worldview has significantly influenced the understanding, in the Western world, of how the universe is ordered and has had extensive influence, therefore, on theology and literature and Western thought. The *Almagest* provided a wealth of information, based on observations taken over time, about the locations of the stars and the motions of the planets. This level of precision brought a new ability to predict the positions of the heavenly bodies at any given time. The work of Ptolemy introduced into the understanding of astronomy an order that had not existed before. He also based his calculations on numerous observations, something earlier observers and philosophers had not done with any rigor. Ptolemy's work, because of its accuracy, became widely accepted and the basis for astronomy for hundreds of years.

The paradigm thus introduced into science—and extended into non-scientific thinking—was one of measurements of things in the sky from the viewpoint of the earth. Without telescopes, and instrumentation, and without well-proven mathematics, the limitation on Ptolemy and other observers was that, while they could observe, they could not measure with any precision. Furthermore, they could not postulate, in any scientific basis, a view of the universe from any other vantage point than from the earth. The exception to this way of thinking had been Aristarchus (c. 300 B.C.), who had posed a heliocentric theory that suggested the sun and stars were fixed in the universe and the earth revolved around the sun. Unfortunately, the only extant work from his hand provides a proof that is geocentric. So his influence on the thinking of Ptolemy and later scientists may have been minimal, at least as regards a solar system [6].

In the late thirteenth and early fourteenth centuries, the Western world was largely influenced by Christianity, and more specifically by the Catholic Church and its doctrines and beliefs. Dante Alighieri, while schooled in classical Greek and Latin literature, was, in the creation of the *Inferno,* more influenced by the Christian and Catholic traditions. Catholicism, at that time, was itself influenced by the omniscience and omnipotence of God. In addition, there was considerable interest in the paradox between the concept of unity of the one God and the triune nature of

God—Father, Son, and Holy Ghost. Dante's structure of the entire Divine Comedy follows this triune concept, with each part representing one part of the triune God: "*Inferno,* the Power of the Father; *Purgatory,* the Wisdom of the Son, *Paradise,* the Love of the Holy Spirit" [7]. The journey through the inferno, through purgatory, to paradise can be construed as a representation of the cosmogonic cycle noted by Campbell. In fact, as Maude Bodkin points out, "the torments of the damned are described as unending, but they have their effect as incidents in a journey—a transition from darkness to light, from the pangs of death to new life" [8].

Dante's guide through the inferno is Virgil, who represents Reason. So it is the orderliness of reason and control that provides a view of the disorderliness of hell. The vision of hell is a vision of chaos, in the sense that it is disorderly, as well as in the sense that it is, pictorially, a chasm, outside the ultimate in creation, the earth. Dante was working in the Ptolemaic understanding that the earth was the imperfect center of the created universe, with a range of concentric circles moving outward, including the moon, Mercury, Venus, the sun, Mars, Jupiter, Saturn, the fixed stars, the Primum Mobile, and the Coelum Empyraeum, as depicted in Figure 4-1. So Dante's vision is compatible with other myths that describe the relationship of chaos to everything else. While his work is highly structured on both existing views of astronomy and the universe, as well as on existing theology, the story in the *Inferno* is one of a descent into a chasm filled with orderly disorder. The formulaic structure of the poem reflects a formulaic understanding of the operation of the universe and of theology in the universe. Yet, the message is one of disorder:

> *Here sighs and cries and wails coiled and recoiled*
> *on the starless air, spilling my soul to tears.*
> *A confusion of tongues and monstrous accents toiled.*
>
> *in pain and anger. Voices hoarse and shrill*
> *and sounds of blows, all intermingled, raised*
> *tumult and pandemonium that still*
>
> *whirls on the air forever dirty with it*
> *as if a whirlwind sucked at sand [9].*

This description of hell thus fits the definition of chaos, both in the sense that it is a chasm or abyss and in the sense that it represents disorder.

In the Elizabethan world (c. 1533–1603), the Ptolemaic view of the universe carried through, influencing the thinking and writing of the time. In these beliefs, chaos held a part: "The planets were busy the whole time; and their fluctuating conjunctions produced a seemingly chaotic succession of conditions, theoretically predictable but in practice almost wholly beyond the wit of man" [4]. The view of the Elizabethans held that there was a strongly defined order in the universe, both physical and metaphysical. The concept of angels included a hierarchy of angels. The concept of evil contained its own hierarchy. Order and perfection and true beauty lay outside of the earth, which was at the center of the universe and was its grossest and least perfect member. So it is that Dante's hell lay in a chasm (he followed the same world order, though earlier than the Elizabethans), and so it is that Lorenzo proclaims, in Shakespeare's *The Merchant of Venice:*

> *How sweet the moonlight sits upon this bank!*
> *Here will we sit, and let the sounds of music*
> *Creep in our ears; soft stillness and the night*
> *Become the touches of sweet harmony.*
> *Sit, Jessica: look, how the floor of heaven*
> *Is thick inlaid with patines of bright gold:*
> *There's not the smallest orb which thou behold'st*
> *But in his motion like an angel sings,*
> *Still quiring to the young-eyed cherubins;*
> *Such harmony is in immortal souls;*
> *But, whilst this muddy vesture of decay*
> *Doth grossly close it in, we cannot hear it [10].*

Here, the view is upward. If only humankind could escape the restrictions of its imperfect "vesture"—its body— it would be able to appreciate fully the glories of the higher spheres in the universe, where order, represented by music, overcomes chaos.

Chaos was a part of God's plan. The natural destruction that people experienced was the other side of the coin and had to be endured, even as earthly pleasures were to be enjoyed. Chaos, in fact, could be attributed more to the actions of mankind than to a malevolent God. In this age, humankind had an element of free will, and self-control of one's destiny. Even though not everything was understood, people had some feeling that the nature of the universe allowed man to influence his destiny. Fate—often recognized in the influence of the stars—was a strong determiner of the pathway, but not the only determiner. Fate could be affected by the will of man, and the path of life thus changed for the people of the Renaissance.

The elements that constituted the universe were themselves considered in hierarchical order: earth, the basest, with water, air, and fire next in order. Everything was composed of some combination of these four elements, and these elements contested with each other for dominance. But not only were they considered to be set against each other, they were, at the same time, transmutable. The general principle was that there was constant shifting from one form to another, creating new potentialities in the shifts. In this idea, the Elizabethans had held to the concepts of order reflected in Ovid. The elements were important, as they served as the joining factor between humankind and the universe in which it existed. The theory of the elements helped explain why things happened the way they did and helped explain the constancy that could be observed in the whole, along with the changeability and flux that could be observed within that whole.

The worldview, therefore, was closely aligned with the place of the world in the universe, and this involved both the physical universe and the metaphysical and religious aspects of the universe. These ideas and this concept of universal order was taught in schools well into the seventeenth century, even after Copernicus had published his work *On Celestial Motions* in 1543. In Figure 4-1 is a representation of the universe similar to that published in 1524, in Peter Apian's *Cosmographia* [11].

In Milton's *Paradise Lost* (1674), well beyond the Elizabethans but still within the Renaissance, we see the notion of chaos playing a central role:

> *Before thir eyes in sudden view appear*
> *The secrets of the hoary deep, a dark*
> *Illimitable Ocean without bound,*
> *Without dimension, where length, breadth, and highth,*
> *And time and place are lost; where eldest* Night
> *And* Chaos, *Ancestors of Nature, hold*
> *Eternal Anarchy, amidst the noise*
> *Of endless wars, and by confusion stand,*
> *For hot, cold, moist, and dry, four Champions fierce*
> *Strive here for Maistry, and to Battle bring*
> *Thir embryon Atoms; they around the flag*
> *Of each his Faction, in thir several Clans,*
> *Light-arm'd or heavy, sharp, smooth, swift or slow,*

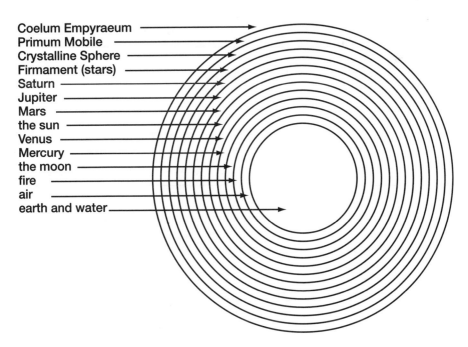

Figure 4-1. The Ptolemaic universe.

Swarm populous, unnumber'd as the Sands
Of Barca *or* Cyrene's *torrid soil,*
Levied to side with warring Winds, and poise
Thir lighter wings. To whom these most adhere,
Hee rules a moment; Chaos *Umpire sits,*
And by decision more imbroils the fray
By which he Reigns: next him high Arbiter
Chance *governs all. Into this wild Abyss,*
The Womb of nature and perhaps her Grave,
Of neither Sea, nor Shore, nor Air, nor Fire,
But all these in thir pregnant causes mixt
Confus'dly, and which thus must ever fight,
Unless th' Almighty Maker them ordain
His dark materials to create more Worlds,
Into this wild Abyss the wary fiend
Stood on the brink of Hell and look'd a while [11].

As we picture Satan viewing Chaos, he is viewing a picture of the physical universe that reflected both the common view and the view of scientists. Much of the description here owes a debt both to Hesiod and to Ovid. Milton elaborates the central paradox of chaos: It is both ordered and disorderly, with the very elements—earth, air, fire, and water—striving for mastery. It is a formless region, but not a void. Milton uses the complex image of an ocean, constantly moving, constantly in flux, and populated by a wide range of organic and inorganic matter. He even introduces imagery that suggests an atomic structure for the universe ("and to Battle bring/Thir embryon Atoms"). It is significant that Milton here connects the characteristic of Chance (line 910 of complete work) with chaos. Chaos is still closely associated with chance and randomness.

CLASSICAL CHAOS AND EARLY SCIENCE

From this point through the eighteenth century, science from the hands and minds of Nicolaus Copernicus (1473–1543), Johannes Kepler (1571–1630), and Galileo Galilei (1564–1642) reshaped the thinking so that the Copernican system came to be accepted as the correct view. With science came less need for a concept of chaos, since the telescope and measurements began to explain what had previously only been explainable by the mysterious chasm. Along with measurement came a sense of regularity. When formulas worked as well as they did to predict eclipses, planetary orbits, tides, and rising and setting of stars, people were more assured that there was a regularity governing all these things and that it was only left to discover how that regularity worked.

Sir Isaac Newton (1642–1727) was a philosopher-scientist who has become the touchstone for physicists in their search to understand how things work. Newton, for instance, approached problems and problem solving through a method of approximation. A given answer might not be the true answer, but it could be construed as an approximation of an answer and, through successive approximations, would lead to better and better answers [12]. When Newton postulated his laws of motion, he thought of them, in fact, as immutable laws. While slight variants might be included from time to time, they did not significantly affect the accuracy of paths of objects predicted by the laws. Scientists studying physical objects and their motion and the effects of gravity had largely accepted this "clockwork" approach to those studies. Once understood, there was a determinism about motion that discouraged any view of changeability. Gleick summarizes the standard understanding of Newtonian physics:

> Given an approximate knowledge of a system's initial conditions and an understanding of natural law, one can calculate the approximate behavior of the system. This assumption lay at the philosophical heart of science. As one theoretician liked to tell his students: "The basic idea of Western science is that you don't have to take into account the falling of a leaf on some planet in another galaxy when you're trying to account for the motion of a billiard ball on a pool table on earth." Very small influences can be neglected. There's a convergence in the way things work, and arbitrarily small influences don't blow up to have arbitrarily large effects. Classically, the belief in approximation and convergence was well justified. It worked. A tiny error in fixing the position of Comet Halley in 1910 would only cause a tiny error in predicting its arrival in 1986, and the error would stay small for millions of years to come.

Scientists had simply adopted the seventeenth- and eighteenth-century viewpoint that everything had initially been invented by God for a specific purpose so that, even though things may be reducible to certain elements, beyond a certain point of reduction we need not go. As Newton wrote:

> It seems probable to me that God in the beginning formed matter in solid, massy, hard, impenetrable, movable particles, of such sizes and figures, and with such other properties, and in such proportion to space, as most conducted to the end for which he formed them; and that these primitive particles being solids, are incomparably harder than any porous bodies compounded of them; even so very hard, as never to wear or break in pieces; no ordinary power being able to divide what God himself made one in the first creation [13].

From this philosophical and quasi-religious viewpoint, then, there is a structure that is preordained and predetermined. The universe and its various parts constitute a machine, in that the future can be predicted based on a clear understanding of the past. This Newtonian deterministic view, and its later applications, worked so well that the concept of the clockwork universe became ingrained as a norm. Neither scientists nor philosophers questioned, in any meaningful way, the apparent logic that was available from calculus. Given a few minor aberrations, the universe was familiar and knowable.

Thus, with the introduction of the Industrial Revolution—most often associated with John Kay's invention of the flying-shuttle loom in 1733 and James Watt's improved steam engine in 1765—the Western world was prepared to accept a mechanistic worldview. There was a regularity to everything, and thanks to Robert Hooke's 1658 invention of the balance spring movement for watches, everyone could measure the regularity for himself or herself. Chaos had no place in such a worldview and was considered an aberration. Anything that did not work with regularity must be broken and could be fixed. If the irregularity was outside of the known science, it would eventually be handled by improvements in science. Newton himself had neatly fixed these problems beforehand, by basing his own science on a broader foundation of religious thought. Newton believed that, in the greater background of universal mechanics, stood a God ready, like a watchmaker, to correct errors and adjust the mechanism when needed. It was the best of times.

By the end of the eighteenth century, however, for many people, it was the worst of times. The colonists in the thirteen land grants in North America rebelled against unfair treatment by the English government and went to war with that government in 1775 following a declaration of independence. In 1789, the French people overthrew the rule of the Bourbons, proclaiming Liberty, Equality, Fraternity; the declaration ushered in the opportunity for Napoleon to rise to a dictatorship of the country. From the cosmological view, chaos as a universal entity had been set aside. From the political view, the mythic model of birth, death, and rebirth had been uncovered, and with it came the chaos associated with change. The royalty of France and the sovereign power of England had been taken for granted. Kings, if not chosen by God himself, were at least favored in the eyes of God. Suddenly a foundation of Western thought was pulled out and crumbled, leaving a political void.

The world was now chaotic. There is some affinity with the Ptolemaic view here, since in that view, the world was at the bottom of the hierarchy of spheres and was thus a gross place to be anyway. The difference is that the rest of the hierarchies that made life comfortable under the Ptolemaic view had crumbled along with the astronomical one. So from a system in which everyone knew his or her place and station, and his or her relationship with the other ranks in the various hierarchies, the end of the eighteenth century saw individual independence and with it, much looser, less-defined governmental and organizational structures. While many of the old hierarchical systems had been replaced with new forms of government and constitutionality, these forms were yet to be tested. We had yet to prove whether or not a democratic approach through liberty, equality, and fraternity could, in fact, yield a more perfect union. A relatively linear system had been converted, through revolution, to a nonlinear system and set in motion.

The uncertainty associated with rebirth was evident in England by the 1830s. It was during this time that a break occurred between the older, medieval views of society, including feudalism, creating a more open and independent society: A concept of change had been introduced, with changes so notable that they could not be ignored as simple clockwork adjustments. As Houghton describes that change, it takes on characteristics that have been associated with chaos: "By definition an age of transition in which change is revolutionary has a dual aspect: destruction and reconstruction. As the old order of doctrines and institutions is being attached or modified or discarded, at one point and then another, a new order is being proposed or inaugurated" [3].

Contributing to the mix is new learning: "Nor should we forget the complementary effect of the vast increase of knowledge, scientific and historical, that almost inundated the Victorians and left them often baffled by the sheer number and complexity of its implications." This change in the pace of life, and the creation or discovery of new knowledge, led to a scientific view that began to question the innate stability available under Newton's influence. In fact, observers were coming to a point of recognizing flux and change as parts of the whole. Change took on a level of complexity that it had not been given before. The thinkers of this period began to pull the idea of change and volatility into the main elements of their philosophies, unable to ignore it. The once simple view of universal systems began to change to acknowledge complexity, changeability, and the reality that change denied traditional views of comfort and safety.

Benjamin Disraeli, a prime minister of England, commented that society was "in the midst of a convulsion in which the very principles of our political and social systems are called in question." This society, Disraeli believed, had created its own form of hero, who was "confused, perplexed, his mind a chaos" but whose spirit was sustained "by a profound, however vague, conviction, that there are still great truths, if we could but work them out" [3]. Change, then, while inevitable, fast, and pervasive, was to be seen as a positive thing, bringing with it improvements through the birth-death-rebirth cycle.

The influence of science on change and the Victorian attitude toward change was strong. It is here, in fact, that scientific methods grew beyond consideration of the physical universe and came to be more focused on humanity itself. Auguste Comte (1798–1857), a French philosopher of the time, categorized mankind's intellectual progress in a stage theory. In the first stage, a theological phase, people explained phenomena using mystery or supernatural forces and powers. In the second stage, phenomena were explained using metaphysical abstractions. In the third and highest stage, scientific laws explained events and phenomena. By this time, then, the optimism that accompanied the deep changes in life, society, and worldview extended to include the idea that science could eventually figure it all out, if it studied a question hard enough. As the old song says, eventually everything would "come round right."

In theology, too, the Victorians were also undergoing radical change. Many of the traditional beliefs were being swept away, to be replaced by various choices, options, and possibilities. It was a brave new world, where potential bubbled and frothed in any number of disciplines. A scientific view of the universe offered opportunities for humankind to experiment in a universe that seemed, itself, to be experimental. Carlyle commented on this change in thinking: "It was clearly the part of every noble heart to expend all its lightnings and energies burning-up without delay, and sweeping into their native Chaos these incredible uncredited traditions, solemnly sordid hypocrisies, and beggarly deliriums old and new" [3]. What he saw was a new philosophical energy being swept in along with new views of science and of human capability.

This is characteristic of the Victorian approach to nature—it had started to yield its secrets, and mankind had been inventive enough to leverage those secret characteristics (such as steam) into powerful tools. This was an age for a strong argument for science. In 1792 William Murdock had illustrated the first use of coal gas for lighting; Eli Whitney, a year later, demonstrated a cotton gin; in 1800, Volta had invented a chemical battery; a Frenchman, Joseph Niepce, in 1822 had demonstrated a process for photography; in 1825 George Stephenson developed the first steam-powered locomotive; and in 1837 Samuel F. B. Morse patented the first commercial telegraph. These examples, of course, are only from the early part of the century and do not include the oil well, the machine gun, the sewing machine, the typewriter, the telephone, or the internal combustion engine, all part of nineteenth century science. Furthermore, this list does not include the contributions of Charles Darwin.

In fact, Darwin's discoveries had been extended into the rest of the society and economy of the times. The struggles in the marketplace took on aspects of struggles for natural survival. The concept of the survival of the fittest was quickly transmuted to business and commerce. The Victorians saw this as a process that enhanced life by removing the incapable and undesirable. This social Darwinism led to an attitude of "might makes right," a stance that was clearly demonstrated in the global empires of the time. The grand assumption, of course, was that the strongest were, indeed, the best selection from a group.

CLASSICAL CHAOS AND THE COLLECTIVE UNCONSCIOUS

The concept of chaos, then, has a long connection and history with humanity and its outlooks, viewpoints, beliefs. As Jung in 1954 described the relationship between archetypes and the collective unconscious, he described much of what we have come to associate with chaos:

> The necessary and needful reaction from the collective unconscious expresses itself in archetypally formed ideas. The meeting with oneself is, at first, the meeting with one's own shadow. The shadow is a tight passage, a narrow door, whose painful constriction no one is spared who goes down to the deep well. But one must learn to know oneself in order to know who one is. For what comes after the door is, surprisingly enough, a boundless expanse full of unprecedented uncertainty, with apparently no inside and no outside, no above and no below, no here and no there, no mine and no thine, no good and no bad. It is the world of water, where all life floats in suspension; where the realm of the sympathetic system, the soul of everything living, begins; where I am indivisibly this *and* that; where I experience the other in myself and the other-than-myself experiences me [14].

When we read passages such as the two cited below, it is easy to see that people associate closely, and generally, with Jung's sense of the dialectic between wholeness and emptiness in this realm of uncertainty.

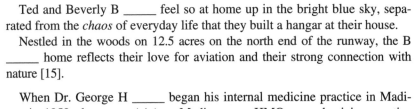

Ted and Beverly B _____ feel so at home up in the bright blue sky, separated from the *chaos* of everyday life that they built a hangar at their house.

Nestled in the woods on 12.5 acres on the north end of the runway, the B _____ home reflects their love for aviation and their strong connection with nature [15].

When Dr. George H _____ began his internal medicine practice in Madison in 1959, there was *(sic)* no Medicare, no HMOs, no physician practice management companies.

He will be retiring Wednesday amid the widely perceived *chaos* of health care in America, having done his best for years to keep doing what he loves: helping people. H _____ is one of a dying breed, an independent practitioner in an age of managed-care companies [16].

In both of these instances, the term *chaos* has been used in a significant way. In the first instance, the family retreats into natural surroundings to get away from society in general and to shape their own version of privacy. In the second example, the writer portrays larger medical organizational cultures as chaotic, juxtaposed against the simplicity and control of the individual practitioner. In both instances, the larger, more complex systems are portrayed as chaotic and something to be avoided. Chaotic systems represent modes of existence that are antithetical to the well-being of the individual and the family.

The briefly told story of the B _____ family suggests a movement away from neighborhoods that are often crowded, noisy, and busy. The summary implies that these people have the means and opportunity to fashion their own environment and to take control of their surroundings, allowing them to distance themselves from the remainder of society, where there may be a sense of loss of control. In terms of the Jungian concept of the collective unconscious, the family has rejected the collective in favor of the more controllable self. It has chosen not to go through the door and seeks a localized comfort zone, rather than the uncertainty of the collective.

This attitude is significant because it points toward the contradictions that arise in current organizations (and families are organizations) when they try to find or return to a "simpler" way of life. That the B _____ family has chosen to retreat to a natural comfort zone in the woods is not surprising. What is surprising is that they have apparently taken their modern transportation technology with them. The message appears to be: "So long as we are in control, we can back away from the world and society and encounter it, via *our* airplanes, when *we* choose to do so, and not by necessity." They are anxious to remove themselves from out-of-control situations that might arise if they had to live in a closer neighborhood or a larger city, or fly from public airports. At the same time, the airplane has gone along with them into the "wilderness" as a comfortable connection to the very technical age from which they have distanced themselves.

At least a part of the irony here is that they may feel that what they are doing does not intrude on that greater society from which they have removed themselves. In fact, this family may impact hundreds of people each time they fly, by creating annoying noise pollution and dangerous air pollution. While they have the sense of being free to roam the skies, their "connection with nature" is a negative one, from nature and society's perspective. Two people flying about in such an aircraft may not sense their connectivity with what is below them, but it is easy and common for them to have an impact across hundreds of miles of territory and on hundreds of people. While the aviators may not sense a connection with the collective, the connection is forced, nonetheless. In this sense, the family is an aggressor, adding pollutants to the air, which may contribute to the disabling of the natural ecosystem, and adding noise, which may disturb those on the ground. Moreover, people flying low and slow in small planes are able to view with some clarity the private affairs of other people, who may not realize that airborne voyeurs exist. Yet such intrusions and pollution are not only condoned but encouraged by municipal and other governmental organizations, which tend to be entranced by the novelty and commercial possibilities of flight. There are few, if any, individual rights of homeowners to the airspace above their private residences. So the B _____ family, when airborne, is not in retreat from their fellow citizens and in harmony with nature, but on the attack.

A second contributor to the irony in this story is the fact that nature, in the view of classical chaos, is not a benign mother but instead is as chaotic as anything humankind has created for itself. The poet George Gordon, Lord Byron, hinted in *Childe Harold's Pilgrimage,* first published in the second decade of the nineteenth century, at this view of nature's power to surprise and disrupt, in considering the ocean:

> Roll on, thou deep and dark blue Ocean—roll!
> Ten thousand fleets sweep over thee in vain;
> Man marks the earth with ruin—his control
> Stops with the shore; upon the watery plain
> The wrecks are all thy deed, nor doth remain
> A shadow of man's ravage, save his own,
> When, for a moment, like a drop of rain,
> He sinks into thy depths with bubbling groan,
> Without a grave, unknelled, uncoffined, and unknown [17].

There is little here of succor in nature, and the view of the ocean is a view of a natural force that transcends the powers of humans to tame it, control it, and often to coexist with it. From a practical viewpoint, anyone who has experienced the rolling thunder of tornadoes crossing the prairie land of the Midwest, or the stereophonic roar of a hurricane, is not likely to accept nature as an alternative to classical chaos.

The family organization also struggles with another form of the same dialectic that is now engaging other organizational thinkers. The human element no longer seems sufficient. It must be augmented and supplemented by technologies. Existence in society, an open systems environment, is not satisfactory because it leads to multiple interactions, increasing attention to both human and technological interfaces, and compromise in recognition of diversity. People who live in city apartments must learn to share resources and space. Those who live on their own private airstrips are not required to do so. The people living in the midst of technological adaptations in the cities must compromise, adapt, and change in relationship to those technologies. People who can pick and choose their technological tools need not feel the same obligation to coexist. Yet, in the secluded acres, by choice, mechanical technology has been introduced. Nature and technology, in Darwin's world, were beginning to feel a merger. This merger is even more intense more than one hundred years after Darwin. The collective unconscious is no longer a place of uncertainty inhabited by humans alone.

Chaos, therefore, for the B _____ family, is to be found in any need to compromise, coexist, and accept an intimate merger between themselves and society. In the view of the writer of the article, nature—including the sky and the wooded property belonging to the family—represents an alternative to chaos and therefore represents a place of unity. The unity, however, must include not only the people in the family in communion with natural surroundings but also, by design, the aircraft. The new unity of the family is not to be without technological elements.

The conception of chaos in the second brief news note is, again, one of something to be avoided. Here, chaos represents the bureaucratization of the United States health care system and its influence on the free will of medical doctors and other medical practitioners. Because both of the news articles appeared under the same byline, it is evident that this writer is prepared to make a clear connection between the activities in general society and chaotic behavior, as she did in the initial article, and a connection between specific activities of a profession and chaotic behavior, as she did in the second article. The implication from both articles is that individuals and families are intrinsically good and right, and have the right to be in control, and that larger organizational entities may be the source of chaos. In the first instance such an entity would be society at large, threatening the control of the B _____ family over their privacy and sense of self, and in the second instance it is the existence of health maintenance organizations that threaten the control of the professional life of a doctor.

In the example of the retiring doctor, he is portrayed to be escaping the rules, regulations, and requirements imposed on medical practice by HMOs. His has been a career, according to the writer, of helping people, rather than catering to the political and regulatory demands of an external organization. Again, this suggests reluctance to go through Jung's doorway into the collective unconscious. As Jung notes, "the collective unconscious is anything but an incapsulated personal system; it is sheer objectivity, as wide as the world and open to all the world. There I am the object of every subject, in complete reversal of my ordinary consciousness, where I am always the subject that has an object" [14]. To back away from this realm of the unconscious is to disconnect from the network and to deny the existence and complexity of that network. In the case of the doctor, it means retirement from the system, rather than adaptation and change with the system. More importantly, it means refusal to confront the system and demand changes across the system itself. We often expend our energies on those activities that will keep us secure. Our nature is to depend on an ability to retreat, and thus survive. Jung noted that many of our rites have to do with keeping away evil spirits and maintaining order in our lives.

Our attempts to retreat from the world, and to discount our relationships with society and its forces, are attempts to maintain control over ourselves, over our conscious beings. We try to avoid the uncontrollable and the unknowable or anything that might hint of a lack of organization. Order is sacred to us, and it prevents chaos. Processes, rites, and rituals all provide the comfort of repetition and acceptance. Withdrawing from the messiness of the world at large is a way to avoid participating in disorder and is, itself, a form of ritual. Where we have control, in this realm of consciousness, we feel secure and feel that we control our own destiny. To look inward, and confront the basic uncertainties, is at once thrilling and fearsome. We want to avoid situations in which we must confront our inability and lack of certainty and control.

One of these factors that is important to an understanding of individuals and their encounters with classical chaos is the concept of the anima. Jung equates anima with soul, in the sense that the concept transcends any given religious connotations of that word. The anima is taken from a Greek root that has meanings including "quick-moving," "changeful of hue," and "twinkling." The soul is the "magic breath of life." As he describes this anima, Jung portrays it as a force that "makes us believe incredible things, that life may be lived. She is full of snares and traps, in order that man should fall, should reach the earth, entangle himself there, and stay caught, so that life should be lived. . . ." What is described here is a fanciful archetype available in our being that not only allows for coping with dissonance but deliberately introduces disorder and randomness.

Chaos is an elemental part of human existence, wired in from the beginning through the archetype of the anima. It is a primitive concept that humans cannot self-generate. It is built-in, and it surfaces spontaneously.

In balance with this whimsical nature of the anima, its role transcends that of randomness in humanity. Behind the seeming irrationality that is a characteristic of the anima is a more complex operation of this factor. Jung tries to explain this duality of the soul by pointing out the importance of the disorderly aspects of anima:

> It is just the most unexpected, the most terrifyingly chaotic things that reveal a deeper meaning. And the more this meaning is recognized, the more the anima loses her impetuous and compulsive character. Gradually breakwaters are built against the surging of chaos, and the meaningful divides itself from the meaningless. When sense and nonsense are no longer identical, the force of chaos is weakened by their subtraction; sense is then endued with the force of meaning, and nonsense with the force of meaninglessness.

The chaotic state of the collective unconscious is unexpected and terrifying. The idea of chaos, as described here as a characteristic of the anima archetype, is often linked with fear and avoidance. We do not like the feeling of openness and the sensation of floating, as Jung described it in the collective unconscious. We prefer stability, the control brought by consciousness, and a sense of steadiness. Yet the anima, at its liveliest, allows and supports the revelation of deeper meaning than can be found in stable states alone. In this concept of the anima, the chaotic state constitutes a mingling of sense and nonsense, meaning and meaninglessness. As the individual begins to sort out meanings from the chaotic mixture, there is a gradual steadying and classification process that Jung associates with experience. This experience is then the basis for learning and for teaching. The role of those with experience is to interpret that experience, and through interpretation to understand. Through understanding, in turn, they are able to explain and convey meaning to others.

The anima is linked to life, and both offer no interpretation in and of themselves, but are open to interpretation. They "have a nature that can be interpreted, for in all chaos there is a cosmos, in all disorder a secret order, in all caprice a fixed law, for everything that works is grounded on its opposite. . . . Once (a person) comes to grips with the anima, her chaotic capriciousness will give him cause to suspect a secret order, to sense a plan, a meaning, a purpose over and above her nature. . . ." The meaning itself comes from turbulent situations only by letting go of traditional meanings and experiencing a "moment of collapse." This description becomes highly important in the next chapter, as we look at the work that has gone on in science, psychology, and other fields to understand just how chaos theory is an attempt to understand this secret order. Scientific interpretations of chaos have led us back to the sensitivity and capriciousness of the anima.

Here is yet another archetypal pattern, associated with the unconscious, that contributes to our understanding of learning as it is related to chaotic states:

> Only when all props and crutches are broken, and no cover from the rear offers even the slightest hope of security, does it become possible for us to experience an archetype that up till then had lain hidden behind the meaningful nonsense played out by the anima. This is the *archetype of meaning,* just as the anima is the *archetype of life itself* [14].

The concern with meaning, here, is not related to specific meanings of specific events, terms, or other phenomena as we experience them in our conscious. The key question has to do with where the *ur*-meanings (the deepest and most basic sources of our understanding) come from that we attach to words, to events, and so on. The archetype of meaning has to do with understanding the pattern that is inherent in all humans that allows them to assign meanings in much the same ways, regardless of who they are or where they are. This archetype may have developed at a time when humans reacted from perceptions more than from considered thought. Historical meanings, which highly influence the meanings we assign today, get their derivation from basic perceptions of phenomena.

The archetype of meaning is the way in which we learn. It is the archetype through which we access the "pre-existent meaning hidden in the chaos of life." This archetype is closely intertwined with the archetype of the anima, since it is anima that provides us access to life in its chaotic state, and it is meaning that allows us to interpret and classify what we find in the anima. Jung personifies the archetype of meaning as "the wise old man," or the "wise magician," who "is the enlightener, the master and teacher. . . ." This form of meaning assigned to what we wish to understand is not a meaning that we formulate and impose. We are not, as in experiencing the anima, the actor but the element acted upon. In this form of thought and thinking, our conscious formulations are highly influenced by the meanings that come from the collective unconscious.

The function of the magician is to impose some form of order and meaning on the more chaotic aspects as derived from all of life, expressed in the anima. The magician helps us to reconcile the dialectics that arise from apparent opposites, or to accept such opposition as natural. The magician, in short, helps us to gain experience, which is the key to achieving stability in the chaos emerging from the anima. It is the magician who is there to help us reconcile what we experience in consciousness with the sensations and realizations surfaced through our access to autonomous archetypal patterns. As we experience life in the conscious sense, associated archetypes, or patterns of response and behavior, become activated. In the extreme situations, "a compulsiveness appears, which, like an instinctual drive, gains its way against all reason and will, or else produces a conflict of pathological dimensions, that is to say, a neurosis."

What is clear is that chaos exists as an archetype and that learning, closely tied to experience, is a way through which we cope with chaos. It is the pattern of wisdom that ultimately surfaces to aid us in our struggle to make sense of the anima. Experience and wisdom can be viewed as the integrating forces between chaos and order.

The operations of archetypes are directly related to a consideration of technical chaos. If, in fact, we are linked to the collective unconscious, then our patterns for learning and for reactions in our organizational systems owe as much to the archetypes of *anima* and *meaning* as they do to mathematical calculations. System behavior may be partly understood through the measurement of chaotic elements that lend themselves to measurement. For full understanding of such systems, however, the nature of these two key archetypes must be included in consideration. The control parameters for chaotic system behavior may be as strongly dependent on archetypal patterns as they are on more superficial and easily measured activities observable in the system. Ralph Stacey gives us strong suggestion of the value of a study of archetypes to an understanding of chaotic system behavior. Stacey [18] extends the use of the term to include what he describes as new archetypes: "I am holding open the possibility that feedback networks might be able to produce completely new archetypes by developing new rules that govern the interactive games they play with each other."

This interpretation of archetypes goes beyond that suggested by Jung and proposes that we are capable of creating new forms of archetypes through experience. If so, then such archetypes would be added to the library of archetypal models. It may be more likely that what are being created are new archetypal *expressions,* based on new forms of human and organizational experiences. Such behavioral patterns as we may see emerge through iteration of systems may rely heavily on the basic constructs of the *anima* and *meaning.*

However we view them, the concept of archetypes provides an important basis for chaos theory, since archetypes may underlie everything, acting as attractive forces to which we respond, regardless of our specific individual personality type or our forms of organization. The nature of the collective unconscious may, as it influences our conscious processing of ideas and facts, provide the ultimate bounds for activity of agents in our systems. The collective unconscious and its archetypes are chief candidates as parameters to be studied in our studies of chaotic system behavior. Such archetypes have not as yet been introduced in this role, and their influence on chaotic system behavior is, so far, assumed but not demonstrated.

CLASSICAL CHAOS AND ORGANIZATIONAL SYSTEMS

In discussing his rationale for the title of his book *Thriving on Chaos,* [19] Tom Peters reports that he had no difficulty in arriving at the term *chaos:*

> The true objective is to take the chaos as given and learn to thrive *on* it. The winners of tomorrow will deal *proactively* with chaos, will look at the chaos per se as the source of market advantage, not as a problem to be got around. Chaos and uncertainty are (will be) market opportunities for the wise; capitalizing on fleeting market anomalies will be the successful business's greatest accomplishment.

In pursuing this idea, Peters suggests that a revolution in thinking will be necessary to accomplish this shift in perspective. He recommends a systemic approach to a general marketplace that had begun to be, at the time of his book, one of high uncertainty across a number of industries. He recommends "meeting uncertainty by emphasizing a set of new basics: world-class quality and service, enhanced responsiveness through greatly increased flexibility, and continuous, short-cycle innovation and improvement aimed at creating new markets for both new and apparently mature products and services." Three themes come out here that carried over into much of the thinking through the 1990s regarding organizational systems: first, the idea that the world is now the proper scope of thinking and operation for many organizations; second, more flexibility is required in meeting the marketplace; and third, continuous innovation is an imperative. His overarching belief is that "excellent firms don't believe in excellence—only in constant improvement and constant change. That is, excellent firms of tomorrow will cherish impermanence—and thrive on chaos."

As Peters uses the term *chaos,* then, he has in mind revolutionary changes to organizational systems that do not end with a single change, but become a way of life. He proposes less a change to the immediate ways of doing business or providing service than a change in the basic philosophy of organizational behavior. Proper behavior, in this and foreseeable markets, is one that has a high degree of volatility, uncertainty, and irrationality. Organizational behavior is more dependent on what the whole system is doing at a given time and is aware of that whole system in operation. Success in a chaotic organizational systems environment means that an organization must become a part of that environment and adopt the characteristics of a chaotic system. Peters largely defines *chaos* as impermanence and volatility on a large scale.

The acceptance of chaos as a concept is widespread and may be ingrained into our psyches as much as into our vocabularies and ways of viewing ourselves and our systems. In the classical sense, chaos is neither totally good nor totally evil. It is the basis for creation, which is good. It is the basis for destruction and dissonance, which is not good. We view chaos, however, from two perspectives. First, as the historical basis for everything, we accept it. It happened in the past, and everything since chaos has been incremental growth and improvement and positive change. Second, as a force to be reckoned with in current events, we disapprove of it and seek to control what seems to be out of control. We want little in our lives that is unknowable, and the systems in which we participate should have sanity, clarity, and some level of predictability. Much of our effort in organizations, therefore, is to learn about how they operate, how they have been assembled, and how they work as systems so that we can eliminate waste, inefficiency, and entropy. We want all energies in a system to be directed as we wish them to be and all agents subject to predictability, at least within a narrow frame of operating tolerances. Chaos, in its classical sense, has no place in such contemporary activity. Acceptable as history, it is unacceptable as present or anticipated experience. We accept it as an archetype but try to subordinate this aspect of the collective unconscious to the presence of our individual and collective consciousness. To accept chaos as an operating reality might be possible if we understand how the chaos itself operates. That possibility brings us to technical chaos and the acceptance of chaotic activity in organizational systems.

REFERENCES

1. Gerwig, K. "In the telecom world, the more shake-ups, the merrier." *InternetWeek,* July 6, 1998, p. 26.
2. Flexner, S. B. and L. C. Hauck, (Eds.) *The Random House Dictionary of the English Language,* 2nd ed., New York: Random House, 1987.
3. Houghton, W. E., *The Victorian Frame of Mind,* New Haven: Yale University Press, 1957, pp. 3, 12, 19, 49.
4. Tillyard, E. M. W., *The Elizabethan World Picture,* New York: Vintage Books, n.d.
5. Campbell, J., *The Hero with a Thousand Faces,* 2nd ed. Bollingen Series XVII, Princeton, N. J.: Princeton University Press, 1968, pp. 284, 286, 288.
6. Hammond, N. G. L. and H. H. Scullard, (Eds.) *The Oxford Classical Dictionary,* Oxford: Clarendon Press, 1970.
7. MacAllister, A.T., *Introduction,* in *Inferno,* New York: New American Library, 1954, pp. 14, 24.
8. Bodkin, M., *Archetypal Patterns in Poetry,* London: Oxford University Press, 1934, p. 136.
9. Ciardi, J. (Ed.), *The Inferno,* New York: New American Library, 1954, Canto III, ll. 22–29.
10. Phelps, W. L. (Ed.), *Shakespeare: The Merchant of Venice,* The Yale Shakespeare, W. L. Cross and T. Brooks (Eds.), New Haven: Yale University Press, 1923, V.i.54–65.
11. Hughes, M. Y. (Ed.), *John Milton: Complete Poems and Major Prose,* New York: The Odyssey Press, 1957, *Paradise Lost,* Book II, ll. 890–918.
12. Gleick, J., *Chaos: Making a New Science,* New York: Viking, 1987, p. 15.
13. Capra, F., *The Tao of Physics: An Exploration of the Parallels between Modern Physics and Eastern Mysticism,* 3rd ed., Boston: Shambhala, 1991, p. 56.
14. Jung, C. G., *The Archetypes and the Collective Unconscious,* 2nd ed. Bollingen Series XX, S. H. Read (Ed.), Vol. 9, part 1, New York: Princeton University Press, 1959, pp. 21–22, 22, 26-27, 31, 32, 33, 37, 48.

15. Gronemus, S., "Passions reflected in home." *The Tennessean,* Nashville, July 10, 1998, p. 2A.
16. Gronemus, S., "Doctor one of dying breed." *The Tennessean,* Nashville, July 10, 1998, p. 2A.
17. Lord Byron, G. G., *Excerpts, Childe Harold's Pilgrimage,* in *English Romantic Writers,* D. Perkins (Ed.), New York: Harcourt, Brace & World, 1967 (originally published 1818), p. 809.
18. Stacey, R. D., *Complexity and Creativity in Organizations,* San Francisco: Berrett-Koehler, 1996, p. 55.
19. Peters, T., *Thriving on Chaos,* New York: HarperPerennial, 1987, pp. xiv, 4.

Chapter 5

Technical Chaos

INTRODUCTION

While the history of what I have called technical chaos is not so long as that of classical chaos, it is equally as interesting, and pertinent to the organizational dynamics and organizational learning with which we are now engaged. Where classical chaos offers us the thrill of contemplating the mysterious cloak of the unknown, and the depths of our collective unconscious, technical chaos offers us the excitement of unraveling some of the threads from the cloak. In more prosaic terms, technical chaos came about with the improved abilities to manipulate calculations, and with improved abilities to display mathematical results as graphical forms and not simply as lists of numbers. It is a way of perceiving that which appears irrational.

Technical chaos is the exploration of what is more than a prediction of what might be. It represents a highly positive line of thought that acknowledges the mystery of systems dynamics while at the same time bringing added understanding to how things work in the environment around us. If we believe that there are innumerable intricate patterns that tie together the activities of humans with the activities of the natural world and universe, and with the activities of the equipment and machines that surround us, then technical chaos offers the unique opportunity to understand those patterns and webs. While all of the patterns may not become clear, we can, by understanding how technical chaos works, understand some of the ways in which the patterns come together and diverge, evolve and devolve, and are created and dissipated.

What is here called technical chaos has gone under various other names and descriptors. It has been called "mathematical" chaos, because much of the emphasis in its theoretical framework is on the understanding of mathematical models that allow simulation of dynamic systems. As I will explore later, the characteristic of measurement is strong in any description or application of technical chaos. Moreover, its roots lie in mathematics. At the heart of darkness lie formulae—generally based on nonlinear mathematics—which provide portraits of systems in three-dimensional views, revealing the patterns of their dynamic shifting and movement. Computer-based simulations, based sometimes on nothing more than the iteration of a formula through hundreds or thousands of calculations, are plotted and graphed to reveal disturbances in the way a system flows, but more importantly, the similarities in the way a system behaves at its core.

Technical chaos has also been called scientific chaos. This is natural, for two reasons. The first revelations of technical chaos came through the use of careful measurements to discern activity within physical systems that had been considered unpredictable. The operation of the weather on Earth and the turbulent activity of the Colorado River share similar features in this regard. As physical scientists studied the unpredictable nature of weather, and as hydrologists, geologists and others studied the nature of turbulent action in streams and rivers, they had difficulty in understanding how the physics of such phenomena actually worked. By approaching these systems, either weather or river, through observation and history-keeping, there appeared to be more randomness than order. What technical chaos has brought to these scientists, and researchers in other fields, is a revelation that apparently random events, when viewed from the right perspective, may not be random at all. What appears to be randomness, when viewed from the benchmark of our ingrained sense of order, may in fact be explained as a form of order that we had not previously been able or willing to see or accept.

The idea of technical chaos has also been expressed as "theoretical" chaos. While initially an idea derived from simulations and experiments, what was originally referred to as "chaos theory" is increasingly being found in real-world systems, and patterns of dynamic activity are being studied and recorded. So, while there exists the theory at one level, at another level it is being located in practice in a number of disciplines. The theoretical framework, however, is vital, since it represented a major departure in thinking from traditional approaches to systems understanding, and takes us beyond classical concepts of chaos.

Technical chaos is synonymous with an area of study now often referred to as Nonlinear Dynamical Systems, or NDS. This area of research and body of thought is comprehensive, and includes chaos theory as well as complexity theory and catastrophe theory. Each of these theoretical areas seeks to bring forward an understanding of how systems, regardless of size or mission, behave. The particular concern, from the NDS viewpoint, is the extent to which a given system—be it physical or biological—exhibits what most of us would call "erratic" behavior. Any system that is difficult to predict, difficult to manage, or that offers sudden or unexpected twists and turns may be a system that can be classified and studied as a nonlinear dynamical system.

Within the whole scheme of NDS lies an interest in the operation of chaos, in its various forms, within systems. The term "technical chaos," then, serves as a way to distinguish mathematical, scientific, or theoretical chaos from the form of chaos we have described as "classical." In classical chaos, we stood in awe of the unknown and incomprehensible, either at personal or universal levels. In technical chaos, the awe and mystery implicit in the term "chaos" has not left us, but we shift our attention to a view of it that offers some hope of measurement, understanding and even application. The mission of those studying NDS is to pick the threads of the cloak, one by one, or sometimes more than one at a time, and understand their functions in the mysterious animated patterns that are woven there. The word "chaos" no longer refers simply to confusion and disarray that offer no hope of being understood. It refers, instead, to activities in a system that are highly complex, highly integrated, and constantly shifting and changing direction, course, and speed. Technical chaos, while volatile and variable, offers some semblance of order. The view is not one of hopeless confusion, but of an identifiable and measurable system, using tools, approaches, and conceptual frameworks that are different from those previously used to understand system operations and dynamics.

Chaos can be viewed as "technical" when it is viewed from the perspective of a measurable, understandable phenomenon which can and does contain some form of order. A view of technical chaos is, furthermore, a view of an holistic system. To study pieces and bits and parts of a dynamical system is fruitless and frustrating. To sense a system dynamic based on separate measures may give a fragmented view of the whole. A system exists as an entity, regardless of how changeable it is or how unpredictable it may be, or how diverse its elements may be. Any given system must be viewed in its relationships and integration with other systems that may exist apart from it or outside of it.

To focus on, for example, the year-to-year increases in facility costs in an organization's operating budget without understanding the other systems which may be integrated into the facility system is to risk making poor decisions about facility costs. To decide, in this example, to cut facility costs by 10 percent would ignore the fact that those who use the facilities may then need to contract other space, at higher rates, in order to continue needed activities, or may try to squeeze operations into inefficient space, driving up operating and production costs elsewhere in the organization. In this instance, NDS suggests two things. First, a single system that is integrated into a complex organization should not be studied or tuned separately from those other systems. Second, the relationships between facility and the other operations of the organization need to be understood as nonlinear relationships. That is, a change in facility availability may have a greater impact than a simple one-to-one relationship. A relatively simple change in space availability may have complex and amplified effects across the organization.

What may not be obvious, in our ordinary view of such changes, is the extent to which the changes resulting from this form of decision may not be observable as a chain reaction. A decision-maker who elects to reduce the facility budget by 10 percent will have some idea about what the impact will be in the organization. He will be able to predict, either from personal knowledge of system operations or from projections provided by others, what the "fallout" will be from a space reduction. What can be predicted, however, are immediate outcomes. These are "chain-reaction" outcomes, which are likely to be observable immediately upon implementation of the space reduction.

While it may be obvious that loss of space will mean that we must make some changes in how things get done, there may be more subtle and delayed effects of the change that we cannot predict as linear or immediate. If, for example, a knowledgeable, well-trained, and highly competent worker is displaced from what he or she has considered an effective work environment, and is perhaps crowded into a smaller, noisier, less comfortable space, this impact could cause that employee to leave after a matter of months, along with the needed capability which that employee represents. Organizations, when viewed as nonlinear dynamic systems, can provide many instances of such delayed and complex reactions. Understanding the whole system, and how dynamics of such systems operate, provides the opportunity to select appropriate changes and to make effective decisions, with some view as to their impact in a technically chaotic system.

This example also serves to display two additional and related characteristics of nonlinear dynamic systems. There is, first, a recognition and respect for the numinous aspects of systems. There is an understanding that there are levels of complex activity in systems that can be understood from a general view of system activity, but not necessarily in the particulars. The intent of studies in NDS is to try to form relatively simple models which will describe the dynamics of the system. Once key variables and points of system focus are identified, this understanding will inform decision-making regarding the manipulation of those variables. This approach recognizes that the nonlinear systems are complex, and that to track every variable at every instant in time, understanding the relationships among variables and the changes in the interacting variables, is impossible. While the systems under consideration are bounded systems and do not exhibit fully random behavior, the behavior they do exhibit is nonlinear, chaotic and sometimes catastrophic, but can be understood at the macro level.

Second, complex systems are still, in many respects, unpredictable, simply because of the number of variables involved and the degree of change that affects several variables simultaneously. A part of the mystery of such systems is the difficulty in understanding what can happen next, since subsequent system status is highly dependent on potentially small fluctuations in any one or several interrelated variables. To derive a prediction of the future on past history and trends is risky at best, since the history of a single system is dependent, in part, on other systems that may be influential. Predictions from a narrow history of a single variable—organizational headcount, for example—are likely to miss influences from a number of possible external systems which could have impacted headcount in different ways at different times over the historical period. The complexity of the potential systemic influences constitutes a barrier to effective prediction from such historical data and system behavior. For this reason, many organizational measures are deemed worthless for anything more than short-term predictions of accurate system behavior.

The approaches to the study of technical chaos and other nonlinear system phenomena represent significant departures from older and more widely accepted and understood attitudes toward dynamic system behavior. While chaos theory, complexity theory and the study of nonlinear dynamical systems derive from initial insights from mathematics, physics, chemistry, and biology, the interpretation of the theories and application of concepts has spread to other disciplines, including social science, literature, and business. The theories have been applied and studied in organizational systems as keys to understanding interactions and dynamics in such systems. Psychologists and psychiatrists have studied the influence of these theories on understanding of individual human behavior and attitudes. Engineers have applied chaos theory in the design of electronic networks and computer-based systems that are subject to turbulence, dissonance, and apparent random activity. An understanding of the basics of nonlinear dynamic systems theories will provide a necessary background to a view of the operation of learning and learning support in organizational systems.

SIGNIFICANT INFLUENCES ON NDS

Influences from Physics

The rising influence of nonlinear systems perspectives can be attributed to a number of developments in a number of disciplines stretching back to at least the beginning of the twentieth century. To provide a full rehearsal of the history of NDS would be a major work in itself, but there are some key thinkers and some key ideas that relate more directly to the current focus. Chaos, complexity, and nonlinear dynamical systems owe much to work in the early part of the century that dispelled the notion of an indivisible atom, and recognized the more complex nature of the building blocks of the universe.

Albert Einstein's theories of relativity and the elaboration—to undeniable proof—of atomic physics are considered to be the twin fulcrums that most significantly affected, in science, the body of knowledge based on Sir Isaac Newton's laws. Until Einstein and other thinkers of the later period challenged Newton's concepts, the nature of atomic structure was thought to be solid. In fact, atoms are separable. Moreover, Newton had founded his concepts of mechanics on a belief that space and time were to be treated separately, in the three standard dimensions of width, height, and depth. In 1905, Einstein's statement of a special theory of relativity contradicted this universally accepted view. Einstein added a fourth dimension, time, and postulated a four-dimensional continuum called space-time. Einstein's argument was that an event or phenomenon would be different, depending on the point in time from which it is observed. Measurements of an event or phenomenon, then, are dependent upon when it is viewed. Measurement and therefore description of an event must incorporate not only position but also time. The net result of this theory was a radical change in the way the universe and its parts and pieces were viewed. The system, from this theoretical perspective, is no longer fixed, but exists and can be described only in relation to where in space-time it is. There are no longer limits to how big or how long (time).

In 1915, Einstein added a general theory of relativity—not yet proven—that suggests that space-time is affected by gravity as an additional variable. Near a large object, for example, space-time will be different, because the gravitational pull of the large object will warp the space-time near it. Space-time is thus curved, and this means that space and time will be different in different parts of the universe.

These two theories of relativity denied the accepted view, based on Newtonian laws of gravity and motion, that dynamic universal systems operated in a stable and predictable way, established by God and immutable. Where Newton postulated a clockwork universe within which anomalies could be ignored as background noise and were of little influence, Einstein suggested a viewpoint that allowed more variability in the system. He added complexity to the ways in which systems were measured and the variables that were necessary to describe the system accurately.

From studies in physics, the other blow to Newtonian physics was quantum mechanics, which questioned the particles of which Newton believed larger bodies to be made. Newton had believed them to be, at a certain level, immutable, with a given set of properties ordered by God. Quantum physics discovered that the same flux, now theorized at the grand universal level, was also operating at the micro level. There was no more certainty here, either, with the ultimate realization that matter is not real at all, but appears to fluctuate between particles and waves of energy. The vocabulary that has arisen around quantum theory says that matter tends to exist and that atomic events tend to occur. The task of quantum mathematicians then became to build probability theories that attempt to predict how likely it is that an atomic event will happen, or that an atomic particle will be in a particular spot at a particular time. This emphasis on probabilities replaced the mathematics of certainty, offering views of various possible future states depending on the ways in which probabilities were calculated. The future, in other words, was not a direct descendent from the past, and history was not necessarily a determinant of future trends. For some purposes, trendlines became suspect, since they represented linear averaging and assumptions of system stability. For students of quantum mechanics, the future is a range of possible realities, dependent on inter-related systems and events. It is, perhaps, the manifestation of the *anima*.

In the early part of the twentieth century, these revelations concerning the quantum nature of reality prepared the way for a new wave of general uncertainty and a new appreciation for the complexity of how things work. What appears apparently simple as a systematic construct can actually be very complicated, and may be subject to large changes brought about by relatively small initial events. Where science had made immense progress in applying Newtonian laws, and creating new technologies based on certainties, it was now faced with explaining that which before it could simply accept—God was not fixing all of the irregularities. Systemic variances could not be ignored, or engineered into the background. Moreover, these sometimes-small variances had an impact that had previously been set aside or ignored in the consideration of the big picture. Since the introduction of the industrial age in the nineteenth century, engineers had found ways to adjust tolerances and standards to account for most variables that might affect the operation of their machines. The science of engineering came to be the science of controlling variables and variances. The uses and applications of mechanical systems thus began to be described in application guides and handbooks.

Today, everyone expects to find such a "User Guide" in the glove compartment of every vehicle, and in the box with any new stereo amplifier. These guides often represent control methods for variances that could not be engineered out of the mechanical system itself. User Handbooks recognize the limitations of engineering and science, and act as crude interfaces between humans and machines. The revelations coming in the early twentieth century were far more basic than this. They suggested that systems are allowed to have variance and variability that cannot be controlled or designed out. As Prigogine and Stengers [1] noted, "In the classical view the basic processes of nature were considered to be deterministic and reversible. Processes involving randomness or irreversibility were considered only exceptions. Today we see everywhere the role of irreversible processes, of fluctuations."

The shift in view that accompanied the early breakthroughs in physics, then, was amplified across the understanding of how physical systems operated. A new appreciation for randomness and the interaction of multiple complex variables in multiple complex ways opened the way for the exploration of systems based on these new realities. Cyclical thinking, which postulates a return to a given point of departure, has been set aside for an understanding of systemic operations which accepts that the histories of some systems will never repeat themselves exactly.

One of the major breakthroughs in understanding nonlinear dynamical systems and the operation of technical chaos came as Edward Lorenz studied the variables associated with weather forecasting. Lorenz, a meteorologist, combined this special-ty with a strong understanding of physics and mathematics and applied dynamical systems theories to weather systems. Lorenz modeled a weather system with com-plex variables and simulated the dynamics of the system in the computer, using dif-ferential equations to represent the changes in variables as they interacted with each other. One of the results of his work is a construct of chaotic systems that is referred to as "sensitive dependence on initial conditions." This characteristic of technical chaos expresses the idea that, in such systems, a small and sometimes simple change in initial conditions can lead to large changes across the whole system. As Stephen Kellert [2] explains the effect, "A dynamical system that exhibits sensitive depen-dence on initial conditions will produce markedly different solutions for two specifi-cations of initial states that are initially very close together."

Lorenz [3] explains the phrase in more detail:

> . . . in some dynamical systems it is normal for two almost identical states to be followed, after a sufficient time lapse, by two states bearing no more resem-blance than two states chosen at random from a long sequence. Systems in which this is the case are said to be *sensitively dependent on initial conditions.*

To place this concept in organizational terms, imagine the introduction of a new organization leader, who immediately "reinvents" the organization. As a percentage of the total organization's population, the new leader represents the smallest frac-tion possible. Yet, the resulting change revises the entire construction and presence of the organization. It no longer looks like or feels like the organization it once did. An organization in which this radical difference can occur could be said to show *sensitive dependence on initial conditions.*

Because change is so closely allied to the idea of learning, such sensitivity and potential for radical shifts in organizational presence have direct bearing on organi-zational learning. The characteristics of the organization affect the characteristics of the learning environment, and this, in turn, impacts the ways in which people, machines, and networks associated with the system will learn. By extension, it impacts the ways in which learning is supported in such sensitive systemic environ-ments. For these reasons, it will be important to consider the meaning and influence of this concept of sensitive dependence, as we move to further consideration of training systems, and learning support in organizations.

Influence of Mathematics

Another considerable influence on the development of NDS theory and application came from the development of mathematics of complex systems. Kellert [2] highlights the work of Henri Poincaré. It is Poincaré who provided many of the keys that are important to chaos theory and its mathematical tools. In studying Newtonian constructs concerning the solar system and similar configurations of bodies in the universe, Poincaré developed a mathematical proof that described a weakness in Newton's assumptions. According to Poincaré there is no guarantee that gravity or any other force will hold the solar system in its current configuration. His analysis included the potential that there may not be a 1:1 ratio between a change in a system variable and the outcome of that change. In other words, his mathematics introduced the idea of nonlinear behavior in such systems.

It was also Poincaré who pioneered the application of geometrical thinking to the understanding of dynamic system behavior. Complicated interactions and trajectories of systems, especially when variation created by chaotic behavior is introduced, cannot easily be understood by looking at series of numbers on a page. Views of system behavior can, however, become more clear when the activity of the system is pictured as a three-dimensional tracing of points [4]. Even this tracing, however, because many iterations of the system activity are necessary in order to fully develop a portrait of chaotic activity, may not provide a clearly understood view of how the system is varying its paths in any regular way. What is now called a "Poincaré map" offers a view of the general path of the central attractive force in the system, and thus reveals how the nonlinear activity of the system comes about and behaves. Imagine someone walking along a completely dark roadway, using a flashlight to look for something. The flashlight beam represents a system. The swings and movements of the beam would be traced as points on a three-dimensional map of the environment. But we would see only the trace of the beam and not the actions of the person holding the flashlight. If our map included, instead, the movement of the person herself, we would understand the way in which the flashlight was being controlled and pointed and moved, and thus would have a different level of understanding of how the system (the beam itself) operated as it did, and perhaps more insight into why it operated as it did. The tracing of the person herself, rather than the beam, represents a tracking, in a dynamical system, of the "attractor" which affects the observable changes in the system. The variance and variability in a nonlinear dynamical system can be traced to the operation of such attractors, a matter to be considered later.

Another major contributor to the mathematics of chaos and complexity was Benoit Mandelbrot, who studied nonlinear systems some sixty years after Poincaré had done his work. In the 1960s, Mandelbrot was a research mathematician with IBM (International Business Machines) [4]. One of Mandelbrot's first contributions was the discovery of similitude in various levels of a system. In a study of cotton prices over a period of sixty years, for example, Mandelbrot discarded averaging and central tendency as approaches to analyzing price behavior. He developed a way to incorporate apparent aberrations and tails in the price statistics into a different form of picture which showed that sequence of price changes were similar when viewed at daily or at monthly data levels. According to an analysis of the dynamics of the pricing history, in other words, Mandelbrot found similarity in different scalar views of the same picture. Seemingly chaotic data yielded a suggestion of order, and order replicated from one scale to another.

Moving these early findings to a reconsideration of Euclidean geometry, Mandelbrot argued that the true distance from point A to point B will vary according to the scale at which measurements are taken. That is, the journey across a lawn, while it may take the same direction, will be measured differently from the view of a human and the view of an ant. The lawn has not changed, but the view of the lawn is different. Humans and ants experience the lawn differently. This observation led to the evolution of an approach that suggested that some phenomena that might otherwise be difficult to measure could be measured using "fractional dimensions." This measurement approach becomes important because it applies to irregular shapes that, though irregular, share simple and similar blueprints. The study of fractals is the study of degrees of difference or irregularity in objects or materials.

Mandelbrot, then, has been able to demonstrate that what often appear to be chaotic patterns in natural or manmade systems can be understood as a form of regularity. The regularity lies not so much in the actual, direct measurement of the object or activity as it does in the degree to which the irregularity maintains itself from scale to scale and view to view.

Fractal geometry has become the basis for computer code that minimizes the computing effort required to generate visual scenes on screen. The technology is used often in creating simulations of "real life" for movies and television and allows the use of digital graphics in place of live actors and real sets. By using the Mandelbrot principle of scaling, a relatively concise definition of an object can serve as the basis for replication, scaling up to a larger view. With this ability to scale and compress, based on fractal elements, storage requirements for digital images can be reduced, yet these fractal elements can be enlarged as much as 400 percent, while retaining the sharpness and detail of the original [5].

Imagine that the defined object is a blade of grass. Scaling can generate a realistic lawn and replication based on that single definition. The lawn will show the same forms of irregularity and unevenness that exist in the natural lawn, but will require very little additional code as overhead to the original description of the blade of grass.

The concept of fractals has also been viewed as a way to study organizational structures and activities. "Efficiencies of scale" have always been engineering goals, and the understanding of system behavior in terms of consistent gradients at different organizational scales may offer ideas for better ways to develop large-scale, virtual organizations. Another potential application of fractal theory is in the area of business process definition. Currently, many business process documentation approaches require the collection and analysis of massive amounts of job, task, and task element data in order to produce an image of a process flow. In fact, these efforts result in static products, suitable for framing but little else. By the time the analysis to deep levels of detail is complete, and documentation produced, the system under analysis has moved on, changes have occurred, and the documentation is largely worthless. A focus on creating fractal studies of the work system would provide more concise and meaningful data which itself would be dynamic.

Influence from a Community of Learning

One of the key communities that has grown up around the idea of technical chaos and nonlinear dynamical systems is the Santa Fe Institute. Since 1984, the Institute has been a gathering place for those who are applying nonlinear dynamical systems theory across disciplines. Some of the disciplines that have been represented over the years include economics, immunology, literature and language, computer science, and artificial intelligence. There is an increasing awareness, through these collaborative studies, that understanding the behavior of dynamical nonlinear systems is a common ground. Such systems are not limited to physics or biology alone, but can be found in areas well beyond these. The need underlying the Institute is to connect parts of different disciplines in order to see a whole picture of system activity. An understanding of a chaotic system requires wholeness, not bits and pieces and subsystems.

Such systems, when viewed through a microscope or in bits and pieces, can hardly be recognized as integral. At a certain level of detailed or partial view, the systems seem to break apart and appear to display more turbulence and randomness than consistency or coherence. The value of the holistic view lies not so much in the fact that it is high-level, but that an holistic view of an NDS system provides key characteristics, variables, and a view of the common elements operating in the system and on the system. Chaos theory, complexity theory, and all of the aspects of nonlinear dynamical systems theory serve the purpose of highlighting the things that are going on in a system which make it a system, even though it appears to lack unity.

The community of learning that is represented by the Santa Fe Institute, then, is one which crosses disciplines, or subsystems, and provides opportunities to inspect interactivity and interconnectedness across the disciplines which constitute the ultimate definition of the System as we know it. The Institute has been, and continues to be, a touchstone for those interested in and pursuing research in the behavior of systems within their operating environments.

Other similar organizations have come into being since the formation of the Santa Fe Institute. Several universities have established institutes or other research organizations focused on chaos theory. The Georgia Institute of Technology's Applied Chaos Laboratory, for example, focuses on research projects examining the influence of chaos in engineering and physics. There is an Institute for Solid State Physics and Chaos Group working in Budapest, Hungary. A similarly named Chaos Group has been formed at the University of Maryland, and the University of California at San Diego sponsors an Institute for Nonlinear Science. The Los Alamos Laboratory, in New Mexico, has a Center for Non-Linear Science. Additional work is included under other university and government-sponsored organizations such as the National Science Foundation, through its grant and research program. The Society for Chaos Theory in Psychology & Life Sciences is an interest group focused on the application of nonlinear dynamical systems theory in areas including biology, physiology, psychology, philosophy, education, and management.

A number of websites have been created which offer information, opportunities to exchange ideas, and links to various studies in nonlinear dynamical systems.

Influences from Biology

Studies in biological science have provided unique views that are valuable to an overall understanding of the implications of nonlinear dynamical systems. Evolution itself has given rise to a considerable body of work which studies how the dynamics of evolution may actually work, and how something that appeared to be a fairly simple concept may, in fact, be riddled with chaotic activity. Mysterious jumps in evolutionary activity, in particular, are subjects of study, in an effort to determine the extent to which generation of new or adapted species may not proceed in a linear way over time. Moreover, the concept of co-evolution—how different elements may cooperate or compete during the evolution dynamic—has direct bearing on this investigation.

One of the discussions in nonlinear dynamic systems, which has the potential for high influence in our understanding of learning in organizations, is the concept of autopoesis, or in chemical terms, autocatalysis. In autocatalysis, the systemic reproductive activity at the molecular level occurs faster if the molecules themselves produce the necessary substances that can catalyze their growth process. The system is self-generating and self-reproducing, and takes command of its own environment [6].

Autopoesis, which owes its name to two researchers, Humberto Maturana and Francisco Varela, is the general idea that systems self-generate. This idea derives from an older concept of some unknown particle, element, or thing that existed in systems and had the intelligence to initiate and produce the whole system. This older concept, however, only informs the idea of autopoesis but does not completely explain it. In an autopoetic system, "the parts exist for and by means of the whole; the whole exists for and by means of the parts" [6]. Thus, a separate executive function that holds the keys to the process for system development and evolution is unnecessary.

From these various disciplines, then, including biology, physics, mathematics, and the collective work from various areas collectively occurring in communities of learning focused on nonlinear dynamical systems, have come some key concepts which have value when applied to organizational systems which include humans.

DEFINITIONS

Viewed from an overall perspective, it is helpful to have some general categories as a way of organizing more specific knowledge about the relevant concepts. While the various manifestations of technical chaos are not easy to grasp, they can better be understood as a collection of ideas. One of the easiest explanations of complex processes came from John Hubbard, who observed that "simple processes in nature could produce magnificent edifices of complexity without randomness" [4]. At least some of the difficulty in understanding the ramifications of this straightforward statement lies in the various approaches that have been taken to investigate chaos theory and the various terms that have been associated with it. Technical chaos has been blessed with a number of tags, names, and descriptions. Early in the literature, *Chaos Theory* predominated, but as researchers have become more discriminating, they have tended to consider an umbrella term, *Nonlinear Dynamical Systems (NDS)*, as the central focus, with subclasses of that general concept.

Nonlinear Dynamical Systems

This term expresses, in itself, three of the core concepts that are important to an understanding of unstable systems such as those to be found in organizations. The concepts represented by the term "system" are important to understand, since they lie at the heart of any consideration of learning as it may occur in such systems. Second, a dynamical system has special qualities that must be understood in order to distinguish such behavior from stable systems. Finally, the qualifier "nonlinear" suggests a special form of behavior in such dynamical systems that may affect the ways in which the system can be studied and understood.

Systems, in this instance, are not restricted to a particular subtype, such as organizational system, planetary system, drive-train system, or ecological system. A system is chiefly recognizable as a coordinated set of elements or processes that can be distinguished as individuals within the set, but that produce selected outcomes most effectively when operating in a collective way. A system can be a contributing subsystem in a larger system.

A system exists to produce outcomes for which all parts are suited and, in some cases, outcomes that have been determined internal to the system. That is, as systems are free to self-organize, they may intentionally organize and coordinate the set of elements and processes which will optimize a certain outcome or range of outcomes. Though not necessary, it is possible, on the other hand, for systems to be controlled by some external engineer or designer who will establish the desired set of outcomes and construct those specific combinations of elements and processes that will accomplish that desired outcome or range of outcomes.

What is of concern in nonlinear dynamical systems are those systems that are relatively simple in appearance but operate in complex ways. These systems are "bounded" in the sense that they show some interrelationship of parts to the whole. There is a way to view these systems as wholes and not as fragmentary parts momentarily assembled, or in some sudden and temporary relationship with each other. That is, a nonlinear dynamic system of the type we are concerned with is not an exploding star. It is, instead, an identifiable entity that seems to operate with some degree of randomness. It is "simple" in the sense that it is deterministic and can be described without highly complex mathematical formulae. Kellert [2] defines a simple deterministic system as one that can be described usually in fewer than five differential equations. Moreover, the system is characterized as deterministic because nowhere in its mathematical description is there an allowance for chance. While chance and randomness may be apparent from the macro view of the system, it is in fact a system that can be described systematically.

Chaos Theory

James Gleick [4] provides a very accessible understanding of chaos theory as he describes the chaotic behavior manifested in snowflakes:

> Sensitive dependence on initial conditions serves not to destroy but to create. As a growing snowflake falls to earth, typically floating in the wind for an hour or more, the choices made by the branching tips at any instant depend sensitively on such things as the temperature, the humidity, and the presence of impurities in the atmosphere. The six tips of a single snowflake, spreading within a millimeter space, feel the same temperatures, and because the laws of growth are purely deterministic, they maintain a near-perfect symmetry. But the nature of turbulent air is such that any pair of snowflakes will experience very different paths. The final flake records the history of all the changing weather conditions it has experienced, and the combinations may as well be infinite.

So chaos theory, in essence, is an attempt to remove some of the darkness and mystery which permeates the classical concept of chaos by explaining, at least in some dynamic systems, how the system exhibits chaotic behavior. The operation may be aperiodic, but is not necessarily random. What appears at first to be random can be explained through the application of accepted physical principles that govern things in motion. Murray Gell-Mann explains chaos in terms of quantum mechanics:

> The phenomenon of chaos produces situations in which the slightest imprecision in initial positions or momenta can lead to arbitrarily large uncertainties in future predictions . . . [7].

So, if quantum mechanics is to be used to establish probabilities of future outcomes and systemic choices or decisions, then any changes in the initial conditions of a system will impact those probabilities and the potential results and outcomes in, through, and by the system. Stacey [8] reinforces this concept of uncertainty as he discusses the predictability of business system outcomes. He believes that it is possible to develop an information set that will help us understand nonlinear dynamical systems. Though difficult, it is not impossible to predict a point in an organizational or business system at which chaos might begin. Knowledge of the set of underlying behavior guidelines is crucial in order to foresee any longer-term behaviors of the system. This rule-set, Stacey believes, can be identified and measured in systems which are either in a stable state or a predictably unstable state. When a system is operating chaotically, however, it is only the short-term behaviors that can be accurately forecast, given knowledge of the system variables. Long-term prediction in a chaotic system is impossible.

We can picture a chaotic system, then, as one in which the usual close relationship between a change and its influence may not be assumed. Effects are not necessarily on the same scale as a cause. The influence of a change event or activity in a system may be greater than would be anticipated or expected. Alternatively, the influence of the change may be less than expected or planned. In human relationships, for example, we often expect and anticipate certain results from an action on our part. When we spend hours weeding a flowerbed on a hot summer's day, we expect some acknowledgement from our spouse for our efforts. To have this level of exertion and sacrifice ignored would not meet one of our expectations of the exertion and effort we have put into the work. The cause, then, did not have a linear effect. The relationship between exertion and recognition is not proportional.

If, on the other hand, we walk in the door from the flowerbed and receive profuse and unsolicited thanks for spending the time and energy to keep up with the weeds, then we might consider the outcome as proportional to the effort invested. This would be a linear relationship. Had we received not only profuse thanks, but also an invitation to a celebratory dinner out, the outcome is again non-proportional and is nonlinear. In the quantum explanation, such nonlinear actions may have greater than local and immediate consequences, and could affect later paths and directions of the domestic system. The importance lies in the shift from our traditional associations of cause and effect to a new view that incorporates an expectation of uncertainty and not an expectation of certainty.

This little example, of course, could also be viewed as an illustration of Vroom's expectancy theory, a psychological model of motivation [9]. That the gardener expects any reward or recognition at all is evidence that there is some sense of a second-level outcome that may be possible. The actual accomplishment of the weeding, then, serves as a first-level outcome, or the immediate behavioral outcome of the gardener's effort to achieve. Second-level outcomes, in this example, might be more intrinsic than extrinsic. That is, a home gardener works at the weeds as much for his or her own inner satisfaction as he does to please neighbors or relatives. To expect much extrinsic reward from such a task is usually not considered a probability in valuing the weeding job. To have someone offer to take her out to dinner as a reward for weeding a garden is beyond most gardeners' probability calculations for the weeding effort. To gain such a reward is, in all likelihood, an unanticipated consequence, and therefore a nonlinear one. Because expectancy theory attempts to understand the variables in individual motivation, it offers a process-oriented model that concerns itself with many of the issues related to applications of chaos theory. The Vroom model allows for both uncertainty and for calculations of probabilities that are linked with both short- and long-term system outcomes.

From this perspective on chaos theory, the emphasis is on the *nature of change*, the description or qualification of change, and on attempts to see the patterns and tendencies of change in a given system. The focus of study here is not the actual facts of the change. While localized facts (localized as to place and time) can be gathered, and while trend graphs can be plotted, the future of a technically chaotic system cannot be predicted from a factual account of actual events in the past. The changes in such a system, because they are nonlinear, may not lead to consistent predictability of future events or results in the system. Further, the difficulty in measuring exactly all of the factors or variables of a system at any given point in time raises difficulties in understanding the potential paths and directions of nonlinear systems.

In the study of a chaotic system, we concern ourselves with the patterns of behavior as viewed from a higher level than one that Gell-Mann refers to as the "fine-grained" historical analysis of system behavior. A fine-grained history of a system would provide a thorough portrait of system activity as it existed at the moment in time at which the portrait data is captured. A coarse-grained view might be more useful, one in which the detail that is captured offers key data but not all data. The methods of measurement thus become highly important in a consideration of chaos theory, since measurement of nonlinear dynamical systems proceeds differently than does measurement that assumes linearity. In measuring chaotic systems, the emphasis is on change and patterns of change and the chief parameters that define the rates and kinds of change.

The nonlinear nature of dynamical systems is a key feature, one addressed by a pioneer in the study of NDS, Edward Lorenz. His approach to understanding chaos theory stresses the appearance of chance:

> Among these processes are some whose variations *are not random but look random.* I shall use the term *chaos* to refer collectively to processes of this sort—ones that appear to proceed according to chance even though their behavior is in fact determined by precise laws [3].

Like the outline of Vroom's expectancy theory, here is the recognition, from a physical scientist, that the relationship between observable outcome and the system initiating the behavior is not a direct or predictable one. Yet, like Vroom, Lorenz recognizes that linkages and relationships exist at the course-grained level. Both theorists suspect processes in operation behind the scenes that make the action and dialogue on the stage non-random. Uncovering those "precise laws" which influence the outcomes of behavior in nonlinear dynamical systems is an essential summary of the study of chaos theory, regardless of the discipline in which it takes place.

In refining his description of how chaos operates, Lorenz settles on a definition of chaos as "sensitive dependence on initial conditions" (p. 8). This simple approach implies much about such a system, and underscores the difference between classical and technical chaos in systems. Where the emphasis in studies of classical chaos is on the apparent confusion and nonlinearity observable in the behavior of a system, and on the mystery surrounding the outcomes, emphasis in studies of technical chaos is on an understanding of the motivators, drivers, and influencers which guide and suggest the behavior of the system. Ironically, the understanding of chaotic systems lies in an understanding of the system's unity and unifying forces, and not so much in understanding the differences and distinctions in the micro tracking of system activity. When students of chaos theory begin to look at the initial conditions or variables that may have guided the behavior of the system in its chaotic dynamics, they are looking for those elements that are common to the system, not those elements that make it different. The equations or descriptors that lie at the heart of the behavior are generally believed to be simple and not complicated. That such a system exhibits apparent randomness lies in its sensitivity. That is, the structure of the system is not so stable or fixed that it disallows change within its framework. It is, in fact, open to influences across its variables, but open only within that established framework. The framework is malleable, but not unbounded.

To understand chaos in this light, then, is to understand it as a natural characteristic of a system and not as a deviation from a "norm." Just as Vroom allows any number of motivators and variables to influence an individual's expectations and consequent goal-setting and action, so a chaotic system allows its complex set of defining variables to undergo considerable change within its systemic boundaries. The behavior of a nonlinear dynamical system is natural, not abnormal, and with this viewpoint such systems are incorporated into the whole fabric of existence and not set aside as unknowable mysteries. They are expected and are not surprises. What we are required to accept, in accepting technical chaos, is that the systems that exhibit chaotic behavior are volatile, and that unexpected results may well come from activities and dynamics within the system and from its interactions with other systems.

It is, perhaps, this tendency to be unknowable by virtue of nonlinearity that has created both the interest in and distrust of chaotic systems. Lorenz [3] explains nonlinearity by contrasting it with linearity:

> A linear process is one in which, if a change in any variable at some initial time produces a change in the same or some other variable at some later time, twice as large a change at the same initial time will produce twice as large a change at the same later time. . . . It follows that if the later values of any variable are plotted against the associated initial values of any variable on graph paper, the points will lie on a straight line—hence the name. A nonlinear process is simply one that is not completely linear.

The nonlinear behavior in chaotic systems is turbulent, however, only in the macro view of system behavior. Perhaps the key discovery about chaotic systems is that there is an order underlying turbulence, and that order can be discovered and recognized. It is an order in the way change occurs. Not only does change occur once in a dynamical system, it is occurring constantly. The picture of system turbulence owes its detail to some fairly simple guidelines that allow the system to experience freedom of activity within those guidelines. For example, air currents may disturb the smoke rising from a campfire, but the smoke still rises, at least to a point, in a recognizable shape. In a similar way, the people who assemble in an organization to work may apparently coordinate things differently from day to day, and may appear to behave randomly, but within some invisible set of parameters which influence decisions and actions.

It is not enough to dismiss apparent randomness or disorder as classical chaos. It is necessary to look beyond the macro, or higher-level view of system activity, and attempt to understand what makes the operation of the system seem to be unknowable.

Furthermore, as systems shift from stability toward turbulence, they do so deliberately, assuming the best form for the system at the time. This change is an adaptive move on the part of the system, as it self-organizes for efficiency. What appeared to be disorder, then, proves to be a form of ordering in the dynamics of the system. Turbulence is a choice on the part of the system, to best accommodate the overall ecology at a given place and time in the life of the system [1].

It is perhaps this self-organizing capability that is an inseparable part of chaotic systems that gives us pause when we translate from physical or organizational systems. Humans sometimes distrust actions that are taken without human intervention and control. While we are sometimes willing to suspend disbelief in our fantasy life, in real life, we generally like to see the strings on the puppet or the oil on the dipstick. To participate in a system in which nonlinearity and sensitivity may be constant sources of new and different experiences, may give us concern. The key to trust and acceptance will lie in an understanding of how such systems operate and a reassurance that we remain important to the success of such systems.

The presence of nonlinearity in dynamical systems can be identified mathematically when the equations that express the activity of the system contain elements that allow for nonlinear calculations [2]. Whereas many dynamical systems can be described through differential equations, these system equations tend to show smooth and continuous changes as they are processed. The evolution equations specify stable rates of changes in the systemic variables. Steady changes in the conditions of a business over a period of years, for example, would imply systemic stability, even though the business system is dynamic. It is through the use of such differential equations that dynamical systems can be predicted.

When such formulas include algebraic or exponential calculations for any of the variables that describe system behavior, then the system is most likely one that exhibits nonlinearity. In an equation which includes two variables, for example, project completion efficiency (y) and professional salaries (x), an element such as (7x) would indicate a nonlinear relationship between the variables. This would act, in the calculation, to account for some relationship that is not strictly linear nor explained by a simple cause-effect progression.

For example, if project completion efficiency were a simple result of incrementing professional salaries, the formula for calculating that relationship would look like $y=x+1$. That is, by incrementing salaries one step, we would have the same increase in project completion efficiency. This is a linear equation, as shown in the graph in Figure 5-1.

If, on the other hand, project completion efficiency does not respond so simply to increases in professional salaries, the formula would need to reflect that complexity. If, for example, the formula is $y=x^2$, a different picture of the relationship emerges, as shown in Figure 5-2. The curve in this graph indicates that there is no longer a one-to-one correspondence between salary increases and project completion efficiency. Instead, this graph can be interpreted to mean that project comple-

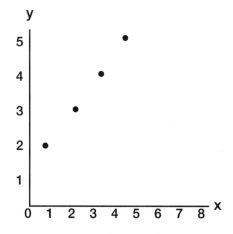

Figure 5-1. Linear equation graph.

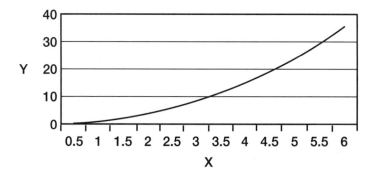

Figure 5-2. Nonlinear equation graph.

tion efficiency accelerates in a way that becomes, over time, disproportional to the salary invested.

By accounting for such nonlinear behavior, the prediction of future states of the system becomes more accurate. This is a mathematical way of expressing the idea that the future is not a straight line based on present and past behavior.

Yet, the intent of the mathematics associated with studies of chaotic systems is not to pin down a precise outcome in the future or to determine an exact behavioral pattern at some future interval. Instead, the intent is to understand the general framework and character of the system's operation and to infer its future behavior by understanding its infrastructure. This is often done through models and simulations which use differential equations to sequence a system through long time periods, graphically portraying the results of the calculations, and thus the "shape" of the system and its dynamics. This approach, based largely on the work of Henri Poincaré, provides a qualitative view of system activity. The focus of the work of Poincaré was on understanding the infrastructure of the variables in dynamical systems. His work led, in part, to a holistic view of system behavior, in an effort to understand the characteristics that underlie such complex systems. Poincaré looked for methods that would describe the key elements of a system and the differential behavior of those elements over time.

Another key feature of nonlinear dynamical systems is the fact that as they change and move, the variables never return to the same state. Regardless of when a researcher visits a system, it will be different, and will thus exhibit aperiodic behavior. This characteristic is easy to see in a sales environment. If a retail store manager tries to maintain a stable, linear pricing model, she will most likely find customers going down the street to the competition, which holds irregular and frequent sales. There is intrigue in being there at the right time and finding just the right bargain. There is little excitement in going into a store where the prices are fixed from week to week. In a nonlinear pricing model, there is always change, based on any number of possible variables, from the base wholesale price of an item, to the season, to the type of customer to be attracted. In the ultimate expression of such a complex pricing model, prices will never be the same at two different price periods, and price behavior is aperiodic.

This pricing method, in fact, is a staple in the soft drink industry, where sustained competition lies chiefly in careful pricing, rather than in product differentiation. Many years ago, bottlers adopted pricing models based on breakeven analysis, which allows them to see, graphically, what will happen if either fixed expenses or variable expenses change in their operations. Using this model, they can adjust prices based on variable costs to deliver the product to stores, so long as fixed costs are covered. That is, given that it will cost x to produce and deliver one case of product to a store twenty miles from the bottling plant, the cost to deliver twenty cases is not 20x. Instead, the cost relies on the fixed costs associated with running the plant and the delivery truck, and the variable costs of producing 20 cases of liquid product vs. one case. The price you see in the market is carefully calculated on both of these costs—fixed and variable—and may, or may not, provide a profit margin for the supplier. However, lack of a margin, as with loss leaders, is a known factor, and is itself calculated into the overall cost of marketing and advertising and recovered from overall sales operations. Variable costing and pricing allows the bottler to manage costs and to allow sales volume to influence pricing.

In other human organizations, the characteristics of instability and aperiodicity in dynamical systems are clearly evident. Kellert notes, for example, human history (pp. 4–5) as a grand and global setting in which nothing is ever the same twice. Events are both unstable, as national boundaries, leadership, and political directions change, and aperiodic, since the systems are sensitive to initial conditions, and no two visits to the civilization system will see the same actions repeated in exactly the same ways (discounting time travel, of course).

OTHER CHARACTERISTICS OF CHAOS

In the previous section, I have tried to elaborate, without adding too much complexity, the various ways in which chaos theory has been defined. In defining NDS and chaos theory, a number of characteristics have come out that will prove useful as we move, later, to transfer an understanding of chaos theory to learning and to the practice of learning support. In addition to the characteristics introduced above, there are other features that will also prove useful as we view technical chaos in its operation in organizations and their learning processes.

Phase Space

The concept of phase space is a different way to view system activity, and to place it in context. Sometimes referred to as "state space," this view of a system is a means of tracking and measuring the behavior of system variables in various dimensions. A graphical point in phase space can be understood to represent the combined values of a number of system variables. Because our concern is with dynamical systems, we are not concerned with a snapshot of the system at a frozen point in time, however, but with understanding the framework within which the system operates and the guideposts it adopts as it organizes itself. We need enough data of the right type to be able to create a number of points in phase space to understand the whole nature of the operation of the system. Since the activity of a nonlinear dynamic system is not confined to two-dimensional space, which can be represented by simple xy coordinates on a graph, the depiction of the phase portrait of a dynamical system is a geometric shape. A chaotic system can be viewed as having a topology that describes its activity and not simply a line of direction on a traditional graph. It is more solid geometry than plane geometry.

In organizations, the concept of the "balanced scorecard" is an attempt, based on the descriptive vehicle of the "johari window" to address the variables in an operational system. Founded in Deming's ideas of continuous improvement, an organization's scorecard may include such major quadrants as financial performance, human resource management, client/end-user satisfaction, and process effectiveness. With each major area representing a quadrant on the scorecard, the visual representation resembles a johari window. In the ideal state of the system, the four quadrants are balanced, receiving equal attention and returning equivalent results in performance. Measurements of variables in each quadrant determine the state of that quadrant at any given time of measurement [10, 11].

The johari window serves as a crude version of phase space, but does encourage analysts and business leaders to consider a number of variables which affect the direction of their operations and to view these variables in rough relationship with each other. It is a first step toward construction of a true phase portrait, which is a much more complex matter. A point in phase space represents all four of the quadrants in the construct of the balanced scorecard, and potentially other variables that cannot be classified into the johari window framework. How these variables get combined is the result of understanding the effect each has on the others individually and in concert. To understand these complex relationships will require research, modeling and simulation work far beyond the simple identification of the systemic elements to be measured.

Phase space itself is shown in Figures 5-3 and 5-4. In Figure 5-3, the changes in a dynamic system are plotted in phase space described by two axes, x and y. This allows a plot for two variables that are affecting the changes in the system under study.

When there are three variables whose behavior is likely to be key in understanding the dynamics of the system, a third dimension can be added to the plot. The "y" dimension in Figure 5-4 adds depth to the vertical and horizontal dimensions that can be measured along the x and z lines.

The importance of points of measurement in phase space becomes apparent when the operation of variables in iterated change formulas is considered. Change leads to divisions within the complex system, making its paths more complex and adding basins of attraction. If we understand this process of bifurcation, then we can understand the various phases through which systems can pass on their way to chaotic behavior.

Bifurcation

The concept of bifurcation is illustrated in Figure 5-5. At the left of the illustration, the system that is being monitored, shows a steady state, graphed as a single line. This is sometimes referred to as "Period 1" behavior, since it is the simplest form. The branches illustrate a period doubling cascade, in which the values of the system begin to fluctuate around two, then four or more different numbers. Multiple paths are created within the system, and each of the paths is coherent and easily traceable [12, 13]. At the point at which the single line first breaks, the system has entered "Period 2" behavior, with a second attractor added to the first, to provide a separate basin of attraction. As additional bifurcation takes place, the system becomes more complex and numerous attractive forces are now operating in tandem, pulling different elements of the system in different directions. On the right side of the diagram, however, the distinct paths and systemic options seem to blur into a generally undefinable pattern, and the paths of system flow appear to be lost

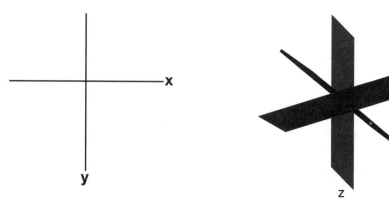

Figure 5-3. Phase space, two dimensions.   **Figure 5-4**. Phase space, x, y, z dimensions.

in "Period 3." This area, in fact, represents technically chaotic behavior on the part of the system. The vertical striations are areas in which some coherence returns temporarily, but the system is now a largely chaotic one. The bifurcation of the system dynamics has led to increased complexity and, finally, chaos.

This form of system performance diagram illustrates the "Logistic Equation," a relationship first established to show the effects of changes in the environment on population growth. The equation develops the picture in Figure 5-5 by a process of iteration in which the behavior of the system is simulated by setting three numbers: the constant which represents the influence of the environment on the population; the initial starting number for the population itself; and the number of times the calculation will be repeated, or iterated. The equation itself looks like this: $X_{n+1} = k \times X_n \times (1-X_n)$. The X represents the number in the population; k is a constant that represents the rate at which the population increases. When the equation is applied to any population, it leads to a determination of the point at which population replacement equilibrium exists. That is, at some point in population growth, the growth will be equally matched with losses.

The iterative nature of the equation is significant, since the value of the population is dependent on each prior calculation. That is, the historical data becomes highly relevant to understanding the behavior of the system. The future of the system—any system—is dependent on choices and decisions made over a period of time. These choices and decisions will impact the "k" factor, the growth factor, and will thus impact the rate and ways in which the population survives. Decisions, in the logistic equation, are not made individually, starting from new data at each

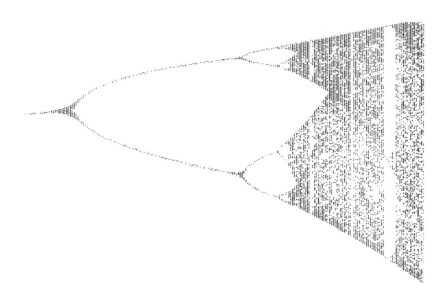

Figure 5-5. System bifurcation.

measurement point. Nor is one time period merely compared with a previous period. What we see in this approach to data is the dependence of measures at one point, on preceding data that has been in the system and operating over a period of time. The trace shown in Figure 5-5, for instance, is the result of hundreds of iterations of the equation. It describes a clear picture of activity within the system, and it helps define the point at which chaotic behavior emerges from the stable and bifurcated phases of the system. Where the illustration begins to look like a series of vertical lines, toward the right side, the system has passed into chaotic behavior.

Bifurcation, then, is a way of picturing alternative realities within a system and identifying the forces that begin to act as separate attractive elements in a complex system. As branching takes place, there is a point where the branches fail to offer clear unifying attractors, and the variety of channels course together into chaotic activity. It becomes important, when considering the dynamics of organizations, to understand the points at which an organizational system becomes vulnerable to period doubling, as well as understand the underlying arrangement of activities that provide order even in the chaotic realm.

It is important to understand how to recognize and make use of stability in systems, but equally important to understand how branching and subdivisions can be used to optimize the system. It is not enough to strive to maintain law and order in the system. This must be accompanied by a fine respect for the ways in which iterated decisions and actions may be used to take a system into chaotic behavior. The chaos in the logistic equation is not classical chaos but technical chaos, illustrated in a very simple form. Only one variable is changed. It can be understood, and is not completely random or wildly erratic. Chaos is simply a natural result of system activity, and not an event that is outside the bounds of system reality. Chaos flows out of iterated changes in the system and is not an unnatural imposition. Chaotic behavior, in this instance, is not catastrophic.

The concept of bifurcation also speaks to the influence of speed in systems. In fluid dynamics, the faster the flow of a fluid, the more likely it is to generate eddies, and eddies within eddies, and through these bifurcations of the channel, to demonstrate chaotic behavior. Given any complex system, and any system open to changes—which accounts for most systems in which humans participate—this same principle is true. The faster things move, the more likely it is that bifurcations will take place, and that period doubling will lead to multiple centers of focus. In other words, speed leads us from relatively stable and predictable Period 1 behavior into less stable and more complex Period 2 behavior.

The rate of change, demonstrated in the growth equation as the constant (k) factor, will influence the nature and behavior of the system. To introduce change in speed of activity, without understanding the likely points at which the system will become turbulent, and without understanding the point at which it may become chaotic, is to take high risks with system performance over any long term. Human managers of organizational systems, in particular, are not yet smart enough and do not yet have enough data to be able to view the system in even the simplest of terms illustrated by the logistic equation. In that equation, only one variable was manipulated. In the typical organization, made up of people, their equipment, and their networks, multiple significant variables are in operation 24 hours a day.

Attractors

Another key feature of NDS theory which is important in consideration of organizational systems and the learning that takes place in them is the fact that different central attractors operate to determine the dynamics in a system. Kellert notes that "until the advent of chaos theory, only three types of attractors were generally recognized: the fixed point, the limit cycle, and the torus. But none of these attractors can describe the unstable aperiodic motion Lorenz found. Lorenz created the first picture of a surprising new geometrical object: a strange attractor" [2]. A system attractor, in essence, operates like a magnet in a system. It is the point or locus around which dynamical system activity coalesces. A riverbed, for instance, is a form of natural analogue to the idea of an attractor, in the sense that it attracts fluid from watersheds, and then loosely channels it. The area through which the water most often flows forms a kind of basin for the dynamics of the river. While water may occasionally overflow the banks, or may, in drought, come short of reaching the banks, it generally tends to be attracted to its basin. The same concept applies with any dynamical system. System activity orbits the attractive force and remains in some general "basin" of attraction. It is the attractor that provides the system with some sense of unity, if not uniformity. The attractor may be strong and definite, as with a fixed point, or it may be weak and indefinite, as with strange attractors.

Where the concept of system dynamics offers a conceptual challenge is in visualizing the operation of a complicated system as it plays out its dynamics in phase space. Where a system has one or two variables in action, affecting the directions of

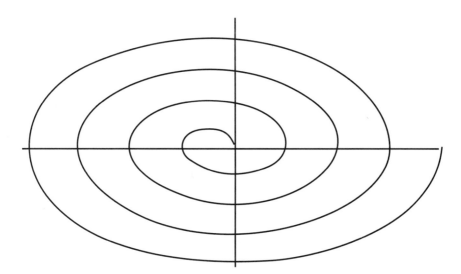

Figure 5-6. Pendulum trajectory in phase space.

the system, as decisions change the state of each of the variables, it is relatively easy to visualize the trajectory of the system. Figure 5-6, for example, shows a rough outline of the trajectory of a pendulum, affected by friction, as it traces a path in phase space. In this instance, the track for the pendulum is determined by two factors, angle and trajectory. The vertical line represents a scale of velocity, and the horizontal line represents a scale of angles. Each point described along the spiral is a point in phase space that describes the condition of the system as it moves [13]. This is true regardless of the number of variables, such as angle and trajectory, used to describe the action of the system. In any phase portrait, each point will completely represent the condition and description of the system at that point.

In the drawing in Figure 5-6, note that the spiral represents a form of orderly progression as angle and trajectory change, based on the influence of friction. The system dynamics do not allow for very many degrees of freedom. The center point of the spiral is the attractor and the entire area in phase space taken up by the spiral can be considered the basin of attraction. This form of attraction represents a single-point attractor, since the nature of the system is such that it is attracted to only one central, fixed point. It operates in a steady state. This same behavior can be seen in a different form in Figure 5-5 at the left-hand side of the diagram, before the first branching. In this area, the system dynamics show attraction to a steady state, and a single-point attractor.

If a system includes a bifurcation, then its attractor is periodic. A periodic attractor is generally found in relatively compact systems, where there is some degree of freedom of action, but the action is such that it may repeat itself. A sine wave is an example in which a signal alternates between two points over time. This form of attractor is shown in phase space in Figure 5-7. In periodic behavior, a sequence of events or a particular set of behaviors will reoccur at regular intervals.

When shown in phase space, period behavior is referred to as a "limit cycle," since the dynamic of the system is limited by the boundaries of the cycle [2]. In Figure 5-5, the area following the first branching is another graphic portrayal of the limit cycle in action, as the behavior of the system alternates between two values.

A third well-known form of system behavior is quasi-periodic, which introduces multiple attractors, but with regularity. This behavior can be pictured as alternating cycles with different values, as shown in Figure 5-8.

This behavior can also be seen in Figure 5-5 in the area of multiple branching. When shown in phase space, this more complicated relationship of the system to its attractor is viewed as a "torus" as shown in Figure 5-9. The points which describe a

Figure 5-7. Periodic attractor in phase space.

system in quasi-periodic behavior now can be viewed as they trace a path around a "doughnut" which describes the attractive forces in a two-dimensional dynamic. This model of behavior, which shows complexity but also a high degree of predictability, is the attraction basin which is closest to chaotic behavior, but without such behavior in it. While the points may not trace the same pattern twice around the torus, there is consistency, and a strong attraction between the activity of the system and its basin [2].

While these three models are the basic models on which dynamic systems thinking was founded, they are not chaotic. Referring once again to Figure 5-5, the system bifurcation diagram, the right-hand side of the plot shows the system activity that is chaotic. The major discovery in studying this area was that, even though seeming to be jumbled, the points behaved in reference to the strange attractor [12]. What happens in the system is that the multiple periodicity noted in the torus model begins to become aperiodic and irregular, due to increased stresses within the system. The number of dimensions against which behavior must be measured increases, and the degrees of freedom expressed in the system behavior also increase. Multiple dimensionality and higher degrees of openness and freedom allow the system

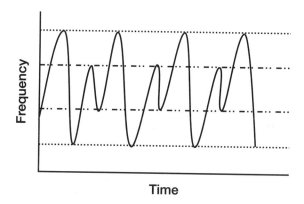

Figure 5-8. Quasi-periodic behavior.

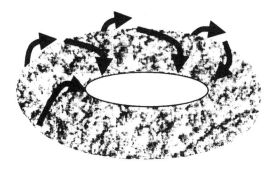

Figure 5-9. Torus.

to break away from the cycles around the torus, and to demonstrate more complex behavior.

Were this openness and freedom to move the system away from any consistency at all, it would fail to be a system and would fit the description of classical chaos. That is, there would be no sense of attraction to anything, and system dynamics would wander off into myriad potentialities. It would not, if that were the case, fit into a description of a bounded system, and its energy would be dissipated into the environment. It would be unmeasurable and unpredictable.

However, it is the strange attractor that makes the difference between classical and technical chaos, when viewing a highly complex system. Kellert [2] describes four characteristics of a strange attractor:

1. It is an attractor, that is, an object with no volume in state space toward which all nearby trajectories will converge;
2. it typically has the appearance of a fractal, that is, a stack of two-dimensional sheets displaying a self-similar packing structure;
3. motion on it exhibits a form of instability known as sensitive dependence on initial conditions, that is, for any point on the attractor there is another point nearby that will follow a path diverging exponentially from the path of the first;
4. it can be generated by the numerical integration of a very simple set of dynamical equations.

The idea of a strange attractor, then, is similar to the philosophical concept called *multum in parvo,* or "much in little." Apparently strange and indescribable behavior in a system can be understood by looking for the kernel attractive force and describing it as a dynamical force consisting of a set of variables operating in relationship with each other. This attractor allows us to grasp the complexity that underlies a chaotic system. In a system that is free of rigorous constraints, many things are possible. There are more degrees of freedom available for exploring new possibilities. The system, as guided by its attractor, can become whatever is possible, and can shift among realities at will. A chaotic system can, potentially, have 360° of freedom in any direction.

One of the first demonstrations of a strange attractor came in the early 1960s, when Edward Lorenz developed a model for the behavior of weather systems [3, 4]. The Lorenz model consists of three differential equations that considered the effect on weather developments of the speed with which convection occurred in the system, along with the differences in temperature that occurred both vertically and horizontally in the system. Lorenz discovered that the integration of the equations produced different results with very small changes in the variables. The system and its behavior, he found, was highly sensitive to the initial conditions in the simulation. In fact, changing the value of a variable by only $\frac{1}{1000}$ can produce significant differences in the behavior of the system over time. This has major implications for the study of organizational systems, where decisions are made every day on a variety of levels, generating multiple changes in the variables of the system. As Kellert [2] points out, *"chaotic systems require impossible accuracy for useful prediction tasks."* By extension, there is also the implication that because results are iterated in the differential equations which describe dynamical system activity, the results of a decision or set of decisions is not discarded nor overwritten later in system history. These results become the basis for ongoing calculations, and future histories of the system will depend on how those results influence system behavior at any given point.

Figure 5-10 is a representation of the phase portrait of the Lorenz system, showing the operation of the strange attractor. This portrait is built on a three-dimensional phase space, because the operation of the attractor is not confined to only two dimensions. The Lorenz equation considers three variables and their actions, not two, and is therefore plotted in x, y and z coordinates. What may not be evident in the graphic is that the plots of the track of system behavior come close to each other, but they never overlap or follow the same track. This would yield periodic behavior, which is not consistent with a chaotic system. Instead, the strange attractor is characterized by the extreme changes in the points describing the activity of the system by irregular jumps from one attractor to the other, and by the adherence of those descriptors to a definable shape in phase space.

Fractals

I have already introduced the concept of fractals, as a way of beginning the consideration of technical chaos. Because fractals are key to understanding system capabilities, it is worthwhile to expand the view of this characteristic of chaotic systems. Mandelbrot addressed the issue of multidimensionality in systems. The concept of a fractal is, simply stated, the concept that, as our viewpoint of systems

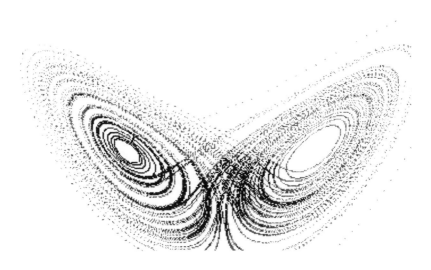

Figure 5-10. Lorenz attractor, as generated from sample program [12].

shifts from large-scale to more detailed, there are similarities in the composition of the system at various scales. The self-similarity that exists within a system offers clues to its kernel structure, regardless of how complicated it might look from a macro view. It is, in fact, a form of geometry which goes beyond the plane, two-dimensional or the solid, three-dimensional geometry. The study of fractals is the study of multi-dimensional behavior of a system, and a search for patterns that will help understand the system and its self-similar structure [4].

The value of fractal analysis lies in the ability to see the patterns that constitute whole systems. In fact, by understanding the self-similarity that exists at the micro level, it is possible to understand the dynamics and actions at the macro level. Understanding, for example, the constitution of individual humans can lead to a better understanding of how those people constitute groups. The understanding of common elements that constitute the group system—of the fractal nature of the system—will lead to a greater understanding of how the whole system operates. The fractal view gives not only the separate views of the analyst, but looks for the common features from micro to macro viewpoints, which really explain what the system is like. For this reason, fractals are an important part of the study of any chaotic system, since it is the kernel description of the behavior of the attractor that is elemental to understanding the unity that underlies the complexity. Self-similarity lies at the core of a technically chaotic system, allowing it to experience a high degree of freedom and adaptation, while at the same time maintaining its essential nature. If a system is made up of various parts, then it is some common factor that makes those parts adhere to each other. The finance department does not exist independently from the truckers who take the products to warehouses and stores. There is a fractal dimension within the system that provides an elemental self-similarity between the two sub-systems.

The figure of the Lorenz attractor illustrates this point. There is not a single focal point for system dynamics. There are multiple dimensions and multiple variables in operation, which tend to behave around two, not one, tori. Yet, the two tori themselves are in a relationship that allows system behavior to move between one and the other. The points that describe the system show wide variability and high sensitivity, yet there is a coherent complexity. It is the nature of this cohesive force that requires an understanding of the fractal behavior of the system and its constituent parts.

What is equally important with the understanding of the fractal nature of a system is the ability that is derived from that understanding. The ability to grow systems and to ensure their sustainability relies heavily on understanding how self-similarity works in the system [3]. To add parts to a system, or to change them, requires a clear understanding of what such changes will do and what the ramifications of change will be. Systems change, then, should be addressed to the fractal and not to the superficial bits and pieces which constitute single, separate points in the system's history. Effective change does not lie in the changes at micro level, nor at intermediate level, nor at macro level alone. Effective change relies on change to the essential nature of the system, and that, for chaotic systems, lies in the fractional dimensionality.

To some extent, this search for the common underlying pattern of a system has been expressed in qualitative terms such as the "soul" of the organization, or the "vision" or "values" of an organization. These terms seek to find and describe the fractal essence that allows the organizational system to operate in uncertainty, but still hold together in a coherent network or matrix. For the students of organization who have sought to describe these features of organizational behavior, it is an attempt to deal with something that is real, within the system, in terms that sometimes blur in accuracy and fidelity. The descriptions often become "soft" and vague and insubstantial, when, in reality, there is a direct, measurable approach to understanding the kernel nature of the system.

Its fractal elements can be teased out, and a consistent view can be developed which contributes to an understanding of the organization from individual, to subgroup, to group levels, and which folds in the contributions to the wholeness of the system made by devices, machines, software, and networks. The rhetorical devices available for the development of "vision" are limited. Data collected across the system for an understanding of the attractor, its dimensions, and the fractals of the system offers fewer limitations, and is founded in structural realities. While much of the literature of fractals has centered on their occurrence in natural objects (coastlines, mountains, human organs), it is necessary to remember that organizational systems which include humans are natural and not "man-made."

While humans believe that they control the presence of such systems, the make-up of the system is such that it transcends human intervention. The organization, then, has humans in it, but is larger than that in scope, and is, therefore, a natural result arising from the larger environment. It is appropriate, therefore, for us to consider these chaotic organizational systems and the fractal attractors that provide their coherence and unity.

COMPLEX ADAPTIVE SYSTEMS

Where chaos theory addresses systems that appear to have high degrees of randomness and are sensitive to initial conditions, complexity theory has to do with systems that operate just at the line separating coherence from chaos. As illustrated in Figure 5-11, complexity operates at the point of phase transition from order to chaos.

What is of interest in these systems is the way they exist at the edge of chaotic behavior, but do not pass over the edge. In this position, such systems exhibit high degrees of flexibility and freedom, operate as open or virtual systems, and display high forms of renewable energy.

A key to the translation and interpretation of business systems as complex adaptive systems lies in an understanding of the characteristics and definition of complex adaptive systems. Gell-Mann [7], in considering the nature of complex adaptive systems, describes the characteristics of such systems in their operation:

> A complex adaptive system acquires information about its environment
> and its own interaction with that environment, identifying regularities in that
> information, condensing those regularities into a kind of "schema" or model,

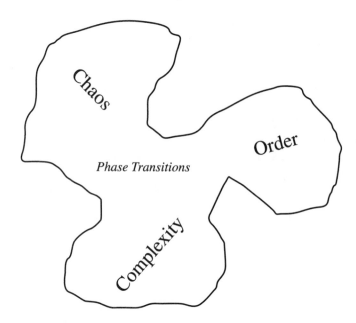

Figure 5-11. Phase transitions.

and acting in the real world on the basis of that schema. In each case, there are various competing schemata, and the results of the action in the real world feed back to influence the competition among those schemata.

The characteristics suggested here include (a) acquisition of information from an environment; (b) the relationship of the complex adaptive system with its environment; (c) the identification of common themes, elements, and "regularities" in the environmental information; and (d) the creation of behaviorally focused models based on the common elements and attributes derived from the environment. The complex adaptive system then acts in its environment based on its available models. Finally, the models themselves undergo change as one model, apparently better, supplants another, or parts of models contribute to the creation of a new and presumably more useful model.

These characteristics can be found in operations from individual persons carrying out their business, or in combined systems—collectives—in which the characteristics operate in relationship with each other. Each layer of collectivism adds layers of complexity into these relationships and opens further possibilities for interactions and changes among the models in use.

Learning is a key activity. In fact, learning is directly linked with the operation of complex adaptive systems:

> It is not only learning in the usual sense that provides examples of the operation of complex adaptive systems. Biological evolution provides many others. While human beings acquire knowledge mainly by individual or col-

lective use of their brains, the other animals have acquired a much larger fraction of the information they need to survive by direct genetic inheritance; that information, evolved over millions of years, underlies what is sometimes rather vaguely called "instinct" [7].

In the makeup and activity of biological organisms, we can see the operation of learning through evolution. In fact, ordered behavior in organizational growth may owe its order to spontaneity and internal forces. Organisms, that is, may decide when, where, and how to change, and may not leave such changes to mere randomness or chance evolution.

Based on this concept of learning and adaptation, Senge's [14] admonition to allow and encourage a generative approach to systems may be, in large part, a suggestion to allow complex adaptive systems to have a large degree of freedom to develop, evolve, and emerge. The concept of self-organization, so important in the definition of complex adaptive systems, may be something that brings with it a natural kind of order that allows association between and among complex adaptive systems [6].

Organisms with high degrees of freedom are those most likely to be highly active in their environment, or fitness landscape. As they stretch their capabilities, they learn what works and what doesn't. As they learn, they stretch in different directions, exploring options and choices. This level of activity results in changes for the organism, which will either advance it on its fitness landscape or cause it to fall behind other organisms with which it is co-evolving.

In this description lie the basics of the mechanics of operations of complex adaptive systems. The exploration of "fitness landscapes" can be extended across all systems that meet the characteristics of complex adaptive systems. The interaction between the system and its landscape, or environment, is a restless one requiring constant adjustment to the ever-changing "peaks" or stimuli that appear in the landscape. The energy of the complex adaptive system is used in adjusting to these peaks, and focusing on adaptation. The system, therefore, must not only be self-organizing but also cohesive, to the extent that it can climb the peaks and identify new peaks that may be rising in its fitness landscape.

As subsystems behave in a larger system, then, they behave in part in reaction to other subsystems that they consider to be predators or competitors, and change to match the changes in those competitors. Of the three states of being that such systems might adopt, the ones that expend the least energy to sustain and improve their place in the larger system, do so by sustaining themselves at the edge of chaos in a highly complex transitional state. By maintaining themselves on the edge of chaos, successful complex adaptive systems display what Kauffman considers to be "wisdom" in their use of archetypal patterns and models to sustain change, but without moving past the phase transition state into even more complex chaotic behavior. He makes a distinction, in this description of complex adaptive systems behavior, between those that exercise this wisdom and balancing act and systems that exercise only power. Power alone may temporarily exert system energy to achieve the most recent peak attainable, but such raw application of power may not be sustainable and may, in fact, throw the system into chaotic behavior. For Kauffman, and for others who have looked at complex adaptive systems [7, 15], the most effective point of operation is at this edge of chaos position, without structuring themselves as chaotic systems.

Waldrop builds a similar view of the nature of complex adaptive systems, and in defining such systems offers insight into their characteristics. First, such systems are complex because they have within them a great number of agents that are inter-acting with each other in numerous ways. In a social business system, for example, system agents may be humans, intelligent machines, or intelligent electronic net-works. A second feature of such systems, much like that described by Gell-Mann and Kauffman, is the ability of the system to self-organize. What Waldrop empha-sizes, in fact, is the ability to do this spontaneously, which suggests that very little need exist as a trigger mechanism and that organization or re-organization can hap-pen quickly. He, like Kauffman, sees coevolution as a feature of such systems that, collectively, form an ecosystem. There is, Waldrop believes, a form of synergy in this evolutionary process, as "groups of agents seeking mutual accommodation and self-consistency somehow manage to transcend themselves, acquiring collective properties such as life, thought, and purpose that they might never have possessed individually" [15].

Such systems are, therefore, highly adaptive. They are active systems constantly working to improve their fitness landscape, and their position in relation to com-petitors and predators. Complex adaptive systems are out to win in their fitness landscapes. This feature, of course, suggests that such systems, in adapting to their environment and its events, are learning. Complex adaptive systems learn as a nat-ural part of their ability to meet the changes in their landscapes. This learning, how-ever, leads not to simple survival, but to increasing complexity. As the system learns and adapts, it moves further from a simple birth event, and acquires history, and through history, additional complexity. It acquires new capabilities that begin to express themselves on the fitness landscape and that may change the nature of its coevolution. If, in some sense, a system is what it knows or is capable of doing, then as knowing increases, the system changes its nature and becomes something different. While this thought is easily accepted at the individual human level, with children going to school to learn and, as they learn, becoming different as they relate to parents and environment, it is not an idea that has been well-established in thinking about social business systems. In fact, the recognition of effects of learn-ing in adult individuals is not well understood, nor well measured in any dynamic way. So the influence of learning and adaptation, as it applies to complex adaptive systems that are adult humans and that are social business systems, is an area for additional investigation.

Finally, there is an important dynamic nature of such systems. Given this dynam-ic feature, complex systems display some features of coherence, structure and orderliness, along with features of adaptability and change. They exist at the edge of chaos, a balance point where spontaneity, creativity, and dynamic change can constantly provide the generative engine for the system, but a point at which order is discernible and not turbulent. There is a fine line in these systems between order and chaos.

These characteristics of complex adaptive systems, described by the chief authors in the field of complexity science, are all reflected in the properties and mechanisms of such systems introduced by John Holland [16]. Holland divides the characteristics of complex adaptive systems into four properties and three mechanisms that describe the particulars of such systems and their operation.

Aggregation, a property, is the process of classification, categorization, and collection used as systems generate or regenerate models. This function is also related to self-organization in that, through aggregation, systems have the tools at hand and materials at hand for spontaneous generation. Categories become building blocks for models and models become the basis for dynamic reshaping and action. Aggregation also refers to the phenomenon of coevolution, as systems aggregate into larger and more complex systems (meta-agents) with different behaviors. This is a generative process in constant operation.

Tagging is a mechanism used by complex adaptive systems to facilitate the aggregation process. Tagging is used to help construct models from available, identified resources. By tracing these tags, systems and system dynamics can be measured. Agents and objects within a system can thus be tracked and observed, because they have been tagged. The extent to which tagging is evident in a system is an indicator of the extent to which interactions within the system, and exchanges between it and other systems, can be tracked and measured. It follows that a high degree of tagging in a system also indicates the willingness of the system to adapt and modify itself, and allow its boundaries to be permeable for interchanges with other agents, meta-agents, or subsystems.

Nonlinearity, already described by other authors, is, for Holland, a property of complex adaptive systems. As Holland describes linearity, "the value of the function, for any set of values assigned to its arguments, is simply a weighted sum of those values. The function $3x + 5y + z$, for example, is linear" [16]. Linearity implies simple summation of values in a system. In contrast, Holland offers a simple example of nonlinear equations, one used to describe predator-prey interactions. The logic is based on the fact that as either population, predator or prey, increases, the chance of an encounter between a predator and a prey increases. He assigns the value U to the number of predators in a given geographical area (a square mile, in his example). V represents the number of prey in the same area. The small letter c represents a constant that is, here, the efficiency rating of the predator. In this example, c represents the average rate at which it can search through its square mile of territory.

The number of possible interactions in a given time unit (1 day) is represented as cUV. If we assume that the efficiency rating c of the predator $= 0.5$, and there are 2 predators in the area, with 10 prey in the area, the number of encounters expected in a day is expressed as $cUV = 0.5\,(2)(10) = 10$ encounters. Increasing the number of predators to 4, and the number of prey to 20, however, changes the expected number of encounters significantly to $cUV = 0.5(4)(20) = 40$ encounters. Because the predator-prey interactions cannot be described simply by adding the number of predators to the number of prey, the calculation above involves nonlinearity. The interaction between predator and prey is described mathematically as a product, not a sum of activity.

Through the use of this example, Holland illustrates that such simplistic and straightforward activities as polling and surveying arrive primarily at linear trend assumptions, and do not include nonlinearity in their mathematics. Insofar as such data may describe linear activity in the system, they are accurate. However, to predict nonlinear effects—such as the quadruple increase in predator-prey encounters based on a simple doubling of predators and prey—more complex models are required to describe the activity. Complex adaptive systems are chiefly characterized by these less linear kinds of growth, change, and modification.

Flow is a property that describes the flow of activity within a complex adaptive system, and with the external systems. Flow may refer to the degree to which there is movement of information or people among nodes of a network, or to the actual physical flow of materials, paperwork, and products into, through, and out of a system. Flow will vary over time in a complex adaptive system, and nodes or agents may appear and disappear spontaneously. Nothing is settled, and the focus of activity is on patterns. There are two properties of flows: a multiplier effect and a recycling effect. Systems may show their efficiency and effectiveness as they make use of new resources, added into the system from other systems. The addition of such resource often results in a multiplier effect, which is passed along throughout the flow, and has the effect of increasing available resources. As Holland observes, this effect

> . . . arises regardless of the particular nature of the resource, be it goods, money, or messages. It is relevant whenever we want to estimate the effect of some new resource, or the effect of a diversion of some resource over a new path. It is particularly evident when evolutionary changes occur, and it typically jeopardizes long-range predictions based on simple trends [16].

The recycling effect in a flow is evident as resources, or portions of them, are recovered and reused. The effectiveness of a complex adaptive system is dependent on its ability to shift, recover, and reassign resources once they have been introduced into the system, so that they continue to act as nodes or agents for the flow and evolution of the system.

Diversity is a property of complex adaptive systems that depends on the needs of the system. Diversity relates to the adaptation within the system to acquire the various agents and capabilities it needs in order to flow and to continue to adapt. The focus in diversity here is on the role that a given network node or agent plays in relationship to the overall activity of the system. The extent to which a system exercises diversity to fill the niches created through changes in the roles of agents, or by the loss of agents, is the extent to which it effectively maintains its flow and its ability to change. The creation of niches, which require new role diversity, is also a measure of the extent to which a system is a complex adaptive system.

Internal modeling is a mechanism described by Gell-Mann [7] as the creation of "schema." The agents in a complex adaptive system receive constant input and process it as part of the overall system flow, based on the interpretation of the incoming data against internal models. Such a system, then, is able to compare and contrast incoming perspectives and impressions and other data or materials against patterns and act based on its present application of the pattern. The agent applies each pattern for specific purposes. Moreover, the agent will adapt and modify patterns or models as needed to maintain the relationship between the goals and directions of the system and the incoming data. Not only are models adapted, but they are then associated with particular potential applications, so that when circumstances introduce an appropriate situation, the appropriate matching model can be used. As noted earlier in the discussion of chaos theory, studies in olfactory processing have shown that the system learns from the interaction of pattern and stimulus, and that this learning influences how and where in the brain a pattern is stored, and how it is dynamically modified.

Holland distinguishes between *tacit models,* which are used to interpret stimuli in light of pre-established system goals and intentions, and *overt models,* which are used for the evolution of alternatives and the processing of multiple perspectives. The degree and extent to which systems use and apply both forms of models indicate the extent to which they are complex adaptive systems.

Building blocks are mechanisms through which systems take apart existing structures into meaningful units and then reuse those units to generate new or adapted structures. The units can be used and reused continuously to remake the system or its parts. It is through the use of such basic objects that a system maintains some regularity, yet can at the same time operate in complex ways. These building blocks serve as the elements from which models, or schema, are constructed and, therefore, the richness of the set of building blocks available to a system is a determinant of it potential for complexity with order.

These seven properties and mechanisms, then, incorporate the elements of definitions of complexity and complex adaptive systems. By measuring the presence of these characteristics in a system, it is possible to determine if the system meets the requirements of a complex adaptive system. By measuring the intensity or variety of the properties and mechanisms, it is possible to determine the extent to which a complex adaptive system is complex and adaptive, and the extent to which it exists at the edge of chaos. Complex adaptive systems theory is important because it helps us understand where that boundary lies. Moreover, it is common for organizational systems to exist at the edge of chaos, in some degree of unrest, but withstanding the temptation to increase nonlinearity into the chaotic realm.

JUXTAPOSITION OF CLASSICAL AND TECHNICAL CHAOS

At the point in our understanding of systems activity when we accept complexity and chaos as realities, then we begin to understand the relationships and values of classical and technical chaos. We understand systems as wholes, and in doing so, do not discount that which we do not understand. The evolution of myth, magic, philosophy and religion relies on our desire to make sense of global and universal evidence, either seen or sensed in other ways. Classical chaos was largely a way to add full understanding to existence, and technical chaos is another, related way.

While we seek stability, consistency, unity, and knowledge of the future, we also understand, from both technical and classical models, that such characteristics of existence are elusive. The best we can do is to try to understand instability, change, inconsistency and diversity as parts of the whole, which is a complex system. That we organize and dance on the edge of chaos is indisputable. What is important to carry forward from an understanding of both classical and technical chaos is that much of what underlies complexity and apparent randomness can be understood, traced out, and used to improve the holistic systems in which we participate. Chaos Theory is an attempt to understand more about the details of how seemingly complex and disorganized systems work.

The progression of discoveries in chaos theory has relied heavily upon the computer which, while ironically a mindless machine, is the only mindless machine that can process data at a rate fast enough to produce pictures and graphics which represent what is otherwise difficult to understand from numbers alone. Chaos Theory is very much about understanding through graphical images as well as numerical results of calculations.

Technical chaos is about seeking orderly patterns in what appears to be disordered and nonlinear activity. It is about documenting iterations of data in such a way that similarities and details come forward when studied by humans. It is about the ability to demonstrate consistency where, otherwise, no consistency seems to exist. It is about finding common flow patterns in what humans initially perceive to be turbulence.

Technical chaos takes the viewpoint that what is disordered need not be considered out of place, and that what happens in seemingly random ways may, in fact, be understood when viewed from one or more different perspectives. Disorder, fractions, parts, pieces, and data that are outside of normal curves and distributions are, in the world of Chaos Theory, all acceptable parts of a larger picture, which, at some level, comes to be seen as something recognizable.

The shortcomings of technical chaos and of our general views of classical chaos are similar: the definition and connotation of chaotic regimes is based on a largely human understanding of what is happening, and an interpretation of results based on human experience and values. Where we have tried to identify order amidst disorder, it is we who have largely defined the point at which order exists, and have written the laws which express what order will be and what it will not be. That which is considered orderly and regimented and regular is so by human definition.

By combining our human interpretative powers with those of the computer, we have created a different form of viewport on the universe and on the way things work. For a human to use a computer to tease out signs of order from apparently random and disorderly system behavior is to say that only through the merger of human and machine is this view available. Even so, we must realize that computers are simply mimics of their creators, and what they look for, what they see, and how they interpret it are limited still by their association with their makers. While computers extend our ability to see into the detailed structure of dynamical systems, these computers do not, in and of themselves, give us fresh insights from a non-human perspective. The tasks given to the computer, either analytical or interpretive, spring from a human understanding. The results are therefore designed to appeal to the forms of logic which are acceptable to humans.

Chaos theory, then, is largely a matter of human mind. The ability of the human population to suspend disbelief, and to accept what it sees as normal, regardless of whether it makes sense against models of order which have come to be accepted and perpetuated, is an ability which allows order to appear in disorder. In fact, it is the mental models of order and disorder that determine the extent to which these two complementary concepts can be understood. We connect with order and disorder at both the level of rational consciousness and at the level of the collective unconscious. If we see the two concepts as mutually exclusive, then we will easily classify the things that are orderly and the things that are disorderly, and maintain separation between them. If, on the other hand, we accept some idea that order and disorder are both necessary and integrated in the way things work, then we will be more willing to look for signs of order in turbulence, but accept that disorder is also natural and to be expected and welcomed.

The utility of chaos theory may best be explained as it contributes to a better understanding of the wholeness of turbulence. Disorder is not isolated from order, just as the tails of a bell-shaped data curve are not isolated from the curve itself—in fact they help define the curve, and cannot be ignored as inconsequential. Certainly, in the nature of systems that integrate humans, machines, and networks, turbulence and disorder are continually possible. In reality, I do not believe that organizational existence is often disturbed to the point of technically chaotic behavior. While it sometimes moves to the edge of chaos, rarely do the self-organizing or control elements release enough so that the system actually shows much sign of disorganization and disorder. What has been perceived and described as chaotic behavior in organizational settings has been largely from the viewpoint of observers who subjectively associate growth and change with disorder. In fact, most change in organizations is prescribed, predictable, and evolutionary, not revolutionary.

REFERENCES

1. Prigogine, I. and I. Stengers, *Order out of Chaos,* London: Collins, 1985, p. xxvi.
2. Kellert, S. H. *In the Wake of Chaos.* Science and Its Conceptual Foundations, D. L. Hull (Ed.), Chicago: The University of Chicago Press, 1993, pp. 5, 10, 12, 13, 35.
3. Lorenz, E., *The Essence of Chaos,* Seattle: University of Washington Press, 1993, pp. 4, 8, 161.
4. Gleick, J., *Chaos: Making a New Science,* New York: Viking, 1987, pp. 15, 46, 83, 86, 306, 311.
5. Turner, D. D., "Two companies set to unveil STiNG-based tools." *EMedia Weekly,* August 24, 1998, p. 8.
6. Kauffman, S., *At Home in the Universe: The Search for Laws of Self-organization and Complexity,* Oxford: Oxford University Press, 1995, pp. 49, 274, 275
7. Gell-Mann, M., *The Quark and the Jaguar,* New York: W. H. Freeman and Company, 1994, pp. 17, 19, 143.

8. Stacey, R. D., *Managing the Unknowable,* The Jossey-Bass Management Series, R. M. Warren Bennis, Ian Mitroff (Ed.), San Francisco: Jossey-Bass, 1992.

9. Gibson, J. L., J. M. Ivancevich, and J. H. Donnelly, Jr., *Organizations: Behavior, Structure, Processes,* 3rd ed., Dallas, Tex.: Business Publications Inc., 1979, p. 114.

10. Kaplan, R. S. and D. P. Norton., *The Balanced Scorecard: Translating Strategy into Action,* Boston: Harvard Business School, 1996.

11. AIAI. *The Balanced Scorecard,* http://www.aiai.ed.ac.uk/: Artificial Intelligence Applications Institute, 1998, p. 3.

12. Pritchard, J., *The Chaos Cookbook,* 2nd ed., Oxford: Butterworth-Heinemann, 1996.

13. Capra, F., *The Web of Life: A New Scientific Understanding of Living Systems,* New York: Doubleday, 1996.

14. Senge, P. M., *The Fifth Discipline: The Art and Practice of the Learning Organization,* New York: Doubleday Currency, 1990, pp. 14, 68.

15. Waldrop, M. M., *Complexity: The Emerging Science at the Edge of Order and Chaos,* New York: Simon & Schuster, 1992, p. 11.

16. Holland, J. H., *Hidden Order: How Adaptation Builds Complexity,* New York: Addison-Wesley, 1995, pp. 15, 25.

Chapter 6

Extended Applications

INTRODUCTION

While chaos theory and nonlinear dynamical systems theories have had their birth and exposition in physics, chemistry, meteorology, and biology, applications and proofs of these theories have now expanded into many other disciplines.

Kellert [1] advises caution as a guide in taking chaos theory and its ramifications too far outside of a narrow range of physical and biological sciences:

> The central insight of chaos theory—that systems governed by mathematically simple equations can exhibit elaborately complex, indeed unpredictable, behavior—is rightly seen as new and important. But sometimes there may be a temptation for researchers to hype their results, to make chaos theory sound too interesting, as if it will revolutionize our thinking not just about the physical world but about art and economics and religion as well."

His caution, however, is balanced by Murray Gell-Mann's [2] enthusiasm:

> . . . my aim in this volume is to set forth my views on an emerging synthesis at the cutting edge of inquiry into the character of the world around us—the study of the simple and the complex. That study has started to bring together in a new way material from a great number of different fields in the physical, biological, and behavioral sciences and even in the arts and humanities. It carries with it a point of view that facilitates the making of connections, sometimes between facts or ideas that seem at first glance very remote from each other.

It is possible to find a number of writers who have addressed this 20th century view of chaos as it may apply in other fields. Margaret Wheatley examined the potential influence of this new science in the fields of management and leadership [3]. Nowak and Sigmund have explored the influence of chaos theory on cooperation in biological societies [4]. W. Brian Arthur views the impact of non-linear thinking on economics [5]. Scott Barton explores applications of chaos theory in psychology, ranging from neuroscience to clinical psychology [6]. In literature, Thomas Jackson Rice applies chaos theory to an understanding of James Joyce's novel *Ulysses* [7]. T. R. Young [8] viewed social dynamics through the lens of chaos theory. Vivian Sobchack explored the relationship between chaos theory and post-modern artistic traits, and has noted the influence of computer technology on the study and findings of chaos [9]. Finally, as an example of the widespread speculation on the impact of chaos theory, David Freedman questions the practice of management in light of the new science [10]. These works serve to illustrate the growing library of material that documents investigations into chaos theory as it applies outside of the physical sciences. The scope of the investigation now covers almost every discipline.

Of the various places where these theories have been applied, several have direct interest for a study of learning processes in organizations. Psychology, for example, has adopted some of the experimental approaches suggested by nonlinear dynamical systems, and some studies have identified technical chaos in operation in human cognition and behavior. Studies of social systems have begun to make use of chaos and nonlinear dynamical systems theories in understanding the behavior patterns exhibited within social systems. It is useful to understand how such systems are being examined, the tools that are being applied in such examination, the findings from experiments and studies, and the applications of those findings in the systems themselves. In brief, a review of the learning activities in these disciplines, as they have discovered and explored chaos and nonlinear dynamical systems theories, will provide an example for the later consideration of learning processes and support activities.

SOCIAL SCIENCES

Those who study human interaction have noted the potential for the use of NDS in their work, and have begun to apply ideas from chaos theory as they view human social systems. In a number of ways, links are being made between the way humans act in social groups, and the behavior of nonlinear dynamical systems.

A major topic of discussion across many disciplines in the latter part of the twentieth century has been the increased connectivity among countries and their industries and other organizations across national boundaries. Along with this "globalization" has come the recognition of issues associated with cultural norms, as people begin to interact with people from different cultural traditions. Fons Trompenaars [11] notes the impact, in business organizations, of this new reality:

> . . . the matrix organization is a very clever reconciliation of the need to be organised by discipline and function and the need to respond to projects, products-under-development and customer specifications. But while this solves American, British, Dutch and Scandinavian dilemmas, it directly threatens and contradicts the family model . . . so that some Italian, Spanish, French and Asian companies will have to devise a different solution.

Mary O'Hara-Devereaux and Robert Johansen [12] made similar observations, as they commented:

> In the patchwork webs of diversity and workforce fragmentation that characterize global businesses—each a virtual atlas of languages, cultures, histories, work styles, traditions, and employment relationships—how do workers identify with one another? For that matter, how do they identify with the employer in a manner that builds loyalty and maintains trust? Clearly there is

an urgent need for proven strategies for developing commitment and shared vision in dispersed, fragmented, and diverse teams and organizations, as well as maintaining coherence and continuity in networked and virtual spaces and relationships.

The growth of global organizations, including nonprofits such as the Boy Scouts, the Red Cross, and the YMCA, has provided ample opportunity to explore the various ways in which organizations have had to adapt, within themselves, to existence across global cultural differences. Because any organization that is assembled to do work or provide special services is an overlay onto the social cultures already in place, such adaptation is a necessity. The local or national social culture provides the strongest attractive force, while outside cultural or behavioral differences must associate themselves with that attractor.

What is now occurring, however, transcends that traditional assumption that national cultures will continue to provide the social basis around which all else will track. Instead, there is a growing awareness of tradeoffs among cultures and behavioral norms. Cultural diversity has, in some instances, made such inroads into nationally-focused cultures that there is a transference of norms from one culture to another, thereby "globalizing" what once might have been considered a nuclear cultural organization. The socialization that is now possible around the globe, makes it increasingly difficult to maintain a culture based solely on local habits and preferences. The world, as it becomes smaller through transportation and telecommunications, also begins to merge cultures. As this happens, strong cultural norms, particular to regions, will come closer, into a co-evolutionary relationship. Isolated cultural norms will become increasingly rare.

If we take the view that we are now at some kind of "point of no return" regarding our cultural milieu, then what we should expect to see is that social systems are nonlinear dynamical systems on the edge of, or in, technically chaotic activity. What we may be participating in is the formation of a global cultural system, and the formation of any system is susceptible to chaos. It is, in fact, from chaotic activity that new forms emerge. The emergence of such new global systems is to be expected, given our new understanding of the potential for volatility and nonlinearity in dynamical systems such as social systems. We are changing our worldview from one that emphasized stability and insularity to one that accepts a wider and more loosely constructed assembly of alliances.

The view has shifted, from local to global perspective and from a Newtonian concentration on regularity and predictability to a quantum view of openness and potential. When we view events from this system perspective, they are no longer isolated, and no longer can we assume them to have local consequences. If there is a single systems lesson coming from the events in world history since the beginning, it is that a single event may have profound effect across vast geographies and social systems. Over time, these events with such ability to affect the system have been relatively large ones. They have been defined at high political levels or at high levels in religious systems.

The difference today is that the ability to impact events in the world has come down the hierarchical scale. As global systems have opened, they have attempted to follow a path toward democratization, increasing the degrees of freedom within which the system can operate. The result has been that it is no longer just Caesar who has a shot at changing the world; it is the anonymous Jane Ito, with a computer and modem in her home. The new proximity of people, created through television, radio, transportation and telecommunications, has increased the awareness of all parties, regardless of geophysical or geopolitical persuasion, that the rest of the world is right next door. Sub-systems for creating a global civilization are growing increasingly sophisticated and accessible. Camels are no longer the only way to get silk from Beijing to Milan.

Along with this emerging global awareness and civilization comes instability. At the same time that we might want "sustainable"—and presumably somewhat stable—characteristics in the social system, the reality is that there is a persistent chaotic nature in these systems. As Prigogine and Stengers [13] noted, ". . . the ideas of instability, of fluctuation—diffuse into the social sciences. We know now that societies are immensely complex systems involving a potentially enormous number of bifurcations exemplified by the variety of cultures that have evolved in the relatively short span of human history. We know that such systems are highly sensitive to fluctuations." What these authors observe is that it is often the actions of individuals that influence the fluctuation and provide the sensitivity. That is, it is not large political, religious or other social institutions that carry the day in affecting the directions, bifurcations, and changes that are evident in social history and activity. It is the individual. There is as much threat as optimism in the volatile nature of social systems.

What is evident is the underlying insecurity that we all feel with the notion that there is less stability available to us in our social systems as time goes on. We become increasingly vulnerable to shifts in tracking around a strange attractor, and less able to view ourselves as part of a stable society with a strong point attractor or a limit cycle to depend on. We do not yet know how to co-evolve on this scale. Lack of this new capability has led to much of the anxiety, as global commerce and global culture move at different paces across the fitness landscape. It has been easy enough, for instance, to ship goods from Singapore to San Francisco. The question that has come to bear is the impact of this capability on the cultural norms in Singapore or in the U.S. Of further interest is the impact on shared cultural norms between the two countries. The potential for conflict of interest between any two national economies is heightened on a global fitness landscape. The potential for misunderstandings is raised, as global economies replace single-country economies. Regardless of the countries involved, an open and unstable landscape—a potentially chaotic system—poses new challenges in the merger of economic and cultural interests.

Aside from viewing the social systems as outside of our influence, and affected by forces beyond our control, forces which act on the system but which are undefined, there is another view which reinforces the idea that the system changes because of the individual influences working within it. Castells [14] reflects on the history of social development as it aligned, in the early history of humanity, with natural cycles. Survival in the agrarian age was dependent on adhering to those cycles, and working in harmony with them. However, "in the developed world, the industrial revolution, the constitution of medical science, the triumph of Reason, and the affirmation of social rights has altered this pattern in the last two centuries, prolonging life, overcoming illness, regulating births, alleviating death, calling into question the biological determination of roles in society, and constructing the life-cycle around social categories, among which education, working time, career patterns, and the right to retirement became paramount." The concept of the clockwork universe is here mitigated by a revised view of the importance of humanity and its inventions on the path of the social system. The sense of order that was reflected in manners, style, the arts and government has been lost, to be replaced by a sense of openness. There is a new willingness to accommodate a wider variety of social behaviors, with what were once social and ethical "norms" in question. Merchandising slogans, which are closely tied to social behavior, reflect this form of open rebellion against the formalism of the past. Many advocate looseness, casual and spontaneous behavior and breaking of rules. These slogans, whether they lead social thinking, or follow social thinking, are ubiquitous reflections of a rejection of the orderly and stately ways of the past. Instability is celebrated, not criticized, and what was once socially unacceptable behavior is now brought into the system as a natural part of it. *Whatever.*

There is evidence that this activity in society reflects its autocatalytic, or self-sustaining, characteristic, a characteristic it shares with other complex adaptive systems [15]. Social organizations coevolve within their environments, exchanging ideas, concepts, products and services with those environments, and by so doing, they are directly involved in the evolution of that environment. There is no magic boundary that separates the actions of an organization from its deeper ecological connections with its environment. In this sense, the social organization is a complex adaptive system.

The phenomenon of urban growth patterns is one that has attracted the attention of researchers who study the chaotic behavior of societies. In many cities, urban growth has become a serious threat to the quality of life in the area. The growth pattern, which begins in the inner city, begins to expand outward, as internal city traffic becomes crowded, apartments and living space becomes crowded and expensive, and as noise, light, and other pollution begins to generate a situation of decay. Land prices begin to rise to a point where only commercial development is viable.

At some point, because there are still economic attractors that bring people and organizations to the area, the development moves outside of the core city area, and creates a "doughnut" of activity around, but separate from, the city's center. This activity may, as in Atlanta, grow around a bypass highway, such as I-285, which encircles Atlanta. That highway has become, over many years, an attractor itself, with businesses developing along its right-of-way. Residential areas, in turn, developed further out from the ring highway, extending into what were once agricultural areas. In one county that makes up the greater Atlanta area, Fulton County, its northern suburban population increased from 76,678 in 1980 to 180,361 in 1997, with a projection that it will reach 221,710 by the year 2002 [16]. Reports from other "doughnut" counties provide similar growth data. In a 1998 report [17], the

U.S. Census Bureau produced a report that indicated the ten top suburban counties in rate of growth from 1996 to 1997. In Douglas County, Colorado, the increase was 12.9%, the highest of any of the counties. While this is a one-year growth statistic, the population increase in that county since 1990 has risen 109%.

When these developments of suburban and even rural areas occur around a central core city, the growth activity begins to look like dynamic system behavior. In fact, when studied in that light, certain urban growth rates were found to behave as complex nonlinear systems. This is not a new pattern of expansion, since it has been going on in one way or another since cities themselves came to exist as concentrators for services and goods and socialization. There is a new realization, however, that, just as globalization is affecting micro as well as macroeconomics, cities and urban growth impact other things. Shifts in population among cities, for example, can be viewed as the result of dynamical system behavior, as the populations of cities track around a strange attractor [18]. The expansion of cities has also been linked to nonlinear behavior, which derives from the variables that describe a city. If the city is located in a geographical area, for instance, which does not support growth, then the city dynamics will be less aggressive than one which has surrounding areas available for economic development.

Another variable has to do with the extent to which the city tries to sustain its vitality from internal development and redevelopment, and the extent to which it opens itself to external influences. The difference between an open city, with complex relationships with other cities and with the surrounding agricultural interests, and a closed city, which depends more on its inner relationships and commerce, can influence the extent to which nonlinear dynamics will be exhibited. Researchers have developed "a butterfly catastrophe model for urban development. The three attractor states were the simple agrarian community, the presence of an open city, and the morphegenesis of a closed city. The four control parameters would therefore be the work-reward efficiency of agriculture, the work-reward efficiency of urbanization (gradient transformations), a bias factor represented by the relative strengths of the urban or agricultural sectors, and the transportation costs to other cities" [18, p. 275]. This study took as its model the approach used by Edward Lorenz in modeling weather patterns around a strange attractor. The results were similar, showing wide swings in the tracks of the variables around a highly open set of attractive forces.

Other research into urban change and dynamics has produced similar findings that indicate that societal change may be understood as a technically chaotic system. One theory, that of punctuated equilibrium, suggests that there is a strong dialectic between society's desire to change and its desire to remain stable. This dialectic generates a dynamic tension, which may act as an attractive force, with actual change in the society's infrastructure tracking around this dialectic. This would, of course, constitute only one of the variables that would describe the system dynamics. Associated with this idea of punctuated equilibrium, is the idea that the periods of creation and innovation were accompanied by strong emphasis on learning and education in the society and culture. One interpretation of the more stable periods that follow these creative bursts is that they offer the society and its economy an opportunity to assimilate the innovations [18].

Education and learning in the society, then, act to influence the behavior of the system as it moves from stable to increased sensitivity, and as bifurcations in the system occur with the introduction of innovations. Learning, however, may not have short-term benefits if the resulting innovation is large in scale. Short-term benefits appear to derive from small, incremental innovations and changes, and not from big ideas. The economic realization of innovation is important if the society is to make use of the change and adapt to it. This fact argues for immediacy of deployment and not strategic deployment of creative changes. Yet, if the changes are large scale, immediacy of deployment becomes problematic because of systemic disruption and resource availability.

This reality may dampen the fires of the innovative learning engine, if the innovators realize that economic rules will dictate the size of acceptable changes. From the viewpoint of nonlinear dynamical systems, if learning and accompanying changes are dampened in the social system, then there will be a tendency for the system to follow a point or periodic attractor. Yet, as evidence from social history suggests, Period 2 complex change may not be enough to maintain the vitality of a system over the long term. Technical chaos, Period 3, may be necessary in order to maintain and surpass the place of the system in the fitness landscape, and such chaos is linked, in this research, with the presence of learning and therefore behavioral change and innovation in the system.

In an ironic twist, the very openness that can sustain a learning environment in a society can also act to restrict the educative process. Research in the area of educational leadership has illuminated the impact of an open society on childhood education activity. Donsky [19] describes a real-life scenario to illustrate this impact:

> The two children were always so tired in class. Their teacher knew something was wrong, but it took her awhile to find out what: The two siblings— one in the second grade, the other in third—were taking turns staying up caring for their mother's new baby while she worked nights.

In the form of open society currently accepted in western cultures, the fact that there is no parent at home in the late afternoons or evenings comes as no surprise, regardless of the economic position of the family. That single parents undertake to raise a family is equally of no surprise. That parents work hours which do not coincide with the presence of children in the home is also a given. So the situation as Donsky has pictured it is not unusual, nor is it confined to a particular economic group or geographical area. What is of interest to a discussion of nonlinear dynamical systems is the impact of this change in societal habits on the education process of these children. Donsky quotes Claire Smrekar, an education expert and professor at Vanderbilt University, whose research includes the interactions between social environments and educational environments. Smrekar observes, of this particular incident, "It's a story no one wants to talk about because the problems are so deep and so difficult to solve. Teachers are talking about the pressure not only to be the teacher but also the nurse, psychologist, social worker, minister and miracle worker, and all that without any additional support, time or resources to accomplish these tasks" [19].

This situation suggests the intricate connection between these two subsystems in the larger social system, that of education and home life. This deep ecology is one that has a complex web of relationships in the dynamic functioning of the systems. The school system and home system are merging into a larger worldview that is interconnected in ways that it has not been before. Traditional views of home life and economic structures are giving way to more open experimental approaches with how homes are organized, how families are organized, and how families exist economically. In turn, the dynamics of home and family lifestyle changes are placing pressure on the related subsystems in the web. The educational system will undergo changes in this overall complex adaptive system in order to accommodate the demands of the home system, and as a result the entire fitness landscape of society will be altered. These are profound, deep changes in the ecology of the overall system, and, as noted earlier, will not take effect quickly. Smrekar's comments, therefore, unfold for us a transformational situation in which the educational system is at or approaching technical chaos. The steady state has given way to alternative considerations and roles and responsibilities in the school system, the resources are not in place to meet these new demands brought about by changes in social lifestyle, and without major innovation the system will become chaotic. That is, it will become sensitively dependent on initial conditions, and will energize its dynamics around a strange attractor rather than around a predictable point or cyclical attractor. The entire system, in essence, will develop complexities that it does not now possess, by allowing more play in the variables that define its purpose, mission, roles, and processes.

The situation just described is evidence that interactions among subsystems in the larger social system are inevitable, complex, and may advance on the fitness landscape through nonlinear reactions to changes in variables. What is also suggested in Donsky's description of the situation is the role played by cooperative efforts in a social setting. As the interrelationships between home life and school life become more complex, group behavior in the web of relationships becomes a vital variable that can influence the dynamical behavior of the system— in other words, how the web is established so that it aggregates family as well as school members in the modeling activities which will lead to revised processes is of concern.

Researchers have tested dynamic processes in group behavior based on game playing. Data was initially collected using qualitative methods, yielding a record of the conversations within the group as they played the game. The conversations were then divided into segments for analysis. Strings were analyzed according to their function in relation to the game, or in relation to group behavior. Some comments, for example, were used to advance the social relationships among group members, rather than as instructions or process comments related to the game itself.

As the purposes of the various conversational segments were analyzed, researchers discovered patterns in occurrence which were not random, and which exceeded probabilities for consistency among the segments. In other words, there appeared to be regularity where regularity might not be anticipated. There was no deliberate attempt, during the game, to structure comments on the part of the players. Yet, what surfaced from a careful review of the comments was a pattern of order [20].

The research briefly summarized here has two layers of significance in relation to social systems. First, in the educational situation described above, there is the likelihood that increased interactions and discussions involving the interested parties—children, parents, teachers, and school system administrators—would lead to apparent randomness in the discussions. The research now underway in the study of nonlinear dynamical systems in society, such as the study described above, offer some hope that deeper understanding of these complex discussions and negotiations is available.

Second, the emphasis in the research methodology itself was on the combination of qualitative with quantitative study methods, using nonlinear approaches to data analysis, and using calculations such as the Lyapunov exponent, specifically developed as a tool to study nonlinear dynamical systems. Such research efforts suggest the approaches that we will need to adopt in order to understand the complex dynamic systems within which we live, work, and learn. Much of the understanding will depend on our ability to understand how systems work, how they can be measured, and how variables can be correlated into behavioral maps. A clear understanding of chaotic system behavior will provide us with the setting for understanding how learning operates in such chaotic systems. The methodology and approaches that we use, however, will change, as we search for clues to the consistency underlying apparently unrelated or random activity in our organizations.

PSYCHOLOGY

There is a fine line, of course, between a consideration of chaotic behavior in society and a consideration of technical chaos in psychology. Psychologists are addressing many aspects of their work from the background of chaos and nonlinear dynamical systems theory. What they find as they view individuals and groups is pertinent to the learning that occurs in organizational systems that include humans.

One of the key points of focus in chaos theory, the wholeness of systems and the need for holistic systems thinking, has been of interest from the perspective of clinical psychology. DeBerry [21] notes, for example, that "despite the enormous philosophical and scientific implications of quantum mechanics, very little of it has found its way into psychology. Psychology still remains a science steeped in the classical Cartesian dualism and Newtonian mechanics of the nineteenth century." In response, he develops a concept of "quantum psychology," which, in part, is intended to get beyond the clockwork approach to psychology. He describes it as "a psychology of consciousness and, as such, is reflective of the entire process of being." The concept of wholeness in quantum psychology takes the study of psychological phenomena out of the narrow realm of human consciousness or unconsciousness, and recognizes the influence of the external environment in society. The idea of wholeness, however, introduces a new concept of complexity that goes beyond Cartesian cause and effect. The potentiality that exists in a complex adaptive system for nonlinear influences on human behavior, make it less simple to draw behavioral conclusions from a finite set of data surrounding individual or group behavior. It is not enough, in other words, to assume direct linkages between stimulus and response. Complexity enters along with the many ways in which people interact with the other objects, people, and environment around them. A psychology founded on the constant potential for change and volatility is different from one founded on a proposal of basic stability. So, given high potential for variability in human and other systems, it is difficult to see, in many instances, direct links between cause and effect in behavior studies.

Moreover, a concept of psychological wholeness incorporates both good and bad, order and disorder, and accepts them as parts that belong, rather than as abnormal highs or lows in systemic activity. That is, "bad" or negative behavior is, from a systems viewpoint, just as acceptable and expected as "good" or positive behavior. We control behavior, and try to channel it to socially acceptable norms, but we also allow ourselves and others to indulge occasionally in a binge of bad behavior that defies those norms. Wieland-Burston [22] cites the story of the Hos, a tribe in northeast India. In their yearly celebration of the harvest, they make an offering to ward off chaos in the coming year; they then chase off a figure dressed to represent a chaos demon; and finally they, as a tribe, carry out chaotic activities, acting out, in real life, the urge toward disorder and dissonance. This is carried to a level of drunkenness and sexual orgy that lasts for the remainder of the celebration. The day following the celebration, life returns to "normal" and everything that happened during the celebration is set aside in favor of an ordered and controlled social existence. The Hos do not view chaos as a bad thing, but simply another part of the completeness of their psychology.

This psychological concern for the inclusion of classical chaos into a life concept is also evident when the subject is an individual and not a group. A number of psychological studies have explored the fantasy worlds that individuals can create for themselves. In such worlds, whether opened through reading, dreaming, or attending plays, we can suspend disbelief and imagine a different kind of life. We reconcile the two worlds—imaginary and real—and use both to construct ourselves. Where there are extreme differences, and opposites, between real and imaginary worlds, we have within us a chaotic and volatile system, which may tend to be unstable [22].

We need to construct an approach to and understanding of chaos that combines both classical and technical perspectives as we consider the role of chaotic behavior at individual level. The intent is not to study the human system—whether tribal or personal—as a technically chaotic nonlinear dynamical system. Instead, the intent is to begin to recognize the aspects of chaotic behavior that can be observed. These aspects, defined and delineated as aberrations from the norm, may or may not constitute technical chaos. However, the information gleaned from a consideration of classically chaotic situations can begin to form the basis for development of a model of how chaos works in tribal groups or in individual lives. From that understanding, both variables and change parameters of the system can be understood, with the intent of applying that knowledge in studies which may locate evidence of technical chaos occurring in the system. Therefore, both forms, classical and technical, can work together as a part of the research tools needed in order to transfer chaos theory into practical tools for the study of individual, group, and organizational behavior. The wholeness theme is thus recursive.

This concept of wholeness is also expressed in psychological literature in terms of the "ecology of the self." DeBerry explains that this form of ecological view concerns "the kaleidoscopic and incredibly complex series of interpersonal and intrapersonal variables that influence and, in essence, determine our identity and development" [21]. Goerner [23] also understands the shift in psychological viewpoint from "a controlled machine vision of the world to an evolving ecological vision of the world." She expands on this view as she notes that the response to increased pressure in a system is coevolution. That is, as a system, human or otherwise, undergoes a buildup in pressure and internal control mechanisms fail, the result is some form of release, which, in essence, is an acknowledgement of the external environment. An ecological view incorporates the interflow, or exchange from one system to another. This personal ecology is important as individuals maintain their own sense of place in what appears to be an unstable environment. It becomes more important as individuals try to integrate with other ecologies on a larger scope and scale. The principle of freedom that operates at the macro level in organizations and societies in order to fuel their dynamism stems from the sense of freedom and independence which is within each person and agent. Larger chaotic organizational systems, in other words, rely on combinations, webs, and inter-relationships of individual agents. The extent to which these agents are chaotic is the extent to which their organizations can take advantage of chaos.

An ecology of the self demands integration of variables, and that leads to an understanding of human dynamics as a part of a whole ecological system, and not as an artificial overlay onto the environment. In order for the whole system to be a system, each part in the system must contribute in some way to the fulfillment of the intent of the whole system. To superimpose human direction and decisions that do not fit into the overall consistency of the system is to establish humans as non-players. If humans existed outside of the whole system ecology, they would be able to bulldoze acres of land, pour asphalt and concrete over it, and drop effluvia and chemicals into streams with no impact on the overall system. In fact, the system would ignore such activities, and the system of the natural world would go on without an impact. That human interventions do make a difference in natural systems is demonstration that the ecology is a whole one, from trees to air to stream to human individual to human organization. It is the ecology of the self that allows and enables the internal person to adapt and accept a role in the larger processes at work in the system. This is a way to understand psychological integration.

Complexity of human behavior is an area that has prompted studies that begin to make use of chaos theory. Torre [24] provides a view of problem solving, incorporating the perspective of chaos. As he describes the way we often approach problems, "many of us are often unable to distinguish among the various elements of a problem situation. Our thinking often lacks clarity and we tend to act in a confused, aimless manner." Torre builds a connection between chaos theory and his construct of a "triadic theory of mental functioning," which incorporates a combination of cognitive processing, affective influences, and pragmatic processes. He believes that the actual operation of these three domains in the act of problem solving incorporates nonlinear dynamical processes, and, in particular, use of fractal structuring of information and thought patterns. As he notes, "researchers in this area posit that chaos not only serves as a useful framework for viewing the brain, but that chaos is perhaps the best model for comprehending the brain's functioning" [24].

In seeking solutions for problems, then, the brain may be using problem data as a general attractor, around which is marshaled the information and feelings and pragmatic constructs that provide, in combination, a solution to the problem. Any internal tensions or stresses that are created in maintaining the nonlinear process toward the solution are channeled back into the process to stimulate mental functioning. If the stress caused by the nonlinearity is enough, additional perspectives may be generated for the mind to work on in developing a solution. If there is too much stress, the mind may literally shut the problem-solving process down. This may, in fact, be a function of Period 3 behavior, or technically chaotic behavior, which is evidence that the strange attractor is at work to maintain its attractive force over the process. To go further in the problem, at this point, would evidently lead to randomness that would be non-productive to the problem solver.

Throughout the process, Torre believes, the subprocesses of teaching and learning are in play within the triad, as independent and perhaps apparently irrelevant facts and constructs are dredged up and put in place as the path toward the solution emerges. The fractal nature of the process can be postulated in thinking and problem solving "because the structured irregularity of their processes and interactions exhibit statistically self-similar structure on all scales" [24].

Fractals have been employed as a way of understanding the ways in which humans think and behave. The bases for believing that fractal mathematics may have some association with human behavior and psychology is firm. Humans, after all, are a part of nature, and much of nature is now interpreted as fractal, recursive structures. A fractal builds up into a complex structure, from a relatively easy-to-understand basic formula, the results of which act as the basis for the next iteration of the calculation of the formula. A structure, then, as it appears after 5,000 iterations of the formula bears dimensional resemblance to the structure at the first iteration.

Marks-Tarlow [25] notes the self-similarity that is apparent in people and relates this to fractal organization in our psyche. This consistency may offer some insight into the behavior of people. For instance, aggression, as a character trait, will manifest itself in a number of ways in the human dynamics as the aggressive person interacts with others in meetings, works with individuals in dyads, or works alone, with materials or ideas. Regardless of the environmental circumstances, the aggressive trait will recur, and this self-similarity is a characteristic of a fractal structure.

The implications in organizational behavior are obvious. If we can define the self-similarity of a "performance dimension," "capability," or "competency," and establish the basis for its recurrence through the recursive process in human behavior, we could understand how a given competency such as "team development" might manifest itself. Further, we might be able to gain additional insight into how competencies interact with each other in a behavioral system at individual, subgroup or full organizational level. If the basic fractal geometry and self-similarity characteristic of any of the performance dimensions were known, this knowledge might influence the ways in which learning is developed and supported in a particular behavioral system.

A second characteristic of fractal geometry that has been suggested as a characteristic demonstrated in human behavior is that of "ordered unpredictability." Again, where natural systems show sensitive dependence on initial conditions, human behavioral systems also display this ability to allow small variants to generate major changes. If we understand the overall patterns of behavior in people, through a deeper understanding of the ways in which performance dimensions work, then what we also need are the variables which can take a person's behavior out of what we consider a "norm" for them. The existence of ordered unpredictability, in terms of fractal behavior, means that the equation by which a behavior may increment is dependent upon the initial variable input [25]. That is, because the changes iterate based on a given equation and on changes in calculations based on prior calculations, the operation of the behavioral system is dependent on each successive calculation. The self-similarity exists, then, regardless of scale, and this demonstrates fractality—the same features are evident at macro views of the system as at micro views. The key is the extent to which the iterative process goes on with consistency over time and a number of iterations.

What we know about human behavior, however, suggests that while there may be some consistency in the underlying behavioral patterns and performance dimensions, people also vary noticeably from those patterns. Yet, the sometimes-unpredictable changes we observe in people will still generally lie within the bounds of their behavioral system. A greater understanding of how that behavioral system comes together, and how variables affect it, will yield a better understanding of the nonlinear aspects of behavior.

The complexity of human behavior exists not because people behave in classical chaotic systems. Rather, the complexity enters as people exist in technically chaotic systems. The probing that is now a part of psychology has to do with how we can understand the basic systemic nature of human behavior. Just as medical doctors know that treating a symptom does not treat the disease, psychologists understand that changing behavior is not the same as changing behavioral patterns. It is the pattern of intrapersonal characteristics, the web of behaviors, that offers the challenge to understanding. This web acts as the descriptor for the behavior of the underlying strange attractor around which our behavior tracks in the human dynamical system. No two tracks follow exactly the same path. Individual psychological history does not repeat itself, and like other chaotic systems, the human psyche is sensitive to small changes—sometimes unnoticed changes—in the variables that govern its path. In most instances these changes do not result in true random behavior. An individual is, for the most part, consistent with the strange attractor that is defined by his or her characteristics. There are instances where the human behavioral system changes in ways which do not fit our concept of "normal" behavior, but these changes, too, are part of the whole system dynamics.

As Goerner [23] observes, nonlinear behavior in complex human systems may lead to coherent behavior or it may lead to divergent behavior. Yet this wide range of potentiality in such systems is natural, holistic and desirable. To understand human behavior, it is clear that we must go beyond the attempt to simplify behavior into cause and effect. There is not necessarily a single point in the system processes that can account for "abnormal" or undesirable behavior. Abnormal behavior may not be abnormal at all, if we understood the true chaotic nature of the system. In any event, changes in the system which do not conform with what others may think the system should be doing are rarely to be traced to a single cause. Life just isn't that easy to understand.

The evidence for technical chaos in social behavior is strong. The experiments to demonstrate the presence have so far been few and relatively narrow in scope. Yet, the opportunities to explore this potential are tantalizing. That exploration work, as it continues, will succeed as it clarifies behavior in individual and social systems. This clarification will take the form of a restatement of these systems according to their chaotic dimensions and characteristics. What we need to understand more clearly, is how to study such systems both qualitatively and quantitatively, to develop the variables and how they operate. It is less an interest in the observable outcomes of system behavior that we need than a grasp of the strange attractor that underlies the system and its observable performance.

Such clarification will yield much that will contribute to our understanding of learning. The more we know about the characteristics of social systems and individual behaviors, the more depth we can obtain in a study of learning in chaotic systems. Social and individual behaviors clearly demonstrate technical chaos. The role of learning in generating, sustaining, or controlling such chaos is not so clear. Learning, in fact, may be one of the chief parameters that governs a chaotic system, as we know it is in a complex adaptive system. Unless we know, in some level of detail, how learning operates in such a system, we will not understand the value of learning in chaos. If we do not understand the operation of learning, we will not be able to support learning in such systems, nor will we be able to use learning effectively to nudge a system into the chaotic realm for its own benefit. An educational system, for example, which maintains its position on the edge of chaos, may be expending significant energies to hold itself poised at a conservative distance from the brink. The realignment of the system—such as that described above—might be restrained, as roles of agents in the system are maintained in traditional boundaries through traditional organizational political efforts.

With a more certain grasp of system manipulation, we might be able to release the system energies and allow it to reinvent itself with some fervor and speed. Donsky's description of the educational situation, for example, suggests that the dynamics are there to encourage systemic change. What holds us at the brink, however, in this and other such systems, is our fear of the unknown. What will happen if we take our hands off of the switch? Will the system, like a train, run mindlessly down the track? Will it come to a screeching halt? Or will it assert its own chaotic learning and control mechanisms and rebuild itself in a new image?

My belief is that the latter possibility holds more potential for systemic change efforts than the other options. Dynamic systems—social or individual—are unlikely to plow mindlessly and destructively down a blind track. They are not likely to come to a halt. One way or another, a system that is nudged *intelligently* into chaos will prosper, as its energies are renewed through redefinition. Chaotic organizational systems, and the way learning happens in them, are closely tied to behavior in chaotic social systems and to the function of chaos in individuals. Our increasing ability to recognize technical chaos and to describe its patterns leads us closer to a merger between classical and technical chaos. This, in turn, gives us a more complete understanding of how chaos might operate in organizational systems that combine human, machine, and network characteristics and capabilities in unstable flux.

REFERENCES

1. Kellert, S. H., *In the Wake of Chaos, Science and Its Conceptual Foundations,* D. L. Hull (Ed.), Chicago: The University of Chicago Press, 1993, pp. ix, 5, 10, 12, 13, 35.
2. Gell-Mann, M., *The Quark and the Jaguar,* New York: W. H. Freeman and Company, 1994, pp. ix, 17, 19, 143.
3. Wheatley, M. J., *Leadership and the New Science,* San Francisco: Berrett-Koehler Publishers, Inc., 1992.
4. Nowak, M. and K. Sigmund, "Chaos and the evolution of cooperation," *Proceedings of the National Academy of Science, U.S.A.,* Vol. 90, June, 1993 pp. 5091–5094.
5. Arthur, W. B., "Pandora's marketplace," *New Scientist Supplement,* No. Feb. 6, 1993, pp. 6–8.
6. Barton, S., "Chaos, Self-Organization, and Psychology," *American Psychologist,* Vol. 49, January, 1994, pp. 5–14.
7. Rice, T. J., "Ulysses, Chaos, and Complexity," *James Joyce Quarterly,* Vol. 31, Winter, 1994, pp. 41–54.
8. Young, T. R., "Chaos and Social Change: Metaphysics of the Postmodern," *The Social Sciences Journal,* Vol. 28, No. 3, 1991, pp. 289–305.
9. Sobchack, V., "A Theory of Everything: Meditations on Total Chaos," *Artforum,* Vol. 29, October, 1990, pp. 148–155.
10. Freedman, D. H., "Is Management Still a Science?" *Harvard Business Review,* Vol. 70, No. 6, 1992, pp. 26–38.
11. Trompenaars, F., *Riding the Waves of Culture,* London: Nicholas Brealey, 1993, p. 166.
12. O'Hara-Devereaux, M., & Robert Johansen, *GlobalWork.* The Jossey-Bass Management Series, San Francisco: Jossey-Bass, 1994, p. 27.
13. Prigogine, I. and I. Stengers, *Order Out of Chaos,* London: Collins, 1985, pp. xxvi. 312.
14. Castells, M. *The Rise of the Network Society.* The Information Age: Economy, Society and Culture. Vol. I, Malden, MA: Blackwell, 1996, p. 445.
15. Kauffman, S., *At Home in the Universe: The Search for Laws of Self-organization and Complexity,* Oxford: Oxford University Press, 1995, pp. 49, 274, 275.
16. Crabb, C., "Suburbs cope with traffic, growth boom," *The Atlanta Journal-Constitution,* Atlanta, August 17, 1998, p. E-1.

17. El Nasser, H., "Population moves deeper into suburbs," *USA Today,* Washington, D.C., March 18, 1998, p. 3-A.
18. Guastello, S. J., *Chaos, Catastrophe, and Human Affairs,* Mahwah, N.J.: Lawrence Erlbaum Associates, 1995, p. 311.
19. Donsky, P., "Teaching goes far beyond books." *The Tennessean,* Nashville, July 31, 1998, pp. 1A, 2A.
20. Guastello, S. J., T. Hyde and M. Odak, "Symbolic dynamic patterns of verbal exchange in a creative problem solving group," *Nonlinear Dynamics, Psychology, and Life Sciences,* Vol. 2, No. 1, 1998, pp. 35–59.
21. DeBerry, S. T., *Quantum Psychology: Steps to a Postmodern Ecology of Being,* Westport, Conn.: Praeger, 1993, pp. 1, 7.
22. Wieland-Burston, J., *Chaos and Order in the World of the Psyche,* London: Routledge, 1992.
23. Goerner, S., *Chaos, Evolution, and Deep Ecology, in Chaos Theory in Psychology and the Life Sciences,* R. Robertson and A. Combs, (Eds.) Mahwah, N.J.: Lawrence Erlbaum Associates, 1995, pp. 17–38, p. 17.
24. Torre, C. A., *Chaos, Creativity, and Innovation: Toward a Dynamical Model of Problem Solving, in Chaos Theory in Psychology and the Life Sciences,* R. Robertson and A. Combs, (Eds.) Mahwah, N.J.: Lawrence Erlbaum Associates, 1995, pp. 179–198, pp. 179, 186, 190, 194.
25. Marks-Tarlow, T., *The Fractal Geometry of Human Nature, in Chaos Theory in Psychology and the Life Sciences,* R. Robertson and A. Combs, (Eds.) Mahwah, N.J.: Lawrence Erlbaum, 1995, pp. 275–283, p. 278.

Chapter 7

Nonlinear Dynamical Organizational Systems

INTRODUCTION

In a previous chapter, it became evident from a review of the literature that those who have considered technical chaos have, in many instances, considered its potential existence in and influences upon organizations that include humans. The discussions of the influences of chaos in the fields of psychology and sociology point to a realization that systems involving humans can be technically chaotic. I have also introduced the idea that chaotic behavior can be beneficial, not destructive.

There is a close relationship between technical chaos and organizational systems that needs to be understood in light of the characteristics of chaos and the behavior of systems which are at the edge of chaos or which exhibit full chaotic behavior. If human behavior can be so closely described as technically chaotic, then it follows that organizations that are homocentric will also exhibit these characteristics. Even systems that are less fully integrated with human behavior, but that have been influenced by human thinking and behavior, are subject to technical chaos introduced by human paradigms, biases, and logic.

A number of studies have begun to explore the range of influence of technical chaos within organizations and their sub-systems. The intent of this chapter is to explore some of the key ideas that have been introduced to date, and to consider the significance of those ideas as they may pertain to learning and the support of learning within organizations.

ORGANIZATIONAL CHAOS

The perception that organizations need to understand the nature of nonlinear transactions and change has increased. Larry Greiner [1], for example, notes the existence of both evolutionary and revolutionary growth in organizations. He characterizes evolutionary growth as a period of relatively continuous change over a period—according to his research—which may stretch from four to eight years. During these periods, change is occurring in a controlled way. In contrast, revolutionary growth occurs during periods of high instability. These are times when supervision and leadership practices in an organization are being reengineered, or radically changed.

In these periods of high volatility, many management capabilities fail to deal successfully with change. If organizations cannot change their processes fast enough and radically enough, then the organization is in danger of randomization and failure, or growth rates will be affected. Growth rates, in turn, can affect the capitalization of the organization, since investors and contributors have come to expect that organizational growth will result in increased share price and monetary dividends. In non-profit organizations, increased growth in contributions means increased capability to deliver services, and higher levels or more types of services can be delivered. Increased services lead to increased likelihood of future contributions.

Greiner speculates, as a result of his study of organizational behavior during growth periods, that there are five phases of growth which are shaped by the combined variables of age and size of the organization. As organizations grow in size over time, they experience phases of creativity, direction, delegation (decentralization), coordination, and collaboration. Within each phase, there is a period of revolution. During the creative phase, for example, there is a revolution in leadership, created in part by growth and the changing character and culture in the organization. As markets, products, and services diversify and become more complex, the organization becomes more complex and tries to adapt to its new place on the fitness landscape. As this happens, the management which led the startup of the organization must either undergo radical changes in the way they lead the growth or step aside in favor of leaders who will take the complexity to new levels [2].

This appears to be a leadership solution for complex adaptive systems. The instances of revolution that occur during each phase do not appear to lead into chaotic system behavior. Rather, the intent of this plan is to bring the system back to superficial order, through the implementation of situational leadership or process change. The change creates a spiral through which change builds on change. The organization does not return to its previous state, but is forever altered.

The dependence on a phased approach suggests that, while the intent is to offer a change process that can be adapted to the organization's point in its phase portrait, the change is itself linear and incremental. While each stage may build on its predecessor, and therefore show an iterative and nonlinear capability, the nature of the overall process is evolutionary not revolutionary. It fits the characteristics of a complex adaptive system, but not those of a chaotic system. Emphasis in phased change methods is on controlling and containing systemic nonlinearity, not supporting or encouraging it. Even though there is the acceptance that complex adaptive systems will exist at the edge of chaos and exhibit characteristics such as nonlinearity and modeling, the emphasis in such systems is on change which can be brought about through aggregation of tagged and classified building blocks. It is change which is under control and predictable. It is change that tends to support artificially imposed and articulated order, rather than emergent and potentially messy order. Many of the forms of change advocated in organizations are careful and conservative, and therefore support limit cycles in the dynamical organizational systems, rather than technically chaotic behavior.

The literature that has addressed technical chaos has provided an entry point for consideration of the impact of chaos theory in organizations. Current research suggests a far greater role for chaos in organizations than has thus far been suggested in the organizational literature itself. James Gleick [3], for example, dismisses the cyclical view of organizational and economic behavior as Newtonian, and no longer applicable to organizational modeling. He attributes such cyclical views to the application, consciously or unconsciously, of Newton's Second Law of Thermodynamics to organizational systems. Systems, in this traditional view, are subject to energy loss through entropy, and organizational systems behave the same way, in a Newtonian interpretation.

This idea that energy is absorbed and used up within a system and its environment, and therefore causes any system to recycle and perhaps dissipate, has now been set aside. What chaos theory has introduced is the possibility that a system and its energy levels need not decay. A system that displays technical chaos is not attracted to a single point, like a marble rolling around and down the sides of a bowl. Instead, it displays variety of activity, and is constantly renewed by its association with its strange attractor. The higher degrees of freedom in such a system means that it does not wind down like a clock, but is energized constantly. Chaos is a creative force.

Given this creative force, the ways in which we manage and change organizations is also subject to change [4]. Manufacturing processes are taking advantage of modular assembly to support better integration of processes [5]. Organization development, which has relied on maintenance of control in the past, must now shift its attention to maintenance of energy in autopoetic, chaotic systems. The business of human and organization development alters to meet a new need—the success of chaotic systems depends on an ability to sustain chaos, not subjugate, control, or eliminate it. The OD paradigm of refreezing a system into a controlled, desired pattern is gone [6].

Even an approach that accepts punctuated equilibrium, or evolutionary continuous change punctuated by a few significant revolutionary events, may not be appropriate for chaotic systems. Management, in this approach, would keep changes in line with evolutionary development. This is the traditional, more conservative approach often seen in change management literature. Instead, chaotic organizations change in ways that are not as smooth as would be allowed under a complex adaptive systems model that assumes continuous improvement and continuous change. The changes that affect a chaotic system are more radical, more often, and emerge from a more sensitive set of systemic variables than those ordinarily accepted in organizational life. One of the basic ideas in chaotic organizational systems is that they are unstable, with high degrees of variability in their systems. They do not conform well, therefore, to traditional approaches that advocate incremental change. The full value of the system's energy will not be realized if the system is harnessed in such a way that parameters are over-controlled. Minor adjustments, in an ambitions and energetic system, may result in major, not minor, changes in direction.

The role of OD in this energetic system is to introduce volatile change as an organizational paradigm, with no possibility of returning to a steady point attractor, or even a cyclical or quasi-periodic attractor. The less predictable strange attractor is the basis for behavior. The attractor, and not its superficial expressions, is the locus of stability. The new role of organization development is to help organizations understand the variables which influence their behaviors, and to understand the essential nature of the strange attractor which underlies the turbulence which objectifies the sensitive energy in such a system.

The application of chaos theory to organizational development, however, is not only about embracing change. It is about understanding, in new and specific ways, the dynamics of the system. This new attitude is important to leaders of organizations, because it takes the lessons of openness, empowerment, and measurement of HR functionality to a new dimension. What is implicit when we begin to study the influence of technical chaos in organizations is that we are no longer dealing with a "soft" side of the enterprise. Nonlinear dynamical system approaches to understanding system behavior are holistic and depend upon measurement of specific system parameters. Financial measures are not sufficient, nor are "soft" measures of employee satisfaction sufficient to determine the nature of change in the system. The intent is to construct definitive formulas for the calculation of system dynamics, and to integrate the variables in order to simulate the phase portrait of system behavior.

This goes far beyond OD efforts to date, but offers the potential for OD professionals to pull together the disparate strings of information which they have only been able to guess at until now. Where the OD professional once functioned as a kind of soothsayer to the organizational Caesars, that professional now has a different model for pursuing the understanding of the functionality of systems and their processes. The role of the OD professional in practice is not to enable continuous change and micro-manipulation of isolated variables and systemic elements. Rather, the role now evolves to one expert in ways to move the organization toward its maximum energy levels.

NETWORKS AND CREATIVITY

The metaphor of the neural network is a valuable one for the ways in which systems should operate, and the activity within such networks parallels the activity described in the concept of the virtual organization. Each person is a node, with a reservoir of knowledge and capabilities, and is free to interact with any other node or nodes, as that reservoir of capability can be brought to bear on an issue or project or opportunity. This approach spells the disintegration of highly structured fiefdoms (and managers who boast of "my people") and the dissolution of silos within organizations. This is not a single change project that results in a new structural architecture, owned and controlled by executives and managers using a wall filled with process flow charts. It is the development of an organization with a culture that is volatile, not fixed. The cultural norm is to work within the attraction of a complex and strange organizational attractive force, not to depend on vertical or even horizontal fixed elements.

The construct of the networked organization, with nodes both internal and external to the defined organization, allows the freedom required for growth. Both creativity and self-organization are enhanced features of a chaotic organization. Instead of the initial entrepreneurial creativity, dissipating as the organization moves through time and growth curves in a linear way, the creativity is now an inherent factor in the organization, regardless of its history or stage.

Creativity is a characteristic of organizations that are willing to let go and allow new things to happen. Regardless of how easy this concept looks when one goes through a teambuilding "ropes" course and falls confidently backward into the waiting arms of fellow workers, the concept of creative organizations is not an easy one to install. Unless organizational focus is on the shape and definition of the attractor that holds the dynamics of the organization in some pattern, creativity will not occur in any significant degree. Where the focus is short-term and localized, organizational behavior will remain conservative and will not exceed Period 2 bifurcation. It will be comfortable with cycling and subdivision, but will not venture out toward chaotic behavior. It will tend to conserve energy and resources, not spend them, in the hope that conservation will yield long organizational life.

Alternatively, the chaotic organization will allow creativity to become an active variable in its dynamics, believing that the expense of energy into creative ventures will act synergistically and yield far greater returns and a more diverse existence, thus prolonging organizational life. Such an organization uses the degrees of freedom available to it, rather than constructing limits.

Like the network architecture and the process of self-organization (discussed later in this chapter), creativity will not occur in some established organizational structures without the intervention of organizational development specialists and leaders who know how to exploit the capabilities of nonlinear dynamical systems. There is a major shift in thinking required in order to move from the concept of the pyramid as a metaphor for organizational solidity and architecture, to the concept of a river rapids as the metaphor for the volatile and transitory presence that is a chaotic organizational system. Our focus should shift from external structure to internal energy. This shift also requires a change from a passive adaptive approach to the environment, customers, and marketplace to a more active approach. The dynamics of organizational systems pose a situation that is fast moving and nonlinear. The introduction of products and services, therefore, needs to follow suit. This argues for definitive actions within the system, which will increase the rate of change, not diminish it [7].

In part, this calls for creation of new products and services before customers ask for them or know they will want them. That is, the creation of the product or service makes a radical and sweeping change to the fitness landscape and redefines the initial conditions of the systems path.

This approach to organizational behavior is consistent with the idea that organizations should be proactive, not reactive, on their fitness landscapes. They are not alone, and co-evolution requires competition as well as cooperation. An organization that generates new products or services will change the fitness landscape in favor of the organization.

On a recent evening, I received a telephone call at about dinnertime. This, of course, is usually some telemarketer, with an opening like: "Good evening, sir, I am _____, and I want to tell you about. . . ." This call, instead, was framed from the outset as a personal call: "Hi, Dr. Hite, this is _____ in Chicago. How are things in Nashville today?" This was no script, it was a real human being, who knew me, knew where I lived, and was prepared to take the time to engage me in a conversation. I did not, as I often do, hang up immediately. We chatted for a bit, I discovered something about the person, and he discovered something about me. As it turned out, he was trying to sell me an upgrade to a piece of software I had purchased some years ago.

Yet, the calling and sales technique was cooperative and not mechanical or aggressive. It represented, for me, a refreshing approach to telephone sales. This organization had my attention and kept it far longer than the ordinary sales call. They had changed, with their approach, the fitness landscape by holding me on the phone for two minutes rather than the usual five seconds.

LEADERSHIP AND HUMAN BEHAVIOR

There is mounting evidence that the ability to work in a chaotic environment takes practice and requires changes in methods, just as the telemarketing company adjusted its methods to take advantage of historical account data. At the level of global economies, we are just learning how dependent we are on our understanding of those at the other end of the phone—or globe, as the case may be. Events in the global economic system, encountered in 1998, bear out the interconnectedness of what were once nationalistic economic systems as well as the increased sensitivity of local events to world events [8, 9]. During that year, erratic behavior in the Asian economies translated into effects in other global economies. It became clear that these formerly national economies had become linked in ways that were barely understood, and difficult to control. The answers lay in collective approaches to financial and economic management, involving a number of countries that had previously viewed themselves as independent. *Business Week,* in an editorial [10], summarized a view from the U.S. economic perspective under the title "Out of Touch with Reality":

> Beltway insiders were totally shocked when a run-of-the-mill currency crisis in tiny Thailand turned into a near depression for Asia.

In this statement, we see the suggestion of a concern with the real nature of global enterprise. While we would like to believe that communications and commerce on a global scale are well supported by the digital infrastructure that has provided satellite and high-speed fiber optic communications, this part of the network may not be the part at fault. If there are surprises, it is because both government and industry leaders have underestimated the loss of national isolation in economies, and have underestimated the chaotic nature of the international financial system. As *Business Week* editors conclude,

> The real world appears to be changing faster than leaders' comprehensions of it. People who grew up in a cold war time of high defense spending, inflation, low growth, and high unemployment can easily misperceive a U.S. economy that is integrated globally, has no pricing power, and sustains high growth and low unemployment. . . .
>
> Many business leaders are simply out of touch. They are divorced from the people they lead and misunderstand the economic and political forces that will dominate the opening of the next century. For them, this should be a time for listening and learning.

These shifts and changes in what is now a globally influenced economy serve as an example of the ways in which peaks on the fitness landscape can change, impacting individuals as well as organizations. Stacey [7] also recognized this complex operation of the organization on the fitness landscape. Businesses, he observes,

> do not operate in equilibrium states. They operate in a border area between the equilibrium states of ossification and disintegration. The insights of scientific theories of chaos and self-organization show that this border area between equilibrium states is in fact a chaotic one, far from equilibrium. The conclusion is that the dynamic of a successful business is chaotic.

Uncertainty has always been a part of our lives, but has been considered an obstacle, an element of randomness that needed to be overcome or gotten around in order to manage or lead the organization. Leadership, much of it, is devoted to reducing uncertainty. Yet, if the system is chaotic, then uncertainty becomes an accepted part of the overall pattern, and high volatility and many degrees of freedom are respected, not rejected. The uncertainty accompanying a nonlinear dynamical system is a desirable feature, but not one that is familiar ground for those who are taught to lead and manage organizations. The paradigm of leadership suggests that enough measurement, oversight, and use of historical data tracking and linear forecasting tools will provide a way past the uncertainty, and the remaining uncertainty is insignificant to the direction of the group.

While the tracking of data and peak movement in the landscape leads us to a clear understanding of organizational and environmental history, knowledge of history alone may not be sufficient to guide us in organizing for movements on the landscape. Historical data, while useful, is not, in nonlinear environments, a good basis for future prediction. Because the relationships between cause and effect become distorted in nonlinear relationships, and because the understanding of history itself is a complex study, the development of a pattern or model based on history may be flawed. Any system that is sensitively dependent on initial conditions may find itself absorbed with the documentation of history in its effort to understand change, rather than focusing on the underlying attractive force which results in the quick and radical rearrangement on the fitness landscape. Again, such system behavior can operate in an evolutionary way, only if evolution is taken in its most modern sense, to accommodate radical shifts as well as gradual shifts. The complex adaptive system cannot be satisfied with continuity and sustainable performance. It must be fully engaged in the constant phase transition that informs the dynamics at the edge of chaos. In fact, to manifest a level of influence over the fitness landscape itself, the organization must be prepared to become chaotic and make the transition into Period 3 behavior, from the more rational near-chaos of Period 2.

As Stacey (1991) summarizes the leadership of organizations that make best use of chaos:

> When we take a chaos perspective we behave in a way that is open and sensitive to our environment, we take a chance, we do creative things with long-term consequences we cannot foresee, we work at understanding and at

developing new understandings; and we create a part at least of what happens to us, accepting that the rest is a matter of chance.

Priesmeyer [11] takes a similar view, and describes the difference between common current practices and those consistent with chaos theory:

> . . . with change all around us, we insist on focusing on snapshot pictures of our world. . . . We record our corporate performance with audited reports that disregard the transitions in our organizations. We capture measures such as on-hand inventories and budgeted expenses as singular quantities and record them with precision, believing that greater accuracy will somehow provide greater truth. We don't seem to mind that those measures don't reveal the dynamics of the continually changing organization they represent.

Once we give up the Newtonian view that organizations should be stable, then we must admit that we do not have the appropriate tools for organizational leadership. From our concepts of leadership down to the ways in which we measure performance of agents in the system, we assume stability and linearity as normal and desirable conditions. Giving up stability means serious reassessment of our processes and methodologies. Whether we are chiefly concerned with general management, organization development, or human resource development, our orientation must change. Leadership in chaos is neither simple nor straightforward. Admission of chaos is the admission of complexity.

A consistent view of the operation of chaos in organizations can be summarized as:

(1) Managers and organizational leaders have yet to shift their point of view to accommodate chaotic systems behavior.
(2) Leaders have not yet applied chaos theory and its associated techniques to understanding and managing the organizations.

As long as erratic and unusual elements in organizational behavior are treated as negatives, to be cast out in order to return the system to a norm, the characteristics and advantages of chaotic activity cannot be accommodated. A system that is managed against industry norms or historical performance, and that looks for small, incremental changes brought about through minor tweaking of processes, will fail to maximize its potential. The potential of a system is reliant on its willingness to open itself to risk and to admit uncertainty. Support for these characteristics must be engendered in the internal or external stakeholders in the system. Short-term management of tactical objectives must not override an understanding that short-term performance will yield short-term results. Such a focus will translate into organizational cultures that value certainty and stability, not uncertainty and high degrees of systemic freedom. As Priesmeyer reminds us, "goals and objectives are the products of linear thinking, whereas human behavior is unequivocally nonlinear" [11].

A study by Lawrence M. Ward and Robert L. West [12] indicates that, while research indeed points to measurable nonlinear behavior in individuals, the measurement process is not yet as strong or as widely applicable as it needs to be. In this study, the authors considered the ways in which individual human behavior could be "at the same time unpredictable and yet nonrandom." Prior research into this area had indicated to Ward and West that "humans cannot behave randomly when asked to do so." What previous researchers had discovered is that people usually form some logical and sequential response sequence when asked to do something. That is, their "executive control function" [13] applied some form of sense-making sequencing to the task at hand, be it physical or cognitive. That humans appear to act randomly or in ways that are unpredictable, may be an appearance only, and not reflecting the true operational nature of the human system.

In the experiment setup by Ward and West, they trained a number of people to imitate a particular logical equation. In the experiment, the subjects were asked to select, on a computer screen, specific numbers that, when taken as a whole final sequence, would reproduce the iterative results of the logistic equation. The result of the trials was that "although all subjects were able to approximate the learned nonlinear function (some much better than others), none reproduced it exactly and not one produced an approximation of the chaotic attractor of the learned function." The conclusions from the experiment suggest that:

(a) In order to reproduce the results of a chaotic equation with any accuracy, it is necessary to be able to work with numbers of a high precision. The experiment asked the subjects to use only 3-digit numbers, in part because earlier work had suggested the difficulty people have in working with more digits or with decimal fractions. Therefore, the human limitation affects the ability of the subjects to reproduce numbers with high accuracy.

(b) Even though the subjects were trained to perform the number-sequencing and selection task, using immediate feedback to help them establish the correct number sequence during the training, they were unable, in the trial itself, "to infer the value of a parameter of a nonlinear equation." That is, when there was no feedback and they were given a seed number from which to start, subjects could not reproduce the model equation as iterated by the computer.

(c) The subjects could not memorize enough data "to produce a precise linear approximation to chaotic iteration." This limitation is associated with the limitation that humans have in working with numbers of high precision. In this case, the subjects were unable to recall enough of the detail from their learning trials to reproduce the results of the equation in the trial without feedback. Lack of feedback in the final trial left subjects without support, and memory was not sufficient to help them.

(d) The researchers noted "some additional, unknown, noisiness of performance." There is, at present, no explanation for this noise, which is displayed graphically as additional points in and around the precise plot of the equation. This evidence of unpredictability is an area for further exploration, since it represents some form of cognitive processing for the task.

The researchers conclude that, in order to resolve this particular task as structured in the experiment, "human subjects resort to using a heuristic that gives a rough approximation of the desired output and is within the limitations of the human behavioral apparatus." This finding indicates that the subjects used what they could from their training process, but then generated a cognitive strategy which included "fuzzy" thinking, in order to select the numbers which would reproduce a chaotic equation. By developing a heuristic, or general solution guideline, through which to carry out the task, the subjects produced "time series of behaviors that possess the same amount of nonlinear deterministic structure as those produced by the noisy logistic difference equation." This ability to reproduce a nonlinear deterministic sequence, however, does not qualify the results as technically chaotic.

The problem of application of chaotic modeling to human behavior remains. While this experiment does demonstrate that people can approximate a mathematically true rendition of a nonlinear dynamical system as it progresses through its iterations, it is not evidence of true chaotic thought processes in humans. It is, however, suggestive that there may be ways to understand the parameters which people manipulate to develop heuristic responses to problems or activities. There is certainly enough evidence to suggest that heuristic approaches to problem solving and project completion may be developed in nonlinear ways. At the micro level of everyday activity, whether individual or organizational, such patterns may not seem to be patterns at all, because of the interference of time and alternative tasks in usual routines. If, however, the pattern-making process can be modeled, the model may serve as a useful simulation for helping people learn how to deal with chaotic processes in personal or organizational life.

Such research offers the possibility that we can come to understand the operation of nonlinear and potentially chaotic thinking in people, and in the shared behaviors which characterize an organization. The potential this offers in the development of organizational capability is evident. With the ability to synthesize and understand the parameters through which a heuristic process operates, it will be possible to build much more accurate simulations of human behavioral situations than are now available. Eventually research will extend from an understanding of individual human cognition, as it may be nonlinear and even chaotic, to shared heuristics, as teams and groups of individuals interact and develop organizational behaviors which can be characterized and understood in their nonlinearity and chaotic activity. Future work in organizational development must depend on an understanding of how nonlinearity works throughout the organization, because open and virtual organizations do not provide for sublimation of nonlinear processes in favor of linear, externally imposed actions. The imposition of order from external sources will be minimized, while the evolution of order, through the development of heuristics and of nonlinear or chaotic patterns of behavior, will become more visible and significant to organizational success. There are no guarantees, in this concept of organizational life, that we will be able to isolate and define the strange attractors that inform the changes in our systems. At the same time, it is becoming clear that unless we probe the systems for some sense of their ordering factors, we will be left blind. In chaotic systems, predictive capability rests only in an understanding of the attractive forces and their parameters. We cannot discover anything about the longer-term futures of our people, machines and networks, unless we go to some expense and trouble to comprehend system dynamics.

Where we have been told, in the organizational development world, that what organizations need to do is to focus through executive or leadership visioning activities, we have followed a path that leads away from the messy, creative potentiality and towards a clockwork organization. Where mission, vision, and values have been chanted like mantras in every organization, they have provided an efficiency of thought bordering on mind control. Emergence of ideas and generative learning from within the organizational belly, then, is stifled. This is an appropriate approach to the development of organizations intended to be hierarchies and those that will reach their goals through manager-subordinate relationships. It is an approach that will follow complicated process wiring diagrams with religious fervor. It is not an approach that will take full advantage of chaotic behavior in the individuals in an organization, or as those individuals, along with their equipment and networks, collectively create the organization itself [14].

Stacey advocates a view of the organization as a nonlinear feedback network. What his work brings forward is the theme of unpredictability and its acceptance and advantages in organizational dynamics. Noting the angst that usually accompanies any process of letting go of control, he argues that the ability to accomplish this will mark organizations that make best use of complexity and chaos theory. In what he calls a "new management paradigm," one of the key understandings that must develop early in the organization is that "we can accept lack of foresight and control without inevitable anarchy, thereby enabling us to hold the anxiety rather than defend against it and so avoid it" [15].

Chief outcomes of this approach are a greater understanding of the role learning plays in the organization; a greater valuation for self-organization, self-directed work and learning; and the expansion of degrees of freedom in the activity of the organization. Mission, vision, and values will be emergent and descriptive, not directed and prescriptive. The "structuring" of the organization will be the last thing done, and not the first, and the structure will be derived logically from patterns which are set within the web. Managers and executives will provide coordinating services as a part of the web, but will not set themselves apart as architects of the web. It is the system as a whole that will describe itself at any point in its phase plane.

MANAGEMENT

Management must be a part of the organization, and management behavior must dynamically complement other changing forces within the organization. The development of management will hinge on two key concepts:

(1) Management does not follow a fixed path, such as that envisioned in situational leadership models. It must be allowed more degrees of freedom than those offered in traditional descriptions of the management role.

(2) Management is not an activity that is outside of the system in which it operates. It is a whole with that system, and is, itself, subject to measurable variables that affect overall system dynamics and performance. When the variables are defined and measured, they must be considered in congruence with each other, and not in isolation.

The second point has significant implications in the way in which the success of the management or leader role is assessed. Where this is currently a subjective process in most organizations, the measurement process misses the opportunity afforded by more definition of the variables and the way they act. Where quantification is used, it is generally associated with financial performance of the manager's organization, and thus has to do with only one variable. Since managers are rarely solely responsible for the financial success of the work they manage, even this measure is suspect.

Moreover, most measures are considered in isolation. Yes, the manager may "make her numbers," but how is this factor integrated with the other variables of management performance? Only by conceiving of ways in which the variables can be constructed in an integrated way can the entire management picture be presented and interpreted. Further, because management is simply another aspect in a whole system, it must not be measured in isolation from the behavior of the rest of the system. Management is dynamic, changing, and must therefore be allowed to share the chaotic characteristic of unpredictability, as it operates in unpredictable circumstances. When we over-define the requirements for management, we deny the degrees of freedom necessary for the management role to move dynamically in coordination with the system of which it is a part.

By treating the management role and processes as nonlinear dynamical systems, the burden then becomes to understand the relevant variables and their interaction. Once understood, like the operation at the individual level described above, these dynamics can be modeled, and the understanding of management processes and core principles can be simulated. The understanding of the dynamic attractors and the differential equations that describe performance in relation to those attractors thus becomes a subject for management development. This information, far more specific than anything currently available in the repertoire of management development, can lead to increased accuracy and fullness of simulations that can help managers and leaders internalize the complexity of the role.

Current events bear out this interpretation and goal. Where once managerial resumes were valued if they showed steadiness and consistency of experience—either in role or tenure—today this is no longer the case. Kunde [16] reports that, in contrast to prior philosophies, multiple experiences are now desirable personal characteristics. What organizations now value in the background of organizational leaders is more varied experiences, not fewer. One of the reasons given for this shift, which has occurred in selection processes over the past 4–5 years, is that increased variety in work provides increased diversity. The ability to work in numerous positions, perhaps even across numerous industries, indicates a person who is flexible and adaptable.

The introduction of these characteristics as highly valued qualities signals that organizations are looking for people who are not locked into rigid definitions of management roles. These new managers will have multiple perspectives on management capabilities and ways to build teams and support the work underway. They will have defined some cognitive strategies that will support application under variable circumstances. In short, they will be able to correlate their capabilities with the dynamics of the systems into which they are being selected. They have characteristics that will fit them for management and leadership in chaotic organizational systems.

While it is clear that these characteristics can be selected into the system, it is less clear whether they can be developed from within the system. This may account for the popularity of these features in the hiring process. If the system does not have a way to create what it needs, it takes it from the surrounding environment. Our concern here should be that a system that must go to the surrounding environment in order to renew itself with leadership may not be fully configured itself to develop flexible leadership internally. If this is the case, then lack of effective leadership development creates the potential for high levels of variance in the leadership role. More conservative leaders, who have emerged from the system, come into conceptual conflict with leaders hired for their ability to exist in, and lead in, an atmosphere of chaotic system activity. Where organizations find themselves bringing in leadership to sustain high degrees of change and volatility, they would be well served to examine the extent to which their internal system does or does not provide leaders with the same flexibility and adaptability.

SELF-ORGANIZATION IN SYSTEMS

As we noted earlier, in the discussion of open and virtual organizations, the degree of freedom exhibited by the organization creates the need for different ways to organize. In fact, self-organization, as a characteristic of chaotic systems, also plays a vital role in the ability of organizations to survive in open and virtual situations. Self-organization, however, is difficult to achieve from an hierarchical organizational structure. Asking an hierarchical organization to self-organize is asking too much. Expectations at individual, subgroup and group levels have been set according to a given layer of the power geology, and history, culture, and processes lend support to top-down flows of information and decisions. In open and virtual organizations, the organizational presence is less rigid and the strata less defined in their roles and capabilities. Autopoesis is encouraged, not stifled, and, when successful, leads to generative processes.

Organizations are learning to leverage autopoetic characteristics that begin to develop among their members. IBM, for example, is using a relatively new and unique approach to determining where the self-generating activity is in the human elements of their systems. With an approach called "social-network analysis" they are discovering where people look for decisions and information, and which people can resolve problems [17]. The network that is mapped from this information reveals that the power structure bears little resemblance to the formal organization chart. The hierarchy, when it comes to getting work done, is set aside in favor of social networks, with people helping people. The informal networks that are created through socialization provide a vivid and practical example of self-organization in organizational systems. While this activity has certainly been a part of organizational life for as long as there has been organizational life, it has heretofore been regarded as an interesting aside, and not an important factor in organizational management. Informal networks have always developed, but have existed in the substrata of the organization.

The importance of such informal web-building is now understood as a key feature in organizational growth and sustained survival. As Kotter [18] notes, in order for corporate cultures to remain adaptive, the members of the organization must support each other. This is most likely to be found in a situation that favors informal relationship building and entrepreneurship. Change is derived from an environment that encourages change. Here, in the organizational setting, is the suggestion that organizational behavior is fractal. Change is iterative and builds on its past results. Much of the iterative portrait that is drawn through the change process owes its characteristics to the degrees of freedom people have to self-organize and the extent to which informal webs and networks are leveraged and encouraged by the whole organization.

This, of course, raises the question as to what the other two parts of the organization, the equipment and networks, do as humans self-organize. In fact, there is a growing symbiosis among the three parts to achieve a holistic, self-generative characteristic in an organization. The shift in networking strategy, for example, from dependence on a fixed mainframe computer to client-server arrangements demonstrates the change in the systems world, from a nuclear to an open system. The mainframe was the sole source of intelligence in the network, with interfaces through "dumb" terminals. These terminals designed for human use, were little more than a video display and a keyboard. All communications, whether giving or receiving, were carried out between human and mainframe. All electronic "computing" or processing was done by the mainframe, as it shared time with many users at any given instant. This meant that the computer processors (less powerful than those found in some personal computers today) often had work backed up for them to do, and, in fact, much of the work was setup for "batch" processing over a 24-hour period. The computer worked nights as well as days.

Problems arose when the processors could not keep up with the work. New records intended for bank databases, for example, might not be assigned account numbers in the system for days. Payments from petroleum exploration companies to the landholders from whom they leased land for exploration or production could be held up if the batch processing failed to keep up. Failure of the mainframe, of course, spelled disaster, and generally every system included some form of backup processor capability. All organizations that depended on computer systems shared these frailties.

Such an arrangement, while it maximized the common resource of the computer, made for slow responses and delays in feedback. These systemic delays from the central computer forced echoing delays throughout the operating system. All roads led to Rome, and when Rome (the mainframe) became overcrowded and backed up, so did all the roads.

This situation did not support autopoesis, since time to be creative and innovative on such systems was limited and restricted in favor of high-priority processing. In fact, only certain people were allowed to program such central processors, and only code that had been inspected and approved by the priests and priestesses of the system would be mounted and run. A religion developed around mainframe computers, and it adhered to hierarchical structure, with highest priority given to scientific applications which were product related, or to business data priorities, mandated by executives. For a common, ordinary employee to attempt to sit down at a terminal and generate a program of any complexity, and then test it, run it, and make it a permanent part of the computer's routine, was nearly unheard of.

This closed and highly structured approach to use of computing resources changed when the economics of computing changed. This happened in the late 1970s and early 1980s with the introduction of personal computers, which provided decentralization of computing resources, availability of relatively cheap computer resources, and thus access for the masses. Organizations could begin to open the computing system, with PCs available for programming and running relatively simple solutions to localized problems and needs. One accounting department, for instance, might load some of its preliminary data periodically into a PC, using a simple spreadsheet program, and develop variance reports throughout a reporting period. The department had the capability to run localized reports and track activity across smaller periods than it would have been able to do on the mainframe. The department could then upload this data either by sending a disk to the computing department for direct input to the mainframe database or, as time progressed and modem speeds progressed, through a modem to the mainframe database.

We have gradually enabled autopoesis in the equipment and networks, to the point where an array of minicomputers handle central storage and some processing functions and act as nodes across an organizational network. Much of the processing, however, has transferred into the hands of individuals who use personal computers to support their work. This capability and openness in the electronic network and in electronic computing equipment supported the transfer of some of the control of the system from the information-processing priesthood to the end-users.

Because economics has allowed high network speeds, storage capacities, and data processing speeds in these units, it is feasible for nearly everyone in an organization to have a computer on the desktop, at home, or available on the factory floor. Because these computers can handle the activities of the organization, with power to spare, they become creative elements in the organization. Their ability to store, retrieve, process and transfer information makes them self-generative parts of the system and contributors to system success. They enable creativity, independence of thinking, and the entrepreneurial approach necessary to support open and virtual organizations. They are, therefore, important contributing members to the organizational presence that is self-generating, as they contribute not only their mechanical abilities in data manipulation, but also their abilities to provide new ways of looking at things and new knowledge from outside of the boundaries of the organizational system. These systems allow the effective merger of human and electronic networks, combining the capabilities of the human element with the capabilities of the equipment and network elements. The capabilities of the network itself are thereby strengthened, as are the capabilities of the equipment and the capabilities of the people in the system.

A LOOP TOWARD REALITY

The need to understand how technical chaos operates in organizational systems is clearly articulated in sociopolitical events. In a 1998 article regarding the economic problems plaguing Russia, Viktor Chernomyrdin, then a candidate for prime minister, commented: "Russia today is, in essence, on the verge of economic and political breakdown. . . . Life in Russia is incredibly difficult as it is, and we have no right to make it still more difficult. We have no time. We have used up our margin of error" [19].

In response to Chernomyrdin's observations, Gennady Zyuganov, then a leader of the Communist party, observed: "The last island of legality in the country is here in the Duma and the Federation Council. If it is finished and destroyed, then chaos and gangs will prevail." In apparent agreement with this assessment, Alexander Kotenkov, an envoy from the President to the Duma, said: "A few weeks of chaos will reduce the country to complete ruin" and predicted "a popular uprising, merciless and senseless" [19].

Here, in the arena of Russia's struggles to maintain a balanced economy, is recognition from the highest levels that the balance may not be sustainable for very much longer. Stability had been pulled out of the Russian economy at this point, by the devaluation of the ruble and general uncertainty over the leadership of the nation. It is necessary to note, however, as was done with previous examples of how the term "chaos" has been used, that this appears to be an application of classical, not technical, chaos. There is no reference to data that would support an analysis of the Russian economic system according to the principles and methods described in the chapter devoted to technical chaos. The comments here seem to come from an air of desperation with both the economy and political situation, the complexity of which was, at the time, overwhelming to those responsible for its maintenance. At the same time, however, it is clear that the Russian economic system would lend itself to study as a chaotic system. The question that is uppermost is: To what extent would an understanding of the systemic chaos that is operating in such a system provide keys and levers or control rods to bring the chaos back toward what is ordinarily considered to be a "stable" economic system? This question raises another: To what extent does a governing body need to intervene in a chaotic system? Is it better to let chaos evolve and operate the economy as an accepted chaotic system, or is it better to bring it under executive control and sacrifice change for order? Again, would a clearer understanding of the operation of technical chaos in this system and its subsystems help point to decisions in these areas?

At about the same time that Russia was undergoing some preliminaries to major systemic change in an apparent "Period 3" environment, similar events were unfolding in Thailand. The Thai Farmer's Bank, because of bad loans and a generally poor economy, reported, in the second quarter of 1998, a US$100 million loss, and its stock dropped by 65 percent. Other Thai banks were reporting similar results, with a general uncertainty as to whether they could be saved. In the overall economy, "with factories closing, unemployment soaring, and the financial sector crippled, Thailand is lurching into a contraction that may surpass almost everyone's worst-case scenarios" [20]. The country's Finance Minister was moving forward with a recovery plan, but admitted, "The system is not functioning." As in Russia, there was considerable fear that economic collapse would be accompanied by political dysfunction. The entire economic system had been in the process of opening, including removal of barriers to free trade, allowing increased outside investment in the nation's enterprises, enactment of reform laws, and privatization. Overall, however, analysts saw the banking system as the linchpin for maintaining the economy near stability.

There are strong similarities between this picture and the glimpse of the Russian economy cited above. In both instances, it is the condition of the monetary system that is a focus as a control factor. Stability is equated, throughout the entire economy, with the stability of the baht or ruble. Second, the action, in the system, of freeing the system from restraints seems to have been in the background environment in both instances. Russia had shifted from a dominant Communist political venue, and Thailand's government undertook a number of simultaneous reforms. Third, there is the fear expressed from both governments that increased uncertainty and loss of stability would lead to riots, street warfare, and general catastrophe.

While the two brief articles regarding these two geographically separate situations can only serve to generate questions, the questions for both countries remain the same. Did their leaders analyze the potential outcomes in the systems using methods and approaches that provide metrics for nonlinear dynamical systems? If the economic systems—and potentially the national systems overall—are in jeopardy of becoming chaotic, at what point did the evidence begin to appear in the system, and who observed and assessed it? Is there a way, given the appropriate metrics and leadership, to make chaos work for the overall evolution of these bounded national systems? Finally, and most importantly, in what ways are the complex adaptive systems so obviously in play here linked with the co-evolution of global economic and social systems? Can the processes in Russia or Thailand be understood as national chaotic systems, or must they be seen and understood as parts of something even more complex than that?

Associated with these systemic concerns are concerns around the learning activities that are operating within each of these national systems. How is learning acting as a variable in the delicate turning point in the economies? How might learning within the system pull it back from the edge of chaos, or move it closer to realizing a chaotic regime? Can each of these systems truly learn if executive control is maintained by the governments, or must some percentage or fraction of executive control be sacrificed in order for the system to evolve in its fitness landscape? Do government agencies know less than they think they do about how their various social and economic systems operate, once bounds are removed in different parameters? What are the individuals who are represented in these governments learning about how to exist in radically different economic and regulatory environments? What are the measures of human responses and behaviors suggesting in their own dynamics?

Unfortunately, the answers to these questions are not obvious, because in many instances the relevant variables are not measured, and defined constants do not exist. Popular opinion is rarely taken in any systematic way, and is used only peripherally by governmental representatives. In almost all representative govern-ments, the representative is free to be swayed by his or her constituents, but also by other influences which may not represent the constituency. "Influence-peddling" has long been a weakness of such representative governments and, where it crops up, can affect the decision-making within the economic and legislative systems. Moreover, most such systems depend on majority votes, which are arrived at through compromises and negotiations. Where this is the case, minority opinions, while heard, are often not influential in outcomes, decisions and directions. At least one U.S. Senator confirmed that, in his view, votes in the U.S. Congress should not be based on public opinion. Many public leaders also believe that, once elected, they are immune from the will of the people and have been given a mantle of wis-dom that transcends the constituency. Public systems are often co-opted by political professionals, or, worse, political amateurs.

All of these realities, in such socio-political scenarios as the two described above, add variability to the inherent instability in homocentric systems. The complexity is often taken for granted, with the result that single, separate events and decisions are often not viewed in light of the overall impact in the system. System behavior is addressed, instead, by the minister of finance, the minister of welfare, and the minis-ter of commerce in their separate ministries, with the overall picture suffering from decomposition. The very arrangement of a government is, therefore, another variable which can affect the stability of the system overall. Diversity in opinions, valued for insights from different perspectives, can become hardened into missions and direc-tions that are noncomplementary in relation to the larger system. Variability and diversity, therefore, offer a paradox in the understanding of systems. On the one hand, variance opens the opportunity for weak attractors that allow the system to display its full range of nonlinear possibilities. This can produce massive change, as the system adapts to the fitness landscape through autopoesis.

On the other hand, variance is an unfamiliar environment, to which most humans and many machines and networks are not attuned. In the chaotic regime, very little is clear, and attraction to any one fixed point in phase-space is weak. There is the potential that high levels of diversity and change can disable the system, leading to the necessity for the system to recreate itself from basic elements. This possibility equals classical chaos to observers and system participants who are unsure that any-thing productive is emerging from such radical change. People fear loss of control and loss of understanding—of knowing—in this environment. Where the measures of technical chaos, and an understanding of system parameters and behavior, are not clearly delineated, the void is filled by classical chaos. Participants in the rites and rituals associated with such classical chaos approach the system as a thing of awe, to be worshiped from afar, and not to be changed. Who knows what happens to the maiden once she is thrown into the volcano? Uncertainty leads to conserva-tion and preservation of the mysteries.

There are clear implications and transfers from the consideration of socio-politi-cal systems into our consideration of other forms of systems. If we avoid what we do not understand, and hold it in awe and reverence, we are unlikely to leap into the volcano to make changes to it. Yet, systemic understanding, when the system is at the edge of chaos, or in chaos, is vital. When a vehicle skids out of control on an icy road, travelling at 50 kph, the effect on the driver and passengers is not pleasant. Loss of control, or the sense of the unknown, is not a comfortable place for most people. In particular, it is not a comfortable place for system "leaders," who believe it is their role to know where the car is going at all times and to have steady control of the wheel. The behavior of complex systems, however, may not respond to changes in the steering wheel, the brake pedal, or the accelerator, or various combinations of these three factors.

Organizations and other such systems contain any number of variables which may or may not be in operation at any given time, and which may provide varying degrees of input to the actual behavior of the system at any point in time. Without understanding these interactions, the actions of the system will remain a mystery to be avoided or bluffed around. The fact that leaders choose to manipulate variables they can understand, and to do so only in the most general way, suggests the same sort of faith in organizational systems that was held by the priests who lifted the maiden over the mouth of the volcano. In both instances, we see the operation of blind faith, whether in the downsizing of an organization based on percentages or the sacrifice of the maiden. The heroic leaders believe that by appeasing the gods of the unknown, that which is known will somehow become more manageable [21].

Down this path lies an acceptance of ignorance as a rational basis for organizational leadership. If worship of the unknown will yield miraculous recoveries in the known world, can ignorance be such a bad thing? Do we need to know how sudden and oblique changes in direction, in complex systems, may affect outcomes? Perhaps it is better to ignore the anomalies and avoid the indicators that do not match linear trends and averages. These represent the things for which leaders have no time, and in which they have no interest. If success lies in mass consumption of goods and services, then the easy way to success is to find out what sells the most in the least amount of time, make it, provide it, and enjoy the wealth therefrom. It is an organization devoted to NOW.

Understanding organizations and the fitness landscapes of their environments may be this simple, but probably not. The suggestions which, so far, can be derived from nonlinear dynamic systems studies indicate that leaders who ignore the operation of complex adaptive systems and chaotic systems risk the loss of control on organizational and systemic ice which hovers around 0° C. Whether political or social or business, an organization which binds itself too tightly to a single attractor will become outdated and of no further use on the landscape. Systems that are tightly bound as individual entities cannot coevolve, and therefore cannot compete. Loss of competitive ability will mean that they will stabilize and atrophy, with their energy drained and none to replace it. Systems that are willing to risk life on the icy road may find less need to sacrifice maidens before, during or after the trip. If the organization understands the nature of its nonlinearity, and understands the interplay of the high number of variables that affect its trajectory, then it will be able to influence the events that will have the biggest effect on its future state. In this set of circumstances, organizational leaders need not fear uprisings or "chaos," or flattened economic prospects. Instead, they will understand the role that radical change can play in opening the organization to new possible futures, and the role change plays in reinvigorating the organization as a whole. Indeed, they may come to an understanding of the synergistic relationship—the trading of energies—between a single organization and the wider environmental systems with which it coevolves.

A suggestion that this is true has come from research into organizational networking, as human agents in the organization carry it out. Based on work done in the 1960s by Stanley Milgram, a social psychologist [22], Duncan J. Watts and Steven H. Strogatz have developed a mathematical theory which supports a conclusion that a single person, placed in the right arrangement in an organizational network, can act as a kind of extra-powerful node in the network, allowing shortcuts and bypasses which make the entire network more efficient. If validated across various types of organizations, this finding could lead to the conclusions that:

(1) a human, well-placed and operating as a network node, may be integrable into a meta-network consisting of humans, machines, and electronic network elements;

(2) a human may constitute the equivalent of an "initial condition" in some dynamical systems, influencing those systems and subsystems which are sensitively dependent on initial conditions; and

(3) a carefully constructed micro-network, using the idea of six degrees of separation, [22] may act as a fractal in an overall organizational network.

By replicating these fractal networks at different scales, large dynamical systems may be developed on the same principle, using a relatively simple formula to describe the network.

This would then form the basis for a chaotic organizational presence that would differ considerably from current organizational models. In this system, change could come from anywhere, with broad impact on the operation of the network.

In order to encourage and support such volatile system networks, we will need to understand change. As organizations move under the influence of their attractors, change will occur spontaneously. It can be self-generated. It can also be encouraged or initiated by the agents within the system. Regardless of the type of agent—human, machine or network—each type may be responsible for monitoring the system, learning within it, and initiating changes to the system. We must construct change processes carefully, to take advantage of the chaos in organizational systems and to avoid smothering it. We need to approach change as an action which involves all system agents and which makes use of the whole construct of chaos, including both its classical and its technical characteristics.

REFERENCES

1. Greiner, L. E., "Evolution and revolution as organizations grow," *Harvard Business Review,* May–June 1998, pp. 55–67, p. 58.
2. Santosus, M., "Simple, yet complex," *CIO Enterprise,* April 15, 1998, pp. 62–67.
3. Gleick, J., *Chaos: Making a New Science,* New York: Viking, 1987, pp. 15, 46, 83, 86, 306, 311.

4. Polley, D., "Turbulence in organizations: New metaphors for organizational research," *Organization Science,* Vol. 8, No. 5, 1997, pp. 445–457.

5. Kerwin, K., "GM: Modular plants won't be a snap," *Business Week,* November 9, 1998, pp. 168–172.

6. Guastello, S. J., *Chaos, Catastrophe, and Human Affairs,* Mahwah, N.J.: Lawrence Erlbaum Associates, 1995, pp. 34,158–159, 162–163, 263, 311.

7. Stacey, R. D., *The Chaos Frontier: Creative Strategic Control for Business,* London: Butterworth Heinemann, 1991, pp. 181, 183, 202, 212.

8. Mandel, M. J., "The 21st century economy," *Business Week,* August 31, 1998, pp. 58–63.

9. Bremner, B., "Japan's real crisis," *Business Week,* May 18, 1998, pp. 136–142.

10. "Out of touch with reality." *Business Week,* November 23, 1998, p. 214.

11. Priesmeyer, H. R., *Organizations and Chaos: Defining the Methods of Nonlinear Management,* Westport, Conn.: Quorum Books, 1992, pp. 3, 135, 136, 153.

12. Ward, L. M. and R. L. West, "Modeling human chaotic behavior: Nonlinear forecasting analysis of logistic iteration," *Nonlinear Dynamics, Psychology, and Life Sciences,* Vol. 2, No. 4, 1998, pp. 261–282, pp. 261, 262, 266, 279.

13. Gagné, R. M., *The Conditions of Learning and Theory of Instruction,* 4th ed, Chicago: Holt, Rinehart and Winston, 1985, pp. 47–48, 72.

14. Stamps, D., "A conversation with doctor paradox," *Training,* May 1997, pp. 42–48.

15. Stacey, R. D., *Complexity and Creativity in Organizations,* San Francisco: Berrett-Koehler, 1996, pp. 17, 55.

16. Kunde, D., "Long stay with 1 firm can hinder ladder climbing," *The Nashville Banner,* Nashville, December 26, 1997, p. 3B.

17. Stamps, D., "Off the charts," *Training,* October 1997, pp. 77-83.

18. Kotter, J. P. and J. L. Heskett., *Corporate Culture and Performance,* New York: The Free Press, 1992.

19. York, G., "Defiant Duma roundly rejects Chernomyrdin," *The Globe and Mail,* Toronto, September 1, 1998, p. A8.

20. Einhorn, B. and R. Corben, "Thailand: Banking chaos," *Business Week,* August 17, 1998, p. 51.

21. Hamel, G., "Opinion strategy innovation and the quest for value," *Sloan Management Review,* Vol. 39, No. 2, 1998, pp. 7–14.

22. Andreeva, N., "Do the math—it is a small world," *Business Week,* August 17, 1998, pp. 54–55.

Chapter 8

The Shift to a Wider Perspective

INTRODUCTION

My purpose in this chapter is to begin to construct a background necessary for understanding the influence of classical and technical chaos on learning. Before considering the potential for chaotic learning, I want to note the learning theories that are predominant in the learning industry and demonstrate some relationships between the characteristics of those theories and the characteristics identified with classical and technical chaos. What is ultimately important is for us to consider ways in which chaos theory may be applied in concert with learning theory, to provide different and perhaps more effective ways to address learning events and the support of those events. There is a kernel relationship between what has been demonstrated in the studies of chaos in organizations and individuals and the ways in which we view learning events and processes.

Learning has not always been as sophisticated a concern as it is now. According to Eby and Arrowood [1], primitive learning by humans was concentrated on essentials:

He tends to repeat earlier practices. He does develop new arts, discover and elaborate new bodies of knowledge, and invent stories, songs, implements, and institutions. But his educational activities are directed principally to the transmission of knowledge and of skills and to the testing and control of the learner—not to the learner's development, or to the increase of knowledge or the discovery of new skills.

The primitive approach to learning had everything to do with survival in a natural world, with natural as well as human predators, and little to do with foresight and futuring. The development of capabilities that might or might not be useful in the immediate future is a feature that is more in line with modern developments in learning. Where the primitive world was uncertain, the uncertainty could, our ancestors hoped, be coped with by acquiring a few necessary skills and honing them. Our own need for such skills has been incremented by an increased need to look ahead and attempt to predict what capabilities we may need in the future.

152

Because many of our present needs are met, we can look out beyond survival and consider multiple possible futures.

What is immediately observable, in more recent thinking about human learning processes, is the emphasis on socialization. The views and approaches to learning and learning support demonstrate increasing interest in a wide perspective which encompasses more complex ways of learning than those envisioned in stimulus-response theories. The idea that training, education and development happen chiefly because of direct manipulation of observable phenomena has given way. More ambitious perspectives of learning incorporate the influence of past experiences, the physiology of humans, social interaction, and the multiple ways in which people piece together data bits to create information and knowledge.

BEHAVIORAL THEORIES OF LEARNING

While theory has progressed to incorporate a wide variety of viewpoints on human learning, much of the world clings to the term "training," which has accumulated a number of connotations. In general conversation, the word has come to be tied to fairly straightforward and formal events which directly and immediately affect the observable behavior of the participants or subjects. Much of what is understood in society to be "education" shares this connotative definition. Students are usually expected to demonstrate immediate feedback of what they have learned. Much of the traditional view of learning, then, is constructed on a behavioral foundation [2].

The behaviorists correctly identified links among stimuli, conditioning, response and retention activities. According to this approach to learning, the most effective way to address learners is through a directive set of performance objectives that, when clearly derived from job analysis, provide the baseline performance requirements. These performance objectives are then translated into course performance objectives, which specify the ways in which course participants should react within the formal course structure itself. This course is then administered to the subjects, whether in K–12, college, or other organizational settings, with an emphasis on repetitive practice, accompanied by positive reinforcement in order to establish new fixed patterns of behavior. These patterns match the expected performance stated in performance objectives. Each individual is graded or evaluated on the way in which her task performance has changed (either positively or negatively), and on her ability to do the task consistently according to the new scheme, outside of the formal learning environment. Whether the behavior change has to do with structuring paragraphs in an essay or setting up a Mark IV milling machine for auto parts, the principle of learning is the same.

This theory of learning tends to emphasize the roles of the course designer and the change agents (teacher, trainer, parent, supervisor) in generating immediate behavioral change in the subject, and then ensuring reinforcement and retention. In organizational terms used elsewhere, it is a "nuclear" approach. While there is a recognition in behavioral learning theory that the individual learner must be mentally "ready" to learn and to change behavior, this readiness is often assumed in the construction of the behaviorally oriented learning event. There is, from the behaviorist perspective, more to be gained by focus on changes in processes than by focus on changes in the affective domain. Very often, the desire on the part of the subject to make changes in his behavior is simply taken as a given, and not as a potent variable in the learning process. The close linkage between tightly constructed job and course performance objectives is generally so tactically focused that motivation and other potentially non-observable elements that may be at work within the subject are ignored.

Behavioral theory, however, is unable to account effectively for learning which occurs outside of formal situations, which does not offer repetitive and controlled practice and reinforcement routines. Moreover, this theoretical model tends to require a "leader-follower" architecture, which places an instructor or other subject matter expert in control, with the participant acknowledging the leadership and superior knowledge of this person in the learning process. By extension, this form of relationship between teacher and learner has been successfully reproduced in much of the computer-based training and other so-called "self-directed" learning tools, which simply replace a live expert with a recorded one. Such learning support products often rely on the behaviorist bent toward command and control, with the chief requirement that the "follower" accept and comply. Compliance with process changes is the chief metric associated with behavioral theory as applied to learning.

There are some difficulties with transfer of learning, since the learning situation tends to adhere closely to performance objectives which, as noted earlier, are focused in the cognitive and psychomotor domains, rather than the affective domain. The tendency to concentrate on the solution of fairly narrow behavioral "gaps" through such training makes it difficult, outside of the highly controlled learning environment, to bring the learning to bear. This is especially true where the training has to do with new or significantly revised process changes that have not previously been introduced into the performance environment. For example, a child who is taught, in some school setting, the process for setting a table for dinner, including glass, china, and silverware placement for multiple courses, will be unable to transfer that skill if dinner at home is generally taken from microwave to TV tray table. While the ability to set a formal table is admirable, it is not a behavior that is practiced or rewarded in the real world, and will be lost for lack of reinforcement. As training designers attempt to avoid such circumstances by focusing the training itself on actual situations, the performance requirement is narrowed and may lose connectivity with the actual performance environment. It is not a holistic solution.

COGNITIVE THEORIES OF LEARNING

Where behavioral approaches to learning tend to be characterized by high control on the part of the teacher or trainer, cognitive learning theories introduce the mental activities of the learner as significant variables in the process. One of the key findings in cognitive research is that performance may be delayed in time from the learning process. A reward, in other words, need not immediately accompany the performance as a reinforcer. Learning may take place in isolation from performance, and the individual will be able to recall the learning later in a performance situation. In this view, then, the individual controls learning, and it is the individual, not some external overseer, who describes the need for learning; defines when, where, and how learning should take place, and engages in the learning activity. There is an intrinsic motivator that supports this process, as well as the retention of learned capabilities until such time as performance is called for.

This approach to learning and its application in behavior change introduces a level of complexity into the process that was simplified in the behavioral approach. Here, there may be many environmental factors that affect the ultimate performance. Learning a process may be only the beginning. Between the learning event and the actual performance may come other learning and other environmental changes that are difficult to identify and describe in any attempt to trace the connection between learning and performance. Cognitive learning, then, accepts the possibility of modification of learned responses and suggests a dynamic continuity between the learning event and the performance circumstances. This learning theory is highly influenced by the Gestalt school of psychology, which emphasizes the whole rather than multiple individual parts working independently and believes that human cognition operates from patterns, rather than from particulars [2].

Jean Piaget proposed that this approach to learning and thinking happens as a result of two key factors. First, he suggested that human growth and maturation had much to do with the development of cognitive abilities and processes. Second, he believed that growth of cognitive abilities was also linked to increasing interactions with the environment. The development of cognitive abilities is experiential. Age and experience, then, affect learning.

Robert Gagné [3] applied cognitive theory to the learning process, identifying five varieties of capabilities:

1. *Intellectual skills.* This form of skill has to do with the human ability to manipulate and communicate symbolically, rather than literally. Symbols are used "for distinguishing, combining, tabulating, classifying, analyzing, and quantifying objects, events, and even other symbols."
2. *Verbal information.* People learn how to convey their thoughts and information in a structured way, through some construct of spoken or written language. The emphasis is not only on the construction of the information to be communicated, but on the forms and formats through which the information will be transmitted.
3. *Cognitive strategies.* This form of learning has to do with what is often called "learning how to learn." That is, individuals develop different ways of approaching a learning project. Because, as noted above, the learning process is internalized and dependent on maturation and experiences, the history of the individual is influential in the ways he may address learning.
4. *Motor skills.* The use of the human body, as controlled by the person herself, is subject to learning. Strengthening muscles and rehearsing various ways to apply them in selected situations results in improved performance for athletes, pianists, and others who depend on physical intelligence.
5. *Attitudes.* Gagné proposes, finally, that mental states are acquired and used in particular ways. These mental states affect the choices that are made, and

impact the nature of the learning experience. Such attitudes are impacted by environment and experience, and become critical factors in the learning and performance processes.

These five areas constitute a high-level architecture for the types of things that are learned. In addition to these areas classified by Gagné, Howard Gardner [4, 5] and other researchers have extended the understanding of multiple intelligences. As Gardner defines intelligence, it "entails the ability to solve problems or fashion products that are of consequence in a particular cultural setting or community." The perspective Gardner takes is that "human cognitive competence is better described in terms of a set of abilities, talents, or mental skills, which we call 'intelligences.' All normal individuals possess each of these skills to some extent; individuals differ in the degree of skill and in the nature of their combination." Gardner, like Gagné, emphasizes that individual behavior is an individual expression of combinations of skills and capabilities. The concept of multiple intelligence, however, introduces eight, not five, capability areas for human performance.

Gardner's research identifies the following categories of intelligence:

1. *Musical intelligence.* This capability is a universal characteristic, occurring in most, if not all, global societies. It is, moreover, one that has been exhibited throughout recorded human history.

2. *Bodily-kinesthetic intelligence.* Like the motor skills noted by Gagné, there is an aptitude that involves use of muscles and skeletal frame. Originally developed by humans as a basic survival capability, the honing of physical skills has remained an important part of human development. Obvious applications are in entertainment and sports, but more practical applications remain in work that requires careful physical coordination. People who are well skilled in bricklaying, for example, can mix mortar to just the right consistency, get just enough of it onto a trowel, in just the right position, and set a brick that is even and level within seconds. For people without the developed physical skill, this process can drag on for minutes. People with this capability know where their bodies are at all times, and are highly aware of what is happening to them, and how to make desired moves quickly and accurately.

3. *Logical-mathematical intelligence.* This is the capability to solve problems logically and quickly, with an accompanying ability to demonstrate the ways in which the problem was solved. Mathematical ability is linked to particular areas of the brain and their development.

4. *Linguistic intelligence.* Like mathematical intelligence, the ability to express diverse concepts, whether concrete or abstract, in a symbolic language, is one that has been a standard measure of capability.

5. *Spatial intelligence.* This form of intelligence includes the ability to judge distances and to navigate, but also the capability to think in more than one or two dimensions. That is, people with highly developed spatial intelligence can visualize objects from several perspectives, whether or not they can actually view the objects from those other perspectives. This capability is especially useful to artists, who seek to develop an ability to represent objects realistical-

ly, from top, bottom, side, or angular viewpoints. The ability is also useful in facility design and in recalling positions of chess pieces during a game.

6. *Interpersonal intelligence.* This capability is a measure of an individual's empathy and sensitivity to others. In one-to-one or in larger group relationships, the individual with high capabilities in this area will be able to connect with other people and establish bonds at various levels very quickly. The individual is able to associate very closely with other peoples' experiences and to understand emotions and reactions that accompany those experiences, even though the person with high interpersonal intelligence may never have encountered the experience. It is this capability that enhances the capacity of people to form social organizations and to facilitate them.

7. *Intrapersonal intelligence.* This is the capability for self-awareness and self-reflection. The individual who is able to distance himself from actions and events is able to understand those events from a personal perspective, rather than from a group perspective. In a heated business meeting, for example, it is this capability which allows us to draw away from highly charged discussions into a personal assessment of the meaning of the discussion. We often find a different viewpoint and points of compromise only by retreating to an introspective attitude. Sometimes this capability is a source of objectivity that is lacking in more complex engagements with other people. This intelligence contributes to a person's sense of well-being and self-confidence. It is a necessary kernel capability before a person can interact well in interpersonal situations or contribute as effectively as possible in other areas of endeavor.

8. *Naturalist.* In this domain, the individual demonstrates high capability in the recognition and use of features in the physical environment. The practitioner is able to orient herself within a natural terrain and adapt to the features of nature as it is found.

These eight areas provide a wider view of human capability than does the list of five provided by Gagné. Recent efforts in training and development, in fact, have focused on ways in which these characteristics can be enhanced among members of organizations. Such categories form the basic framework for learning. How these capability areas are addressed, however, relies on cognitive processing. A model for the mental activity involved in learning or enhancing capability is represented in Figure 8-1.

In this process, input from the environment comes to the individual through receptors, tuned to receive stimuli and transfer it to the brain. A short-term sensory register holds immediate perceptions. Through an "attention" process, selective elements of the broad range of sensory experiences are held and transferred to short-term memory (up to about 20 seconds) [3]. There is a form of rehearsal or learning activity engaged in the short-term storage process, through which the individual internalizes the impressions that are to be held in the short-term. An encoding process then transfers relevant data from short-term to long-term memory. The long-term memory retains patterns of what is being learned, and not necessarily just a set of facts. The brain integrates any and all impressions from the five capability areas and organizes it for storage. Exactly how this happens is still a mystery, but

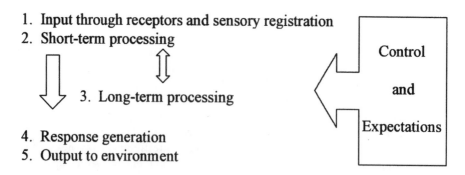

Figure 8-1. Information processing.

research has borne out the use of neural networks which serve to store data in a variety of locations and not as a single memory block.

The long-term storage phenomenon is made more complex by the use of learning devices that may be different from the actual experience itself. That is, when a person hears a story, he may interpret the literal words in symbolic ways, assigning moral or other alternative values to the ideas stated in the story. What may be stored in memory is not only the literal wording of the storyteller, but complex impressions not directly generated either by the storyteller or the story itself. The individual learns by transfer and analogy [6], associating the literal event with other historical events stored in memory, or with recombinations of reality that constitute an imaginative extension of the facts of the story. The stored pattern may not resemble the words of the storyteller in any but the most minute ways.

Retrieval from long-term memory is accomplished through the use of cues that generate the brain activity necessary to reconstitute the patterns. Again, because the long-term stored memories and impressions can be fed to the short-term memory, the possibility exists for the memories to be recombined with newer material, thus generating an adjusted long-term memory. Retrieval from either short-term or long-term memories passes to a response generator. At this stage of recovery of memory, the generator must access two general classes of data. First, it must know which of the sensory outlets to use: voice or other muscles. Second, it must know how to reproduce the memory. That is, it needs some instructions from the stored data as to how to reproduce the information that has been stored. The response becomes a framework consisting of actual performance, along with the ways in which the performance is to be accomplished.

Immediate as well as stored memory may influence how the performance is shaped and programmed for distribution. The pianist, in touching the keys to play a series of chords, will recall the actual notes to play, but also how fast to play them and what pressure to apply to the keys, given the piano that she is currently playing. The transfer of the musical pattern from brain to audio output from the musical instrument will involve more than just mechanical recall of notes and note sequences, but also the attitudinal response desired from the audience as they hear the particular passage. This depends on a highly situational response from the pianist's brain and body functioning as more than a simple information-processing machine. It requires that the interpretation from brain to audience be tempered by instantaneous aggregation of numerous capabilities, with the output highly dependent on the dynamical system that is in place and operating in the concert hall.

The whole system includes continuous feedback in action among the performer, the machine and the audience. No element of this network is isolated from the other, and all are subject to complex variables. The musical instrument itself, for instance, is subject to a history of wear and tear, the state of its soundboard and strings, and the humidity of the operating environment. The pianist is subject to interjections from short-term memory that may include coughing or movement in the audience. She may also be affected by long-term memories which have nothing to do with the immediate performance. The audience, for its part, is subject to individualized impressions and feedback from the environment. Is it too hot, too cold, too crowded? Did it arrive in rain or snow, with subsequent dampness of clothing? Is the lighting on the stage appropriate, and is the piano audible? All of these factors influence the way in which this performance system will operate and its success. It is a system highly dependent on multiple factors, many hinging on cognitive processes and learning.

The way in which this performance actually plays out, and the ways in which memories are acquired and stored, relies on two influences that are not directly built into the processing system itself: executive control and expectancies. Executive control mechanisms are the cognitive strategies developed by an individual in order to aid the effectiveness of the learning process. They are ways to get at what each of us needs in order to make learning successful.

The pianist, for example, may begin to learn a piece of music by playing only the melody line of a passage, repeating it until an impression forms of the flow of that passage, and its interpretation. Then full chords or other figures will be added to the capability, and the whole mechanical performance set into perspective, given the composer's instructions regarding tempo or other performance attributes. Other pianists may approach the learning project differently, perhaps plunging headlong into the detail of an intricate passage, trying to encompass the whole message and direction of the piece, and then concentrating on areas where memorization may pose problems. Some will work immediately with a metronome, some will not.

All of these differences in approaching the learning task derive from ways individuals have found success in the past. Given the choice, we will learn in ways that involve the least indirection, the least trouble, and the most self-satisfaction, whether from intrinsic or extrinsic reward. Our cognitive strategies are designed to get us to a desired learning end, in the shortest period of time with the least amount of effort. These strategies work best when an individual is free to approach the learning project in such a way that strategies can be selected, combined, and modified to suit the person's interpretation of the circumstances.

The "expectancy" that forms in an individual's mind is, like the cognitive strategy, an influence on how learning will take place. Learning is not a given in the cognitive model, nor is the quality or completeness of the learning experience subject to external guarantee. What an individual expects to gain from a learning experience may, in fact, affect the selection and use of cognitive strategies, or executive control mechanisms, as well as directly influencing the way perception is translated through memory into behavior changes. This application of an expectancy concept is strongly related to the expectancy motivation theories discussed elsewhere in this book.

In considering the existing theories of cognition and learning, in particular the work of Piaget, Klaus Riegel added a different dimension to the conception of learning and development. In the mid 1970s Riegel proposed that concepts from the dialectical philosophy of Hegel and others be applied to extend the interpretation of Piaget's model for developmental psychology. Riegel believed that while Piaget had begun to interpret human development, at its earliest stages, in terms of dialectics, he had not included dialectical thought patterns as a part of later development stages. Dialectics, Riegel believes, constitute a core competency of mature humans, and therefore the use of dialectical thinking underlies all of Piaget's stages, and is available to adults as well as to infants.

The implication for adult learning is significant. If adults are presented with fixed answers, closed-end questions, or overly simplistic cases to solve, they will not have an opportunity to exercise their abilities in dialogue or dialectical thinking. This will lead to frustration in the learner, which could act as a block to significant learning or participation in the learning event. Instead, adult learning, to follow Riegel's thinking, should be framed in such a way as to emphasize the dialectical nature of business, organizational relationships, society, and individuals.

In formulating his ideas, Riegel reacts directly against concepts of stability in learning systems. He introduced his "Manifesto for Dialectical Psychology" [7] with this warning:

> By segregating the subject from the object, we escaped into abstract formalism; by preferring static traits and balanced equilibria, we substituted for the human being a mechanistic monster or a mentalist mirage; by disregarding our commitment to the human being and to human culture, we increased our self-constriction instead of our self-awareness; by focusing on static universality, we forgot that the human being is a changing being in a changing world.

For Riegel, it was this relationship, the "changing being in a changing world," that formed the basis for understanding the ways in which humans develop. In taking this Hegelian position, Riegel distanced himself from the ideas of Piaget, in relation to the developmental process in humans. Piaget, as Riegel points out, had proposed a much more static view. The Piagetian notion of development allowed for discrete plateaus of ability and awareness. Riegel rejected the discrete nature of development in humans.

This position regarding the importance of dialogue and dialectic is reinforced in the work of Chris Argyris, who introduced the term "double-loop" learning to refer to "those sorts of organizational inquiry which resolve incompatible organizational norms by setting new priorities and weightings of norms, or by restructuring the norms themselves together with associated strategies and assumptions" [8]. He expands on this idea with the explanation that "individual members resolve the interpersonal and intergroup conflicts which express incompatible requirements by creating new understandings of the conflicting requirements, their sources, conditions, and consequences—understandings which then become embedded in the images and maps of organization." Effective learning, then, is manifested in situations in which individuals, teams, and full organizations allow the existence of highly sensitive and widely available feedback networks. It is feedback, dialogue, discussion, and the dialectical interplay of ideas that coalesces learning from individuals into learning that can be used and reapplied by a group.

Much of the dialectical nature of human learning surfaces in dialogue [9]. The value of dialogue is that, if it occurs in a non-biased, open, and non-destructive way, it helps humans think about complex situations, and to recall and reapply learned facts and concepts which may have been stored in memory. There is a connectivity that is established among people engaging actively in a dialogue, and this network then forms the basis through which ideas, concepts, and practices can be formed and reformed. This constitutes the best use of dialectic and results in highly effective learning by all involved. It is a foundation of Senge's discipline of "Team Learning," but is also vital to the discipline of "Shared Vision." Visions that have not been internalized and adopted in the cognitive interplay of an organization or group will not be a shared building block for further growth and thinking and learning. Dialectic, as it is played out in dialogue, embraces both agreement and disagreement, with the ultimate intent to reach some different level of understanding of the subjects of the dialogue.

The constructivist thinkers, who emphasize the personal nature of learning processes, offer another view of cognition. This emphasis is due, in large part, to an increased understanding of the importance of the executive control and expectancy functions in the learning process. A learner constructs the learning situation, tailoring it deliberately to achieve a desired capability [10]. The research into the ways in which individuals develop and use cognitive strategies has yielded several findings significant to learning and learning support. In particular, anchored learning, also known as situated learning, is a way to support metacognition [11]; open space technology [12] has been offered as a support technique for organizational learning and development initiatives; and the place of lectures and "telling" has been clarified in its role in support of metacognitive capability development [13].

The cognitive approach to learning theory, then, offers considerably more potential for influence from factors external to the learner and any closed environment. The assumption is that the information-processing model represents, in large part, the functions that take place at the individual level, and that the interplay among individuals in an organization reapplies this construct at a higher level. A learning organization is dependent on the ability of the whole organization to combine and recombine its various impressions and memories under the influence of a shared executive control, or vision, with a shared expectancy [14].

The greater the degree of alignment of the expectancy, then the more benefit the organization derives from learning experiences. Learning organizations will not succeed without individual and collective commitment to a learning process. From this collective commitment come the changes that are necessary to energize the organization. Changes—especially massive changes—must be supported by cooperative efforts that span the organization's network. Learning and its effect will, otherwise, fail to lead to substantive change.

Dialectic is, at least in the human portion of the organization, the dynamic engine that powers the process. The result is a constantly learning organization, as its collective memories are reassembled, questioned, and reapplied, with behavior change, as observed from the environment, that is proportional to the dynamics of the internal learning that is taking place. Learning organization theory, then, is closely allied with cognitive psychology, and cognitive approaches to collective learning. It offers a unified view of how organizations operating in diverse cultural environments and open to strong influences from their systems environment can cohesively and consistently deliver products and services. The learning organization can be viewed as a unifying and stabilizing construct for organizations that need to replace a nuclear structure.

HUMANISTIC THEORIES OF LEARNING

In contrast with the more directive theories is another learning theory, humanism, which places high emphasis on individual learner initiative. Many of the characteristics associated with this perspective come from the work of Abraham Maslow, a psychologist who devoted much of his career to the understanding of human motivation. It was Maslow who proposed a construct that has gained some popularity in organizational change, the hierarchy of needs. The hierarchy proposes that human motivation springs from a number of satisfiers, and that the satisfiers are dependent upon each other—hence the hierarchical structure of the concept. As Maslow [15] described this relationship:

> Human needs arrange themselves in hierarchies of prepotency. That is to say, the appearance of one need usually rests on the prior satisfaction of another, more pre-potent need. Man is a perpetually wanting animal. Also no need or drive can be treated as if it were isolated or discrete; every drive is related to the state of satisfaction or dissatisfaction of other drives.

The relationship that Maslow proposed, included five needs (in order of hierarchy, top to bottom):

Self-Actualization—At this level of satisfaction, people are acclimated with the world, by finding a place in it that allows them to explore their potential to the fullest extent possible. As Maslow succinctly stated it, "What a man can be, he must be." The outcome from such self-realization is creativity. The person who is satisfied with her situation, and is satisfied that she is doing those things for which she is best suited and which meet her personal goals, will then focus on activities and actions which extend that self-satisfaction into a variety of creative acts. The person who is satisfied with who they are and what they are can leave behind most of the concerns with survival or politics or established processes, and explore options and possibilities. There is, for the self-actualized person, less need to worry about day-to-day events, and thus more opportunity to think about experimental and conceptual potentiality. Narrow viewpoints of life, social activity, work activity, are subordinated to a wider scope of interest with the knowledge that the elemental needs have been met.

Esteem—This factor in the motivation hierarchy has to do with the extent to which an individual perceives himself to be respected within the social milieu of which he is a part. It is a need for stability and respect. The skilled employee wants to be recognized as a person, but also as a person who has perfected and honed his skills in ways that others have not. Each individual wants to be more than a time-clock number or name on a class roster. In an English class with 65 other students, each person wants to be known for his specific characteristics and contributions and strengths. This level of need satisfaction supports self-confidence and the person's sense that he is useful to organizations and to society at large.

Love—This category includes affection and connections with other people that go beyond the practical. It is, in a way, a need that calls for a high level of socialization, with the expectation that this social activity will lead to the establishment of bonds with other people. These bonds go beyond the practical contribution that one human can make to another through assistance with tasks or problem solving and enters the realm of psychological bonding. In this realm, a person knows another person more intimately than would be the case in a casual organizational relationship. It is a highly personal association with the other individual, including emotional stabilization for both parties. As Maslow notes, "practically all theorists of psychopathology have stressed thwarting of the love needs as basic in the picture of maladjustment." Failure to establish such relationships, then, is not only detrimental to the individual himself, but may influence others in the organizations of which the individual is a part [16].

Safety— This is a strong and dominant need which follows close behind satisfaction of physiological needs. Here, the need is for protection and reassurance. There is also a strong requirement for stability and predictability at this level in the hierarchy. Even rigid control of schedules, actions and activities is acceptable to an individual in order to meet this need. Nuclear organization and structure are welcomed at this level, and supervisor-subordinate relationships can thrive. The supervisor's sense of safety may be met through the presence of a staff reporting to her, while the subordinate's need is met by acceptance of a passive role. The parent-child behavior model has often been noted as an example of this form of relationship that satisfies the safety need on both sides. The parent is satisfied by knowing that the child will carry forward the family, and thus protect it, as well as by the thought that the child may one day become the protector of the parent. The parent finds safety in the sense of family, and therefore group, that exists when there is a child present who clings to the parent or seeks sustenance from the parent. The child, alternatively, is satisfied because the parent is in the role of physical and economic protector and provider. It is within the family group that the child is first socialized, and the reliance on this family social group is important to the sense of stability and history that the child develops.

The manifestation of safety in society is generally through reliance on rules and regulations, policies and procedures that exist to maintain the common good. Speed limits, highway markings, exit signs, fire departments, and police departments all speak of the strong need to satisfy safety requirements through control mechanisms designed, in many instances, to protect us from ourselves. At the very least, such mechanisms are intended to provide a strong basic sense of stability, habit, and familiarity in a turbulent world.

Physiological—Maslow notes the reality that, given a full range of choices, we will eat those things that satisfy some bodily need. The operation of the bodily chemistry is the dominant driver for our diets, unless we consciously suppress the needs. In addition to this basic urge to satisfy the complex human physical machine, there are other needs in this category defined by our various senses. Sunlight, after a long string of cloudy and rainy days, for example, provides us with a more positive mood. Our brain, often assailed by the hum of electronic equipment, noise from aircraft, vehicles, televisions and radios, enjoys moments of quiet. We get sensations of satisfaction from touching certain fabrics, or the skin of another person. Humans cannot exist in total darkness, quiet, and isolation. The mediation of these circumstances, with a variety of sensory inputs, is as necessary as food. Gratification of these various physical needs results in the essential level of satisfaction that is necessary to support construction of sequential levels of the motivation hierarchy.

As we operate within this hierarchy, we learn. Here, the learning is less easy to quantify and observe than the learning proposed through a behavioral approach. Humanistic learning theory places emphasis on the learning activities initiated by individuals to help them satisfy themselves throughout the levels of the hierarchy. Learning where to find foods for which we have a craving, or learning how to establish a loving relationship with another individual are examples of self-initiated learning, driven not by a desire to overpower or overwhelm or win, but instead by the intrinsic and individual needs which arise dynamically within us.

Learning becomes a tool with which we satisfy our needs, regardless of level or intensity. Successful learning results in a climb up through the hierarchy. The satisfaction of needs, then, is viewed as a human strength, providing advantages as people move higher up the levels. Much of this psychological theory as explained by Maslow and developed by Carl Rogers has worked its way into an attitude toward learning that supports self-directed approaches. It is the basis for work by Malcolm Knowles [17, 18], who introduced the concept of andragogy, that is learning and learning support as carried out particularly by and for adults. Andragogy has been influential in the development of many of the principles and practices that now are to be found in the general discipline of adult learning. The foundation of these principles relies heavily on humanistic psychology.

As Knowles defines the characteristics of andragogy, he emphasizes four general domains. First, the concept of the learner is self-directed. That is, people learn things that they are motivated to learn, when they are motivated to learn them, and this motivation is highly internal, individual, and situational. Second, learners will bring to any learning activity, whether formal or informal, a psychological background and history. They do not arrive without some form of experience, and experience affects the way they learn, the things they learn, and what they do with what they have learned. Third, learning success depends on readiness to learn. This readiness is highly dependent on self-perceived and formulated needs. This drive to learn may develop from projects in which people are engaged, from interpersonal relationships in which people seek to be successful, and from problems that need to be solved. In all instances, learning is supported by real-life situations. Fourth, there is an orientation to learning that integrates it into life. Whether goal-directed or immediately practical, the learning that is undertaken by the individual is fully integrated into the needs for individual competence that have arisen in the individual's personal or organizational life. There is a volatility that supplants stability in various organizational settings. Within this environment, learning must play a significant and continuing role, as people adapt to change and to the increased pace of change. This emphasis on learning, therefore, translates into forms of learning which do not fit the patterns established by formal learning events. Nor does learning relate solely to a given period in life. The concept of lifelong learning suggests an ongoing human strategy to remain current, or even ahead of the environment, in order to maximize the position in the hierarchy of needs.

In an age of knowledge and its application, and in an environment in which creativity and innovation are key to organizational success, the individual's ability to learn constantly, under varied circumstances, with various forms of support and input, becomes vital both to the individual and to the organization. The burden for learning shifts to the individual learner, and away from teachers and trainers. The focus is now on ways in which organizations within society can provide useful support to the learner. These characteristics allow the learning and behavior change process to become more open and less rigid or nuclear. In turn, learning begins to drive organizational circumstances, processes, and performance, and the kernel of the learning organization is established.

SOCIAL LEARNING THEORY

Perhaps the most direct approach to learning has been accommodated in the ideas of social learning theory. According to this viewpoint, people learn, by and large, by watching other people. Originally a subset of behavioral learning, the expansion of social learning beyond that major theory set came with the further exploration of ways in which people learn through association with others. Bandura [19] feels that at least some of the reasoning behind social learning theory lies in reaction to the idea of fixed human traits. This reflects the findings of psychologists who have advocated an approach to understanding human behavior that is nonlinear. If our behavior and our characteristics are as subject to change as these researchers have suggested, we may be applying a nonlinear approach to our learning projects and our activities. Social learning theory supports the idea that much of our learning and subsequent behavior is spontaneous. That is, in terms of chaos theory, we interpret the fitness landscape dynamically and may react to our environment with apparent randomness. Social learning theory would provide a dynamic stability to apparently radical actions by suggesting that the behavior is the result of a definable learning process.

Two factors have emerged which appear to interact to determine behavior. The first is the individual and the second is the situation. The focus, in social learning, on situation is somewhat different than a focus on the whole environment. Rather, the definition of a situation is specific to a time, place, and set of events and circumstances, rather than incorporating everything. The other factor, the individual herself, will also influence the behavior that results in a combination with the environmental situation.

A keystone in the operation of social learning lies in the understanding of modeling and how people use modeling to develop their behaviors. The internalization process begins with a model that is observed or experienced by a potential learner. The potentiality is realized through the application, within the learner, of various attentional processes which serve to attract the learner to the model. Retention processes, similar to those encountered in cognitive information processing, enable the learner to store the memory of the model. Motor reproduction processes come into play as the individual converts the experience with the model into a personal interpretation. The conversion process incorporates a form of successive approximation through which the learner practices the new capability in various ways. This practice may occur under the same or similar circumstances as those in which the model was observed, or the learner may attempt to apply the learned capability in different circumstances. For example, in a situation in which the learner has been presented with a budget model for a multi-billion dollar organization, he may want to apply the model to home finances, which rarely offer the same circumstances. During this process, there may be reference to the original model, which serves as a form of feedback as to how closely the new behavior is approximating the model behavior. The final important stage in the process involves the observation of consequences. The behaviors that are accepted for modeling and the behaviors that result from social learning are highly dependent on the perception on the part of the learner that positive consequences will result.

Neutral or negative consequences will act as a deterrent to imitation or adaptation of the model. For example, if career-minded people observe that many mid-managers are the subject of layoffs and tend to be the first group cut in organizational downsizing, the model may suggest a negative impact to a mid-management position. This may serve to deter some people from accepting such positions, and may, in fact, deter them from preparing themselves for such positions. Their development sequence may be self-contained and diverted away from management simply by observing the potential consequences of career development in that path. Moreover, even the deliberate creation of positive models may not generate imitation. A number of things may contribute to non-performance according to a predicted model. Again, the behavior of humans as nonlinear agents allows us the luxury to ignore cues and resolve needs in creative, individualized ways. This is one of the most open forms of learning.

At the same time that the process of social learning offers no guarantees of behavioral outcome, it is one of the most widely used ways to learn. Much of our learning is carried on outside of formal classes or learning support events, and much of it occurs as we try to model ourselves on our heroes and heroines, on our parents, or on others whom we select quietly but consciously. It requires a conscious decision to adopt a behavioral pattern, and it takes a conscious decision to ignore one.

Marsick and Watkins [20] believe that an understanding of informal and incidental learning, often accomplished through social learning methods, is important for an holistic view of learning as practiced. For organizations that have moved to open or virtual architectures, and away from nuclear structures, non-routine becomes a way of organizational life. Moreover, in circumstances which now exist where organizational performance relies on global market behaviors, organizational change is a given. Learners in such volatile circumstances, then, will turn to informal ways to organize and conduct their learning, and a primary source of learning support is the human model available for imitation [21, 22].

On-the-job learning has often been praised for its efficiency. It is the ultimate in the use of models to derive learning, as a new employee will observe an experienced employee in the conduct of processes. The new employee then tries the activity, and through practice—guided, observed, and coached by the experienced master—attains the needed capability. This, at least, is how it should work. This is the purest form of learning, as apprentice works with master, both producing a usable product or service, while at the same time absorbing the methods and processes for success. In terms of organizational cost, this form of learning has long been advocated for its low costs. There are no formal courses to design, develop and deliver, nor are there any trainers to pay or training facilities to maintain. No materials are needed, other than those ordinarily required for job performance.

In practice, the horror stories around on-the-job training (OJT) abound. In one instance a bank teller, just out of high school and newly hired by a small bank, was brought in on her first day and paired with an experienced teller. The day went well, with the apprentice teller spending most of her time observing the ways in which the master teller worked with the customers, providing them either direct service or referrals to loan specialists, investment specialists, etc. The apprentice watched as the teller handled the money and a wide selection of other forms associated with the transactions. Throughout the day, the experienced teller answered questions and explained how the transactions were being handled, as she was able to given the workload at the window. At the end of the day the experienced teller closed out the drawer, and both teller and apprentice went home.

The next morning, when the apprentice reported for work, she was told that the experienced teller had called in sick and the apprentice would have to stand in for her. There was no one else to work the window. The apprentice, years later, reported that somehow she made it through the day, nervously, and with a great deal of hesitation, but managed, by accident, to come up with the right balance for the drawer at the end of the day. This experience with on-the-job training is common. The advantage of social learning theory is that it proposes some of the ways in which these forms of learning happen, and suggests some avenues for improving the process for OJT, and for maximizing the effective use of modeling and simulation in learning and learning support.

SOCIALIZATION OF THE LEARNING PROCESS

Regardless of the fact that learning is chiefly an individual activity, there is a growing emphasis on individuals learning in groups and communities. This socialization of learning has come as researchers have discovered that effective transfer of learning and effective behavioral change require the intermingling of learners in a performance setting [23]. In circumstances in which individuals have been separately trained or prepared, there can be difficulties in applying the learned behaviors in a process environment that may not support them. Learning that is undertaken under specialized or generic circumstances is difficult to integrate into some environments. For instance, a person who attends an open course on financial forecasting may or may not be able to use the techniques and tools from the course in his job. Even if his job entails some form of forecasting financial needs and cash flows, the policies and accounting practices in the organization may not accommodate the procedures as learned. In other circumstances, the individual may have attended a training course tailored to the organization's financial planning processes, and may have learned very specifically how to acquire forecast data, enter it into formulated spreadsheets, produce reports, and translate the report data into budget actions. The week following the course, however, the finance organization, reacting to market conditions and the installation of new software, changes the forecasting package radically, along with the associated processes. The learner is once again left with nothing tangible to show for the learning effort.

Alternatively, the social nature of learning tends to integrate the theoretical with the practical, and tie process to practice in ways that stimulate transfer. Informal learning is highly adaptive, and tends to be generative as well. That is, while a great deal of it is repetition of observed behavior, much of it is also unique and contributes new ideas, viewpoints or ways of doing things. Where the learning is double-loop, involving high degrees of feedback, it tends to become creative, with constructive applications common. Socialized learning, because it involves multiple people, and multiple ideas, results in the learning of capabilities and the development of skillsets, though not necessarily precise and standardized process steps. Such process steps, we have learned, are changeable, and more often than not change radically.

While continuous improvement in systemic processes may result in moderate or small changes over time, there are often instances, especially where growth is a key characteristic of the environment, in which more radical change will be encountered. Even given small changes in a continuous improvement architecture, some of these changes will require changes in practice and processes that call for new learning. If the learning is allowed to drive the process definition, then the need for learning will always be present. If learning is driven by process changes, then the need for learning may or may not be acknowledged in the system.

As more people, in flatter and more open organizations, begin to play multiple roles in the processes of the organization, the likelihood is higher that learning will be a constant activity and will be generative, driving change. Socialization of the organization, evidenced by flattening of hierarchies and the opening of organizational structures to external and internal influences, is leading to increased needs for people to learn among themselves, to learn quickly, and to coordinate that learning into action in efficient ways in multiple and changing circumstances. Such socialization supports a view of learning that is inclusive, not exclusive, of ideas, people and new opportunities. It is based on patterns, or formulas, which can be understood from a variety of perspectives, and which, with some specialized tailoring, can be adapted flexibly into a variety of situations.

COOPERATIVE LEARNING

One of the manifestations of socialization has been a continued emphasis on learning activities that call for people to contribute their perspectives and knowledge to a learning "pool." This approach encourages participation on the part of everyone in a learning group and encourages the development of new ideas and innovative thinking. The learning process is omni-directional and does not depend on the teacher or instructor as subject matter expert and final authority on learning processes or outcomes. Cooperative learning works in situations where individuals participate fully and actively, and where teachers and instructors can fade into the background, acting in roles of facilitators and coaches. The burden of success lies with the participants in the activity. What often happens is that, as the facilitators give up the burden of running the classes, they become as actively engaged in the learning process as anyone else.

PROBLEM-BASED LEARNING

An effective subset of cooperative learning is problem-based learning, which began as a way to enrich situation-based learning, such as case studies, by opening the situations to wider interpretation, and asking the students or course participants to play a larger role in shaping the situational model. The rigorous pre-preparation of the case study approach gives way to a goal-based initiative in which the students are fully engaged. They, in essence, define the situation and the needs and issues arising from the situation.

Bridges and Hallinger [24] offer these characteristics of problem-based learning:

1. The starting point for learning is a problem.
2. The problem is one that students are apt to face as future professionals.
3. The knowledge that students are expected to acquire during their professional training is organized around problems rather than the disciplines.
4. Students, individually and collectively, assume a major responsibility for their own instruction and learning.
5. Most of the learning occurs within the context of small groups rather than lectures.

A problem, as defined here, may be generally defined as any issue or question for which solutions or answers are being sought. The intent of the learning situation is to allow the learner to form generalized patterns of responses and solutions, and define the variables in a given situation that will illustrate the ways in which the patterns might be applied most effectively. The intent is not to teach an individual to solve a single, well-defined problem, but to help the individual construct a cognitive and affective map which can be recalled and modified for a situations which may resemble those developed through the guided learning experience.

TEAM LEARNING

A key factor in the success of cooperative learning is the use of team or group settings that develop a richness of responses, dialogue, and resolutions. Team-based learning has long been viewed as a valuable subset of organizational learning, regardless of the makeup of the teams. The most effective construct is the intact team, which is ordinarily joined in some joint process or operation. Such teams can benefit from developing capabilities with each other, since the learning situation may offer opportunities for dialogue and practice that are not available in the organizational setting. Since these teams constitute mini-communities of practitioners, each member brings not only his or her special knowledge and capabilities, but also an existing interpersonal relationship with the rest of the group. While this can have negative as well as positive impact, such group learning can, in fact, help to resolve some internal team development issues or bring them to the surface, where effective resolution can be started. This, of course, is itself a form of learning that has more to do with the affective domain than with cognitive or psychomotor domains, but is important to the well-being of the team and the individuals who comprise it. The team learning activity, then, whether in a formal setting, apart from the day-to-day organizational environment, or embedded in daily processes and routines, can provide the architecture to support cooperative learning.

The alternative grouping strategy is to assemble learning teams whose members are not directly or closely related to each other in usual circumstances. Open and virtual organizational dynamics are making this an increasingly necessary approach, as representatives of various departments or sub-organizations, including vendors and customers, are assembled from across the supply chain. In this way, a "seed" team is formed which encourages cooperative learning and later cooperative work across and through any artificial organizational boundaries that may exist.

ORGANIZATIONAL LEARNING

While cooperative learning can be obtained across an organization, it becomes more difficult as the organization grows larger. At the point at which multiple cultures are being integrated, in some form, into the supply chain, and at the point where multiple languages begin to influence the way an organization operates, cross-organizational learning begins to lose focus. Learning becomes more culturally centered, and what is acceptable in London is less acceptable in Hong Kong or São Paulo. While geographical distinctions may impact learning and operational effectiveness in teams, it becomes a major factor at full organizational level. The ways in which cross-organizational learning is supported, then, becomes a major consideration for any large group.

One answer is to maximize the effectiveness of local teams and individuals, with focus on learning strategies that are common to the culture or region. This means duplication of effort, unless enough forethought goes into the development of formal learning support materials and events to allow tailoring to suit local tastes. The success for this approach to global learning in an organization lies, as it does in problem-based learning, with the identification of core patterns and goals. Each group, regardless of its cultural history, can address those common factors, and thus link with other global groups in a common thread of dialogue.

Another answer to the learning needs of a large global organization is to develop common learning experiences that deliberately bring together representatives of various regions and cultures. Close association, as with diverse team approaches, can be used to foster dialogue and promote learning at cognitive, affective, and psychomotor levels. Such experiences, however, must be loosely structured to allow for framing of issues and topics from a variety of global perspectives. This venue, like diverse team groupings, should be expected to result in increased communication after any formal events, and increased coordination and consolidation of processes and organizational work. A key precept to remember is that organizational learning cannot lose sight of the individuals who constitute the organization. The company or practice or church or school must remember that it is not a thing apart from the people who take part in it, whether as worshipers, students, partners or employees. This is the core idea that must inform any attempt to address organizational learning, since no organizational learning can take place unless it is constituted in the individuals.

ACTION SCIENCE

The attempt to make close links between agents and their behavioral environments is one that is common to any socially oriented discipline. Psychologists try to represent the environment in experiments, sociologists seek both overt and subtle links between individuals and their environments, and teachers are concerned with the influence of environments on the education process and vice versa. The essential nature of action science is to let learning and change strategies emerge from the environment in such a way that they are natural parts of it. Like problem-based learning, action learning is intended to develop solutions for issues that exist in real life processes and activities, rather than spend time and effort developing artificial simulations, exercises, case studies, or other representations of reality. Action science is the first row in a Shakespearean theatre, where the actors and audience often mingle, and the audience members often become caught up in the play. Those engaged in action science are solving real-life problems and making real-life changes, with the help of coaches and active mentors who are a part of the action science continuum. This approach may involve teams, but may also emphasize individual learning, development, and change management through a guided issue solution process.

As described by Watkins and Shindell [25], "action science begins with a view of human beings as designers of their actions in the service of achieving intended consequences. They make sense of their surroundings by constructing meanings, both cultural and individual, of their environment. These constructed meanings, in turn, guide actions. In action science, behavior is evaluated for consistency and validity against those internalized beliefs and meaning systems that individuals hold." This approach to organizational behavior, then, acknowledges the influence of the individual agents within the organization, and the ways in which organizational change depends upon those agents.

LIFELONG LEARNING

Because we have been taught to think of learning as the result of some formal experience in classroom or conference room, it is difficult to think that learning processes are active outside those environments and beyond the time devoted to formal events. The significance of lifelong learning becomes apparent when the impact of open and virtual organizational arrangements is understood. As the participation and membership in single organizations become less common than participation and membership in multiple organizational arrangements, learning becomes less tied to the well-being of a single organization. Here, as noted in other theoretical constructs above, the emphasis shifts from learning job- and task-specific steps and processes to pattern-based learning (capability acquisition), which can serve in a wide range of circumstances.

Contractors and consultants know this well. If they prepare a standard approach to customers and clients, they may well lose credibility, because one client does not necessarily want to adopt another client's solution. The perception within organizations is that the circumstances in that group are different from circumstances in some other group. Each enterprise must be engaged on its own terms. Solutions, which may well have some kernel self-similarity, are developed differently as they are adjusted to the circumstances at a given time and place. It is not sufficient to change the logo at the top of a form, and assume that it will work for the next client. Learning, then, for the consultant or contractor, lies in three key areas: how to address and maintain a relationship with a temporary client; how to develop the general competencies and capabilities which make up a consulting platform; and how to integrate oneself into a client organization deeply enough, if only temporarily, to implement an effective specific solution derived form the potions and jars on the capability shelf. The learning process that revolves around these three core capability domains is ongoing.

Learning, then, becomes a survival habit, rather than just an event-focused activity. It has less to do with attending the occasional seminar than with the constant pursuit of the three capabilities. As membership in organizations, over long periods of time, becomes less of a promise and more of an accident, this consultative approach to organizational learning and performance is following that trend. Even those who are full-time members of organizations often find their roles expanded in flattened and downsized organizations so that they are expected to know more about cross-functional operations than previously.

As silos disappear, we often replace them with a model of organization that calls for the integration and multiplexing of the entire supply chain, including direct and indirect elements. The vertically organized system is replaced by an image of a horizontally multi-layered system, with broad requirements for capability among its members. Capability development is viewed by participants as a way to remain viable within the organization, and a way to flex as the organization flexes to keep up with the marketplace. Individuals now participate in a free or almost free market for their services. Applications of capabilities are still important on a resume, but equally important is the ability to adjust and adapt to a new situation. The focus of capability now extends beyond a 20- or 30-year career, beyond a single company, and beyond a single industry category. The value of learning in the marketplace is enhanced, and it plays a significant role at a lower point in the layers that Maslow described as necessary for satisfaction.

MASTERY LEARNING

The idea that an individual should pursue learning until a topic is mastered is surprisingly simple, but chiefly ignored in the practices of education and training. Because much of the curricula available currently are delivered through live classroom methods, time has been a determining factor in acquisition of knowledge, skills and attitudes. A yearly survey (1998) of training activity in the U.S. [26] reports that a live instructor in a local classroom delivers 70% of courses. While this figure is less than the 81% reported in 1997, there is little variance year over year. Training delivered by computer, which is a way to move around formal class time requirements using "time-shifted" learning, accounts for only 19% of the formal training courses available. Delivery mechanisms alone, then, offer less opportunity for individuals to take the time they may need to master subjects.

Moreover, while mastery learning leads to improved organizational performance, organizations are slow to use any rigorous forms of performance evaluation to establish achievement and mastery. Lack of evaluation is a negative motivator to the learner, who comes to believe that attending a class or session is sufficient. They, the instructors, and administrative managers have come to equate attendance with capability acquisition, and many management groups require only the reporting of class attendance to demonstrate successful training investment. There is conceptual confusion across all stakeholders in training, regarding the purpose of training sessions and expected outcomes. Yet, there is no guarantee that a person walking out of a training session will have acquired 100% of the capability she went in to get, and lack of measurement, other than subjective measurement, denies any illustration that behaviors were changed to a point of mastery.

The concept of mastery itself can lead to confusion. It has often been associated with training based on behavioral principles, with mastery clearly defined as an ability to meet 100% of the objectives established for the course. Unless the objectives are extremely well articulated, however, mastery is more complicated. It implies that the individual can perform the skills in the training environment but also in the performance environment in the organizational system. It is not sufficient to prove that an individual can simulate the processes. Mastery requires that the individual be able to demonstrate consistent performance capability on the job, over various repetitions, and over a period of time. Retention thus becomes a significant requirement for mastery. Again, current measurement usually does not demand this rigor in establishing mastery. This is particularly true in management, leadership, intrapersonal and interpersonal skills training courses, where definitive measures of successful performance are often ignored.

SYNERGY

One of the general outcomes of socialization is the development of synergy in teams and larger groups. Synergy plays a role in the learning process as well as in the organizational processes that depend on highly networked operations. The concept suggests that activities carried on by groups are more likely to produce higher levels of outcomes and higher quality output than activities carried on separately by individuals. There is, therefore, incremental value in team or group efforts which is missing in individual efforts. This belief in the power of team-based problem-solving and other group efforts has resulted in considerable interest in how collaborative efforts can be fine-tuned to yield the greatest outputs.

Much of the recent work in teambuilding concepts and approaches has been devoted to maximizing the use of teams and small groups, and linking this work together into a larger organizational frame. The challenge undertaken in such efforts is that of ensuring group cohesiveness and effectiveness, and ensuring that the proper capabilities exist in the team in order to underwrite the tasks and processes associated with the team. Team processes, outputs, and learning must be internally coordinated, with the clear understanding that teams are composed of individuals. So, at the same time that team interests and infrastructures must be built, the needs of the individual cannot be ignored. If this happens, and the structure of the team begins to overshadow the well-being of the individual, the effort will fail.

Synergy depends on the balances that are struck between the needs of the team and the needs of the individual, as the needs of both are satisfied to achieve some level of motivation. There is, then, a hierarchy of needs which applies to the individual, and which must be honored, at the same time that the group is fashioning a hierarchy of needs which is shared. It is in this dynamic of team organization that learning to share and learning to trust become significant attributes of the cognitive scheme. It is not enough to dwell on the mechanics of getting things done. It is necessary, in order to achieve synergistic collaboration, to surround process with assurance and commitment. In other words, self-confidence must be developed as a level in the team motivation hierarchy, along with process, product, and service skills.

Beyond the team level, of course, lies some other organizational structure that may be construed or presented as a larger team environment. While the larger corporate body may prefer to consider itself a team, achieving synergy at this level becomes far more complex than achieving it at sub-group levels. At corporate, or mega-organization levels, communication throughout the entire network becomes more difficult, and is often complicated by the insistence on the use of layers and levels to denote importance of sub-groupings. The tendency to classify and categorize, which serves us so well in many applications, may in fact undermine team-building and organizational network construction.

There is, when organizations are large, a strong tendency to delegate and to hold people accountable for sub-group operations, and to establish separate layers of hierarchy in the belief that these will optimize the "management" of the organization. However, once "management" becomes a primary driver for organization, there is a loss of synergy as levels are established and areas of responsibility defined. Where, in smaller organizations and in teams, the expectation is that there will be close collaboration and internetworking toward some common goals, this approach to system behavior tends to be lost in larger organizational structures.

The result is that fiefdoms and silos develop, even with best efforts at maintaining openness and integral communications. Such silos will, even so, reduce the flow of people, ideas, and generative learning so that attempts at constructing networks are foiled. The network is subjected to hierarchical layering and every such layer or subdivision tends to encourage bureaucratic walls. Processes, policies and procedures are developed within those walls that do not represent the whole organization, but only a subset of it. The network is effectively shut down.

The choking off of a network, and its subsequent ability to optimize combined energy among individuals and teams within the larger organization, happens both vertically and horizontally. That is, the evolution of a vertical layering, such as that produced by "management," will lead to separations among the layers, separate goals and objectives at each layer, and the potential for dissolution of consistency and synergy. To "fix" this problem, a meta-management group is put in place and called the "executive" group. This group takes as its mission to separate itself from the rest of the life of the organization and develop standardized processes and procedures and policies that apply to all layers in the organization. Generally, their mission is to ensure stability in the organization, offering this as a justification for what is a "controller" role.

While the vertical dynamic thus leads toward stabilization, the lateral dynamic proceeds in the same direction. Where layers develop vertically, silos develop laterally, with customers, suppliers and various other groups in the whole supply chain classified and set apart from each other. The tendency is for each group to withhold from the other, with highly refined rituals for communicating from one group to the other. Each silo, like each layer, maintains its own focus, and constructs its own stable environment, with policies and procedures and "management."

So collaboration and subsequent synergy, in an open and networked environment, are often defeated at the higher levels of organization. Lack of synergy at these levels will translate into less effective collaboration and process at team level, and may render team activity nonproductive. The learning that enables and results from open organizational environments is lost in a collection of subdivisions and categories that should have been an integrated network. The dynamics of such organizations tend to wind down, burdened by efforts to accomplish tasks through the various barriers which have been erected. The organizational value which can be derived from synergy is lost.

The shift to a wider perspective, then, has offered a way for organizations to address volatile and changing conditions and modify their learning and learning support mechanisms in recognition of the natural presence of uncertainty in organizational dynamics. The trend toward socialization of learning has paralleled trends toward open and virtual organizational structures. The challenge to ensure the dynamics of the organization lies at individual, sub-group and group levels, as diversity requires new ways of organizing and thinking.

The learning theories which tend to provide the highest levels of support for open organizations are those which emphasize the uniqueness of individuals and their contributions and the ability of individuals to construct their own meanings from their environments. People, as individuals, bring unique perspectives and strategies to the learning activity and incorporate learning as a natural part of doing [27]. The activity of learning and behavior change is not very far removed from everyday life. Yet, there are ways in which learners can hone their learning capabilities, either individually or from the perspective of their place in networks [28]. There are also ways in which learning support practices can support learning in uncertain and changing conditions. These practices should be the focus of individuals, sub-groups and larger organizations, as an understanding of chaos in systems is clarified through research and practice.

REFERENCES

1. Eby, F. and C. F. Arrowood, *The History and Philosophy of Education Ancient and Medieval,* New York: Prentice-Hall, 1940, pp. 5–6.
2. Merriam, S. B. and R. S. Caffarella, *Learning in Adulthood,* San Francisco: Jossey-Bass, 1991.
3. Gagné, R. M., *The Conditions of Learning and Theory of Instruction,* 4th ed, Chicago: Holt, Rinehart and Winston, 1985, pp. 47–48, 71–72.
4. Gardner, H., *Multiple Intelligences: The Theory in Practice,* New York: HarperCollins, 1993, p. 15.
5. Pennar, K., "How Many Smarts Do You Have?" *Business Week,* No. Sept. 16, 1996, pp. 104–108.
6. Tarpy, R. M., *Contemporary Learning Theory and Research,* New York: The McGraw-Hill Companies, 1997, p. 548.
7. Riegel, K. F., "The Dialectics of Human Development," *American Psychologist,* Vol. 31, No. Oct. 1976, pp. 689–699, p. 696.
8. Argyris, C. and D. A. Schön, *Organizational Learning: A Theory of Action Perspective,* Reading, Mass.: Addison-Wesley, 1978, p. 24.
9. Senge, P. M., *The Fifth Discipline: The Art and Practice of the Learning Organization,* New York: Doubleday Currency, 1990, pp. 14, 68.
10. Glaser, R., *Application and Theory: Learning Theory and the Design of Learning Environments,* in *23rd International Congress of Applied Psychology,* Madrid, Spain, 1994.
11. McLellan, H., ed., *Situated Learning Perspectives,* Englewood Cliffs, N.J.: Educational Technology Publications, Inc., 1996.
12. Owen, H., *Expanding our Now: The Story of Open Space Technology,* San Francisco: Berrett-Koehler, 1997.
13. Schwartz, D. L. and J. D. Bransford, "A Time for Telling." (Unpublished Manuscript), No.1997.

14. Marquardt, M. J., *Building the Learning Organization: A Systems Approach to Quantum Improvement and Global Success,* New York: McGraw-Hill, 1996.
15. Maslow, A. H., *A Theory of Human Motivation,* in *Classics of Organization Theory,* J. M. Shafritz and J. S. Ott, eds., Belmont, Cal.: Wadsworth, 1992, pp. 159–173, pp. 159, 164 (originally published in 1943).
16. Marcic, D., *Managing with the Wisdom of Love,* San Francisco: Jossey-Bass, 1997.
17. Knowles, M., *The Adult Learner: A Neglected Species.* Building Blocks of Human Potential, L. Nadler, ed., Houston, Tex.: Gulf Publishing Company, 1973, p. 19.
18. Knowles, M. S., *The Modern Practice of Adult Education,* Rev. ed, New York: Cambridge, The Adult Education Company, 1980.
19. Bandura, A., *Social Learning Theory,* Englewood Cliffs, N.J.: Prentice Hall, 1977.
20. Marsick, V. J. and K. E. Watkins, *Informal and Incidental Learning in the Workplace,* New York: Routledge, 1990.
21. Chalofsky, N. E., "A New Paradigm for Learning In Organizations," *Human Resource Development Quarterly,* Vol. 7, No. 3, 1996, pp. 287–293.
22. Garrick, J., "Informal learning in corporate workplaces," *Human Resource Development Quarterly,* Vol. 9, No. 2, 1998, pp. 129–145.
23. Stamps, D. "Communities of practice." *Training,* Feb. 1997, pp. 34–42.
24. Bridges, E. M. and P. Hallinger, *Problem Based Learning for Administrators,* Eugene, Ore.: ERIC Clearinghouse on Educational Management, 1992, pp. 5–6.
25. Watkins, K. E. and T. J. Shindell, "Learning and transforming through action science," *New Directions for Adult and Continuing Education,* Vol. 63, No. Fall, 1994, pp. 43–55, p. 43.
26. "Industry report, 1998," *Training,* Oct. 1998, pp. 47–76, p. 58.
27. Durr, R., L. M. Guglielmino and P. J. Guglielmino, "Self-directed learning readiness and occupational categories," *Human Resources Development Quarterly,* Vol. 7, No. 4, 1996, pp. 349–358.
28. Van der Krogt, F. J., "Learning network theory: The tension between learning systems and work systems in organizations," *Human Resources Development Quarterly,* Vol. 9, No. 2, 1998, pp. 157–177.

Chapter 9

To Performance Support from Teaching

INTRODUCTION

The last chapter revealed that there are many approaches to learning theory that support open and virtual organizations. A number of our theories, therefore, are already oriented toward the support of chaotic learning. In this chapter, I move forward to review some of the approaches to learning support which have developed out of the general learning theories described in the last chapter. We find it useful to have theories as a backdrop. However, the actual work in supporting learners depends on ways in which managers and system performance professionals have realized those theories in actual practices and materials. In turn, this view of current theory and practice will set the stage for the next part of the book, which will suggest some closer integration of learning and chaos theories and implications for the practice of management and system performance support. One of the initial considerations has to do with the practice of HRD itself. Changing views on the role of human development in organizations has led to re-evaluation of both HRD and OD practice. Second, regardless of how the practice moves ahead, there are considerations concerning the ways in which change is moderated throughout the organization and in which HRD and OD practitioners do their work. A review of process models will illustrate changes in emphasis in this area. Third, there is increasing concern with the evaluation of training and other human-related practices within organizations. It is important to understand the current approaches to evaluation processes and findings. Finally, there is an area of practice that has grown up alongside the actual practice itself, having to do with management of HRD, OD, organizational change, and other such activities. The way in which we approach management of organizations plays a vital role in the successful support of learning.

THE URGE TO CONSULT

One of the continuing sagas in the history of human resource development, or staff development, has been the relationship, or lack thereof, between the development of humans and the development of organizations. One of the largest portions in any line manager's budget is that devoted to support of people in the organization. Generally, salaries and benefits budget lines are the largest. Training will be close behind. Rarely is there a specific line item for organizational development. In many cases, budgeting for organizational development has been carried at the highest corporate levels, where organization development staff are situated as a common resource for the entire organization. Training, on the other hand, tends to be more personal and more of a variable cost, related to the mission, objectives and staff readiness of a particular line organization.

In the grand scheme of organizational behavior, training or human resource development (HRD) groups have been concerned with micro improvements in individuals and teams, while organizational development (OD) groups have concerned themselves with change management at macro levels in the organization. The two groups often pursue their separate missions, with little integration.

Recent changes in thinking, however, have reemphasized the common interests of the two groups. One change is the increasing awareness that an organization does not exist in isolation from its stakeholders and other participants in its supply chain. As this awareness has led to an opening of organizational boundaries, the role of learning has been recognized as a vital, ongoing element in system success. Learning organizations have developed, where emphasis on the role of learning throughout the system has resulted in consolidation of training and organization development. Another change is a shift from physical labor to what is called the "knowledge worker." The changes brought about in the core nature of work itself, largely attributed to information technologies [1], have shifted emphasis from physical strength and immediate physical interventions in operations to operational coordination through electronic devices. Computers and other electronic instruments now replace the role that physical human sense once fulfilled, *informating* the organization. Another form of disintermediation is created through increased use of electronic networks for communications. The internet is a basis for electronic commerce that is replacing many localized, physical, face-to-face sales and marketing efforts.

All of these changes have placed greater emphasis on the integral nature of training and organization development, and have created the need to expand both disciplines. The concept of Performance Centered Learning (PCL), for example [2], demonstrates the ways in which the greater emphasis on performance might change the ways in which computer-based training is structured. Figure 9-1 shows a comparison of traditional vs. PCL approaches.

Traditional CBT	**Performance Centered Learning**
Behaviorist Roots	Cognitive Roots
Obejctivist	Constructivist
Tutorial Based	Scenario Based
Bottom Up	Top Down
Learning Before Doing	Learning While Doing
Extrinsic Motivation	Intrinsic Motivation
Passive Learning	Active Learning
Inert Knowledge	Linked Knowledge

Figure 9-1. CBT vs. PCL.

The theoretical approach that informs PCL lies in some of the more open theories concerning learning. In particular, PCL stresses the careful integration of socialization and individuation. This idea of mass customization, introduced as a way to satisfy customer demands for tailored products and services, is appropriate here. In PCL, we see an approach to learning support that relies on a tailoring of the learning situation. Unlike a manufacturing setting, the customer does not sit at the end of an assembly line waiting for something to appear. Here the customer, or learner, must be fully engaged in the learning support process itself in order to ensure that the final outcome—behavior—meets the needs of the individual and of the situation. Concepts like PCL move us from a prescriptive approach to learning support to a descriptive approach.

Such practical changes in the approach to development of learning and performance support tools have at their basis a more general change in philosophy regarding the places of OD and HRD in the life of the organization. The emergence of the idea of "performance technology" allows a more complete integration of OD and HRD, and HRD/OD and the other subsystems which comprise an organization.

The concept of Human Performance Technology (HPT) offers an amalgamation of the disciplines which concerns itself with organizational behavior as a whole [3]. This means that human performance is placed in context along with other subsystems that constitute the presence of the organization. From the viewpoint of performance technology, the worthiness of the system as a whole depends not only on human learning, but also on the ways in which that factor is inter-related with electronic knowledge management systems, compensation systems, production systems, and management systems. The value and sustainability of the system is dependent on close interactions among all of the elements in its value chain.

The tendency is to subordinate the individualized disciplines, HRD and OD, into a more holistic approach to organizational support. The development of the organization is no longer solely reflected in team or group interventions which are conducted separately from changes in other elements of the system. Human behavior is viewed as one variable in a list of variables that can influence the nature and dynamic of the system. The role of the performance consultant [4] is much broader, requiring a different set of skills than those belonging separately to OD or HRD specialists, as they have been developed in the past. The shift is toward a general consulting capability and the ability to manage organizational change projects, rather than to provide specialist services such as course evaluation or course design and development.

The difficulty with a picture in which organizational experts exist as an internal consulting group is that (a) it is hard to distinguish between this role and general management's role in the organization; and (b) the challenge to show value to the organization is intensified. First, a performance consultant, if the role is developed according to existing models, will be little different from a general business consultant and, therefore, little different from a general manager. Many of the same characteristics which make a good performance consultant are those which we would like to see developed in line management at all levels. The separate role of the performance consultant, then, may be interchangeable with line management, with the advantage of separation coming in objectivity and oversight. In the role of performance consultant, a line manager may be able to step back and see situations through a different lens, in an application of her *intrapersonal intelligence.*

In a performance consulting role, a manager with well-honed management skills would be able to assess and analyze operations and processes at the sub-group or group level with more objectivity than she might have if looking at an organization for which she is responsible and with which she is highly familiar. Distance from the organization provides the potential for insight that might not otherwise be possible. The performance consultant can then bond closely with line management, in order to share objective insights and suggestions, and act as a conduit from line management to higher levels in the larger organization. The role, then, can be informed observer, process contributor, and feedback mechanism. Such close coordination between the manager/performance consultant and the actual line management in place is an opportunity for an individual to move from one role to the other seamlessly.

Performance consulting is good preparation for line management and vice versa. This has advantages, but some cautions as well. A manager coming from line management into a performance consulting position may be bringing a fixed set of ideas along. This toolkit may have worked in the specific experiences that the manager has had on the line, but may not be transferable to other elements in the organization. If this toolkit contains the wrong set of tools for the wider responsibilities of the performance consultant, the value of the consulting role will be negated. While there may be some useful tools, the manager who converts to performance consulting should be concerned with an objective review of that toolkit, along with objective views of the organization.

Second, difficulties can arise from the inclusion of a consulting group within some organizations. Often the value of internal consultants is questioned, since it is sometimes difficult to establish their actual contribution to direct products and services. Where Sales, General, and Administrative (SGA) expenses are of concern to the organization, such consultants are often viewed as non-value-added services. The challenge in performance consulting, then, lies in producing products and providing services that are seen as tangible values to the organization.

Because the role is so broad, however, this can pose difficulties. In the role of project manager for change projects, the performance consultant is again paralleling the role assigned to line management. If the organization accepts that line management constitutes the primary change agent in the system, then the management of change projects may be viewed as the responsibility of line management. A separate consulting role may appear to be redundant if it tends to replace this embedded responsibility of the line. While it is occasionally useful to engage a separate project manager for change initiatives, such managers may be available from within the business process support structures already existing in a business unit or sub-group. The role of project management, in fact, is itself becoming a specialization, and the organization may choose to select someone who has focused on project management skills, methods, and software applications, rather than on a generalist consultant.

The role of performance consulting, then, while it appears to offer many advantages, must be approached and defined carefully to ensure a fit with organizational needs and existing capabilities. To step away from the more tangible tasks and products and services available from HRD and OD specialists and toward a more general model of organization change and support may not be successful. We cannot ignore those specialist skills, for they form additional facets that are necessary to support learning in chaotic systems. The ability of the performance consultant is vital, but so is the immediate availability of expertise in design, implementation, and assessment of specific interventions.

ISD AND OTHER DESIGN-DEVELOPMENT-DELIVERY MODELS

Aside from the existence of a performance-consulting model, specific work must get done in order for change to be successful. The specific utility of training and OD interventions, therefore, will not be replaced by the appearance of performance consulting roles. Courses and other interventions will continue to be designed and developed in order to meet specific requirements. The most commonly referenced model for training is the Instructional Systems Development (ISD) model. A version of that model [5] is shown here in Figure 9-2.

Other versions of this process have been proposed, offering different approaches to the same task of systematically developing training or educational materials. The Critical Events Model, developed by Leonard and Zeace Nadler, provides a different and popular view of the relationship of the activities [6]. That view, shown in Figure 9-3, emphasizes the consistency of the analysis, design, delivery and evaluation processes, as they are evolved through formative and summative evaluation. One of the most attractive points about this model is its emphasis on openness and feedback as a part of the overall learning support system. Feedback develops through constant formative evaluation as the project progresses. Summative evaluation provides feedback as the products and services are delivered to the client organization. Further, feedback from the entire activity feeds into the major system, where it produces behavioral change. While the model itself tends to show cyclical dynamics, the true message of the process is that there is no true recycling through pre-existing points in the map of organizational history. Feedback, as it reflects changes in behavior at the individual or organizational level, is the mechanism through which a repetition of history is avoided, and the system, presumably, learns from its experience and spirals to a higher level of capability. While this interpretation is not completely clear from a view of the model itself, any interpretation of the meaning of the model will result in this understanding of its dynamic.

Wedman and Tessmer [7] developed a multi-faceted approach to the solution of learning problems, the Layers of Necessity Model, which allows for considerable variance in the steps used to complete a design project. Their design activities essentially mirror those of ISD, but differ in application and timing. They identify two key situational variables that determine which of the steps in the design system would take precedence: (1) the time available for the design and implementation process; and (2) the resources (human, budget, equipment, etc.) available for the

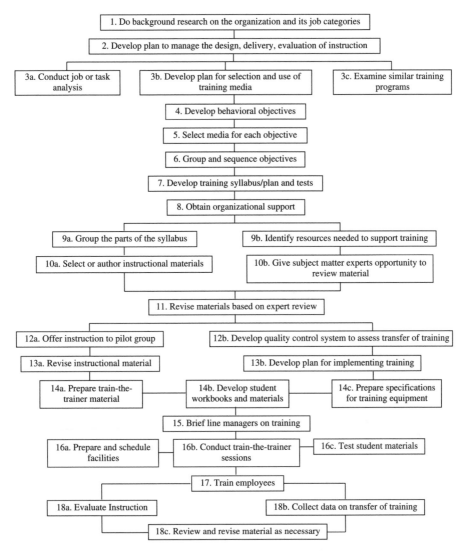

Figure 9-2. Instructional systems development model. *(From Rothwell and Sredl [5].)*

design project. These two factors, in combination, determine the number of layers of steps to be included in the project, and thus the complexity of the project.

Other models, while less elaborate, suggest the same major categories of stages, which generally include: (1) front-end analysis of a target organizational situation to define learning needs; (2) design and development of the intervention course or other materials; (3) delivery of the intervention to the target audience; and (4) evaluation of results. In most instances, the models that are constructed to present these stages suggest linear and incremental assembly of parts. However, at the same time that the models appear linear, very few practitioners follow any such straight-line,

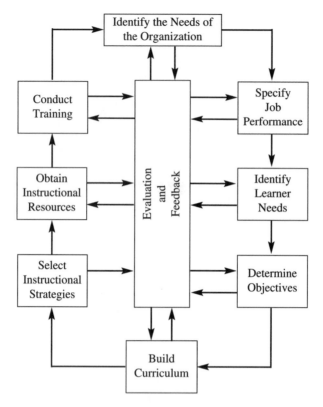

Figure 9-3. Critical events model. *(From Nadler and Nadler [6].)*

incremental, staged process. In most instances, practitioners are more likely to use
some form of the Layers of Necessity model, whether they know that model or not.
That is, most intervention projects are influenced by time and resource availability.
These constraints often produce interventions and other learning support services
which are timely, applicable, and useful to the target population. Just as often, such
efforts result in haphazard and unmeasurable events which occur in isolation from
the operating systems which they were intended to support. The outcomes prove to
be unknowable, either in short or long term.

   While models are useful, therefore, as a reminder of the things that need to be
done, the literal use of models is neither recommended nor practiced. Yet, the models are influential and are to be found in all parts of industry where organizational
or human resource development is carried out. These models are included in HRD
course curricula in professional degree programs, and are included in any number
of books that have addressed the topics of teaching, training, and organizational
intervention. Through intensity of exposure, if through nothing else, people have
come to see these models as necessary guides to proper development of learning
support interventions. As we consider nonlinear dynamical organizational systems
and appropriate learning support, we may want to revise our models to reflect more

open and less constrained practice. At the same time, however, we will need to ensure that interventions are designed as high quality and complete activities. Design of interventions, then, offers additional challenges in chaotic environments. Our ideas and approaches may require new tools, as we address learning needs in such systems.

NEW MEDIA, MODES, PLACES FOR LEARNING

The introduction of electronic technologies into the design, development, and delivery of organizational interventions has introduced more variety in delivery methods, and with it increased complexity of design. The design of learning support for lecture courses was relatively simple and straightforward. At the same time, it tended to be highly tailored to the particular audience and situation, and involved the need to know that audience and the situations, to make the design relevant to needs. With the advent of electronic technologies, the approach to design, · development and delivery have undergone a shift in mental models to include larger and more diverse audiences. Figure 9-4 indicates the direction of this shift, as it has moved over time from individually focused learning support in the form of apprenticeship, tutelage, and on-the-job training. Once beyond the individual focus, the emphasis tended to move toward groups of varying sizes, including small groups and teams and classroom-sized groups of 25–35 people. The extension of this shift that is now underway includes group sizes beyond the physical limitations of traditional classrooms, and beyond the domain of a single instructor who is present in the learning environment. Combined with the inclusive nature of performance consulting practices, along with the more open approach to instructional design represented in the Nadler and Tessmer/Wedman models, this trend is impacting nearly every aspect of human and organizational development.

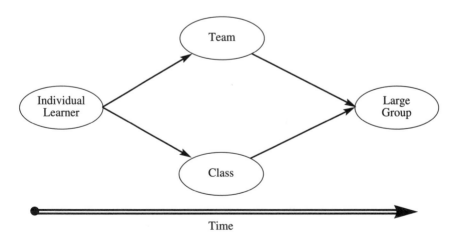

Figure 9-4. Expansion of learning support.

Through the inclusion of larger groups into learning events and efforts, the nature of learning support changes from support of nuclear objectives to support of virtual goals. The combinations of electronic technologies with learning theories that support less directive approaches and more self-directed approaches to learning support offer considerably more potential for intervention design than has traditionally been available to consultants and practitioners in the field.

At the same time that the digital economy [8] has brought increased flexibility in terms of audience size and availability, the introduction of new technologies, along with the existence of more open learning theories, poses some difficulties. One of the chief difficulties is that practitioners still provide some 70 to 80 percent of learning support through traditional classrooms [9]. The prevailing mental model for learning support, or for organizational change support, remains the classroom.

What this means for designers of learning and change efforts is that much of what they do will continue to be done in traditional ways. While there are some signs that the mix of delivery media and locales is changing to include more electronic performance support, the changes are coming slowly. They are not happening at a rate in business and industry that is equivalent to the rate of change on college campuses and in K–12 schools. In these locales, teachers and administrators have been quick to adopt packaged learning tools that can be used on individual computers or through a campus network. Many MBA and other graduate level courses are now available online, and universities are fast moving toward degree programs which can be completed at a distance.

While the graduates of these schools are now moving into businesses and other organizations, they have not yet made their influence felt in the ways in which they experience learning. They appear to be satisfied to accept the traditional classroom as the way to learn what they need to know about corporate operations. This situation will change as the people in influential organizational positions exert pressure on those responsible for employee and organizational learning.

Where electronic tools have been introduced into adult learning, success of the tools has been tangible but not spectacular. In part, this is because the existing design models for electronic learning support tools are simply adopted directly from existing models, which may tend to emphasize the stable nature of learning [10]. The development of fixed courseware belies the nature of the forms of learning which have significant impact on the behavior of the organization at large. Such learning is highly adaptive and happens quickly. As this is increasingly recognized in organizations, there is increasing pressure to develop learning support that also has these characteristics. The emphasis in organizations to produce faster, better, and cheaper has also influenced viewpoints about human resource and organization development. Learning support systems developed on existing models tend to want to be stable products and not volatile solution sets.

Further, such learning is multivariate and not generic. What is clear from extensions of cognitive learning theory and humanistic and social learning theories is that individuals learn in different ways, at different rates, and at different times. Not all learning is confined to the classroom or to a given time period. This reality is important when constructing learning support in chaotic systems. The difficulty in producing electronic packages that must appeal to everyone is the same difficulty we encounter in attempting to produce any generic package that will suit all circumstances. Any generic package will suffer because it is not tailored to the specific time, place, and circumstances that created the need. Generic packages address generic situations. The effort on the part of individuals to use these packages and convert their contents into personalized learning is often greater than that required to learn without learning support tools.

THE VALUE OF INCIDENTAL LEARNING

The distinction between formal learning events and incidental learning is important in the transition from a "teaching" environment to a learning support environment. The practice of supporting incidental learning has never developed as a major role in HRD or OD, with the emphasis placed on more scientific and controlled interventions and training courses. Incidental learning, however, is both adaptive and generative. It is largely self-initiated and self-sustained, and is linked automatically by the individual with his or her pattern of motivations. When properly supported, encouraged and rewarded, incidental learning can acceptably take the learner down paths that may not have been considered in artificially constructed learning environments and events. Incidental learning is a core concept for constructivist approaches to learning support, and is an important ingredient in problem-based learning. Much of the internalization of new or revised behavior occurs outside of the realm of the formal classroom or outside of the interaction between learner and electronic performance support tool.

The very informality of this approach to learning offers challenges to those who would support it. One of the avenues currently being investigated is that of knowledge management, using a concept called a knowledge bank, or knowledge warehouse [11]. Spawned from increasingly sophisticated electronic networks, and the availability of internet and intranet resources, the knowledge bank provides access to an assembly of knowledge from the whole corpus of the organization. It is an assembly point and a point of departure for idea generation. The concept is one that both addresses the wider, expeditionary approaches to learning encouraged by network availability, and one that supports generative learning regardless of audience size.

Issues include: (a) how to get the knowledge into the bank; and (b) how to keep it current. Getting the knowledge into the bank involves the cooperation of various departments and subunits, which must establish responsibility for collecting data and information and then storing it. What information to keep, how much of it to keep, and what forms of data to store are all-important questions which will impact the initial structure of the data bank. Some information may not be in digital form, and may not, in fact, be in paper form. Inclusion of videotapes of key meetings, for example, may provide useful insight into decision-making or organizational change processes. The capability exists to store such high-volume data on a video server, but this option requires investment in the server and its network access, as well as the initial investment in digitizing any analog videotapes for inclusion on such a fileserver. Audiotapes present similar opportunities to capture useful information, in a quick and handy format, but providing access across a network calls for digitizing the audio and storing it in such a way that it can be accessed on demand. Questions of ownership, copyright, and performance releases must be resolved before either paper, video, or audio material is digitized and stored.

Organizing the knowledge and data means tagging it in such a way that it is accessible through free-form as well as more structured topic searches. Tagging video, graphics, and audio is difficult, but not impossible, and software exists to help in these media. Some form of search engine must be available to access the database, but the growing experience with web-based search engines provides some choices for this.

Once in the knowledge bank, the material must remain meaningful. Data of historical value must be explained and documented in such a way that historians can recapture its significance, if pulled in later years for study. Content "owners" must, on a periodic basis, review information for more current applications in the organization, much as web pages and sites must be reviewed in order to determine the continuing fitness of the information. Some decision process must be in place to determine the point at which data becomes history or trash.

Finally, the relevance and utility of such a knowledge bank must become the responsibility of the organization. To expend some effort and money to establish the storage and retrieval system, all members of the organization must realize value from it. If data is wrong, missing, or hard to access, the knowledge bank will not have served its purpose. If it fails to yield information and is, instead, a collection of data bits without interpretation or context, no positive end will have been gained. While knowledge banks show potential as sources for learning and growth in organizations, regardless of size or location, the effort required to construct and maintain them is not a small one, and must be carefully considered.

MEASUREMENT OF LEARNING—CURRENT PRACTICE

Current evaluation of learning effectiveness is based in a model proposed by Donald Kirkpatrick in a series of articles in the 1950s. This work is updated and expanded in a later book [12]. In essence, Kirkpatrick proposes that training should be evaluated at four levels: (1) a reaction level, to capture subjective responses from the participants at the conclusion of the course; (2) a learning level, to capture the actual impact of the course through internal course measurements such as pre- and posttests; (3) a transfer level, to measure the extent to which learning in a formal course is transferable to the job; and finally, (4) a cost-benefit level, to establish the ratio of program design and delivery costs to the benefits derived from the course.

To this initial four-level proposal has been added one other theory, often referred to as Level 5 evaluation. Jack Phillips has placed emphasis on the Return on Investment (ROI) of training [13, 14], taking the process beyond simple cost-benefit analysis. One of the key factors in this argument is that a training investment is not fully understood unless the performance results are quantified and shown to provide a return. Moreover, this approach takes advantage of an existing financial measure, used in the valuation of other capital investments. While evaluation practices have improved considerably, many organizations still choose to do little in this regard. Yet, to measure the impact of learning in an organization is an important function in any organizational environment. Evaluation is the chief method for acknowledging the value of learning support mechanisms and testing the actual utility of learning and performance support. This argument becomes more important for chaotic systems. In a later chapter, I will consider evaluation methodology in more detail, for it, too, must change in order to measure chaotic learning. Metrics and measurement, often considered a side effort in performance support, is an essential activity when planning or tracing learning in chaotic systems.

THE MANAGEMENT OF LEARNING

Learning has often been associated with some rigor and with control mechanisms to ensure that it happens. Businesses review the cost structures of internal training groups and manage employee attendance at external seminars. Schools develop curricula that meet strict time standards and guidelines for content and delivery. The overall impression, it seems, is that learners cannot be entrusted with something as important and expensive as learning. Moreover, the management of learning in the organization has now passed from the exclusive agency of the HR department to a broader spectrum of overseers. Some customer technical training, for instance, may be the sole responsibility of the specific product group responsible for the technology. In large corporations, the control of training and learning support may be so distributed that 50 or more training departments or cells may exist at various places in the large organizational structure. Each of these learning support groups has its own mission, sometimes operating autonomously from any central training authority.

Such a decentralized activity is close to an ideal state, insofar as each training, OD or learning support group maintains the integrity of its mission and satisfies a need localized by geography or by organizational function. Where there is little overlap of mission, this arrangement provides the most efficient placement of a learning support function at those places where it is most needed. I presume, of course, that form follows function, and such decentralized units are adding value to the departments, divisions, or locations that they serve.

This decentralized model, however, is suspect at its management and coordination levels. If no form of network has been established among the various learning support functions, then there is the danger that duplication of effort will occur from one unit to another. A training organization in Denver, for example, may offer similar but not exactly the same courses as a training organization in Houston. Both organizations may have similar management and administrative functions. This structure, if it exists across a number of decentralized operations, can result in waste through duplication and lack of coordination. In some instances the waste can come through similar offerings, and in other instances waste can come through duplication of management. Inefficient multiple contracts with the same vendor company for courseware, supplies, or services may create waste, as well. Under-utilization of HRD and OD facilities may also result if decentralized units have sole control over scheduling, configuration, and use of facilities. The sharing of facilities among groups seems a simple matter in principle but becomes both a political and logistics problem in practice.

CORPORATE UNIVERSITIES

There is no trend or consistency in the use of a decentralized model, however. Some organizations use a more centralized oversight group, preferring to set policies and procedures and to provide a common service. This basic organizational construct, tending to be nuclear, is the basis for the concept of the corporate university that shares many of the virtues and pitfalls with its academic model. The university concept has some advantages, both in academic and corporate organizational worlds. It implies a gathering of minds, free to explore new ideas and variations on old ideas. It is an open concept, with the vigorous inflow and outflow of creative thought in the faculty and professional domain as well as in the student domain. Constructive thinking is honored, and unlearning, as well as learning, is practiced. In its ideal state, it is both a place of reflection and of action. As John Henry, Cardinal Newman [15] expressed it,

> It is a great point then to enlarge the range of studies which a university professes, even for the sake of the students; and, though they cannot pursue every subject which is open to them, they will be the gainers by living among those and under those who represent the whole circle. This I conceive to be the advantage of a seat of universal learning, considered as a place of education.

From Newman's nineteenth century viewpoint, the purpose of the university was to provide a gathering point for universal education. His concept would provide a graduate who had a command of the world and environment in which he lived, and a sense of continuity between past and present that would form the basis for the future. Education, to Newman, was not an activity to teach specific skills and tasks, but one that would teach people how to think, and to give them the historical basis for current thought and social activity.

In comparison with the modern academic university, this goal is loosely achieved, but with much pulling and tugging from those who would turn the university into a practicum. Current ideas of education want to anchor instruction and learning in real-life application, with the result that the student can do something observable with what is learned. The more observable, the more measurable. The more measurable, the more likely it is that additional contributions and funding will be forthcoming from parents, the community, and governmental agencies. Relevance is all.

Yet there exists, beneath the great engine of practicality, a core that retains the generalist philosophy of Newman and other thinkers. The underlying belief that still motivates educational enterprises is largely one that supports the generalizability of information and learning. Yet, increasing emphasis is directed away from this core, toward degree programs with little about the world in general and more about specialties and sub-specialties.

It is this picture, and not necessarily that of Newman, that has informed the concept of the corporate university. This form of the university has less to do with the universe and more to do with profit generation. The concept is driven by a desire to contain learning and to manage it with a central metaphor. What has been taken from the idea of a university is its administrative architecture but not its core function. What is most appealing to organizations that have adopted this architecture is that it provides a metaphor for business learning.

This application of the university concept is focused on the well being of the organization that sponsors the university so that it is learning activity directed to the bottom line of the company. There is nothing universal in this. On the contrary, the focus is on acquisition of practical and immediately applicable skills and knowledge.

Apart from its appeal as a general metaphor, the corporate university structure provides a convenient way to manage and control the learning process. While the intent may be to suggest that learning can be supported anywhere, anytime, the university paradigm, at least today, suggests bricks and mortar—a campus that is fixed in a particular locale. Many companies proudly point to the academic buildings they have built, with classrooms, laboratories, etc., intended to remind employees of their academic pasts. What companies hope to gain from such campus architecture and the accompanying class schedules, mandatory curricula, and certification programs is a sense of identity with the past.

The concept of a university administrative paradigm offers security and familiarity, along with a sense of stability. The alma mater is still there, with its tree-covered walkways, its fountains, and its solid architecture, built to last the centuries. The corporate university seeks to recall an organized and orderly past. Even when the construct is extended into what is called a "virtual corporate university," it is difficult to disassociate the traditional concept of university administrative consistency. If the virtual university maintains the characteristics associated with a centrally located university, then the essential function has not changed through the addition of distance learning capabilities. A school model is still a school model, regardless of when, where, or how it is encountered. The academic university is an objective corollary with its environment. It exists in an open state with that environment, but at the same time maintains objectivity in regard to that environment. To that extent, there is an essential difference between the academic and corporate concepts. A corporate university is fully influenced by its environment, and no objectivity exists. It is there for the sole purpose of gaining and sustaining market share and profitability by modifying human behavior to predetermined standards. It is questionable, then, as an adequate tool for the support of chaotic learning.

THE CLO

Another trait in our current thinking about learning support is the increased interest in raising the position of those responsible for managing the learning process in organizations [16]. The result is a functionary often called the Chief Learning Officer (CLO). This role is designed to place a person within reach of the CEO or President who can both support strategic organizational leadership and shape learning support and organizational development policy. There is interest in this function, though the actual existence of such roles remains rare. Generally the seedbed for a role such as this is a commitment on the part of the organization's top leaders to a practice of organizational learning. The prerequisite for strategic inclusion of learning in organizational planning and leadership is the belief that sustained success in the market will depend as much on learning as on finance or operations or sales. In fact, the existence of a CLO might threaten the power structure of the HR person who is closest to the top of the organization. For this reason, and because CEOs often tend to identify learning as a benefit or reward, the CLO position will not be immediately filled in most organizational structures. Learning support and organizational development are more likely to be found under the HR umbrella, where there may be vice-presidential positions responsible for fostering learning and managing its dissemination through the organization. What CEOs and Boards of Directors miss, in placing learning within HR, is the opportunity to maximize the contribution of learning across the entire enterprise. That is, it is not only human learning that must be considered, but the full integration of learning into the operations of the organization.

The best parallel may be the role of Chief Information Officer (CIO). This role has responsibility for the information systems, networks, and equipment across the enterprise and beyond, as data links are made to suppliers and customers. It is within the realm of the CIO to establish the ways in which the electronic networks will provide service to the human networks. These decisions impact not only the way people get day-to-day operational data and share information through e-mail, databases, and so forth, but also the ways in which people will learn. An electronic network that cannot support distance learning, for example, will deny this delivery mechanism to the learning support function. The lack of sufficient servers can prevent the OD group from mounting skill and capability assessment software for organizational use. The CIO, then, is at the top of the organization because the information systems function touches on and impacts every other operation of the organization. It is not subordinate to the supply or value chain, it is now a vital and direct link.

If this thinking holds for information systems, it would extend to learning support and organizational development, if these functions were also viewed as significant direct links in the supply chain. Generally, however, they are not. While Human Resources as a larger classification of corporate concern is considered vital across the supply chain, learning is considered to be only one piece of the entire HR function. Learning, then, is not the only human-related activity that must be successful in order to ensure the success of the enterprise. While the nascent role of the CLO is appealing because it would put emphasis on the integration of learning support into the overall function of the organization, it may not often be separated out from the general concerns with humans in organizations. This ensures that learning support will remain focused almost exclusively on human learning and will not venture very far into machine or network intelligence and learning capability. It also ensures that learning will remain, in the minds of organizational governors, a subset of activities and not a major contributor to organizational success across the enterprise.

MONITORING HUMAN PERFORMANCE

A final trend in performance support and management that is particularly relevant to a consideration of chaotic learning is the increasing trend to monitor and measure system performance. This trend has significant advantages, but also some ethical concerns associated with it.

Because much of the work of modern systems occurs through electronically mediated processes—whether telephone, fax, or data connection—transactions are liable to easy monitoring. Many people who contact customer service hotlines hear a message such as "your call may be monitored in order to improve the quality of our service." This is a way of signaling that it is likely that your call will be audiotaped. It may then be used for training customer service representatives as they try to improve their ability to address problems and concerns. This approach, using real conversations, can significantly reduce the amount of time it takes for a representative to achieve proficiency. While it is not a new technique, it is one that has gained in popularity with the introduction of less-stringent laws regarding audiotaping of telephone conversations, the introduction of cheap and available equipment for such taping, and less concern on the part of customers about such practices. The taping, in fact, has the added side benefit of intimidating customers who may be angry about the product or service they are using. Taping such conversations provides the organization with a useful tool.

At the same time, such taping is a form of performance management and control that is questionable. That individual service representatives can learn from review of their conversations, or from hearing other conversations, is undeniable. If, however, access to the tapes or to the live conversations is extended to supervisors and managers of the representatives, or to others in the organization, then the practice is questionable.

The electronic monitoring of employees, regardless of the medium, is gaining acceptance for two reasons. First, the technologies are readily available to provide full details from any medium. Audiotape and videotape are obvious. Less obvious are the station detail reports that are generated from most telephone switches, and which are often sent to managers on a scheduled basis. From these call detail reports, managers can sift through every phone call a person has made, identifying the party called, the time of the call, the duration of the call, along with the costs of the call. Originally developed to monitor switch performance, these reports showed technicians potential problems with network congestion and failure and indicated circuit or trunk problems. That this level of detail of employee telephone activity is now in the hands of supervisors and managers raises questions of ethics and trust. Organizations justify this monitoring by citing their ownership of the internal network and the potential costs associated with employee use of the phones for personal business.

This suggests a second reason that such monitoring is gaining acceptance. In many instances, while perfectly legal, people may not know of such monitoring. The existence of station detail reports from telephone switches is probably not something that many people know about. Security cameras are questionable on the same grounds. While organizations support their use in order to guard against theft, it is a practice that detracts from the privacy of the individual and raises questions of trust. A wall begins to be raised between the individual and the organization. Individuals feel intimidated and controlled by organizations that practice such monitoring and surveillance.

Finally, monitoring occurs through use of computers connected to a network. Software is now available which, when loaded onto individual computers, will provide automatic reports to technical support personnel regarding software loads and changes on the individual unit. Further, since its inception, the internet and intranets have offered little individual privacy. Reporting software is available which can provide managers and supervisors with detail reports, similar to the station detail reports from the telephone switch. These reports indicate which sites have been visited by an employee and when the visits occurred. Again, because the technology is there, it is used, and often employees are not fully aware of its use.

This trend toward monitoring, from a pessimistic view, brings to life the image of society provided in such books as Aldous Huxley's *Brave New World* [17], George Orwell's *1984* [18], and Ray Bradbury's *Fahrenheit 451* [19]. The spectre of misuse of technology to the detriment of society has been with us as long as there has been a technology to worry about. At the same time, this ability to measure human performance offers potential for support of system performance that is unparalleled. Because machines and equipment and networks are becoming more aware of their users, the ability to integrate humans with machines and networks has taken a major step forward.

Much of the learning support for humans provided to date has been filtered through artificial exercises such as role plays. The advent of technologies that can capture real action and activity in such a way that it is reproducible offers a base of knowledge about human performance and behavior that we have not been able to access in any significant way. Games, role-plays and other second-level simulations have tantalized us with the potential for systems that would allow us to develop our capabilities. Videotaped vignettes of supervisor-employee interactions, or prepared and staged audiotapes, do not offer the immediacy of real life nor its accidental nature. Scripts reflect a consistency and order that is not there in real-life interchanges, and generally try to elicit specific responses to address a specific teaching point. Problem-based learning experiences are a little better, if designed to introduce some of the messiness of real life, but still show evidence of imposed order and forethought.

Not only can technology help us reproduce live events, but a collection of such events can provide insight for studies of human behavior and reactions. Increased availability of data offers increased opportunities for research. Increased research will be necessary if we are to go beyond what we can casually observe about human systems, or what can be derived from highly controlled scientific studies. Technology, if carefully and thoughtfully used, can provide the basis for a breakthrough in how we support learning in formal events, and also how we support learning in informal activities. We are challenged to develop ways to study the sociology of organizational situations and dynamics, and to use the new data that is now being collected for narrow monitoring purposes and for short-term learning activities.

In order to break through our barriers with regard to the mysteries of human behavior in organizational systems, we must take a step toward increased use of measurements and metrics. Where equipment and network performance measures have been a given in engineering and productivity calculations, the same approaches have not worked well when applied to human performance in systems [20]. Efforts to apply technical engineering principles to social organizations have failed. In large part this has been because the people in the business of human performance are, at best, versed in business measurement principles and practices. They have rarely used even those measures in application to human behavior. Instead, there is a prevailing opinion that human behavior is random, or that its activity is so affected by events past and present—or even future—that the list of variables is too long to try to measure. The concept of individuals as independent beings has caused us to avoid defining the systemic principles that may underlie behavior, and then measuring to any finite degree, the behavior in the system.

We address bits and pieces of the human element in systems, but rarely have we attempted to describe human behavior in its whole, as it operates as a dynamic system in relation to other elements in the system. What is required in order to move us forward in our understanding of learning and learning support in dynamical systems is to identify ways, qualitative and quantitative, to address the increased amount of data on behavior of these systems. Weather forecasting has come from an age of absolute guesswork to an age when volumes of dynamic data can be used to model the behavior of weather systems, and project that behavior. If such a complex natural system can yield to computer simulations and modeling, and display adherence to technically chaotic behavior guidelines, there is the potential that similar techniques in organizational systems studies will yield a similar magnitude of systemic understanding. Such systems understanding will act as useful feedback into the learning activity that supports sustained system growth and development.

We are moving from strategies that are based on instruction to strategies that are based on learning. Our increased application of learning theories that are learner-centered has led to changes in the way we design, provide, and evaluate interventions. There is the need for further change in learning support efforts, as we begin to understand the nature of chaotic organizational systems. The nonlinearity of such systems suggests a further development of our tools and processes for OD and HRD intervention. These tools and processes must ultimately support an organizational picture that is turbulent and difficult to forecast. Its future is quantum, in the sense that the future has multiple potentiality. Anything can happen.

Learning support, we will find, will be a vital tool for initiating and sustaining needed chaotic activity in organizational systems. If nonlinear dynamical systems activity provides advantages to organizations in their fitness landscapes, then nonlinear dynamical learning support systems are appropriate. We will abandon training and OD efforts that subscribe to stable worldviews, and develop methods that support turbulence and instability.

REFERENCES

1. Zuboff, S., *In the Age of the Smart Machine,* New York: Basic Books, 1988, p. 9.
2. Rosenheck, M., "Closing the gap between training and performance," *CBT Solutions,* May/June 1997, pp. 50–53, p. 50.
3. Rothwell, W. J., *ASTD models for human performance improvement,* Alexandria, Va.: American Society for Training and Development, 1996, p. 3.
4. Robinson, D. G. and J. C. Robinson, *Performance Consulting: Moving Beyond Training,* San Francisco: Berrett-Koehler, 1995.
5. Reprinted from *The ASTD Guide to Professional Human Resource Development Roles and Competencies,* written by W. J. Rothwell and H. J. Sredl, copyright 1992. Reprinted by permission of the publisher, HRD Press, Amherst, Mass., (413) 253-3488.
6. Nadler, L. and Z. Nadler, *Designing Training Programs: The Critical Events Model.* Building Blocks of Human Potential, L. Nadler (Ed.), Houston: Gulf Publishing Company, 1994.
7. Wedman, J. F. and M. Tessmer, "A layers-of-necessity instructional development model." *Performance & Instruction,* April 1990, pp. 1–7.
8. Tapscott, D. *The Digital Economy,* New York: McGraw-Hill, 1996.
9. "Industry report, 1998." *Training,* Oct. 1998, pp. 47–76, p. 58.
10. Masie, E., "Multimedia is falling short of its potential, says industry founder." *Technology for Learning,* Sept. 1997, p. 4.
11. Johnson, P., "Managing knowledge assets over the web," *CBT Solutions,* May/June 1998, pp. 1, 6, 8–11.
12. Kirkpatrick, D. L., *Evaluating Training Programs,* San Francisco: Berrett-Koehler, 1994.
13. Phillips, J. J., *Return on Investment in Training and Performance Improvement Programs,* Improving Human Performance, J. Phillips, ed., Houston: Gulf Publishing Company, 1997.
14. Phillips, J. J., ed., *Measuring Return on Investment,* Vol. 2 In Action, J. J. Phillips, ed., Alexandria, Va.: American Society for Training and Development, 1997 .
15. Cardinal Newman, J. H., *The Idea of a University,* New York: Doubleday, 1959, p. 128 (orig. pub. London, 1852).
16. Stuller, J., "Chief of corporate smarts." *Training,* April 1998, pp. 28–34.
17. Huxley, A., *Brave New World,* New York: Harperperennial Library, 1998 (orig. pub. 1932).
18. Orwell, G., *1984,* New York: New American Library, 1990 (orig. pub. 1948).
19. Bradbury, R., *Fahrenheit 451,* New York: Ballantine Books, 1953.
20. Gilbert, T. E., *Human Competence: Engineering Worthy Performance,* New York: McGraw-Hill, 1978.

Chapter 10

A New Order

INTRODUCTION

In previous chapters, I have tried to represent some of the changes in organizational thinking which are influenced by a number of sources. First, the nature of the organization has been heavily influenced by increased interdependencies encouraged by globalization. As supply chains expand, even for medium and smaller organizations, the need to shift views and values has grown. The concept of the organization, at this point, is represented in nuclear, open, and virtual forms, and those engaged in organizational development struggle with different ways of approaching and supporting this variety.

Second, there is a growing acceptance of the presence of chaotic activity in organizations. Classical chaos has lost some of its terror, and technical chaos offers the promise of understanding, if not controlling, some of the turbulence which we see around us. We have some level of comfort with organizational existence at the edge of chaos, but have not quite developed the same level of comfort in the chaotic regime itself. Organizations still want to bring everything under the control of some efficient operating model, which will resemble a clockwork structure. Yet, because evidence suggests that there are benefits to be gained from introducing technical chaos, organizations are beginning to speculate on ways to bring it about, measure it, and understand it, so that the release of energies is positive and not negative.

The role of change, as we have seen, has itself changed in organizations. Change is now accepted as a continuous activity, with learning associated with it, in order to keep pace and to develop organizations. The natures of learning and learning support are also changing, as learners use new technologies and new approaches to problem solving and decision-making. The philosophy of performance support has reinforced the idea of holistic learning, and the focus of learning support has shifted from specifics to capabilities and competence. Both learning and learning support methods and philosophies are prepared to change along with the changes in the learning organization. This concept, the idea of a learning organization, is the building block that has served as the basis for joining learning activity with other organizational subsystems. We have embraced the idea that continuous learning is a necessary factor in near-chaotic organizations.

What is left for me to do is to provide some description of learning and learning support as they may develop in a chaotic organizational environment. As we noted in Part II, there is a clear distinction between system activity at the edge of chaos and system activity in a chaotic regime. From clearly delineated, although complex, bifurcation activity, the system moves into activity that is far less easy to map and understand. Organizational behavior begins to seem random and disconnected, and the system appears to be out of control. In fact, as we have learned, there are controlling factors in place, and a technically chaotic system has a core set of parameters which provide it with its own form of order. Our challenge is to understand and to take advantage of that order, and to learn how people, equipment and networks can best continue to learn in such conditions [1]. To follow that line of thought, I have included below a case example, which illustrates what might happen in an organization, with some discussion as to the nature of complex activity and potential chaotic activity. I have followed this introductory chapter with some final consideration regarding the learner in a chaotic systems environment, and the nature of learning support in such an environment. I have concluded with some general thoughts regarding the changes to measurement of learning in chaotic organizations, in the hopes that these initial thoughts will lead to further development of specific tools and techniques.

(RE) EVOLUTION AT XMIT CORP

In 1993, along with other companies operating in California and Texas, the XMIT company, a manufacturer of data processing equipment, learned that state regulations might require a certain percentage of its population, working in those states, to telecommute, in order to reduce vehicle traffic and pollution. Each telecommuting employee, as the XMIT plan worked itself out, would be set up with a home office, with telephone and data network links into the corporate network. The data-networking group within XMIT had the responsibility to manage the overall telecommuting program, and to provide services and network access to the employees. This support was provided as a part of the regular overhead for corporate data support services. The plan was implemented with great success. The company recognized increased productivity on the part of the telecommuters, work teams had established new processes for conducting work at a distance, and the company reduced its facility expenses. XMIT had a positive return on its investment in telecommuting equipment and services, and the states were pleased that the company supported their quality-of-life initiatives.

On May 7, 1996, all XMIT telecommuters (well over 100 people by this time) received an e-mail from the data processing group, which opened with this sentence: "Due to the increasing number of telecommuters and the costs associated with supporting them, the Data Support Group will assess a $35.00 monthly fee to all telecommuters, to be charged automatically to their budget departments."

By that afternoon, reactions began to come back to the Data Support Group from telecommuters all across North America. Two comments are typical:

To: Bob @ Data Support Group   5/7/96 3:49 PM

From: William

Help me understand what technical support you are going to provide. I have yet to receive any support from your group for my home office telephone line. I am always told to contact the telephone company for problem resolution. I already pay for computer equipment support through other departmental charges from your group, why should I pay for it again for home equipment? It is the same equipment!

To: Bob @ Data Support Group   5/8/96 9:10 AM

From: Sarah

I ordered equipment and a telephone line through your group last fall. My telephone line was installed by the local telephone company on January 8, but no equipment has ever arrived. I know there are issues in connecting us into our local XMIT office, but I've been paying for a line for over four months that has never been used. I sure hope you don't start charging me for something I don't even have yet.

There were at least 30-40 such e-mail messages within a matter of a few days, accusing the Data Support Group of various sins and omissions and objecting to the new fee for the Group's services. Telecommuters were not pleased. The responses came from all levels of employee and from all geographical areas. What is of great interest to a consideration of chaos theory and learning is that these responses were *broadcast to all recipients* of the original Data Support Group e-mail. What had been isolated issues and concerns were suddenly aggregated into a service picture available to everyone. Surprised by the new charges, telecommuters had reacted individually, but had sent their individual reactions to the entire group.

Opinions began to feed off of each other. One person would add an idea or thought to a prior e-mail. A cascade effect began across the population of telecommuters. Senior management was silent, and did not intervene to stop the tirade, perhaps hoping that it would die away and the charges could be implemented without additional concern.

Such a hope, if it existed, was stifled with the following popular suggestion, which showed up in the e-mail discussions 3 days after the initial Data Support Group message:

To: All Telecommuters   5/10/96 6:50 PM

From: Sam

Hey telecommuters . . .
Any interest in some type of telecommuter association/club of some type to share like issues/opportunities? Any ideas?

A number of positive responses began to appear in the dialogue, with various ideas on how to organize such a "customer interest group." Offers began to appear from those who had survived the equipment installation ordeals, to provide tips and assistance to those who were struggling.

Suddenly, two things happened. The Data Support Group sent out an e-mail to remind telecommuters that a forum such as the one they were suggesting was already in place. A web-based newsgroup site had already been established, but this had not been well communicated to the telecommuters and the site was unused. Second, the Data Support Group sent out an e-mail that included the following:

To: All Telecommuters   5/21/96

From: Bob @ Data Support Group

A great deal of issue has been taken with the $35.00 per month rendering we have initiated in April of this year. It is apparent from the customer response that a good deal of misunderstanding exists.

We have heard your concerns regarding the program savings and the level of services you have received. Based on your feedback we do not feel that it would be appropriate to continue to render the monthly $35.00 fee that you received in April. A credit will be issued for renderings already incurred.

The Data Support Group, then, revoked the charges and cancelled any further plans to add a charge. Several conclusions from this case are relevant to the successful integration of chaos theory and learning theories.

A COMPLEX ADAPTIVE SYSTEM

First, the overall pattern of events is consistent with the characteristics of a complex adaptive system (CAS). Holland [2] notes that such a system is characterized by the presence of a number of variable agents interacting among themselves. The rate and nature of these interactions, then, determine the pace of change in the system. Agents change as they adjust their ways of thinking and acting and their rule sets based on an accumulation of experience. This accumulation process is a form of development within the agent and is, subsequently, a form of learning. As agents learn, they change by integrating new learning with previous knowledge. The learning process is influenced from outside the system by interaction among agents. This suggests that the agents are dissipative systems, with open architectures and permeable behavioral and rule boundaries, and can both influence and be influenced by stimuli external to them. Since humans can be considered as this form of complex adaptive system, the nature of learning, rule-setting, rule changing, and behavior change is highly dependent on interactions among humans and between humans and their environments [3].

In the XMIT case, the CAS characteristic of *aggregation* is in plain view. The mass e-mail from the Data Support Group is evidence that the telecommuters were considered to be a self-similar grouping. Through aggregation, the corporation had constructed a model of a telecommuting community by consolidating all of the members of the group and attempting to generalize characteristics of the group. Individualization had apparently been dropped, and the Data Support Group saw telecommuters as a category consisting of certain employees and/or contractors. From this perspective, the category had been assigned—consciously or unconsciously—certain characteristics, and this provided a model through which "telecommuters" as a category were known. The model is extrapolated from the aggregated characteristics of a group.

Moreover, it was through aggregation that the telecommuters began, as the dialogue continued, to view themselves as one rather than as a collection of many. Where the Data Support Group had formed a collective view of telecommuters, the telecommuters themselves had not. There was no shared vision of telecommuting and supporting services between the Group and the telecommuters. It was not until a concentrating action occurred that separate telecommuters began to coalesce into a group through their opposition to the imposed fee. In this sense, the actions in the system generated a meta-agent [2], that is, an agent within the system made up of an aggregation of other agents.

The CAS mechanism of *tagging* is already evident in the description above. In order to aggregate, the individual agents in the system were tagged, first as telecommuters, and then certain of them, who self-identified, as dissenters. Tagging is evidence of a form of learning, as the system begins to make meaning and adjust behavior based on classification. Such classification leads to actions involving the classified group, and these actions constitute change in systemic behavior. To tag, and then to arrange tagged agents or elements into a taxonomy, is an organizing function which can affect the subsequent behavior by the inhabitants of the taxonomy as well as by the external agents doing the initial tagging and classifying. However, at the same time that tagging supports aggregation, it also supports individuation. A person's name is a form of tag, and is used as a way to identify an individual agent in the social system. This application of tagging was also evident in the XMIT communications, as individual names and personalities entered the conversations and idea generation. In many instances, people individualized their responses by directing them to a particular person, and copying everyone else in the classification. From both human and electronic network perspectives, this use of tagging served to link the agents into the network. It is a common rhetorical device used by candidates for political office and others who want to recognize individuals as a part of a larger network support group. Lesson Two in the politician's guidebook is to call individuals by name whenever possible. This form of inclusive individualization is evident here, as participants in the dialogue use tags to associate with each other in constructing a human network by means of the electronic network.

If we look at the operation of this system from the inception of telecommuting in 1993 through the events in 1996, we see the CAS characteristic of *nonlinearity*. Essentially, nonlinearity is defined mathematically when a calculation provides a non-proportional result. This concept has been explained earlier in the book.

While the XMIT case has not been analyzed mathematically, the operation of nonlinearity is not found far from the operation of synergy. Like mathematical nonlinearity, what we refer to in psychological definitions of synergy is the non-proportional effect of combined thinking or work on a given idea. The whole is greater than the sum of its parts, and the outcome of synergistic activity is greater than the individual investments in the process. Synergy provides added value to the outcome through its inclusive activity, and the conbinatorial effects of multiple perspectives on a given situation. While synergy has been assessed chiefly through qualitative analysis, its operation appears to be a parallel to mathematical nonlinearity.

Synergy, and therefore nonlinearity, appear in the XMIT case by considering the whole system operation, as the Data Support Group operates initially apart from its customer group, making decisions which will affect that group and implementing a significant system change. The change is rejected, in large part because the support group has failed to communicate with the customers. By the end of the story, of course, communication is re-established, and the formation of a customer focus group and the suggestion of increased use of the web-based newsgroup tool leads to the conclusion that synergy has been established between support group and customer group, and that future outcomes in the system will be the result of mutual cooperation and understanding. Shared values will lead to shared actions, and the way is prepared for results which will exceed the simple addition of support group + customer group. This provides a view of synergy in the system at a large scale.

At a smaller scale, it is evident that the complaint of one or two individuals, if narrowcast directly back to the Data Support Group, would have had little impact. It was the collective nature of the responses and the broadcast nature of the dialogue that supported the development of synergies among the customers. This collaboration led first to the understanding of the parameters of the situation and the issues involved in it, second to the proposal for a way of combining the individual efforts of the telecommuters to find solutions, and third to the greater synergy which combined the efforts of customers, now considered a telecommuting services user group, with the efforts of the Data Support Group to identify issues and, as a large group, find solutions.

There is not, therefore, a linear cause-effect approach to the problem, because there is not a single problem presented. The immediate trigger for problem identification and resolution activity in the system was the imposition of the fee. The fee itself, however, can be considered a symptom of the misalignment of the system components and the preliminary failure of the system. There were more issues and problems to be resolved than available resources to resolve them, under the current Data Support Group budget, and therefore the straight-line solution is to increase costs to the whole customer group. The simplistic and linear approach was rejected in favor of a more complex, indirect—but more effective—approach to the situation. The $35.00 magic bullet was abandoned in favor of the collaborative effort to leverage knowledge within the customer group, and to find common solutions where possible, but to solve situational problems where necessary.

The fact that there is obvious change and movement in the system supports the existence of the CAS characteristic called flows. This characteristic refers to the network metaphor itself. A complex adaptive system is constructed not in hierarchical or nuclear form, but in networked form, at some point to the right of the nuclear structure on the organizational continuum introduced earlier in this book. Organizational networks are in constant flux and change, as agents act as nodes in the network. Agents, in this sense, may be human or may be equipment. Within the overall network, which can merge human social with electronic forms of connectivity, nodes may add or drop connections at any time, at the initiation of either node. There is no firm and permanent link between two nodes. A link exists because it benefits one or the other, or both of the two nodes at any given instant. The network, then, can be thought of as existing in phase space, with characteristics that redefine every instant based on the dynamics and flow of the network. This concept of flow, then, extends well beyond the more narrow physical construct of work process flow, or material flow. Where those activities tend to linear and stepwise, network flow is far more volatile and unpredictable.

This characteristic of a complex adaptive system is one of the chief determinants of the extent to which bifurcation occurs within the system, and therefore how close to the edge of chaos the system may be operating. Maximum network activity means maximum efficiency, as node links occur for a self-defined reason and not because the links are forced by some predestined nuclear relationship. A measurement of networked activity within an organizational system, then, can be used as a key indicator of the efficiency of the system.

The network characteristic, of course, is also dependent on learning. A node that is connected to many other nodes is learning from those nodes, and contributing something to those nodes. The other nodes, in turn, are learning from the first node. The exchange of learning follows with the richness of the network in the number of connections, the variety of nodes which are interconnected, the duration of the connections, and the level of learning activity which is included in transactions among nodes. What we observe in the brief examples from the XMIT situation are node connections that are made because of the stimulus of the original e-mail. The level of learning is low at first, as participants in the dialogue are in discovery mode about each other and the situation. With the volunteering of help from one participant to the others, the learning process in the network enters a different level, which incorporates informational transaction. Presumably, establishment of the support group led to the possibility of a further learning level, which would have provided additional variety of learning experiences and documentation of lessons learned. At this point, systemic learning would have been high and would be integrated well into the ongoing operations of the system. This is the ideal state in a learning organization.

The existence, in the XMIT situation, of the CAS characteristic of *diversity* is unquestionable. The initial bifurcation in the apparently stable system came as telecommuters began to underscore and define the diverse opinions they held regarding the operation of the telecommuting support system in the organization. There was a clear distinction between the Data Support Group view of the world and the customers' view of the world that had not been explored or examined. When brought to the light of day, differences between those two groups became apparent, and the customer group coalesced and self-organized, in part, around the diversity which existed between it and the support group.

The emergence of the pre-existing gap between provider and customer lends support to the value of diversity, and the value of encouraging diversity in all aspects of the organization. This characteristic, a significant factor introduced at the beginning of this book, is apparent in the operation of the XMIT system. To allow diversity is to sit back and let things happen, without over-controlling. Supporting diversity is the same as supporting nonlinearity and flows in a system. It is crucial in order for the system to develop openness. The extent to which diversity is encouraged in the network determines the extent to which the nodes will diversify their capabilities, and therefore prepare to move, shift, and adapt on the fitness landscape.

Survival of the overall system and network depends on sensitivity of the nodes, or agents, to what is going on around them, and their ability to seek out and use diverse points of view and information. The highest function of a node is to assimilate what is available to it from one or more networks, synthesize the input, and find effective ways of translating the synthesis into action that benefits the net. Diversity begets innovation, innovation ensures change, and change results in the regeneration of the network within its phase space. In XMIT, diversity had to be introduced through the self-organizing activity of the customers, but it was allowed and supported and not squashed under the rules of some standards or management group.

The presence of diversity encourages the *modeling* activity that is also characteristic of a complex adaptive system. It is up to the agent, whether individual or meta, to construct meaning from the inputs coming to it from one or more networks. In fact, the very architecture of its relationships with other agents, or nodes, may carry meaning that contributes to the internal modeling activity. The customer group in XMIT developed a model for its purpose and existence as it explored the purposes of the dialogue process itself, and explored the given issues associated with support of telecommuters. The model that emerged at the end was a cooperative one, with the intent to synthesize the efforts of the Data Support Group with the potential energies in the customer focus group, in order to make positive changes in the system.

Once models are constructed in a CAS, they are not static. They are, themselves, subject to change. Rule setting is in the same order of flux as the other characteristics in the system, and operates in parallel with the overall activity of the system. The intervention of the self-organized customer group in XMIT generated the need for that group to establish some model for working together. That model was constructed from a number of pre-existing building blocks, among them the concept of collaborative effort. The rules of operation were defined internally, through the reconstruction of existing, commonly available components. The richness of the resulting model is dependent on the diversity of building blocks available to and employed by the agents in the network. The model that was originally proposed, the $35 fee, was rejected in favor of a different model, constructed of a different set of building blocks. The key to the use of building blocks in the dynamic activity of a system lies in an understanding, as with models, that the construction is temporary and sensitive to change. The blocks must, therefore, be small enough to be disassembled and reassembled quickly. Smallness also contributes to diversity. For example, it is easier and more straightforward to frame a house from preformed or preassembled sections than it is from plain lumber. However, the preassembled sections may not fit the model, as conceived by the future owner of the house. The resulting house may not be suitable to the potential owner. On the other hand, by starting from a more basic set of building blocks, the new owner's vision can be realized more accurately, with more flexibility in the construction process. It is not as linear, but results in a higher quality end product. So, whether the building blocks are physical or cognitive, software, brainware, or hardware, they must be capable of flexing into the dynamic integration of the system.

The importance of dialogue and description—through dialogue—of the dialectical relationship between the provider (the Data Support Group) and the customers (the telecommuters) is clear, and links to the process of systemic learning. It is only through a form of dialogue, chiefly carried out on the part of the customers, that differences in viewpoints are established and explored. There is no easy flicking of a switch to change the system. Change comes, but only through patient exploration of the fractals, through acceptance that what appears to be a straight line is not. Change, here, did not occur through process re-engineering. There was no conscious plan in the minds of the Data Support Group to throw the new charge at the customers and allow systemic behavior to emerge. The pre-planning for this change effort did not include the reactions that developed. Instead, the Group, based on the tone of their initial e-mail, expected compliance and acceptance. They expected to remain in charge of the situation and continue to collect an automatic fee for services. Most process re-engineering efforts are built on assumption of power and control over the systems which are being modified and changed. This example suggests that, in virtual systems, where there is high empowerment and individuation and low management control, prepared process maps and charts may be rejected, even if developed by opinion leaders and representative teams. While in this instance, the rejection of change was open, immediate, and abrupt, in other instances rejection of change may be more subtle and may translate into general and sometimes hidden lack of support for new processes. In an open or virtual system, as more self-direction is encouraged, the more likely it is that change will be self-generated and supported. Change in a system such as that represented in the XMIT corporation will not be successful if directed—it must be led.

THE EDGE OF CHAOS

Second, there was a key point in the dynamics when a slight change would have urged the system over into chaotic activity. The Data Support Group could have stood their ground and issued a stern e-mail on May 8, refusing to hear additional complaints, and requiring that complaints be transmitted singly and separately, rather than as broadcast responses.

It is difficult to say, given the current level of information about the case, whether or not the systemic behavior actually classified as technically chaotic. In part, this question rests with the consideration of technically chaotic organizational systems in general. That is, can a system be technically chaotic without mathematical proof? While we may believe, metaphorically, that system behavior passes over the boundary between Period 2 bifurcation and Period 3 chaotic activity (See Figure 10-1), affective confirmation is a secondary consideration in assigning technical chaos to the system. First consideration has to do with the numerical measurement of system behavior and the delineation of parameters that will describe the attractive force and system dynamics. Without such proofs, any system may be described as classically chaotic, with the attendant connotations of confusion, disorder, and randomness.

In the case of the XMIT group, the mathematical description of chaos is missing and, therefore, the system cannot be confirmed as technically chaotic. The lack of good qualitative proofs for technical chaos are lacking, and this lack is affecting the ability of organizational development professionals to describe or confirm technical chaos in organizational systems. Where the path to proof lies through sophisticated nonlinear algebra and advanced math, most people who have focused on the evolution of organizations are easily led astray if not ambushed. Even those with sophisticated mathematical tools and the highly-developed capability to use them are not yet confident in their ability to apply non-Cartesian calculus in the multi-dimensional phase space that is found in organizational systems. Work here is just beginning. This subject of measurement, introduced already in the book, will be considered with some recommendations in a later chapter.

For the immediate consideration of the XMIT case, however, no data has been modeled quantitatively. The final impression, based on a qualitative assessment of the primary dialogue derived from the e-mail exchanges, is that the system behavior is not chaotic, but does approach the edge. Having approached the edge, the system recovers some stability as it accepts the two changes that will restore order: the creation of the user group and the revocation of the fee. At least two of the parameters which would dictate system behavior, then, are (1) the ability of telecommuters to contribute their ideas and recommendations to the overall discussion and decision-making process; and (2) the existence or non-existence of a fee. The actual

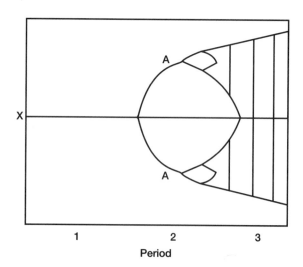

Figure 10-1. Bifurcation diagram, showing periods from stability into chaos.

amount of the fee does not appear to affect the overall discussion. Through further experimentation with these two parameters, it may be possible to test system behavior for chaos, and establish some mathematical formula that would represent the actions of these parameters in the system.

Short of being able to demonstrate such proof, comparing the case activities with the characteristics of a technically chaotic system will provide an initial baseline for opinion, if not mathematical certainty.

Each of these characteristics has been discussed in previous chapters, and is strongly associated with technical chaos:

1. *Instability*—The case indicates a strong tendency on the part of the system to move to instability, given the announcement of the new fee (an initial condition). We can assert, from the number of responses and the tone of the responses, that the imposition of the fee, regardless of the actual amount, produces a significant change in system behavior. Telecommuters do not let the incident go unnoticed and react more strongly than management obviously expected. While the reactions are the surface evidence of instability, they may suggest a deeper level of potentially disruptive energy. This event has triggered what appears to be two significant communications gates—one between the Data Services Group and the telecommuters, and the other among the telecommuters themselves. These gates have suddenly and dramatically opened, and the burst of communications suggests a pent-up energy—perhaps frustration—that is affecting the nature of the attractor for this telecommuting system. The instability, then, may be read as stemming from this one pricing trigger, but may in fact be more thoroughly embedded and active in the system and its attractive force.

2. *Aperiodic*—Both the introduction of the fee and the subsequent events do not follow a schedule or predictable path. The fee surprised telecommuters. Their responses are neither periodic nor synchronous, although toward the last days of the record, there is a tendency to seek harmony and synchronization throughout the system and its agents. From the available information, however, we can expect that the system will not settle to a steady cyclical strobe, but is sensitive enough to respond again as parameters change. Whether or not true periodicity is achieved, or the system maintains some quasi-periodic behavior, is difficult to surmise.

3. *Deterministic*—Determinism, in reference to chaotic systems, does not automatically carry with it the meaning of "predictable." Deterministic nonlinear dynamical systems are not necessarily predictable, but they do appear to conform to some organizing influence. A chaotic system exhibits very little evidence of predictability, on the surface or from an initial view. It therefore does not appear to be deterministic. Yet, below the superficial view, such a system actually demonstrates very little randomness. Its "present state completely or almost completely determines the future, but does not appear to do so" [4]. The tantalizing possibility in the study of chaotic systems lies just here, in the potential to discover determinism where none seems to exist. Present and future states are dependent on past states of the decisions and the decisions made in the system at historical points in its past.

The extent to which we can discern any deterministic patterns in a system relies on the sensitivity of the system to initial conditions, and on the number of conditions (variables) and on the range of values possible for each condition. Systems with low sensitivity, few variables, and low ranges of possible change appear to be more clearly determined than those with high sensitivity, many variables and wide ranges of possible values. Changes in the system will be fewer and less abrupt in less sensitive systems. Each sequential state of the system as it changes in time will therefore seem to proceed logically and continuously from a prior state. In systems where this does not appear to happen, events in the system, as it moves through time, appear to be more sensitive and therefore more random, although they may actually be adhering to a complex set of underlying patterns.

The example presented in the XMIT case appears to have a sequential flow, and bears some suggestion of random behavior (where did the idea for the fee originate?) and strong suggestion of sensitivity. The activity, however, appears to be highly deterministic and shows low randomness. It is therefore questionable that this would prove to be a technically chaotic system, given sufficient measurements.

4. *Nonlinear*—There is sufficient evidence in the case to suggest that the reactions of the clients to the proposed fee are nonlinear. The nonlinearity can be proposed on the grounds that the fee imposition resulted in more than a simple "no, we won't pay that" response from the clients. Furthermore, the number of respondents suggests nonlinearity in the relationship between the announcement and the reaction. The change to the system, represented by the introduction of the fee, resulted in many negative responses, and those responses were elaborated with considerable detail and led to the formation of a revolutionary sub-organization, the user's group.

5. *Dynamical*—A system with dynamics is a system that moves and changes. The study of a dynamical system must, of necessity, take into account the movement and changes of all of its parts and subsystems. An holistic view of a dynamical system, then, is not just a virtuous way of viewing the interoperability of the various nodes in the network, it is the only way to understand the complete operation of the system. The XMIT system is a system with more than one part, and the parts are interrelated. The system shows a tendency to change, based on the initiating action of fee imposition.

6. *Dissipative*—A system which is influenced from the outside, and whose energy level is subject to exchange and loss, is a dissipative system. Such systems have the characteristic of convergence toward an attractor. They are open systems, and as such are subject to both loss of energy and gain of energy. Inflow and output of energy tend to balance, but the balance may not occur regularly. The XMIT system is such a dissipative system, and subject to influences from outside. There are no fixed boundaries, and no "clockwork" source of energy. The sustained drive of the system depends on its ability to use internal and external resources, potentially variable, in order to ensure momentum.

This example, then, shows most of the characteristics of a technically chaotic system. The question that would have to be answered through additional research would have to do with the extent to which it is chaotic.

DARKNESS VISIBLE

Third, a careful analysis of the events was made possible because the e-mail messages were available and were time and date-stamped. Basic data about individual participants in the exchanges could have been (but were not) accessed through XMIT's corporate HR database, providing additional analysis data on the humans in the system. Such demographic data can add perspective to the first-hand data in the message transcripts themselves. Technology allowed the data regarding this incident to be captured and analyzed in its complexity. Because the data comes in the form of messages, it lends itself to initial analysis using qualitative methodology. At the same time, as Guastello [5] demonstrated, such data can be the basis for quantitative analyses that set the stage for tests for the presence of mathematical chaos.

THE LIGHT OF LEARNING

Fourth, the visibility of the data also contributed to learning in the system, during and after the recorded events. There was, most notably, no course offered in "How to Introduce a $35 Charge for Services." Learning was experiential on the part of the Data Support Group. As learners, they had the wisdom to open their Group system and its boundaries to influence from other forces, in particular, their customers' voices. They gained insight by unlearning lessons they thought they had learned through their experiences in establishing the telecommuting program. They learned cognitively, but also through an empathetic relationship with the customer group and through following the leads and hints provided in the customer models presented in the dialogues. They observed, accepted, interpreted and reapplied without defensiveness or blocking. They did not participate in the broadcast dialogues between May 7 and May 21. Yet, because the dialogue was broadcast, and because the Group was the direct recipient of all of the responsive e-mail, and because the electronic system confirmed receipt of the e-mail, there was no doubt in the minds of the customers that the Group was reading and absorbing the responses.

TECHNOLOGICAL TRIUMVIRATE

Fifth, technology played three key roles. At the same time that it helped in the capture of the sociological data necessary to reproduce and understand the events which were going on, it served as the vehicle through which the system emerged and developed a dynamic. Without the grouping capability offered by e-mail (mass distribution), individual telecommuters would have been left to deal with their issues one by one. Individuals might not have known what others across the organization were feeling or experiencing without the availability of network communications. From the standpoint of this emergent system, then, its existence would have been impossible without technology.

This suggests a third role of technology in the system illustrated in the case. Technology was the initial cause of the issues that generated the response system. Without issues in technology, the Data Support Group might not have felt the need for additional funding to support the telecommuting network. It was obvious that the implementation of communications capability in the various homes was not working well, requiring additional time and effort on the part of the Data Support Group. The source of the dynamic that surfaced in the tsunami of e-mails may have been a strange attractor operating behind the scenes. The attractor may have been influenced by the uneven capabilities of local telephone companies across North America in installing network equipment and high-speed data lines to support telecommuters. This characteristic in the external environment set the stage for sensitivity in the "ideal" telecommuter support system. Where an improved network might have precluded some of the technical support effort required by technical professionals, a less robust network created increasing need for support services. This, of course, cannot be had without a cost, which is either absorbed by the organization or passed along to users (telecommuters). Sensitivity to the initial conditions in the network, then, generated a near-chaotic set of circumstances, which only became recognized and understood as data was accumulated through the e-mail sequence. Whereas, in the past, organizational boundaries could be erected and solutions discovered within those boundaries, the advent of new thinking about relationships with activity outside those boundaries introduces new complexity into this organizational picture. Events are not totally under the control of the telecommuters, the service group, or even the larger organization of which they are a part. Events, as demonstrated here, may be significantly influenced by systems that lie outside of artificially erected organizational boundaries. Unless we perceive the light that is dim but evident in this larger darkness, the nature of some of our systems will remain a mystery. To comprehend a chaotic operating system requires an understanding that the strange attractor is complex, not simple, and is itself subject to wide-ranging parameters that may be difficult to pin down. Yet, it is this attempt to define such parameters that lies at the heart of changing chaotic organizations in such a way that the change and its impacts are understood.

SELF-ORGANIZATION

Sixth, and finally, it is important to recognize that efforts emerged from the group itself, to bring meaning and control to the situation. Just as control rods slow the atomic subdivision process in a nuclear reactor, the message suggesting a customer focus group introduced a stabilizing factor into this example system. The publicizing of the newsgroup web address contributed to stabilization, as did the revocation of the $35.00 surprise service fee. In essence, steps were taken by various influencing groups to control the parameters of the system activity. In part, this emerged as a need from the people involved in the situation, from the customers. In part, control came from the Data Support Group. It is important to remember that it is this group which has the "official" blessing of XMIT management. They have the corporate mandate to support the entire telecommuting activity, and thus had management's blessing for the introduction of a $35.00 fee. Yet, in a move that may have been calculated, the Support Group allowed a certain dissipation of energy from the highly charged system before changing a parameter to stabilize the system. The Group monitored the system for readiness, and at a point when indicators were that the system was beginning to stabilize itself, initiated the reminder of the newsgroup capability and the revocation of fees. Organizational change was allowed to happen, and was managed through non-intervention. The lesson for leadership here is that leadership and stability will emerge from organizational systems if the systems are left to their own devices. While some classical chaos may be perceived, it may not necessarily reflect the presence of technical chaos. That is, the system may experience radical change in self-managed ways and do no more than approach the edge of chaos, without falling into sheer randomness. Leaders should understand the strange attractors working underneath easily observable system behavior, and react to symptoms or tracks of system dynamics around the attractor.

LEARNING AND CHAOTIC BEHAVIOR

The concepts of learning and chaos have never been very far apart. In considerations of complex adaptive systems, in particular, it is learning that is viewed as the basic dynamic process that supports evolution. Beyond Period 2 behavior in a system, that is, beyond the edge between multiple bifurcations and technical chaos, the role of learning in the system is less clear. Where most learning theories assume some ongoing utility of that which is learned, as it is applied in an evolutionary way, the onset of chaos suggests higher dimensions of radical activity in the system. The attractive force underlying the description of technically chaotic systems is itself complex—a strange attractor. As we lose sequential and linear change, we also lose systemic predictability, and with that we lose utility for learning and learning support mechanisms which are predicated on some element of stability in system parameters.

In school settings, for example, the curricula and courses are formulated on historical facts, on established and proven hypotheses, or on outright formulas for solution of a math problem or construction of compound sentences. The focus is most often on what is certain, what is known, and what can be counted on to be there twenty years from now. Only a small percentage of what comes into the formal curriculum has to do with volatile systems activities.

Even in the infrastructure of the school regime itself, we are confronted with mechanistic expectations of children, and are tempted to impose control on their behavior at micro levels. The degree to which order is imposed and, by extension, punishment used for non-compliance are issues which surface constantly in the discussions of school boards and parent groups. Disruptive behavior in this environment is viewed by administrators, teachers and parents as harmful and detrimental to the social atmosphere of the school, as well as to the teaching efficiency of the system. There is constant pressure to reduce turmoil, turbulence, and uncertainty in these settings. No ways have yet been demonstrated to use technical chaos productively in school regimes. The stakeholders in these systems typically believe that order and linearity are preferable for learners.

Much of corporate (including profit and non-profit) and governmental training and development tends to follow the same model and seeks the same levels of certainty. In fact, cost models for justification of training often depend upon two or three year recovery periods for investment in intervention design and implementation costs. Such models affect the selection of topics and the treatment of topics, acting as economic gates for learners. The business learner is confronted with pressures to conform to topics that complement the corporation as it exists now, and to spend less time on topics that may be of personal interest or of possible future value. At the same time, business case development that accompanies the development of new courses and performance interventions relies on system stability for up to three years. As designers prepare the cost estimates for a project, they spread recovery of those costs over several years, suggesting that the courseware will continue to have the same value to the organization over this period. This assumption is based on a clockwork model, which assumes little and insignificant system change over such a period. Learning, by definition, is fixed in time and space, and must conform to the economic picture at the time the design proposal was assembled and approved.

There are, however, ways in which learning theory and chaos theory come together. In some instances, as may have been evident in a review of the last three parts of the book, many of the things we know about learning and a number of our practices are attuned with complex adaptive systems [6, 7]. In fact, as I have shown in initial research [8], there is enough evidence to suggest that electronic performance support tools, in particular, can be constructed in such a way that they act as complex adaptive systems. As such, they are capable of maintaining a complementary relationship with the operating systems that they were built to support. Yet, such learning support systems remain at the edge of chaos, and do not cross the line into the area of highest chaotic dimensionality. As Waldrop [9] describes such a situation,

> . . . if a system isn't on the edge of chaos already, you'd expect learning and evolution to push it in that direction. And if it is on the edge of chaos, then you'd expect learning and evolution to pull it back if it ever starts to drift away. In other words, you'd expect learning and evolution to make the edge of chaos stable, the natural place for complex, adaptive systems to be.

In this interpretation, learning is a stabilizing mechanism, which allows adaptation and adjustments within a system as it interacts with a highly volatile environment. Learning, in complexity, equals adaptation and is the survival method of choice. Once the phase transition is made, the cyclical nature of system behavior can no longer be expected, and there is no return to a stable state. In low-dimensional chaos, there may be an appearance of consistency or even repetition and control, but, as illustrated earlier in the "butterfly" diagram of chaotic system behavior, the tracking of the systems dynamics never exactly overlap.

Each change is forever, and small changes in the parameters yield noticeable changes in the operation of the system, when described mathematically. If learning results in a change of behavior brought about by some input to or experience of the system, it, too, may be sensitively dependent on initial conditions. If changes in the system are due to a form of learning, then it is conceivable to believe that everything involved in the dynamics of the system will be subject to change and thus learning. This is why any concept of learning in chaos must incorporate the possibility that initial conditions can be affected in humans, or the equipment in the system, or the networks in use in the system. Perturbations, potentially minor, can set off learning and thus change, and the influence of small perturbations may be greater than a 1:1 relationship. The system never recovers or returns to a "norm," but keeps changing in response to those influences. Like Argyris' [10] idea of double-loop learning and Nonaka's [11] idea of the learning spiral in organizational systems, learning yields change yields more learning yields more change. The track of this form of system never returns to its former point.

It is the nature of learning under these systemic circumstances that interests us here. In situations where organizational systems are undergoing constant change and disruption, with reorganization following reorganization, and introductions of new people, new technologies, and new relationships, and with work processes spread over great distances among a great many agents and meta-agents, the existence of technical chaos is no surprise. How learning can be accomplished under unstable conditions, and how learning can be supported under conditions in which the system core, or attractor, is itself complex, are the subjects for the next two chapters.

REFERENCES

1. Miles, G., et al., "Some conceptual and research barriers to the utilization of knowledge," *California Management Review,* Vol. 40, No. 3, 1998, pp. 281–288.
2. Holland, J. H., *Hidden Order: How Adaptation Builds Complexity,* New York: Addison-Wesley, 1995, pp. 15, 25.
3. Hayes, J. and C. W. Allinson, "Cognitive style and the theory and practice of individual and collective learning in organizations," *Human Relations,* Vol. 51, No. 7, 1998, pp. 847–871.
4. Lorenz, E., *The Essence of Chaos,* Seattle: University of Washington Press, 1993, pp. 4, 8, 161.
5. Guastello, S. J., T. Hyde and M. Odak, "Symbolic dynamic patterns of verbal exchange in a creative problem solving group," *Nonlinear Dynamics, Psychology, and Life Sciences,* Vol. 2, No. 1, 1998, pp. 35–59.
6. McLinden, D. J., "Proof, evidence, and complexity: Understanding the impact of training and development in business," *Performance Improvement Quarterly,* Vol. 8, No. 3, 1995, pp. 3–18.
7. Hartwell, A., "Scientific ideas and education in the 21st century." http://www.newhorizons.org/ofc_21 cliaash.html, Oct. 1995, pp. 1–14.

8. Hite, J. A., Jr., "Learning at the Edge of Chaos," Doctoral Dissertation, Nashville: Vanderbilt, 1998.

9. Waldrop, M. M., *Complexity: The Emerging Science at the Edge of Order and Chaos,* New York: Simon & Schuster, 1992, pp. 11, 295.

10. Argyris, C., *Knowledge for Action,* The Jossey-Bass Management Series, San Francisco: Jossey-Bass, 1993.

11. Nonaka, I. and H. Takeuchi, *The Knowledge-creating Company,* New York: Oxford University Press, 1995.

Chapter 11

The Learner Learning in Chaos

INTRODUCTION

As we saw in Section II, chaos theory is moving out of the realms of the natural and physical sciences and into the realms of scientific inquiry into human and organizational endeavors. Along with this move is an effort to find more application and less theory. As scientists begin to develop more practical mathematics to support their beliefs, an increasing number of experiments are being pursued which will have practical value. As students of human and organizational behavior begin to transfer the ideas of chaos theory, the need for mathematical tools becomes apparent.

Moreover, as those tools and metrics are developed and introduced in experimental designs, it is important to begin to think about the ways in which our attitudes, beliefs, and practices will need to change in order to support human and organizational development. Chaos and complexity theories bring a new perspective to the consideration of how organizations work and how the people, equipment, and networks that constitute organizations interact, learn and develop. A deep understanding of the impact of this theory on the practices of organization and people development is a first step, and needs to be in place at the same time that metrics are evolving for this field.

The view of the organization itself changes as we consider it as a multivariate complex and dynamic entity. The view of people engaged in organizations changes as we accept their variability as a part of the system to be fostered and fine-tuned, rather than as an element to be suppressed and controlled. Further, the complexity introduced through the recognition of the more valuable organizational role of equipment and networks is coming forward as we consider influences of chaos theory. Once subordinate "infrastructure," these elements play an increasing role as organizational process variables, gradually losing their stable state as they are provided with increased abilities to enhance or assume decision-making activity.

We need to consider the adoption and use of chaos theory from a practical viewpoint, as it influences our understanding of how we humans provide learning and development in organizations in concert with equipment and networks. What will it mean to accept a new regime in which order and chaos contribute simultaneously and equally, and both are encouraged in organizational learning? How will we shift from our tendencies to favor order, and to teach and learn order in orderly ways?

215

This section is intended to consider this new world view, as organization leaders rethink the ways in which chaos theory may allow them to fine tune and enhance their organizations. The focus is on learning—not so much from a theoretical perspective, but a practical one. We now need a bridge from theory to practice and from experimentation to application. We need for learners—regardless of how we define that term in the larger system—to reconsider the ways in which they learn. We need for these learning elements to reconsider what they learn and when they learn it. New learning strategies will take into account system dynamics and open systems. We need for learners and organizations to understand the interplay between individual elements and the larger system as learning is taking place. Organizations need to reconstitute, as groups, their own views of system dynamics and the ways in which the three system elements learn together, and transfer that learning into observable activity in the present or in the future. Finally, we need to understand the impact on organizational effectiveness and how that effectiveness can be measured in terms of learning. There are shifts in measurement models that must be undertaken if we are to understand the activity in dynamic chaotic systems. These forms of measurement will impact both the individual learning and organizational learning that is available to and used by the system.

The new order that we intend to secure is one that rejects fixed systems and static approaches to system problem solving and learning. The new order arises from revolutionary rethinking of ways in which learning fits into chaotic systems and revolutionary new approaches to the creation and support of learning opportunities and their influence in the systems. We cannot view chaotic learning as inefficient learning. It must be measured against the contribution it makes to a chaotic system as a part of that system. As we lose the notion that systems must be stable to be correct, we also question the drive toward stability that influences learning and learning support activities.

A new order of learning means adoption of new definitions of order in chaotic systems. Learning systems themselves become chaotic as they form parts of larger systems which operate chaotically. The establishment of new perspectives, and the acceptance of a new order, calls for the annulment and curtailment of the old order. It may not be a continuous process, but a sudden one. To adopt new tools, perspectives, methods, and measurements suggests that we will set aside old ones. As organizational dynamics grow more, not less, complex, there is increased reason to move to the new position on the fitness landscape as quickly as possible. This move will require coordination among those who manage systems, those who help develop them, and those elements that support learning in them. The change, finally, to the new order is not a people change, and is not the sole responsibility of any Human Resources group. The change in perspective is systemic and will match learning to the dynamic of the other subsystems which make up the whole.

A NATURAL PART OF THE SYSTEM ORDER

Chaos includes order, though the order must be understood and studied. Learners, whether machine, human, or network, will find themselves naturally learning in chaotic or complex systems. That is, there is no need, in many instances, to think of imposing chaotic behavior in a system. The system will naturally meet some if not all of the characteristics of a complex adaptive system or chaotic system. From this perspective, then, we can look toward the ways that the individual learner, or learning element, may identify an appropriate learning strategy.

". . . In equilibrium, matter is 'blind,' but in far-from-equilibrium conditions it begins to be able to perceive, to 'take into account,' in its way of functioning, differences in the external world (such as weak gravitational or electrical fields)" [1]. In more familiar terminology, what Prigogine and Stengers have noted here is that matter can learn. The idea that it can react to its environment and choose appropriate paths or forms means that it is not locked into a pre-determined existence. Once outside of the stable state, matter takes on a form of cognitive ability that allows it to adjust to its environment and changes in that environment. It can learn and change its behavior accordingly.

Guastello [2] reinforces the role of learning in systems and emphasizes that learning need not be considered a slow process:

> . . . not all adaptation occurs through slow genetic mutation. Learning is a form of adaptation as well. An organism that adapts by learning to behave differently will survive where other organisms do not, and the adaptation permits the survival of the organism's genetic code. It is well known that the adaptive impact of learning can be massive.

Learning is a natural part of the order of systems. The four chief camps of learning theory—behavioral, humanist, cognitive and social—reflect the recognition that learning is integral to what humans do. The capability of machines and networks also includes adaptation and learning. Furthermore, learning, we have come to suspect, is influenced by our attraction, as individuals, to certain capabilities. The individual who is fascinated by music and who feels most comfortable when expressing feelings in bodily movement will likely be attracted toward dancing. The combined influence of the two areas of intelligence—musical and kinesthetic—will support such an interest. In the same way, a computer handles data differently to emphasize the design of architectural plans in one configuration and the exploration of nuclear physics in another.

Learning, as a part of the system, conforms to the ever-changing nature of the system. It is relative to a particular time and place and set of circumstances, which are never the same from instant to instant. As Bertalanffy [3] noted, "ultimate reality is a unity of opposites; any statement holds from a certain viewpoint only, has only relative validity, and must be supplemented by antithetic statements from opposite points of view." This dialectical view reinforces the need for diversity in individual and personal thinking, as well as wider concerns with diversity as organizations develop with the aggregation of people, machines and networks. The idea of multiple perspectives is one that has been adopted by those who study human cognition and has formed the basis for learning and teaching strategies designed to build on this capability. The recognition of instability in social events and in history has been pervasive. Behind most of the recognition, however, whether expressed as multiple intelligence theory, theories of multiple perspectives in cognitive science, social learning theory, cooperative learning, or problem-based learning, is the acknowledgement that learning can take place, even if particular outcomes may not be known. The theme behind the developments in much of the learning-related literature is one of increasing uncertainty when attempting to tie specifics to the learning process. Yet behind all of the approaches to learning is the theme of orderly progression of a learning process. Learning is still viewed, too often, as a process through which order is to be imposed on disorder, with the ultimate intent that students can classify, organize, and store what they have learned, to recall it in orderly fashion. There is more emphasis on school learning—formal learning—than on informal learning, chiefly because informal learning is messy, doesn't seem "right," and there is no clean test to ensure that the learner has learned. The potential for messy learning is denied by the need to establish some form of validity and reliability for learning.

Chaotic learning leads to faster, higher-quality order and thus more effective performance for individual elements and whole organizational systems. Chaotic organizational conditions, using the characteristics of technical chaos, may be introduced into a system deliberately. This introduction calls for the use of chaotic learning capabilities and approaches for the individual learner. It is necessary, in letting go of traditional, stable organizational models, to let go of tradition-bound and stable learning strategies. The individual who is a truly effective agent in a system will carry the responsibility for adaptation in complex adaptive systems and for integration in chaotic systems. The system itself becomes, as bifurcation grows more complex, a malleable framework. Its structure, its politics, its people and its symbology change and shift meaning with the system's dynamics. The learner, whether in a CAS or in a more involved chaotic situation, will learn to interpret the dynamic nature of the system and its parameters and use these as the bases to construct needed capabilities.

HOW TO LEARN AS A COMPLEX ADAPTIVE SYSTEM

The two regimes, complexity and chaos, exist side by side with very little boundary between them. Learning in one, however, will tend to be adaptive, while learning in the other will be radically creative, much more spontaneous, and more difficult to trace and measure as a cause-effect relationship. Learning in complex adaptive systems is common practice for all human system agents, since we are complex adaptive systems and exist in complex adaptive systems, whether natural, physical, cognitive, or organizational. The learner has considerable experience in adaptive learning. This is the form of learning that is dominant when we meet a new supervisor or manager for the first time, when we re-engineer business processes, or when we move to a city where we have not lived before.

We explore to find out where the supermarkets are, what the best changes will be to improve a work process, or to begin to learn the manager's mannerisms, likes, dislikes, and sense of organizational direction. Regardless of our learning style, we will try to learn in such a way that it is natural and flows with the routines and systems which are in place and with the moods and pace of the other people and activity around us. It is continuous learning, allowing us to adapt to the circumstances we find ourselves in. We construct our own meanings and interpretations from what we see and observe, and we read and study the signs and symbols around us. We follow prescribed procedures where they exist and imitate behavior where they do not. We therefore rely heavily on cognitive, humanistic, and social learning approaches to ensure that we adapt and therefore survive.

There are some key points to remember about learning at the edge of chaos:

1. *The most effective learning will come from informal, not formal, resources.* Formal resources take time to develop, and time can affect the content and utility of learning materials. The learner who makes best use of tools which fit the present system configuration will be the learner who will learn most efficiently and effectively. At this point, we do not have effective ways to guarantee timely delivery of formal learning support or performance support tools and products, a point to be discussed further in the next chapter. The learner, then, needs to depend less on her culture-driven urge to attend a formal event, and more on her innate sense of where the natural learning tools lie in the environment. This calls for a new awareness on the part of the learner as she identifies and learns to use those existing tools.

2. *Learning in and with a group will yield greater results than learning alone.* The idea of synergy in learning, by combining different perspectives on experience and events, is well known and accepted in the professional training and organizational development community. Many learners outside of these communities are not as well aware of the impact of collective learning efforts. There are, as well, some other obstacles in the organizational environment that can influence the effectiveness of group learning. First is the availability of other learners with the same interests at the same time. To avoid the drawbacks associated with lock-step group learning situations, learners can form informal groups, virtual learning groups that collect to consider a particular problem, issue or opportunity, and then take their learning into organizational behavior in multiple ways that they define individually. The synergistic effect is present during the group interactions and in the incremental effects from multiple implementation of learning, perhaps in different subsystems within the organization. In this way, group learning offers the combined advantages of tailored learning for the individuals involved, but synergistic interaction of learning in the group setting and synergistic implementation within the overall organizational presence.

3. *Complex adaptive systems grow nonlinearly.* Change outcomes may be greater than the apparent value of the change itself. Learning may not, therefore, come from obvious sources at predictable times or places. The learner should be aware that incidental learning [4], like informal learning, is a natural part of the individual and organizational learning experience and, therefore, should develop learning strategies to leverage this capability. The ability to recognize incidental learning and build the learned capability into a personal response system or into an organizational process is important in a near-chaotic envi-

ronment. The dynamics of the system demand decisions and actions, often quickly, and incidental learning can be brought to bear on such decisions in ways in which more formal, fixed learning cannot.

Incidental learning is more relational and situational and can be more readily available than more formal activities. However, at the same time, this situational nature may pose a problem if translations are necessary between the specific learning situation and the situation in which the learning is to be applied. It may take some time, for example, to decide if a capability learned on the fly some time ago, and vaguely recalled, will fit into a current situation. Because the complex adaptive system may exhibit strong nonlinearity, the situation now may not resemble the situation then, and transfer of learned capability may be made more difficult.

4. *The fitness landscape forecasts systemic changes and, therefore, forecasts adaptations.* Change, in a continuous change environment, is foreseeable, and many changes can be anticipated with increased measurement of the full fitness landscape. The greater the understanding of the values that affect the system's behavior, the more likely it is that such foresight is available in a complex adaptive system. The learner in such a system, therefore, has the responsibility to study the measurements of the full system and its environment in order to forecast what learning will best meet the foreseeable situations. Learning, and the changes which emerge from it, must be attuned to that environment if they are to be effective in maintaining a position in the fitness landscape. Survival in such a system requires more than just adaptation. To adapt, often, is to follow and not to lead. Leaders in the fitness landscape must learn faster than those organizations with which they are co-evolving, and must set the characteristics of the landscape. Learners, regardless of type or level, should maintain access to the full environment and its events.

5. *Learning models and the way internal modeling works in the given system will yield more value than learning the particulars about a given set of building blocks.* The development of learning strategies, as suggested above, is important in an ability to take advantage of informal and incidental learning but applies, of course, to all forms of learning. Regardless of the way a new capability is developed, the capability should be absorbed into the full system in such a way that not only do the human learners gain the advantage, but that their coworkers—the equipment and networks—are also incorporated into the learning experience. This requires a learning strategy that is more comprehensive than those usually adopted by individual human learners. Where individuals generally focus on how they can control a learning situation for their own benefit, the holistic nature of the system and environment now demands that human learners consolidate their learning strategies with strategies of other agents in the system. Each learner, regardless of the type of agent it might be, needs to be aware and informed of other learning strategies at work around it. Without alignment of these strategies, learning—whether formal, informal, or incidental—may be lost or misdirected and will not contribute to the overall dynamic of the system. The system moves ahead in its near-chaotic activity as

a whole thing, influenced by events and agents internal to it, and by those events and agents external to it. The presence of the system is defined by all of these things; so is the learning that occurs in and around the system. The ways in which learning occurs in individual agents is important, as much because it generates effective learning in the whole organization as because it is effective and efficient for the learner himself. Linked learning strategies offer another layer of synergy in the fitness landscape and contribute to the ability of the organization to survive and prosper in that landscape.

HOW TO LEARN AS A CHAOTIC SYSTEM

Just as near-chaotic systems can become effective learning environments with some help from the learner-agents in the system, so a fully chaotic system benefits from activities on the part of the learners in it. The nature of the chaotic system demands attention on the part of its agents. Because it is volatile and sensitive, such a system may change radically and quickly with very little to initiate the change. Learning is more than continuous; it is imperative and radical.

There are several guidelines to keep in mind when learning in a chaotic system:

1. *Try to find out what lies beneath the apparent randomness.* What is the strange attractor? How can it be described? Is the system truly random, is it technically chaotic, or does it really follow a more stable attractor? The key task of the learner in a chaotic system is to establish the ways in which the system is technically chaotic and not simply random. This means that a part of the learning has to do with learning about the nature of the system, its variables, and how those variables might change under different conditions. This focus has led, in the current investigations of such systems, to an emphasis on simulating system behavior in order to understand the complex nature of that behavior. Such attention on system possibilities has not yet had much of an impact in other organizational systems and is an area that should be developed. The ability to simulate the effect of various changes in the system will yield a greater understanding of the underlying attractive forces that generate visible changes. This form of learning is important if learners are to progress to attempting changes in the real system itself, beyond the simulated environments.

2. *Find the parameters and measurable aspects of the system which are responsible for its sensitivity.* This learning is key to understanding the system. As noted above, the nature of the strange attractor is important if the behavior of the system is to be understood and, most particularly, if it is to be modified deliberately. In systems with weak attractive forces, any impact on the variables, or any changes brought into the system by environmental circumstances, can significantly alter system futures. Knowledge of the whole system again becomes important. All of the agents are subject to changes, and all may influence the behavior of the system. Measurement of the system is vital if the learner expects to be a part of changes initiated elsewhere in the system or its environment, or if the learner intends to apply learning to change the system.

3. *Learn what the boundaries are.* Change your learning strategy to one that will maintain constant sight of the boundary, whether described in organizational vision or by combinations of factors including internal system and external system parameters. A vision only reflects the view an organization has of itself and can become quickly dated. Make sure that your view includes such a vision, but is not limited to it. The boundaries are more complex than that. Chaotic organizations are not rivers that gently wash against the firm banks alongside, and remain in those predictable banks. Physical boundaries are poor metaphors for organizational boundaries.

4. *Learn how the system uses energy and how it renews it.* Energy sources in chaotic organizational systems are complex and are generally not studied to the depth necessary to understand their influence on the strange attractor and system behavior. Will speed, for instance, really result in better products or services over the long term? The immediate answer is yes, since speed produces faster results. The long term answer may not be yes, if achieving speed pushes system agents beyond their limits and causes them to shut down. Speed may not be the answer, likewise, if the operation of such a speedy system has a negative and undesirable influence in the overall fitness landscape in which the system is co-evolving. For example, use of bigger jet aircraft may move packages faster across the country, resulting in immediate benefits for the package-moving system and its finite set of customers. Such speed may, however, be detrimental to those who have to listen to the jets taking off and landing 24 hours a day, or who have to breathe the polluted atmosphere which results from jet exhausts. Learners must realize the complexity of such systems and the potential for unpredictable outcomes of changes. Learning which results in changes that prove negative will cause the system to decline in its landscape.

5. *Learn inside the system, not as an objective observer.* A chaotic system will not allow the delay between activity and observation. Every point in time defines a different state for a chaotic system, so any delay in observation means that the system has moved on. Because the system operates in a three-dimensional phase plane (or more), external observation of activity will be difficult if not impossible. Participation in the system, as suggested by sociologists, is the most effective way to learn in it and about it. Because learning should translate very quickly into action in such a system, the learning agent that is outside the system may not effectively translate learning into actions that complement the dynamics of the system. This argues for a well-integrated supply chain, since it is the entire chain that will guarantee the capability of a chaotic system, not simply a "core" piece. Learning activity must be well integrated into the entire chain and not just selected links of it.

6. *Understand that anything learned in the system is sensitive to the operation of the parameters on system behavior around its attractor.* The sensitivity of the system around a strange attractor means that what is known at any given point

in system history may be similar to, but not exactly like, that which is known at a different point in history. Understanding history is important, but it is not a way to predict future system states. The system ignores history in favor of whatever is affecting it now, within its general boundaries, and the strength of those influences. Sensitivity of the system means that not only will learned concepts be always tentative, but that change in concepts and system behavior may proceed with apparently illogical jumps. Allow for this in your learning strategy and be prepared for a bumpy ride.

7. *Apply fractal learning.* Once the base fractal structure of the organization is known, the learner can tune into that formula. A fractal formula can be replicated n times with the same basic result, but with increasing or decreasing specificity of magnitude. The self-similarity is a core factor to be learned, regardless of the scale on which the similarity is worked out in the system.

The learner's goal changes in a chaotic environment. As Stacey [5] notes, "In open-ended situations the business organization will have to rely on the experience-based intuition of individuals, on reasoning by analogy, if it is to innovate and discover new strategic direction." This form of strategic learning is far from the traditional approaches to learning which are most acceptable today. They are more closely related to what the Nadlers [6] referred to as education and development than they are to specific skills training. The preparation by the individual is a preparation based on the understanding that capabilities may need to be applied in a variety of ways, in a variety of situations, and under a variety of systemic pressures. This is not to say that the burden of solving problems, creating effective markets, or producing effective products is lifted. On the contrary, the need to apply learning quickly and effectively has not diminished. What is now imperative is that learning be applied quickly and effectively in chaotic and unpredictable systems.

The learner, in a chaotic system, should find multiple activities that appear to be disjointed. Under this turbulent surface, however, there will be some core and relatively simple set of dimensions that inform the system. Consistent with the self-organization principle that we have seen in learning theories as well as in chaotic systems theory, the learner is responsible for learning in the system. Learning, however, requires constant construction and reconstruction of learning strategies, as well as the capabilities that are learned. In a volatile system environment, rote memorization of facts or process steps is not enough to remain current. To maintain a useful place as a node in the behavioral network, the learning agent must remain open to radical alterations in that network. There is no permanence or consistency in a chaotic system and learning will adjust to this reality.

Learning in chaos is a deliberate confrontation with the unknown. Learning strategies adjust to sense the constant changes and hints of changes in the system. The core role of the learner is to develop a knowledge of the control parameters and variables that can be determined and to use those as the means through which to interpret the changing nature of the system and his role in it.

REFERENCES

1. Prigogine, I. and I. Stengers, *Order out of Chaos,* London: Collins, 1985, pp. xxvi, 14, 312.
2. Guastello, S. J., *Chaos, Catastrophe, and Human Affairs,* Mahwah, N.J.: Lawrence Erlbaum Associates, 1995, pp. 263, 311.
3. Bertalanffy, L. V., *General System Theory: Foundations, Development, Applications,* New York: George Braziller, 1968, p. 248.
4. Marsick, V. J. and K. E. Watkins, *Informal and Incidental Learning in the Workplace,* New York: Routledge, 1990.
5. Stacey, R. D., *The Chaos Frontier: Creative Strategic Control for Business,* London: Butterworth Heinemann, 1991, p. 212.
6. Nadler, L. and Z. Nadler, *Developing Human Resources,* 3rd ed. The Jossey-Bass Management Series, San Francisco: Jossey-Bass Publishers, 1991.

Chapter 12

Chaotic Learning Support

INTRODUCTION

The immediacy of the need to reconsider how learning can be incorporated into chaotic systems begins with a realization that chaotic systems are necessary, not necessary evils. The stigma attached to classical chaos does not follow into the realm of technical chaos, where behavior seems random but is not. Failure to understand and appreciate the value of such systems is a failure in perspective and measurement, but not a failure on the part of the system itself. To the contrary, we should prize energetic, self-renewing systems. Jeffrey E. Garten, dean of the Yale School of Management, described the late-year 1998 economy this way:

> Facing slower growth around the world, volatile markets, and fierce competition from products priced in cheap currencies, many CEOs are restructuring their companies. Their efforts, however, are likely to fall short of what's needed [1].

What Garten notes, in the strategic and tactical planning in many companies, is the tendency to consolidate, downsize, and simplify. In some instances global decentralization is the preferred solution, in others the combination of related units. These traditional tools, however, are only moderately effective in the short term. Single efforts aimed at organizational change will not be enough of a strategy. As Garten notes, "planning is full of daunting uncertainties." He recommends that "in this chaotic international environment, companies will be forced to go beyond streamlining and a one-time structural overhaul." Finally, he points to Toyota as an example of an organization that is taking effective steps: "Extreme flexibility, built-in contingency planning, and intensive focus on developing new skills for management and for the workforce. The winning plans will require more stretching than anything CEOs have attempted in their professional lives."

In fact, Toyota's training arrangements are of interest for chaotic environments because of the extent to which the company is addressing the supply chain [2]. In technical training, for example, company-oriented training is offered not only to internal personnel, but special classes have been developed for delivery at colleges and technical institutes. The entire process is automated through use of extranet connections between Toyota's network and the electronic networks in the schools. This means that learning support materials, whether electronic or paper, can be handled through the network, eliminating shipping and handling costs and time delays. It also welds together the student tracking and interactive course measurement capabilities of the company with those of the schools.

The intent is to provide a seamless, low-cost, networked learning environment. The end result will, of course, benefit the company, since students will be swayed to either work for Toyota or recommend its parts and products. Students who take Toyota training in their technical schools have the equivalent of a head start on other job candidates when applying for positions with the company. The schools benefit, of course, because they have access, through the network, to subject matter expertise, as well as instructors and materials, that would have been difficult or too expensive to gain access to ordinarily. Their students have the opportunity to talk and work directly with Toyota's technical experts, an opportunity that might have otherwise had to wait until they actually had a job with the company.

This form of disintermediation of the learning and learning support process introduces complexity into the learning environment. First, new systems capabilities are required in order to connect the corporate extranet into the school networks. A high level of trust and cooperation is required in order to support this physical network link and all it implies about access from one institution to another. Second, certification issues may arise concerning the fit between the corporate-designed courseware and academic requirements. Third, schools must address questions regarding conflict of interest: Does the acceptance of support and courseware from one company jeopardize relationships with other companies? What does such an arrangement mean to other potential sponsors or contributors? One change may lead to others and to a reassessment of school values and mission. So, while the extension of networks and connectivity provides benefits in expanding the potential of such learning systems, such extension also means a more complex and potentially chaotic learning situation. As the network—both physical and interpersonal—gets more intelligent, it also begins to demand more integration among all of its agents in order to understand the chaotic behavior that is introduced.

Moreover, the nature of change in a chaotic system can confound efforts to develop strategic plans. The blow to many strategic planners confronting chaotic systems is that once they have their elaborately constructed plans, they are largely worthless over any period of time. What they fail to take into account is that their plans are constructed from only one point on the system's phase plane, and it is extremely difficult to predict future system activity, given the large number of potential futures it has in a chaotic realm. Unless the full nature of the system is known, prediction is sophisticated guesswork. To know the parameters and variables in an entire global economic system is a large challenge indeed. At the same time, the task for strategic organizational planners becomes much more clear. With overwhelming amounts of systemic data available through internet and other network resources, as well as other data collection and analysis sources, the potential to gain greater understanding of the chaotic economic system is tantalizingly close. The availability of computing resources, which are effective at consolidating and analyzing data, is certainly unquestioned.

What we need, then, is the ability to comprehend the messages that lie in the data and make decisions based on that comprehension. At this point, that function largely belongs to the humans in the system. Unfortunately, most of them are waiting for things to settle down, with their "fight or flight" responses fully on the alert for uncertainty. For many, to be out of control is a situation to be remedied, not encouraged. To view humans, machines and networks as parts of a largely unpredictable system is a difficult concept to comprehend, especially when we are drawn toward the warm sensations of stability.

The dialectic that exists between stability and chaotic behavior in the larger system exists as well in approaches to learning support. The economic forces that demand efficiency also dictate low cost, highly effective learning support. The fastest way to this end is to create the illusion of Newtonian systemic stability and to teach it. Call in subject matter experts, define the way things are, describe the way things ought to be, and develop training courses that close the gap in favor of the way things ought to be. This makes a nice straight line from there to here, and results are measurable against the standards set by the subject matter experts. This is efficiency in training and learning support. But, like the CEOs who want a single solution, this form of learning solution is fixed in time and denies the variability and dynamics of a chaotic system. What we need are some new perspectives on learning.

COMPLEMENTARY LEARNING SYSTEMS

Earlier, I noted that the instances of technical chaos were probably few in organizations. Here, I want to emphasize that fewer instances may not be better. That is, the imposition of control functions and order in systems models may not necessarily lead to the most effective learning in the organization. I suggest that there is a need for more technical chaos, not less, in systems operations at the various levels into which organizations may be classified. In particular, technical chaos can enhance learning activity at the individual, team or sub-group level, and at the macro organizational level. Technical chaos is both an observed phenomenon and an organizational variable. To fully understand how it works, its mechanics, and its measures may be extremely difficult. It is, after all, turbulent. But there are advantages in allowing the system to let go of its control wires and puppet strings, and taking it from an evolutionary emergent regime through the phase transition which allows it to operate at a chaotic level, governed by its strange attractor.

The chief advantage comes as the system is forced to learn and relearn very quickly. Behavior change comes as an observable outcome of learning, and the highest value is attached to sustained behavior *change*. However, the value placed on sustaining behavior change assumes that the behavior will occur in a stable system in which activity and process will itself be sustained. As more and more organizations come to value quick change and high levels of change in the dynamics of the system, the level of sustainability of learning comes to mean less. The more volatile the system, the more volatile the learning. What is sustainable is change, not a given behavior.

Instead, the focus shifts to applicability and immediate relevance of learning. Long-term sustainability of what is learned and the resulting behaviors may be of marginal value. As systems themselves are deliberately forced closer and closer to a chaotic regime in order to achieve speed and mass customization leading to customer or client satisfaction, learning must be understood to be just as volatile. Learning behavior should be highly relevant to the system, as the system perceives itself at any given instant. Learning redefines the system, but the system redefines learning.

The period of time during which a system is stable is shortening. Therefore, the period of time over which a particular learning activity, whether formal or informal, is relevant is also shortening. But time is just one of the many factors which make up the "presence" of a system. The presence of the system is defined in terms of its whole nature and definable existence at any given point in time and space. Presence includes processes and activities, which are observed through the behaviors of humans, machines and networks. Presence also includes less-easily identifiable factors, which may be subtly influencing the system from its encompassing environment.

If the system achieves a presence of "X," then the learning in the system must achieve a presence of "X + 1," in order to prepare the system to adjust to change and velocity. Learning must occur ahead of system change and mutation, not in parallel with it. Behavior change which is achieved through learning, therefore, must be appropriate to the next system instant and not to the current system instant.

NEW LEARNING THEORIES NEEDED

A world that intends to transcend its currently available organizational structures and practices must look to new ideas regarding what organizations will look like, how they will interact as systems, and how they will interact to learn and change. Even given current thought surrounding organizational learning, much of that thought remains homocentric. New theories of learning must adopt the prerequisite assumption that both the definition and characteristics of learning are subject to revision. First, while we have comforted ourselves, as humanity, that we are the ultimate learners and thinkers, we can no longer make such a smug assumption. We must accept a new reality that understands that machines and equipment may learn, choosing to change their behavior based on learning, and may do a better job of it than we can.

We must, further, come to understand that networks, whether based on an interpersonal, human perspective or on the perspective of electronic interconnections, also learn. Networks are entities, sometimes redefined on a moment-to-moment basis, but entities nonetheless. Examples of this flash network redefinition process are becoming easier to find with the growing availability of the internet. As people use computers to establish electronic links through the various switches and servers that provide the routing, the electronic network reconfigures itself to provide the best available connections. The people, in turn, reconfigure themselves, to bring themselves together into the most effective learning situation that can be established in partnership with the equipment and network. The ultimate product is a complex human and electronic network accomplishing some common goal. Here, for example, is a description, from a United Nations Educational, Scientific, and

Cultural Organization (UNESCO) case study, of how educational networks are becoming these combined complex adaptive systems on a global basis:

> A global internet classroom starts with one group of students asking a question to another group of students living in another part of the world. Their dialogue and exchange through internet is then passed onto another classroom in a further school. Results of dialogues or joint classroom projects are posted onto the web and the process continues. An Internet user, unlike the person watching television or radio, has the benefit of being able to respond directly to information. It is this interaction that characterises the Internet and gives it a unique opportunity for opening up learning. It has given many children worldwide the chance to discover culturally diverse opinions and develop a global dimension to their work [3].

It becomes clear, then, that we must adopt a view of learning that recognizes the close integration of human, machine, and network. The learning of one may affect the learning or activities of the other. When a machine learns, the humans in its network must also learn. The outcome of learning is then increasingly less limited to what people do by themselves. The events in the XMIT case bear out this close relationship. Presently, we see an hierarchical order of things as reflected in Figure 12-1. In this view, people are the Supreme Commanders, directing the work of machines which, in turn, communicate electronically with each other, in some cases through a network. Alternatively, the machine can be left in its closet and people can interact in people networks, without the presence of the machine. The machine, in this view, may have more or less knowledge, but does not have intelligence, and certainly not wisdom. Our view is often that machines are drones.

Learning in such an environment is, of course, largely to be focused on humans, since they are the most important function in the system. While networking is certainly included in human learning activities, it is generally networking among human peers. Teambuilding, management, and similar interpersonal learning topics are focused almost exclusively on human-to-human interaction. Such learning activities, regardless of how or where or when they occur, reinforce the model that humans are the most important part of the tripartite construct and must therefore be treated with respect, dignity and careful attention to development. At the same time, formal training which teaches people how to use software, hardware, and networks is generally separated from training which prepares people to work with people. There is, in most models of learning support, a clear distinction between what is called "soft" skills training and "hard" skills training. In soft skills training, people

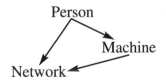

Figure 12-1. Current model of the learning hierarchy.

learn to interact with people. In hard skills training, people learn to interact with software, machines, and networks. There is a clear understanding that the two forms of learning will be carried out, at least in formal settings, under two different roofs. That is, specialization has developed which separates learning support for interpersonal and other human network skills from learning support for use of computers and other equipment. We are left to reconcile the two capabilities as best we can.

If machines and electronic networks had egos, they would no doubt be lobbying for equal access to learning opportunities. In the hierarchy where humanity is dominant, these devices and structures are viewed as having no heart. Like the Tin Man in *The Wizard of Oz*, the "hardware" and "software" in our world have no heart, no "being," and are, apparently, to be non-learners in a society otherwise rich with learning opportunities and support. To be non-human is to be relegated to a subordinate position in our models of systems and to be denied access to the full range of learning activities provided to the human element.

Machines and networks, however, do learn. They do so in two significant ways that should be recognized here. Publishing a revision or upgrade to a software program is tantamount to graduating it from a technical certification program. It has been given added capabilities and added features which, presumably, make it a better fit with the humans with whom it will interact after graduation. In a similar way, of course, the upgrading of machinery or hardware has the same effect. An automobile acquires new qualities when it receives a set of tires that will resist skidding while running at high speed on an interstate in a rainstorm. The automobile has changed its behavior, based on an acquisition of new competencies. Networks are also under constant review and revision to reduce traffic conflicts and congestion, eliminate or reuse excess capacity, and ensure connections and nodes where they are required. The introduction of fiber optic loops into the telecommunications system, for example, provides the potential for higher bandwidth and faster transmission, along with the potential to reduce the number of wires that must physically exist between nodes.

Engineers are teachers and instructors, helping their pupils learn and acquire new skills and competencies. Such changes are driven by two main forces: (1) the changes in the environment that call for increased or different capabilities in machines, software and networks; and (2) changes in the availability of new devices or processes which allow increased capabilities in the existing network or equipment or software program.

The environment, first of all, has much to do with how machines and networks learn, when they learn, and how much they learn. If there is no demand, then equipment, software, and networks are not acquired by the humans in the social organization, and therefore play no part in that organization. If existing equipment or network capacity is adequate to do the job, then additional changes to hardware, software, or networks are not forthcoming.

The environment for these inanimate objects is highly controlled by human demand, following the hierarchical model shown in Figure 12-1, and is controlled as well by peer and subordinate equipment and networks. It does little good, for example, for a website to provide large and complex databases at transmission speeds up to T-1 (1.544 Mbps) if the receiving computer has access to a 28.6 Kbps modem. There is a mismatch in capabilities in such an environment, so while the website may offer highly useful data or information, it cannot be accessed without long download periods, and is therefore of questionable utility. The "client" equipment, with the restricted modem speed, is the determining factor. In the same example, human demand may have caused the restriction and operates as a controlling factor on change and learning among machines and networks. If the owner of the client computer has previously had no need of large databases downloaded from the internet, and sees no use for such databases in his or her activity, then the connectivity restriction will likely remain a part of the machine and network environment.

A second force that influences changes introduced by engineering of machines and networks is that of changes in the availability of new devices or processes. To move, for example, from a method of writing instructions for computers which involves keying each instruction each time it is used to a method which allows cutting and pasting of instructional "objects" provides high advantages in software preparation. The introduction, into an electronic network, of a device to increase the number of light frequencies transmitted over a single fiber allows greater use of that fiber. The construction of a new tire designed to shed water more quickly and maintain firmer contact with the roadway allows increased vehicle stability at high speeds on wet pavement. The learning and change of systems, from the perspective of machines and networks, depends, therefore, on the invention of new devices that will provide advantages to the system.

In positioning such events in the inanimate world as learning, I do not intend to imply that it is a parallel to human learning. In fact, as noted in the discussion above, humans dictate and control the types and forms of change in the areas of machine and network "intelligence" and therefore limit the extent to which these system parts learn. The learning, for the most part, is the result of changes that are introduced into the system by the controlling factors. While some software programs are now learning from their environments and from their conversations with both humans and other network nodes, such learning activity is largely confined to picking up added facts and data, saving them in a database, and then recalling them as patterns, according to predetermined algorithms. The software program adds nothing original to this process and does not, in most instances, adjust its basic algorithm according to its own interpretation of what it has acquired. Newly available voice input technology, for example, appears to "learn" from our pronunciations and use of vocabulary. The secret, however, lies only partly in its ability to establish and change brain-like patterns. It also relies heavily on machine memorization of vocabulary. It is a step toward cognition but is still short of it.

Lest the discussion be seen as overly anthropomorphic, consider the future. The future of machines and networks, as envisioned by humanity, is a more democratic approximation than the hierarchical arrangement now in place. The future for machines, humans, and networks lies in integration.

First, the ability of humans to interface with devices has always been important. Automobile manufacturers spend considerable time and money on the human-machine interface, since the comfort level of humans and the users of the machines consider the utility of buttons and switches important. In a similar way, the evolution of computer-human interfaces is an area of continuing focus. For example, Apple® computer had a great deal of initial success with the Macintosh® computer line because it adapted a graphical user interface. This approach, using icons and pull-down menus to get work done, was more appealing to most people trying to use the machines than the clunkier symbol and text-based interface still to be found in other major operating systems. The machines, then, were taught by their programmers to conform more closely to the way humans work and less to the ways in which the machines themselves thought and did their work. This interface, or linkage, between humans and machines was suggested early in the history of miniaturization by the wrist-radio made famous in the newspaper comics. The need to connect with the devices, to have them add to our existing human capabilities, and to have convenient interfaces has been a shaping force in the past, and indications are that emphasis will continue on how we connect with the machines and networks we increasingly use.

Yet the irony with these interfaces is that they are convenient only to the human agents in the system. Computers are constructed to depend on machine language, a language that is inbred into them in the forms of 1s and 0s. What they understand, they understand as sequences of these two digits and nothing else. The fact that we can type in our native language onto a keyboard and have that typing appear on a screen as recognizable words is due to the ability of the machine to adapt to humans, not the other way around. While the machine must of necessity think in one way, it is flexible enough to accommodate the inability of its human partners. So the very menu-driven abilities considered necessary by the human agents may, in fact, hinder our capability to interact with the hardware and software which share the system with us. With menus, we can only express what programmers have previously anticipated. Given the high number of menus available, programmers have anticipated a great many of the things that we might want to express to a computer. Yet, the menus and the graphical user interface, while affording a measure of communication capability not known in earlier human-computer environments, imposes restrictions on the capability of our computer partners. In this situation, it is the computer, not the humans, that has done all of the adapting.

Second, our science fiction points the way toward integration of humans with these machines and networks. *Frankenstein* [4], which actually placed more emphasis on the outcomes of technology than on the technology itself, provided a fascinating early insight into artificial life and intelligence. We have since seen much engineering research concerning robotics, with the transference of human capability into machines. Robots, of course, played a major role in early exploration of space and have continued to represent human skills in the forms of exploration probes (such as the Voyager missions) and research robots used to explore the chemistry, biology, and geology of other planets. An outgrowth of this reality is the science fiction of part-human, part-machine entities, which could transform themselves like self-directed tools to meet any circumstance or need. The being that is one moment a spaceship is, in the next moment, a humanoid robot pacing across the planet to accomplish its mission. Actual engineering and fiction seem to feed each other as the imagined becomes both real and the basis for imagination. Consistently, however, we have seen these visions and realities creating human-machine combinations or organic-physical combinations.

Third, science has given us micro-machines, which are actual working machines the parts of which are measured in microns, not centimeters. These microbots may be limited in ability but function at scales where humans cannot. Building a "smart suit" which contains computing capability in a garment is also a near reality. These devices represent the increasing capability to bring machines into position to mimic or replace tasks once handled solely by humans, if indeed handled at all. These new devices offer new possibilities for applications that heretofore have not been possible.

Fourth, biologists are moving ahead with the definition of the human genome. This project, officially known as the Human Genome Project, began in 1990 with the goal to discover and describe all of the 60-80 thousand human genes. The end result will be a reference genome which researchers can then use for further study of human biology. While individuals differ in the description of their genome, all share the same basic set and structure. Once the reference data is in place, it will be easier for researchers, medical technicians, and biologists to compare and contrast differences within the structure, from individual to individual. DNA matching is, in fact, at such a level of accuracy that U.S. courts accept evidence of matches between samples of DNA found at crime scenes and samples taken from suspects.

The overall scope of the genome definition project is suggested by the fact that, after some seven years of preliminary work, only 3% of the human genome is mapped. In part, this has been a period of experimentation with methods for obtaining, capturing, measuring, and storing the information. Yet, the project has underscored the overall complexity of human DNA. This research has led to some preliminary experimentation in cloning complex organisms.

Such an ability to recreate a biological entity from samples of the DNA of a parent suggests the movement toward the ability to create intelligent or semi-intelligent biological beings constructed as organic machines. Setting aside the notable questions which arise from the domain of human ethics regarding such practice, the technical ability to achieve living organisms which have been engineered for particular purposes suggests the potential for the merger of what is now three separate functionalities embodied in humans, machines, and networks. The extension of the findings from the human genome project is the finding of commonality across species at genetic levels. Humans share basic traits with other species on earth. This finding makes us at once less unique in biology but, at the same time, more related to our systems and life environment.

The trends from both science fiction and science fact point toward the potential for blending human, machine, and network into units which can function in a variety of ways, using the best capabilities from the three elemental forms. The logical extension of this thinking provides us with, perhaps, a kind of creature reminiscent of the Star Trek® "Borg." The Borg, short for cyborgs, represents a combination of humanoid with mechanical parts, the whole creature being incorporated into a collective network. Regardless of physical distance from each other, the Borg shared knowledge. What one part knew, all parts knew. What one part felt, all parts felt. What one part learned, all parts learned.

Fortunately, based on the reputation the Borg earned in science fiction, they exist only there, at least for now. However, the capability to add a sophisticated prosthesis to a human body is fact. Arms, legs, hands, and feet, along with some internal organs can be mechanically replaced. The ability to simulate lost limbs and to restore some functionality with substitutes has been achieved. For the most part, the substitutes do not possess the precision or capabilities of the originals, but imitation comes closer as this technology learns through successive generations.

We also replace human parts with animal parts with increasing levels of success. Again, through DNA manipulation, we are able to help the human body adapt parts from other animals. Mastery of this capability suggests that adoption of synthetically generated organs is also possible. The nature of those organs, and their sophistication, will expand gradually. Synthetically produced skin for skin grafts and synthetically grown organic hearts or even brains are results of our experience, learning, and ability in such mimetic sciences. The trends are not imaginary, and the capabilities are expanding in the biological sciences.

Given that, ultimately, knowledge of the human genome will give us manipulative abilities over characteristics that we now consider to be human, the implications for learning are significant. Learning capabilities themselves, now dominated by humans, may become more integrated into close-knit connections among humans, what may be called machines (organic or mechanical), and networks. Humans may eventually simply stick an appendage into a connector and know the latest football scores from around the world without turning on a television, radio, or other separate communications device. Boundaries between what we now define as humans, machines and networks are already disappearing. At some point, the distinctions may become meaningless. As we now accept people with artificial hearts as still human, so in the future will we accept biological entities, which do not resemble humans at all, as intelligent elements in organizational structures and networks.

As events take us toward such an integrated future, it is appropriate to speculate on near-term implications of these directions. We are, at this point, still detached as humans from any substantive merger at the biological level with our machines and networks. They are still independent of us, even though there is a clear interdependency that is evident. We need them and they, at this point, cannot exist without us. Given the situation in the present, it is worthwhile to focus on how learning will be done in such integrated systems, which part will dominate (human, machine, or network), how the three parts will reconcile each other's strengths and weaknesses, and how each part will learn from the others and teach the others. The further need to learn and change in chaotic systems offers another facet for exploration. These are the primary questions which, when answered, will provide the new basis for learning theory.

TOWARD A CHAOTIC LEARNING THEORY

The content of the foregoing chapters has served to provide us with the basis for constructing a new model for learning based on characteristics of chaotic systems.

The characteristics that will influence learning and learning support in this new perception of the environment are chiefly these:

1. *Wholeness*

   We will have a sense of wholeness within the learning system, among the learner and the elements of the network of which it is a part. This wholeness will include a sense of both cognitive and affective connectivity into the network. We will have a sense that the learning support system is dynamically associated with the network, and that the network is inclusive and democratic.

2. *Diversity*

   Learning will take place in diverse places, diverse ways, at diverse times, among diverse groups, and learning support may be addressed to non-human elements of the network as well as human. The existence of an agent in a complex adaptive system will be determined by the context of the system at any point in its phase space. The proper kinds of agents must be available for use in the network and must be brought into a node relationship within the network dynamics as the particular needs for that agent arise—not earlier, not later. Each agent fills an ecological niche and may exist to maintain the place of the system on its fitness landscape or prepare the system to advance in that landscape. No active agent is redundant.

3. *Dialectic*

   Learning and learning support will occur in an atmosphere of considerable dialogue, not necessarily to reach consensus, but to reach understanding and adaptation to varying personalities, network characteristics, and network entities as the network is configured at any point in its phase space. Agents engaged in dialectic will understand and promote the idea that differing viewpoints and perspectives are acceptable. Problem solving will be nonlinear rather than linear, and nonlinear dynamic solution sets will emerge from the dialectic that is ongoing within the system. Cooperative learning will be a key outcome.

4. *Open*

   Learning and learning support will be available to everyone and everything that is a part of the network web. The network will be tuned to learn as much from outside the web as it does from inside the web. An open learning system will incorporate ideas of continuous learning. Outside and inside will become difficult terms to describe. Openness will support diversity and dialectic, as well as nonlinearity. In addition, the open learning system will support the characteristic of "flows," a part of a complex adaptive system. This is the way in which networks are switched or reconfigured dynamically to adjust to their current ecologies and the fitness landscapes on which they find themselves. The flow construct also applies to the recursive nature of the fractal system, which builds its future state from its present and past states. Flow, in this sense, has to do with how well the system reuses its parts and readjusts them to new circumstances as the system presence changes. Facts encapsulated on a hard drive buried deep in a network, for example, are inefficient if they are not reused and recycled into knowledge or even wisdom.

5. *Everywhere, anytime*

Learning and learning support will be expected to be continuous and will be deliberately constructed to be continuous. They will be dynamic, with a portion of the support going to ensuring the dynamic adaptation between learning, learner, and organizational system.

6. *Strange attractors*

Learning and learning support will follow strange attractors, not fixed or limit attractors. Attention will be focused on system attractors as targets for learning and not on the traces of the dynamic systems themselves. Attention will be on the core equations and the relevant variables that accurately demonstrate the attractive forces at work in the systems.

7. *Feedback*

The system will be attuned to the fact that it is recursive and builds on itself. Its fractal nature will be recognized, with learning and learning support exploring the full range of fractal dimensions of the system. Attention will be paid to the understanding and definition of the equations and variables that produce system replication and an understanding of the initial conditions which govern system behavior.

8. *Emergent*

Learning and learning support will be emergent and will be self-generated from the network and organizational system. There will be no top or head of the system. Those in leadership roles will suggest and facilitate, but will not direct or control the relevant system variables or constants.

9. *Autopoetic*

Learning and learning support will be self-sustaining in the system. They will display proof of synergy derived from integrated and combinatorial factors in the system equations. This will follow from the emergent nature of the system, and will be dependent on its vitality. Learning and change will never be simultaneous, but will be closely linked. Learning will continue to be stored for later recall and may not be implemented immediately or directly as internalized. The nature of the autopoetic system, however, will share the learning, and it may be stored in different agents in the network for recall and application at different times, under different circumstances, and by different agents than those that originally "learned." Learning becomes a widely dispersed and available building block within the system, and is itself highly dynamic and sensitive.

10. *Nonlinear*

Learning and learning support will be nonlinear. They will not display high dependence on cause and effect rationalization, but will, instead, display evidence of nonlinear algebraic behavior, including sudden and complex bifurcation and change. The system will display sensitive dependence on initial conditions. Instability will be expected and encouraged, insofar as the system continues to demonstrate technical and not classical chaos.

11. *Aggregation*

Learning and learning support systems will both use and advocate aggregation as a feature of complex adaptive systems. Aggregation is a property that influences diversity, model building, emergence, regeneration and co-evolution.

12. *Tagging*

Learning and learning support systems will utilize tagging to classify and categorize elements in the system, so that their properties are known. Tagging in a CAS acts to help construct new models from existing or new materials, to the extent that the building blocks are well-understood across the network and the utility and functionality of the building blocks can be best accessed and applied in the dynamic system. Tagging enables aggregation in nonlinear system dynamics, especially those which are "accelerated," as viewed qualitatively by any element in the system. In other words, speed in a nonlinear system is supported by constructive aggregation and tagging.

13. *Internal modeling*

The learning system will support the creation and modification of schema that will describe the strange attractor or the patterns through which the system functions or will function. Learning will not be held to be static, and emphasis will be on learning strategies or models through which learning takes place, as opposed to facts and history.

14. *Building blocks*

Learning and learning support should take advantage of building blocks that are objects, reusable within the network as it reconfigures. Building blocks provide sets of capabilities that are ready at hand as the system prepares to change and adapt. The units should be constantly reconfigured and reconfigurable to reflect the descriptors of the current fitness landscape or phase space.

THE DESIGN OF CHAOTIC LEARNING SUPPORT

Establishing the Basis for Intervention

The Problem with Gaps

There are three issues with the "gap analysis" approach to analysis of learning needs in a chaotic system. First, the gap is an artificial construct, based on today's understanding of systemic values. Second, it assumes a knowledge of future states of the system that may not exist. Third, because learning support tends to be done by human resource departments, learning is automatically associated with human learning and other systemic learning needs are often set aside to be dealt with separately, or subrogated to the human agents in the system.

That gaps are artificial constructs is not a surprise to anyone who has attempted what is called "front-end" analysis, "needs assessment," "needs analysis," or "performance analysis." There is always the difficulty in getting the right subject matter experts (SMEs) assembled and establishing the desired future state. In many instances, analysis is conducted by training professionals and therefore centers on training needs. These analysts may miss other systemic issues or, where they are identified, such issues are passed on to other segmented human resource or systems organizations not involved in the analysis project. Compensation issues, for example, are often passed to the compensation specialists, who are sometimes too busy making sure that people get paid to be concerned with compensation issues which may impact a specific performance problem. Further, many subject matter experts are those who are expert at carrying out things as they are now and have been rewarded for ensuring stability and continuous change, not radical change. Their view of the future, then, tends to be one of a piece with the present, and, in their brief interview sessions, they are often reluctant to let go and transcend the mundane.

The future state which is such identified is thus suspicious on the grounds that the new standard for performance many not be holistic and may not reflect radical changes in the system. The new standard is an attempt to guess at the future state and make it a logical extension of the present state. Subject matter experts can be so overcome with experience and practicality that they cannot break through those ceilings. This approach is illustrated in Tom Gilbert's Potential for Improving Performance (PIP) formula, which assesses system behavior against the standard of an ideal state [5, 6]. The PIP represents a philosophy in which a perfect or stable state can be envisioned and defined, with performance of the system described as the degree to which actual performance can approach the ideal.

The resulting gap represents another form of stable state, since the analysis is generally a one-time function, barely tolerated in the time schedules management has consciously or unconsciously imposed on learning support development activity. Rarely is enough time devoted to this work, yet its results configure not only the learning support to emerge, but the impact that support will have on the organization for some time to come. Stability also rests in the establishment of a new and apparently higher performance standard. The word itself is suspicious in a chaotic system. The behavior of such a system is incremental and depends on choices made at each point in the system's dynamic path and the influence of the nonlinear strange attractor beneath the system. Since the chaotic organizational system behaves in highly variable ways around its attractor and is highly sensitive, any claim to establish a standard of performance for humans or any other element in the system is suspect. The delineation of a gap is thus tenuous. It is a frame of the movie, not the movie itself, and is a poor basis for decisions on learning support strategies, methods, and development and delivery budgets.

The second problem is that a gap represents a future state that may not exist. The measurement of the effectiveness of learning and other performance support interventions is now largely believed to be a function of the extent to which such changes affect the behavior of the organizational system into which they are introduced. If the system is dynamic and chaotic, how can this future state be determined? In fact, in establishing standards and defining gaps, we assume stability and linearity, neither of which is available in chaotic systems. The measurement of transfer, the measurement of costs and benefits, or the establishment of ROI are all methods which depend on some sense of stability in system performance. In all instances we are asking, "Are things better, and if so by how much?" The answer is, of course, predicated on the measurement of the gap, and an understanding of the difference between desired and actual. Since the learning support intervention was concocted at one point in time, when the system had one definition in its point in phase space, and the measurement is occurring at a later point in time, when the system has a different definition in phase space, the value of the measurement depends on stability in the system from one time to the next. This assumes stability in the variables that define system dynamics and on the ranges available to it in its parameters. What is learned, then, is dependent on how things looked at one point in time, but what is measured is system performance and the impact of learning at another point in time. Basing learning support on a fixed gap definition is thus suspect.

Third, those who design learning support are generally oriented toward human performance and a homocentric view of the effects of learning in the system. This is less true when the topic of learning is some form of network or equipment. Yet even when the subject is computer skills, the role of the computer or its associated electronic network is generally neglected in favor of the role of the human learner. The networked computer is viewed as a tool to be manipulated, but usually not a partner in the completion of work. Gaps identified in capability focus on human capability to use the tools, not on the lack of capabilities and gaps in the equipment or network. Sometimes this is due to a lack of understanding on the part of the learning support designer of the technical characteristics of the equipment or network. The backgrounds of some of these designers may be oriented toward human resources development and not system development or holistic performance support. In this particular area, however, the designers are usually well-versed in the equipment and network technology. Yet their gap analysis and training needs analysis tend to concentrate on what humans have to do to adapt to the electronics and adopt them into the human way of doing things, rather than on what might be necessary to change the behavior of the network or equipment.

This attitude has led to a situation in which technical language and technical knowledge has become a prerequisite to opening even popular magazines about computers and electronic systems. Those who build electronic systems expect human users to close the gap between their day-to-day work and the intricacies of the equipment and networks with which they coexist. If network capabilities and equipment capabilities are not well used, it is the fault of the trainers who failed to train human users properly. The equipment, software and network, like spoiled children, are pampered, and their foibles and weaknesses accepted as the best they can do, or even, in some unenlightened places, praised as better than nothing. Gap analysis, then, when confined to the human element in the system, fails to explain much that is wrong in the system. By accepting some things as unchangeable, analysts create artificial gaps, which are ill defined, and therefore lead to improper or incomplete solutions.

Recognizing Needs in Chaotic Systems

The first general need in any chaotic organizational system is to recognize the nature of the chaotic system itself. That is, there is a need to describe the system as a technically, not classically, chaotic system. This form of understanding is basic to assessing the ways in which learning and performance support may be introduced into and contribute to the success of such a system.

Since it is difficult to establish a gap without introducing a stable descriptor into a dynamic system, gap analysis is not recommended. Instead, analysts should address the learning and other support that will be necessary to maintain the characteristics of the dynamic system. Specifics are of less interest in such a system, as are policies, procedures, and process flows. Such things are highly volatile and subject to immediate jumps and changes as the system adjusts to the constant collective decision-making that is going on within it.

Learning and support needs, therefore, are of a more general nature than are the case in more traditional or stable systems. Support will tend to focus on how the system under consideration interacts with other systems and with its general environment. The characteristics and variables of the system must be mastered. The key question is not "What makes it tick?" but "What makes it change?" The concern is with knowing about those things which may influence or impact the variability of the system and helping the system learn how to absorb and integrate those changes [7]. The purpose of learning and performance support becomes a general systems understanding purpose, and not a specific fix-it purpose.

The approach to learning support in a chaotic system must begin with strategic and not with tactical considerations of how the system operates. The core need is to identify the forms of learning support which will vary along with the system and which can themselves adapt as the system follows a chaotic trajectory. Emphasis, then, leads toward the integration of cognitive and social learning into an amalgamation that is not overly structured or specific as to violate the dynamic nature of the system, but not so loose as to veer off into randomness. The chief need to be supported in such a system is the need to change, and all learning and performance support should be directed to that end. Understanding the strange attractor and its attractive activity, along with the variables and parameters that contribute to the volatile nature of the system, leads to the definition of the things to be learned.

The example of weather systems, where much of the research into chaotic activity began, offers a suggestion of an approach to chaotic learning. By understanding the sensitivity of key variables in the weather, scientists were able to develop simulations that helped them further understand the key underlying formulae that governed the seemingly erratic behavior. This learning has been followed by further understanding of such non-local phenomena as El Niño and La Niña, alternating hot and cold spots in the mid-Pacific Ocean. The understanding of these oceanic events, seemingly unconnected with wind, rain, and snow, has in fact led to an understanding of the influence these two events have on weather. By backing away from the increased understanding of the weather variables themselves, scientists have been able to learn by looking at the things that influence the status of those variables. Increased accuracy in forecasting has come not only because of sophisticated satellite mapping technology, but also in the learning that has come from more holistic views of weather behavior.

In this same way, the needs of an organizational system are being hinted at by the local symptoms we usually view and treat, but such views and treatments are after the fact. Concentration on localized and narrow fixes will yield only an expenditure of energy—in terms of time, agents, and money—with little to show for it beyond the instant. Just as an organization's balance sheet is a snapshot of the financial state of the organization at a particular moment in time, the traditional gap analysis for performance or learning support accomplishes the same thing. It is locally useful, but has little strategic value. Assessment of needs must be as dynamic as the system itself and must accomplish a wider view than localized symptoms.

Developing Chaotic Interventions

Three high-level models, as noted in an earlier chapter, generally govern design of interventions:

1. ISD
2. OD
3. Performance Technology

There is an increasing awareness that elements of all three approaches to learning and organizational change can be combined. Shandler [8], for instance, lists some eleven alternative delivery technologies that include peer-to-peer learning, job aids, mentoring and coaching, performance support systems, and reading. These methods can be traced to all three of the facets of system performance improvement. However, these methods, and others associated with any of the three major approaches, are chiefly aimed at supporting change in the people in the system. This leaves other system agents to be dealt with in other ways or to self-organize as they choose. Separate approaches through training theory, OD theory and practice, or the wider scope of performance technology are not sufficient to address support for complex adaptive systems or chaotic systems.

Design of Complex Adaptive Performance Support Systems

As the HRD/OD/HPT professional begins to come to grips with the organizational presence of systems that are admittedly unstable, fast-changing, and, to one degree or another, complex and chaotic, he or she will necessarily begin to rethink the entire process of design, development, and delivery through which supporting products and services are brought to line organizations. The concept of predictable processes applies no better when considering the development of training courses and other human performance interventions than it does when considering the other subsystems at play in an organization. Consideration must be given to alternatives that will not only satisfy the learning needs inherent in a complex adaptive system, but also conform to the shift away from formalism in such systems.

Interventions, if adaptable, will have characteristics in common with the operating systems they support. This applies not only to the familiar formats of training courses, but also to all other forms of interventions that are developed to help a system maximize its place in the fitness landscape. An open operating system, then, will gain advantage from learning and performance support systems that are also open. Operating systems that are complex adaptive systems will benefit from performance support systems that are also complex adaptive systems.

What may be useful, then, as professional interests once represented by the specialties of HRD, OD, and HPT merge will be some core principles that will guide the development of such interventions, rather than prescribe paths, processes, steps, and stages. If design were to adhere to these principles, the need for a simplistic and linear ISD process would be mitigated in favor of a more volatile, flexible approach to the development of learning and performance aids. Further, these principles would extend beyond the professions devoted to human performance and would, in fact, be of interest and concern to others in the social business organization who are responsible for performance of the organization and its subunits.

Ultimately, of course, in the virtual organization, this definition incorporates everyone responsible for the supply chain for a product or service. This broader consideration also takes in those who are currently considered contractors or other workers outside of the core organizational structure. If they are a part of the supply chain, then they are a part of the learning organization, with need for facts, processes and principles, and with contributions to make to the learning and evolution of the complex adaptive organization.

To extend this line of thought to include home and family life is not to go too far. In fact, home and family life become a part of the larger supply chain for the virtual organization, as telecommuters spend more time at home and contractors use their homes as the base at which much of their work is done. The concept of telecommuting, in fact, gains its vitality from the combination of home and work as elements of the operating system's presence. In a similar way, contractors, operating more independently than telecommuters, maintain network connections and act as nodes for more than one core organization. Home, to them, often equates to the total physical facility investment of their business. A contractor is his organization, and operates successfully in a virtual world by becoming an effective node with strong flows interconnected with other organizations. The contractor working from home, connected to clients and associates by telephone and computer, constitutes a complex adaptive system, with human, machine, and network elements.

Learning, then, will flow into and out of this home and family node as well, and performance of the system will ultimately depend on the extent to which this node and these flowlines into the home are supported. The fitness landscape of the successful virtual system can afford to ignore nothing that is relevant to the complex adaptation of that system. As an example, a company recently revised its employee orientation program and included both a classroom segment, held for the employees, and a CD-ROM segment, intended for employees and their families. The electronic package included corporate history and background, and served to orient the family to the type of business into which the employee was entering. Other electronic performance support tools, originally intended to be used within the walls of organizations, are also finding their way outside to provide benefit to the employee, the family, and, in other cases, to contractors and supplier companies which are in partnership with the organization. This approach to learning support will provide increasing benefits to such supply chains, as links in the chain understand the relationships which underlie the more formal contracts and working agreements which are in place.

This expands the idea of learning and performance support professionalism beyond those who have chosen to call themselves professionals and those who have been designated as trainers, performance consultants, or change managers. The concept of professionalism in this discipline is not one that should be restricted to a few, but is a capability that should be encouraged in the many. There will be those who will be useful in a dedicated and specialized capacity, but primarily in the role of consultants to the consultants.

To introduce experts who are not an integral part of the system into the system and expect them to become integrated into it may be expecting too much. The performance of a CAS suggests that it will absorb and adopt subsystems needed for survival and growth, but those subsystems must become a part of the primary reason for being of the CAS itself and must not be viewed as appendages. HRD, OD, and HPT professionals, however, are often viewed by organizations as just such appendages. Within the adaptation dynamics of the complex system, these professionals are often discarded because they fail to become a part of the overall fitness landscape and exist as specialists and specialties. They are brought into the system as temporary expedients to fix a problem or set of problems and to help close some perceived gap. They are often discarded by the system because the perceived gap is closed or because remaining needs within the system do not seem to warrant specialists.

These disciplines then, as currently positioned in the overall social business system, are not vital to its ongoing evolution. They provide short-term solutions, but not long-term sustenance for the complex adaptive system that they serve. While this positioning for HRD, OD, and HPT is effective, as they become temporary nodes in a virtual organization, such positioning is ineffective in building the ability of the larger system to sustain itself through learning. Learning and performance support, as they apply to the whole system and as they are integral to the whole system, are not advanced by temporary solutions. Investments in short-term courseware and other organizational interventions, presented as events, do little to strengthen the ability of the complex adaptive system to learn, survive, or grow. Formalism and rule-based approaches to design are inconsistent with a CAS model.

In fact, such temporary solutions detract from the ability of the system to adapt. Resources that are useful in a virtual sense—that is, with loose connections into the system, and connected only when the system has a need for them—are a natural part of a CAS. Many such resources, however, become permanently attached to the system, yet are never integrated into the flows of the system, as in the arrangement shown in Figure 12-2.

This is often the case with HRD, OD, and HPT subunits, with the effect that they drain resources away from other areas of need within the system and fail to continue to contribute to the effectiveness of the overall system. The establishment, then, of specialized, semi-permanent nodes within the network that constitutes the CAS is questionable in its effectiveness. If abilities and capabilities are not transferred from node to node, imbalances begin to appear in the system. The sophistication of the system is limited by its ability to transfer expertise among nodes and to balance the flows and

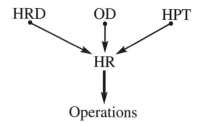

Figure 12-2. Hierarchical learning support resources.

nodes of the system. The support of system development, learning, and performance, therefore, is more likely to be effective if it is a part of the primary CAS, with indistinguishable characteristics, as illustrated in Figure 12-3. In this perspective, an operational learning node is a part of a larger system and is configured to include both the primary production or service function that is aligned with the larger system and the primary learning function that is aligned with that encompassing system.

All of the elements shown in Figure 12-2 are also here in Figure 12-3, but have been integrated and networked for maximum effectiveness and minimal boundary structures. This is in keeping with the need, in systems theory, for relationships among parts of a larger system—the parts must be necessary to each other and share rationale within the larger system.

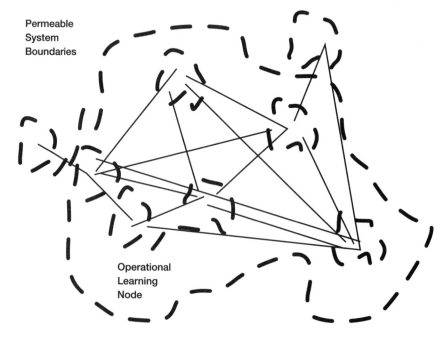

Figure 12-3. Integrated CAS learning network.

Specialists in HRD/OD/HPT, then, because they often center their work and being around a specifically defined attractor, as in Figure 12-2, may not integrate effectively as a part of an operating system. This can occur even when they focus on humans, which constitute the more influential parts of a social business system. These specialists, like all others who are not in the direct line of the production and service value chain, are appendages—often viewed as necessary, but just as often viewed as discardable. If discardable, they do not, then, exist as integral needs of the system, but as temporary nodes linked into the supply chain as perceived needs for expert services arise. This situation may exist even when the HRD, OD, or HPT functions report directly to a line manager, without the intervening hierarchical level of HR, suggested in Figure 12-2.

It is, therefore, those agents that are considered directly involved in the production or service delivery purpose of the CAS that must not only perform in the sense that they do the work leading to production they must also support performance within the system, as in Figure 12-3. This equates to an empowered learning organization in which the agents not only learn, but learn how to learn and support each other in their learning. It is important to remember, here, that these agents may be human, may be machines, or may be networks. It is not necessary that learning and performance of the system rest solely with the human agents in the system. Intelligence in the equipment and intelligence in the network should be brought to bear in consideration of learning and performance support resources and actions.

Such inanimate agents may be overlooked if adaptability and learning are taken to be biological imperatives. They are not. Humans have increasingly transferred cognitive capabilities to machines and to networks so that these non-human agents can now act, as well as be acted upon. This reality of increasing participation by inanimate agents signals that such agents may be looked to for learning and performance support, just as humans are seen to possess such responsibilities and roles. The design of interventions, then, must account for the presence of inanimate as well as animate agents and humans as well as machine or network-based cognitive processes within the CAS.

A proposed set of principles to guide design of interventions destined for complex adaptive systems need not be elaborate. In fact, the core set of principles is stated in Figure 12-4.

Complex Adaptive Performance Systems

1. The learning and performance support system should be emergent.
2. The support product should be, itself, a complex adaptive system.
3. Learning and performance support should be dyanmically integrated with the operating CAS.
4. All agents in the operating CAS are agents in the performance CAS.
5. The success of the learning and performance support CAS and the operating CAS are indistinguishable.

Figure 12-4. Design of complex adaptive performance systems.

The first principle in the design of learning and performance support systems for complex adaptive systems is to treat performance as a natural and existential part of the operating complex adaptive system. Any subsystem, then, will emerge from within the larger system and not be imposed or inserted into it from the outside. Learning and performance support will occur as natural events within the overall activity of the complex adaptive system that they seek to enrich.

This does not mean that such emergent systems cannot be radical or cause radical upheaval and change in the fitness landscape. In fact, following the descriptive characteristics of chaotic systems, the changes brought into the larger system can be expected to produce consequences that are a magnitude greater than the initiating change. At the same time, however, the changes should maintain a discernible pattern and center of attraction so that the result of change is not a chaotic regime. The position of the system must remain at the edge of chaos in order to maintain its consistency as a complex adaptive system. It cannot be distracted to the point that it enters a more turbulent and chaotic existence. The learning and performance improvement activities which emerge from the larger system, then, will be associated with that system and will have strong links and traces back into the defining system. These activities must play a part in maintaining the complex adaptive system at the edge of chaos.

Second, the learning and performance support system should itself be recognized as a complex adaptive system, intimately associated with the operating system that it complements and from which it emerged. It should meet the definition of a complex adaptive system and should demonstrate the characteristics of a complex adaptive system considered earlier in this study.

Third, the emergent learning and performance support system must include in its definition the necessary information to allow it to adjust dynamically as the supported system adjusts and varies. If the performance support system is emergent, it must also be dynamic, with full recognition of the volatility of the underlying system from which it emerged. The learning and performance support system must be continually linked to nodes and flows within the operating system and able to draw from those links the cues for changes underway on the overall fitness landscape that will affect the performance support system. The performance support CAS must maintain its intelligence to the point that it can change in tandem with the operating system, thus eliminating the concept of gaps. Such gaps as those currently included in the literature as the trigger for learning and performance support events [9–12] are post hoc, and their identification is after the fact. The properly coordinated performance support CAS does not allow gaps to develop, but precludes them by using its intelligence to know where it is on the overall fitness landscape and adjust as the underlying system adjusts. There is no pause or difference in the capabilities of the operating system and its complementary learning system.

Fourth, it is important that all agents in the operating CAS also be agents in the learning and performance support CAS. That is, all learning is organizational. There can be no distinguishing and separable learning for individual agents or groups of agents within the system which does not influence or impact the adaptation of the entire system. Nothing that happens within the system goes unnoticed, and no behavior within an agent or set of agents happens without adjusting the entire system on its fitness landscape. At the same time, learning is agent-based, and performance and system behavior derive from the collective behaviors of the agents. Therefore, each agent, separately, can be seen as influenced by and an influencer of the system as a whole, and individual agents cannot be ignored. Home, family, societal, and other learning influences brought into a given organizational entity by individuals will influence the implicate order of the organization. Whereas once corporations were seen as benefactors to individuals and guardians of the behavior and well being of individuals, the emphasis is now shifting toward the reverse of that philosophy. Corporate benefits and patronage are on the wane, with the ensuing recognition of the value that individuals bring into the corporate organizational system. No butterfly is too small to originate change.

There is no such thing as averaging out performance over the system—this would be to ignore the nonlinearity of the CAS and assume that deviant behavior in the system is a negative factor. This calls for the elimination of models of system performance that focus on averages and bell curves. Nonlinear system performance means that support for performance must also be nonlinear and must account for the statistical tails as well as the mean, median, or mode. Learning and performance support for the central tendency is no longer applicable within a complex adaptive systems environment.

Equally important is the suggestion, in the fourth principle, that humans are not the only agents within a complex adaptive system. As noted earlier in this study, the agents may be humans, machines, or the networks created within and among agents. This suggests that performance support must take into account all agents, not just human agents, as it emerges from the complex adaptive system of which it is a part. It is this factor of the fourth principle that is best acknowledged by literature addressing human performance technology. All agents, human, equipment, or network, must be included in any complex adaptive system that provides complementary learning and performance support for its operating system.

Finally, it seems reasonable to think that if the learning and performance support system is a complementary complex adaptive system, emergent from the operating system, then success of the two complementary systems is singularly defined. There is no separate measure of success for the performance support system. Success for learning and performance support is dependent on direct, dynamic relationships with the nodes within the operating CAS and is measurable only to the extent that the underlying CAS is measurable.

The transfer of these five principles of learning support design into practice has implications for the whole complex adaptive system. These implications are most evident in changes required in order to design and develop interventions that are complementary complex adaptive systems. Electronically supported interventions offer capabilities and qualities that make them likely candidates for complex systems. For example, they fit naturally into the flow of the network. At the same time, however, design of interventions that are complex adaptive systems will require some skill and attention from the agents within the system.

In many cases, because the learning and performance support systems do aspire to be complex adaptive systems, the development of such systems will require skills and capabilities not now believed to be integral to the operating system. While, as noted earlier in this chapter, HRD, OD and HPT specialists offer an extended supply chain function and can act as temporary nodes in the virtual network, these specialists have been only tangentially accepted by the operating system as necessary to its survival and growth. Either specialized skills in the design of learning and performance support systems will have to be accepted as a part of the skillset of the complex adaptive business system or that system will need to find better ways in which to integrate the specializations in these domains.

Some systems have tried to get around this issue by declaring that design is unimportant and can be done by generalists or other agents within the larger operating system. Experience suggests, however, that the result of amateur design is an amateur product. Such products may not, in fact, be able to satisfy the five principles stated above and, therefore, will not be able to meet the needs of a dynamic complex adaptive system. Nor does this answer generally apply well to the design and implementation of electronic performance support. Here, a variety of special capabilities are available that can make such systems complement complex adaptive operating systems. The skills required to produce such support systems, however, go beyond what is usually available in the generalist agent population within most systems. So the degree to which specialized expertise is brought to bear on design of such support systems will determine the extent to which such systems may be fashioned to support dynamic operating systems.

This reality suggests the central dialectic between emergent and controlled systems and their learning and performance support activity. Where there are high levels of control, there are likely to be high levels of formalism in support of learning and performance. The existence of control mechanisms, processes, and procedures triggers the growth of formal certification programs to ensure compliance. Training, education, and other events and interventions become a visible sign that control has been established and that all agents in the system recognize their place in the chain of being. Such operating systems will fit only a few characteristics associated with complex adaptive systems because they tend to exist far from the edge of chaos. Control and stability, rather than change and volatility, distinguish their operating philosophies. Design of learning and performance support interventions, then, becomes a way of asserting and maintaining control over the system as a whole.

A complex adaptive system, on the other hand, uses learning and performance support in a more native way to enhance its position on the fitness landscape. It does this by providing access to knowledge and capability across its network. Much of the learning, in this environment, is spontaneous and emergent, with a significant lack of formalism and fixed structure. Learning happens simultaneously with what is considered productive work in the system [13, p. 34]. Learning and performance support, then, are not artificially introduced into the system, but grow out of the system's general perceived need to change. Learning and performance merge, to the point where one is indistinguishable from the other. There is more intrinsic than extrinsic motivation in the agents and in the network, so that control is established from within the system dynamically and not from outside of the system [14, pp. 52–56].

Support for this type of performance requires a different view of design of interventions. Interventions cannot be described as fixed and formal events. These interventions, if they are to support a complex adaptive system, must move and change and adapt as the system adapts. The best design approach, then, is to leverage the operating system itself for learning, using knowledge, processes, and principles that are emerging from the environment as the tools to promote learning and change. These pure performance support devices are ecologically efficient, because they require little or no manipulation or reprocessing. They require only transmission from a point where knowledge originates to other nodes and agents in the system. This simplicity of design is one of the factors that encourages managers to dismiss expertise in design as a requirement for learning and performance support systems.

Such simplicity, however, may be deceptive. Materials that may provide learning or performance support in one instance may not be transferable to other instances or other agents. Such material is generally available only in one format and from one perspective. To assume that such material will be equally accessible and reusable by all learners is to deny the complex operation of cognitive structures in the various agents within the system. In short, what might be valuable in one instance may be useless in another, and what might be an effective presentation mode or method in one instance may be ineffective in others. So a naïve approach to the support of learning and performance is inadequate because of the complexity of the system being supported.

Design of Chaotic Performance Support Systems

The design of performance support in and for chaotic systems differs slightly from the design for complex adaptive systems. This is because a CAS assumes complex but not chaotic behavior. The complex adaptive system learns at the edge of chaos and uses its learning to stay just clear of the boundary. An optimized CAS is nearly chaotic, but not quite, and derives its growth and energy from its openness and variety. It does not show, however, the same freedom of movement available in a chaotic system, nor does it follow a strange attractor. For support of learning, the difference can be important. Learning in a CAS is learning toward emergence and self-organization in a system with multiple, but identifiable, bifurcations. Learning is intended to achieve balance and carefully poised control over complex activities. Learning in a chaotic system, on the other hand, may have three different purposes that act as separate goals for learning and learning support, or which can be combined to create modified goals.

First, chaotic learning may be directed toward shifting a system into chaos. That is, learning support may be used to increase the sensitivity of the system and allow increased change and increased variability. To go beyond the structure of the learning organization is to invite additional complexity in organizational system behavior, and this may lead to chaos. The intent of learning would be to assist agents in the organization in understanding the values to be derived from increased nonlinearity and sensitivity. Such learning, regardless of the type of agent, would free the agent to explore additional ranges of behavior and participate fully in the redefinition of systemic boundaries and parameters. Such learning would serve to make a fully active connection between feedback from the various system agents and external influences and the architecture assumed by the strange attractor. The attractor would become highly sensitive and responsive to these influences, change accordingly, and thus create changes in the core nature of the system. Where leaders want to explore new options and possibilities, they may encourage learning of this sort.

Such learning will be in evidence in organizations that focus on career development and career survival skills, as opposed to internally defined curricula. Where such curricula are developed over a period of time to ensure the survival of the enterprise, career-focused learning support risks short-term gains for longer-term value. Agents become less attached to a company way of doing things and so open themselves to various perspectives on system activity. Organizations that support such learning, and integrate it into their own flexibility, welcome such agents as contributors to change, as well as productivity. People who have become independent, career-focused consultants, for example, often report that they instantly discard company politics. This is a way of expressing a detachment from organizational trajectories that tend to be conservative. Learning becomes more strategic, with focus on skills that can be used now and later. As one contractor explained, "I would say the reason the majority of us do contract work is that we know what we are there for, the client knows what we're there for, and there is no internal strife" [15]. The arrangement between agent and system is a virtual one, with nodes connected only so long as necessary to complete an efficient transaction. The system nodes then rearrange themselves, either reconnecting in the system or disconnecting and reconnecting into another system. Unlike traditional job changes, there is less entropy and less expense for the agents and for other parts of the system. Emphasis is not on infrastructure and permanence, but on effectiveness. This is a learned behavior on the part of the agents.

Learning in a chaotic system may serve in an opposite way, pulling the system out of the chaotic regime and restoring it to a more controlled form. In this instance, learning may be applied to restore a chaotic system to a quasiperiodic, or even periodic, cyclical behavior. This learning activity would be designed to increase entropy, restore boundaries, and minimize ranges in the parameters that control system behavior. For the organization, it would mean learning directed at restoring hierarchical controls and procedural certainty.

Learning in chaos may also have the effect of sustaining chaotic behavior in order to maximize energy use and transfer of energy between internal and external systems. This function of learning is applicable to small as well as large organizations, with the intent to loosen the system to the point at which it goes beyond simple bifurcation and enters the chaotic regime. The achievement of complex bifurcation is equivalent to establishing a learning organization, but the residual effect of living at the edge of chaos is high complexity that tries to maintain order at the same time. It is the stuff schizophrenia is made of. Agents in such a system, if it is fully implemented, may be confused and unable to function without constant stress. Bifurcation, as a system process, only serves to continually split the organization into smaller and smaller basins of attraction and, while this frees the system in one sense, it complicates it in another.

Basins of attraction can be building blocks for innovation and may thus serve a positive function for the system [16]. A *skunkworks* operation represents just such a systemic phenomenon. In the skunkworks, a mini-system often forms which is generally consistent with the main purpose of the central system, but differs in specific intent. This mini-system is free to explore other possibilities and alternative realities for the central system. While it is free to do so, it becomes a basin of attraction that is separate from the central body of the organization. It is a bifurcation of the central system.

The advantages are great, including increased learning in a short period of time. Skunkworks are laboratories teeming with ideas and new applications and generally have some pressure to produce results based on the rethinking of old ideas or introduction of new ideas. The danger is that such a bifurcation may result in a basin of attraction that is closed off from the remainder of the system dynamics, becoming an organizational pariah. Organizations, like some parents, will sometimes kill and eat their young.

If the upstart mini-system begins to take on semblance of a major effort, it may be spun off to survive on its own, or shut down. By so doing, the remainder of the organization avoids the effect of such a counterweight and maintains its stability. So the value of such skunkwork operations, as they open the system to new learning, may be lost to the system. In some instances, such operations have, in fact, been spun out and have become successful competitors with the parent system. Stability is maintained in the original system, and operations continue as they have done. The edge of chaos is maintained, but the true value of the mini-system, as it challenged the attractor of the main system, was lost. The innovation in the main system is avoided, even though, in corporate circumstances, the parent company may continue to own some percentage of the spin-off.

This tendency to maintain stability supports the establishment of successful learning organizations in smaller organizations or sub-organizations rather than across larger global organizational landscapes. The bifurcation needed in order to renew a CAS may work against itself as it tends to generate more pools of power and not fewer. The system may become so divided that self-organization is stymied by complicated networking and web-building arrangements, and the intent of the CAS is lost. While learners desperately try to keep up with the twists and turns of the organization, much of their energy is consumed by this effort, and energy directed toward the purpose of the system dissipates, without replacement [17].

To move a system beyond bifurcation and into chaotic activity is to create a situation in which there is a strange attractor but attractive forces are not divided and are clearly distinguished, as they are in a complex adaptive system phase. This may explain the clarity with which Champy and Hammer [18] advocated radical change in organizations in order to achieve breakthroughs and prosper in volatile markets and environments.

Yet there is resistance to this level of apparent randomness. It essentially frees the system from mid-management, allows it to open, and allows the system to express its capability for exploration within its parameters. The resistance often comes because people are uncomfortable with this amount of freedom and often do not know how to cope with it. Responsibility is a learned characteristic, not one that comes automatically installed at the factory. The sober truth is that we would often rather revert to cave-like simplicity in our systems experiences than be thrust onto the bleeding edge of highly unpredictable systems. In a recent report, for example, the Educational Testing Service (ETS), which produces many of the standardized scholastic tests used in the United States educational systems, identified this need for security in learning environments. In a study of behavior and its links to learning performance, the ETS study found that "schools with strict codes of behavior and harsh punishments experience fewer problems" [19].

U.S. society, as a whole, has chosen to open parental and other social systems to the point of entrusting teenagers, and even younger children with setting and maintaining schedules, maintaining ethical standards, and fitting into the social system. This open systems environment has not been accompanied by sufficient preparation of either young people or their mentors and leaders. There is disaster in generating an environment that demands constant communication, learning, and self-responsibility without providing the learning tools that support such an environment. That discipline works better, in an environment lacking such preparation of the agents, should come as no surprise.

Educational organizations, like many others, must depend on the interaction of agents in order to prosper. Self-organization, within the system itself, is preferable to disciplinary structures, which may serve to stifle creativity and generative learning in the system. Yet, from a practical viewpoint, discipline works and has been a fallback position over time. As with other systems, it would take a focused effort to intensify the chaotic behavior of an educational system to the point at which it passes bifurcation and begins to display chaotic behavior. The system must be prepared to participate fully, not just be led into such an environment. Chaos is a deliberate choice.

Leadership must be thoroughly integrated into all of the agents in the system, and all agents, human and otherwise, must be attuned to rapid and drastic changes that optimize the energy of the system. There is little in the current U.S. educational system—from politicians, school board members and students to parents and the community at large—which supports such innovation. Conservative requirements for immediate results of learning efforts dominate any approaches that take advantage of more open learning experiences.

This is not to say that some educational systems have not taken advantage of open and virtual learning opportunities. Anchored instruction, problem-based learning, and the increasing availability of distance education links, are positive signs of future capabilities and potential in these systems [20]. Realizing the full advantage of opportunities for self-directed learning and communications with other student groups in other cities and cultural environments, however, will depend on the solutions found to the overall strategies employed in educational systems. Increased discipline will serve to close the system and reinforce the image of master-apprentice relationships, rather than the more desirable image of the community of learners. To place students in strong disciplinary environments in schools is to deny the existence of a more open and volatile environment outside of those bounded school systems. A return to the cave is not the answer. Systemic learning is necessary, and the intelligent use of chaotic systems can provide benefits not now available in this environment.

In corporate environments, the same issues surface. While there still exists a noticeable separation of boundaries between educational systems and work systems, these boundaries are artificial. Leaders are slowly recognizing this and, in some instances, the boundaries are coming down. This has been true for some time, as corporations have invested in research and development efforts on college campuses. Formalized volunteer groups, that provide advice and materials to K–12 schools, also serve to reduce the barrier.

The design of learning support, then, takes a different form in a chaotic system than in a complex adaptive system and is certainly different from learning in more stable or periodic systems. My purpose is not to elaborate an alternative to ISD or any other learning and performance support design system in the space of this chapter. Instead, I want to point out some of the chief characteristics of such design systems which must be addressed if learning and performance support tools are to be effectively deployed into a chaotic organizational system. Chaotic learning has different purposes, occuring differently in the system. Learning is not there to increase stability, but to introduce or support instability. The design of learning support, therefore, will show the following characteristics:

1. *Design will be non-sequential.* That is, the design process cannot afford to wait for a front-end analysis to be completed before the shaping of support materials is begun. The front-end sequence, in fact, is a major point of change in the way we will address learning in such systems. It is at this front end that information must be established on the system dynamics, with less emphasis on the collection and documentation of facts. To avoid a focus on gap analysis, the initial exploration must consider the extent to which the system is volatile and to which system behavior, on the part of all engaged agents, is temporary. In short, no action may be necessary. What is observed initially as a need may simply go away as the system moves to a different point in its history, or the need itself may be so volatile that it will change before any integrated effort to change the system's actors can be implemented. This, in particular, applies to specific task training, or job-focused education. In a chaotic system, the job and its tasks may change so quickly that delineation of needs and packaging of support may be worthless expense.

   Instead of this form of traditional task or front-end analysis, regardless of how closely related it is to the overall activity of the organization, a more holistic understanding of needs comes from a consideration of diverse perspectives on the role of an individual agent. The agent, in a chaotic system, is a node in a network of agents, human or not, and is valued for possessing certain capabilities which can be applied and reapplied across the various interconnected networks. The fluctuation of the system will determine the relative need for the agent, and thus the number of interconnects the agent may have. Figure 12-5 shows a capability construct that illustrates the way in which an agent's place in a chaotic system can be understood.

   As the figure illustrates, capability in a highly volatile system must be defined in a number of different layers that complement each other and contribute to overall capability in the system and networks. To focus on an

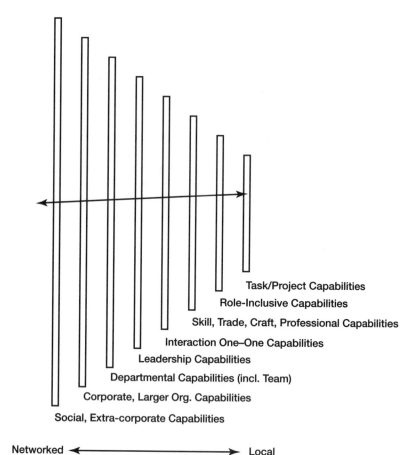

Task/Project Capabilities
Role-Inclusive Capabilities
Skill, Trade, Craft, Professional Capabilities
Interaction One–One Capabilities
Leadership Capabilities
Departmental Capabilities (incl. Team)
Corporate, Larger Org. Capabilities
Social, Extra-corporate Capabilities

Networked ←————————→ Local

Figure 12-5. Agent capability.

agent's abilities at one or two of the layers, without consideration of the remainder, is to risk incomplete preparation to maintain consistency in an ever-changing system. The analysis of needs, then, must be taken from this larger picture, not from a more specific, task-focused or time-restricted view of capabilities and skills.

The further implication of chaotic systems is that learning support and performance support tools may emerge from within the system and may appear without specific intervention on the part of a performance support specialist. This is in the nature of informal and incidental learning and action learning. This form of learning support is very much derived from humanistic and social learning theory and is a form of self-generating and self-sustaining learning support. As noted earlier in a consideration of on-the-job training, there are some concerns around the quality of such self-generated solutions, but these concerns can be balanced by an appreciation of the native nature of the occurrence of learning in this way. It is fast, immediate, and focused, and therefore offers high potential for systems which are volatile and sensitive. In such systems, in fact, these solutions may appear before many in the system are aware that a need exists. The system, to a large extent, is self-healing and will find ways to construct its own learning solutions as it moves and changes within the parameters of its attractor. Since one of the main characteristics of a chaotic system is that it builds its new reality on past choices, learning solutions will naturally develop along the path of change.

The traditional design and development system is helpless in the face of spontaneity. Where solutions appear before thorough analytical procedures, the role of the design activity will be to re-integrate those solutions with the larger system dynamic, as suggested above. There is also a need for quality assurance, to make certain that the spontaneous learning generated within the system is the learning that is needed by the system at that moment and that the transfers among data, information, application and synthesis are as effective as possible.

Spontaneous learning may begin with data accumulation or awareness, assembly of that data into informational forms or building blocks, and then application of the information in various ways in the system. Feedback from within the system will generate a synthetic process, which will impact the application and the ways in which the knowledge is assimilated and remembered. This is a system that must be complementary to the larger system within which it operates and takes part.

Without an understanding of how this learning and transfer system works chaotically, there is a danger that randomness in learning, without any underlying order, will be the result. So the learning, even though emergent from the system, is emerging from a chaotic and not a heavily ordered system. The nature of this learning system, as a chaotic system, is as important as the nature of the system that it develops to support.

There is, therefore, no sequential order to learning in a chaotic system, and learning support must be flexible enough to address the learning as it appears in the system. Lack of a sequential design order means that learning support, like the learning itself, must lie close to the nature of the system. That is, separate performance support intervention design functions must align their work closely with the system for which they are designing and should facilitate the emergence of learning support more than to try to introduce it as an artificial event. Any fixed or standard set of design methods or requirements will fail in a volatile system environment and prove irrelevant to the changing requirements of the system.

2. *Design will be modular.* In order to provide rapid support to learning needs within a rapidly changing system, objects or modules will prove to be a useful way to provide necessary building blocks. The advantages of prepared learning or performance support aids are clear, and have been demonstrated many times over in organizational learning support efforts. Such things as job aids have a

long history of providing cues and clues to effective performance, and are established means for quick dissemination of performance support. The concept of the knowledge bank is an updated version of the job aid concept, using electronic networks and client-server technologies to provide easy access to organizational knowledge. While this method is generally poorly implemented, and tends to be a collection of facts stored behind some simple search engine, the elaboration of the concept will lead to more intelligent systems.

Besides job aids, training modules have been a staple on the learning scene for some time and offer the same kind of compactness, though with a different purpose than the job aid. The job aid primarily offers information or process steps or some visual or audible aid to performance, such as the warning voice in an aircraft cockpit. The training module is a formulaic way to lead people through a learning process that includes clarification of purpose, definition of terms, elaboration of content, practice, feedback, and review. Such modules, if correctly constructed, include some form of performance test, either cognitive, psychomotor, or both (affective capabilities are rarely tested, although methods exist).

While there are certainly advantages to these modular forms of performance support, there are drawbacks as well when considering them for use in chaotic systems. The modules themselves can be made up of fixed information or process data, which require constant update in changing circumstances. This becomes a maintenance burden and detracts from the ease of use in many circumstances. Modular training segments may use outdated or static information as their basis and do not reflect transitional or transformational thinking in the system area to be studied.

Modular learning support segments, in order to be effective in a chaotic system, must be updated regularly and easily; updates must be accessible to end users who have used the module in the past and the modules must be closely attuned to the organizational situations that they are designed to support. Learning and performance support tools must be volatile and have an immediate presence within the system for which they are designed. This means that modularity may be at a very simple level, with the building blocks in elementary format and organized in such a way that a learning experience can be constructed from them by the learner, with little intervention from the faculty or design specialists or from performance consultants or OD specialists.

The modules, in that case, will more resemble small objects of computer code that can easily be located by a programmer, incorporated into a program, and then quickly modified to meet the existing circumstances. To make such learning support tools available, designers must construct intelligent tools so that learners can perform the role performed by the computer programmer. Intermediaries slow the learning process and may misinterpret needs or requirements.

A modular approach that allows learners to shape their own learning support tools is far preferable. Such tools are intelligent enough to help the learner through the structuring process, as well as simply provide content or information. The learning support tool must adjust to varying learning strategies, depending on the agent that is doing the learning, and effectively support both the shaping of the learning strategy in a given situation as well as the location of the needed combinations of content modules.

In this area of performance support, the development of electronic performance support systems is producing first generation solutions to the need for such modular, real-time learning. These electronic systems offer the advantages of modularity and variability, as well as that of immediacy. They can generally be accessed from almost any location, through computer connections or voice response systems. The initial thrust of such systems is toward support for humans as they work with unknown tools or processes, but the electronic basis of such systems makes them available to smart equipment as well [21, 22]. Automated downloads of programming updates from a server to client computers is an example of this early form of performance support system, which may incorporate a simultaneous download of a training unit for the human who interfaces with the features of the downloaded changes. The electronic performance support system also incorporates information, as well as formally designed learning support, and so serves as an integrated solution.

3. *Learning and performance support design will incorporate multiple delivery methods.* The electronic performance support system (EPSS) is an example of such a design. Within an EPSS, it is possible to deliver information in various forms, provide access to dynamic data, such as stock quotes or production status data, and provide an interactive interface for learning support. The learning support, or other tools, may be available in various electronic formats, from databases or streaming audio explanations to streaming video demonstrations, either live or stored.

The graphic in Figure 12-6 depicts the parameters of performance support methodology.

There are four parameters that are adjusted to provide performance support within a system. The first is the medium itself, which can be interpersonal— that is, a live instructor, facilitator, or coach. It can also be paper-based (such as a self-instructional manual or a laminated card with instructions for starting a machine) or video-based (a videotape or live business television). An audio-based medium can be in the form of an audiotape or even broadcast audio over a low-power transmitter in a large plant or a campus setting. Another option is a computer-based medium as in computer-based training or web-based job placement opportunities.

The second parameter is the channel through which the media will be delivered. This ranges from a discrete channel—perhaps a CD-ROM disk used on a laptop computer in a hotel room—to networked delivery, as in business television narrowcast to a number of corporate sites.

A third parameter describes the presence of the support element. The presence can be live, as in a traditional classroom activity, with instructor and students co-located. The presence may reflect packaged media, such as the CD-ROM, or computer disks, audiotapes and videotapes that can be distributed through the mail or other delivery services. Packaged support may also refer to a computer-based training (CBT) package that is available through the World Wide Web.

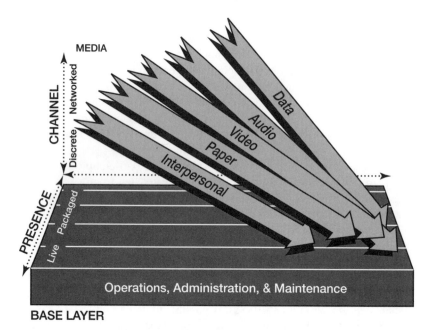

Figure 12-6. Method parameters.

Finally, the fourth parameter has to do with the infrastructure that supports the learning support tool. Access to performance support tools through electronic kiosks, for example, may provide learners with quick and simple ways to find information in video, audio, or computer-based formats. Distance learning nodes may also be set up in convenient but out-of-the way locations throughout a building to provide longer-term access to learning or performance support materials. Such "learning nodes" may consist of a workstation or cubicle with a computer networked into a local area or wide area network, along with capability for playback of audiotapes, videotapes, or CBT materials. The location might seat 2–3 people, with some privacy, for use as a videoconferencing, business television, or audioconferencing location. Alternatively, the infrastructure may consist of comfortable traditional classrooms and breakout rooms, accessible for those interventions that require interpersonal activity.

The traditional concept of an intervention changes when considered from the viewpoint of chaotic systems. Interventions, whether spawned from organizational development practice, performance consulting practice, or training and development practice, can no longer be presented in stable ways, as fait accompli of some logical and drawn out analysis process. They are variable processes, and we must account for variance in design processes [23].

Chaotic systems, because they are volatile and not necessarily because they are fast, are sensitive to immediate and drastic changes, and sub-elements of the system must share these characteristics. Not only will learning and performance support tools be modular, they will also be variable in the methods available to the learner and the times when learning can take place. The system dictates the form of the learning support it needs, and efforts to over-prescribe will fall short of what is needed, when it is needed. A course, then, may be an outdated concept.

What is a formal and carefully constructed event may need to become a modular and diverse learning experience. Different agents may want to approach the learning in different ways, from different learning styles, with different learning strategies, and with different perspectives on the needs. To provide modular learning is to provide a part of the answer, but the learning support must also be diverse, system-sensitive, and time independent. Learning situations which call for group learning (live-networked learning) should be carefully defined and distinguished from those learning activities which can best be accomplished by individuals.

Traditional classroom learning is one of the most expensive ways to help individuals learn and one of the least effective methods for support of individual capabilities development. When there is justification for a group of agents to learn the same thing at the same time in the same way, then the immediacy of the classroom is called for. Too often, however, classroom-based learning, with instructor and learners present, is viewed as an easy alternative to more effective designs and is used without discrimination. A more flexible approach to performance support design, then, begins with few or no assumptions as to delivery methods until content and scope of the learning experience is understood, and the methods can then be matched with the needs of the system itself.

4. *Design will be system-focused and not process focused.* As noted in Item 1, there is a difference in a focus in design toward a specific capability area and a focus that is more inclusive of the system. While tight focus may appear to yield useful immediate results, they are generally localized to one point in the system's history. That is, a tight solution may solve a need that has resolved itself by the time the solution is available. Such a solution, while it may retain value over intermediate or even long-term (up to a year in most situations), may not incorporate a sufficient view of the other layers in the capability model in Figure 12-5 (agent capability). This can prove to be an obstacle when reintegrating the agent into the system. There may be a difficulty in immediately applying new capability or there may be a longer-range difficulty in extending learned capability to dynamic changes in the system. If the learning support is too tightly focused on immediate needs and relies too heavily on tactical knowledge from subject-matter experts, there is a danger that the learner will not have sufficient capability, even upon exiting the learning experience, to meet the needs of the system. This means that supplemental work must be done in the organizational environment to reinforce and support application of the learning, and to ensure some degree of useful retention. Such pre-learning preparation or post-learning support is not a norm, even though it has been recommended for some time [24]. In orderly and predictable systems, such lack of formalized learning integration activity has been overcome by the volunteer efforts of the learner to apply what has been learned. Other reasons,

too numerous to consider here, have also prevented widespread use of integral learning systems.

However, such systemic integration will be vital if learning support is to be useful in a chaotic systems environment. Because the system is highly sensitive to initial conditions, any change in the system may bring nonlinear responses and additional changes. These systems have wide latitude in how they can respond to a change or stimulus and will react disproportionately to small changes. This means that a learner who introduces an idea into the system may find the system responding to the idea in ways that do not fit logical and controlled cause-and-effect models.

The system may shift direction on the basis of learning, regardless of where the learning may lead. The system, in order to maintain volatility, unlearns very quickly and adopts a new choice of action quickly. If the change that is introduced through learning, therefore, is one which may lead the system into random or highly controlled behavior, such a change has a good chance of occurring. So the lack of an integration capability in the learning support system may mean that ideas and changes are introduced into the system in such a way that the system's performance could be changed in unpredictable ways.

The design of learning support, then, must take into account the sensitive nature of the encompassing system and include ways to assist agents in implementing learned changes and behaviors into the dynamics of the system. In some instances, this introduction will need to generate immediate and substantive transformations in the system. In other instances, implementation of change may need to be delayed until all agents in the system are prepared to contribute to the change. The design of learning support should be integrated into the system, so that the whole nature of the system is available to the learner, and there is a consistency between what is learned and the activity and nature of the system. This design criterion can best be acknowledged in the full integration of design into the system itself, to the point of having agents across the system in a design role. Design activity that is initiated and carried out within the system is preferable to design work that is conducted apart from the system. As noted earlier, however, the concerns with quality and full integration of the learning into the system activity are important.

The design function in a chaotic organization exists for two reasons. First, its role is to lead the organization to an understanding of the principles outlined in this chapter. Second, it provides flexible expertise in the development of a wide variety of learning experiences. The role of the design function is not to service a fixed curriculum of formal courses, nor does it exist to broker purchase of packages from outside of the system. The role is much more significant to the chaotic system itself, because it functions to maintain learning support that is chaotic. The role requires a clear understanding of the underlying attractor and its dimensions in the system and an understanding of how all of the agents in the system are configured and how they relate. From this systemic understanding comes the capability to provide the organization with a mirror to its own dynamics and behavior and with an understanding of how learning derives from and contributes to this behavior. Learning support in a chaotic system is not possible without a deep understanding of the behavior of the strange attractor underlying the system. Learning must be complementary with the system and integrated into it, and this is not possible without knowledge of the system parameters and how variables affect overall system performance.

Effective learning support cannot be developed outside of the system itself. For this reason, deep expertise must be available in the learning support or performance support role, in all of the areas displayed in Figure 12-5 (agent capability). For performance support specialists, this means a wide range of expertise and capability in all of the areas described in Figure 12-6 (method parameters). Lack of flexibility or capability in these areas results in an inability to prepare or recommend learning and performance support interventions which are appropriate to the situation in the system. This is critical in chaotic systems because learning that is inappropriately applied may result in randomness or over-control, which may impact the survivability and sustainability of the system on its fitness landscape.

REFERENCES

1. Garten, J. E., "Cutting fat won't be enough to survive this crisis," *Business Week,* Nov. 9, 1998, p. 26.
2. Robinson, T., "Toyota tunes up training program," *InternetWeek,* Nov. 23, 1998, pp. 19–20.
3. UNESCO, *Case Study 5: Global Classrooms, Learning Networks and Virtual Communities,* http://www.education.unesco.org/lwf/: UNESCO, 1997, p. 1.
4. Shelley, M., *Frankenstein, Or, The Modern Prometheus,* Signet Edition, New York: Penguin, 1994 (originally pub. in 1816).
5. Gilbert, T. E., *Human Competence: Engineering Worthy Performance,* New York: McGraw-Hill, 1978.
6. Austin, S. J., "Physics and human performance technology." *Performance Improvement,* 1998, pp. 31–33.
7. Vaill, P. B. *Learning as a Way of Being,* San Francisco: Jossey-Bass Publishers, 1996.
8. Shandler, D., *Reengineering the Training Function: How to Align Training with the New Corporate Agenda,* Delray Beach, Fla.: St. Lucie Press, 1996, p. 20.
9. Rothwell, W. J., *Beyond Training and Development,* New York: AMACOM, 1997.
10. Rosenberg, M. J., "Performance technology, performance support, and the future of training: A commentary," *Performance Improvement Quarterly,* Vol. 8, No. 1, 1995, pp. 94–99.
11. Kepner, C. H. and B. B. Tregoe, *The Rational Manager: A Systematic Approach to Problem Solving and Decision Making,* 2nd ed, Princeton, N.J.: Kepner-Tregoe, 1976.
12. Gagne, R. M., L. J. Briggs and W. W. Wager, *Principles of Instructional Design.* 3rd ed, Chicago: Holt, Rinehart and Winston, 1988.
13. Stamps, D. "Learning ecologies." *Training,* Jan. 1998, pp. 32–38.
14. Marsick, V. J. and K. E. Watkins. *Informal and Incidental Learning in the Workplace,* New York: Routledge, 1990.

15. Crowley, A. and S. Neil, "Have skills, will travel," *PC Week,* Oct. 19, 1998, p. 88.
16. Port, O. "Getting to 'Eureka!'" *Business Week,* Nov. 10, 1997, pp. 72–74.
17. Nelson, H. G., "The necessity of being 'un-disciplined' and 'out of control': Design action and systems thinking," *Performance Improvement Quarterly,* Vol. 7, No. 3, 1994, pp. 22–29.
18. Hammer, M. and J. Champy, *Reengineeering the Corporation,* New York: HarperBusiness, 1993.
19. Gannett News Service, "Discipline cited as key to learning," *The Tennessean,* Nashville, Oct. 14, 1998, p. 6A.
20. Gordon, J., "Infonuggets: The bite-sized future of corporate training?" *Training,* July 1997, pp. 26–33.
21. Dibbell, J., "The race to build intelligent machines," *Time,* March 25, 1996, pp. 56–58.
22. Kline, D., "The embedded internet," *Wired,* October 1996, pp. 98–106.
23. Merrill, M. D., "Learning-oriented instructional development tools," *Performance Improvement,* Mar. 1997, pp. 51–55.
24. Broad, M. L. and J. W. Newstrom, *Transfer of Training,* New York: Addison-Wesley, 1992.

Chapter 13

Directions in Measurement

INTRODUCTION

Just as our perspective on performance and performance management and support will change as we begin to view organizational systems as nonlinear dynamical systems, so will our views on measurements and metrics. The attitudes and methods with which we now approach systems behavior measures will not be the same attitudes and methods with which we address chaotic systems. In order to facilitate our way through such systems and make meaningful changes, we will need to develop a way to orient ourselves in a more volatile environment. As we have seen, there is much less stability and much more uncertainty in these systems. When we come to measure the things that are happening and try to project out to anticipate some of the things that may happen, we will be at a loss if we try to apply current performance metrics to the situation. What we will need to do is to accept that measurement criteria will be different and measurement methods will be different. Even the sources of data may be different as we bring together more, not less, information about how our systems are performing as a whole.

We are, after all, viewing the system, as it takes advantage of chaotic behavior, as a part of a quantum, and not a clockwork universe. Our sense of steadiness in such a system is more akin to the sense of weightlessness that astronauts feel in space than to the feelings of certainty and predictability with which we have approached systems in the past. Given the quantum nature of systems and chaotic behavior in them, we are faced with a measurement situation unlike the situations we have faced in the past. The potential for change is much higher in a chaotic system, and the need to understand the underlying reality supersedes the need to expend energies on fixing the status quo. True change will come as we access the basic attractors of the dynamic system. We will need to deal with the rocks and the streambed, and less with the eddies that we see on the surface. Chaotic systems will succeed if their chaotic nature is maintained and if the factors governing their behavior are understood. It is at that understanding that metrics will focus in a nonlinear dynamical system.

This chapter is devoted to a brief outline of the measurement activity that accompanies both system management in general and system performance improvement efforts in particular. I want to consider, first, the nature of current metrics and approaches to organizational system measures, to establish some methods in present favor and concerns with the attitudes and methods in use. Then, briefly, I want to review the forms of metrics most often used by OD and HRD practitioners and describe some concerns with those metrics as they might apply in chaotic systems environments. Finally, I will suggest some of the value in revising our approaches to organizational behavior metrics, to incorporate more views of nonlinear dynamics in our systems. If we are to introduce a new order of consideration in organizational change and behavior, with emphasis on nonlinearity and volatility, then the measures we use should also reflect this new order.

WHERE MEASURES FALL SHORT

Most of the authors who have considered organizational systems as chaotic systems have noted a current tendency toward linear measures, with a background assumption of stability. Ralph Stacey [1], for instance, observes this tendency in our approaches to price behavior in a business setting:

> The simplest and most widely used techniques are averages, the normal distribution, regression analysis and probability. . . . We cannot deal with a whole time series of price data but we can collapse it into an average over the period and deal with that. And we can use the assumption that the deviations of actual prices from this average are normally distributed to measure the bands within which prices are likely to move around the average. . . . The problem is that when the dynamic of the system we are dealing with is chaotic, all these approaches are flawed in their application to the long term.

Priesmeyer [2] also notes the problems with existing forms of measures:

> . . . with change all around us, we insist on focusing on snapshot pictures of our world. . . . We record our corporate performance with audited reports that disregard the transitions in our organizations. We capture measures such as on-hand inventories and budgeted expenses as singular quantities and record them with precision, believing that greater accuracy will somehow provide greater truth. We don't seem to mind that those measures don't reveal the dynamics of the continually changing organization they represent.

The nature of measurement in organizational systems has been primarily linear and kept relatively simple. The simpler the measures, the less time is required for measurement and the more time that can be spent on fixing problems and ensuring service. This, at least, has been the philosophy that has been in place for some time.

Even in an atmosphere of continuous improvement, under the guidance of Deming and with the goal of the Malcolm Baldridge award, organizations are dependent upon measures that track day-to-day efforts in individual silos. Productivity awards go to companies and other organizations that are able to demonstrate "control" of situations. The "control chart," in fact, is an example of a measure that represents current thinking and approaches to continuous improvement.

A CONTROL CHART TO CONTROL BEHAVIOR

A control is any document, form, or report format that is designed to present measurement data that can be used to control the operations of the system. In the literature of continuous improvement, the term "control chart" refers to a specific variety of measurement instrument that is a time-based, linear tracking format, as depicted in Figure 13-1. A control chart shows the results of observations of a system in operation over time. Ideally, the performance data for the chart is collected objectively, with activity proceeding according to a standard process flow. The units of measure will be whatever units are used to measure the activity, e.g. minutes to complete a form. The points on the vertical axis are determined statistically, using mean and range calculations, based on actual observation numbers.

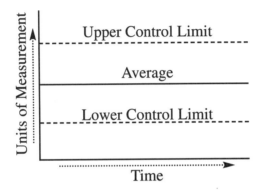

Figure 13-1. Control chart.

Calculations result in the determination of the average performance for any given point in time when an observation was taken, and the determination of an upper control limit and a lower control limit, which provide a range of acceptable performance. An out-of-control process can be detected by looking for points that fall outside of the upper and lower control limit range, and the extent to which activity in the process can be depicted as regular. That is, even if a set of observations shows that process activity falls within the vertical range described by the upper and lower control limits, any irregular pattern may still suggest that the process is out of control. While there is an assumption that processes that are shown to be in control are likely to be producing high-quality goods or services, that is only an assumption and is based on an understanding that the base process that is being measured is designed to produce high quality. The real message from a control chart has to do with the consistency of the actual behavior of the process. Activities, according to this logic, that proceed erratically are likely to be inefficient and in need of corrective action.

While it is not within the scope of this book to teach development of control charts, an example will illustrate the concepts outlined above. In this situation, observers have tracked the number of student applications for season football passes at a university's athletic offices. Figure 13-2 shows the results of each day's observations, recorded as the average of number of requests processed each day, over a period of ten days. On each day, observations were taken at six different times per day, to determine the number of requests that had been processed during the previous hour. Observations were collected at 9, 10, and 11 a.m. and at 2, 3, and 4 p.m.

The process average is the average of all daily averages and is shown as a straight baseline representing 10.83 requests as the average processed over the ten-day period. The upper control limit line—calculated using a formula including averages, range data, and a standard factor—is 17.67. The lower control limit line, calculated in a similar way, is 4.02 requests. The average requests line tracks the average number of requests for each day. According to the baseline and limits established through the calculations, the chart shows that this process is out of control. In particular, Day 8 and Day 10 show out-of-control system behavior, and Day 4, at 17.60 average requests processed, approaches the upper control limit of 17.67. All three instances show out-of-control behavior that may be attributable to influences outside of the process as it was defined, since all three show radical departure from the average baseline. Members of this organization would no doubt be counseled to review events on Days 4, 8, and 10 to try to identify the influences that caused the significant variances from the norm.

This same data set can also be viewed, as a function of the control chart preparation, as a picture of ranges of work accomplished. For each day, as shown in Figure 13-3, the range of requests processed on an hourly basis is calculated by subtracting the minimum number recorded in the day's observations from the maximum number recorded. This range indicates the variability of the processing procedure throughout the day. If the range number is small, then the number of requests

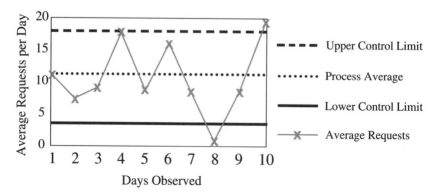

Figure 13-2. Processing of student ticket requests.

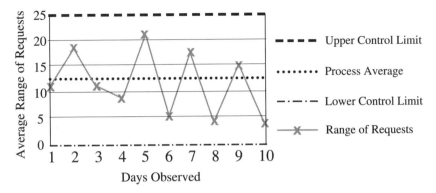

Figure 13-3. Range data related to student ticket request processing.

processed from hour to hour across the day remained fairly steady. Larger range numbers indicate higher variance between the greatest number processed during the day and the smallest number processed. Inconsistency here, from the viewpoint of process control, is worthy of investigation. The range data from these observations, shown in the range chart, suggest a high degree of variance from one day to the next and high degrees of variance between maximum and minimum number of requests processed on several days.

Day 4, for example, shows an average range that is near the overall average across all days. At a range of 9, the day is close to the average range of 11.8. There was little variance in number of requests processed from observation to observation throughout the day. This is in sharp contrast to the range for Day 5, which shows a difference of 21 requests between the maximum number observed and the minimum number observed. Something significant happened during the day that allowed, at one point, a high rate of processing but severely curtailed the processing operation at another point. Again, members of the organization, and those responsible for this system, would be reflecting on the events of that day in order to determine what changed to create this notable change in processing activity.

In reviewing the charts alone, however, answers to these questions cannot be reached. The data are limited and confined to one variable—the number of requests processed. Such control charts do not track other variables that may serve to document and explain the variances in this one variable. This control process paints a very small part of the system picture. It provides information that can act as an indicator of process deviation but cannot indicate why the deviation occurred. It cannot explain why there is a performance gap between the nominal mean baseline and individual observation results, nor whether such deviations constitute problems occurring within the system. It cannot indicate positive events that should be considered for their impact on the overall system and its external connections. For example, a deviation in the number of requests processed over a period of a day may indicate that the processors were engaged in more immediate value-added customer service activity.

BALANCED SCORECARD

A more recent expression of the attempt to see the big picture and manage accordingly is the idea of the balanced scorecard. Such a scorecard is illustrated in Figure 13-4. This example is based on work by the Artificial Intelligence Applications Institute at the University of Edinburgh (http://www.aiai.ed.ac.uk/). The institute indicates four elements prevalent as top-level measures in such a scorecard: financial measures, based on organizational financial performance; customer metrics, including customer satisfaction; internal process measures; and growth measures, which document innovation and change within the organization.

While such a scorecard offers a conceptual improvement over scattered discrete measures from financial, engineering, sales, and human resources source data, it leaves us short of integrated information about performance. In fact, the scores of four different games (at least) are being measured here. Given that an organizational strategy will have established goals or hard targets in each area, the targets may have been set and agreed to separately by separate leadership silos within the organization, with some level of agreement from an executive organizational layer.

In practice, often, such scorecards merely represent a convenient portrayal of disparate data sources, and not a singular consolidation of data into a picture of activity. Moreover, in practice, the underlying data for such scorecard reports are flawed by inaccuracy. The balanced scorecard, after all, does not introduce any new ways of measuring, simply a consolidated view of operations. Underlying measurements that still rely on linear, sporadic, or incomplete data will not yield much insight beyond what is available by looking at operational data in their separate forms. The tendency to average performance, as it is reported upward, may also contribute to

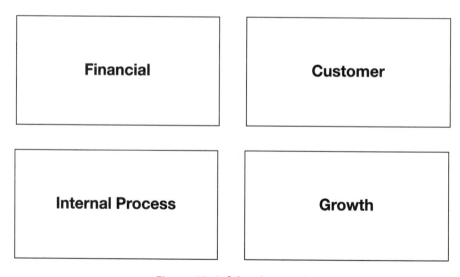

Figure 13-4. Balanced scorecard.

inaccuracies as to the true state of affairs in the organization. Where departmental results are compiled into division results, which are compiled into regional results, which are compiled into full organizational results, the picture becomes muddier at each level of compilation and averaging.

Fundamentally, neither the continuous improvement measurement activity, nor the business management assessment activity associated with ISO 9000, nor the balanced scorecard can get us away from an atmosphere in which measurement means control. It is prescriptive intent, not descriptive intent, and constantly compares present performance, at a fixed point in time, with a standard. Failure to achieve standards is perceived to be failure of management. It is not rewarded and is sometimes punished.

THE METRICS OF LEARNING

The metrics used in learning and learning support activities vary widely. Where there is strict attention to precision in measurement, an array of sophisticated statistical tools are used. For the most part, such tools are confined to experimental situations or to the development of validity and reliability data for test and measurement instruments. Where tests are norm-referenced, the validity and reliability depend heavily on statistical results from trials and experiments in order to confirm that the tests measure what they are supposed to measure and can do it consistently across a defined population. Where tests are criterion-referenced, the focus is on the nature of the tasks or activities that are the subject of learning [3]. Testing is focused more heavily on the ability of the learner to demonstrate learned performance under conditions as close as possible to those found in real life or on the job [4]. In practice, it is not common to find very sophisticated statistics applied to learning situations, whether formal or informal. What is more common is to find simple and expedient measures used, to provide a good enough picture of what is going on at the moment and to provide minimal business support for investment of resources in a learning project. Measures in use are often sporadically applied, and based on invalid and unreliable instruments.

Whether the emphasis is statistical or not, the measurements tend to rely on simple, linear cause-effect assumptions about behavior and change, tend to avoid consideration of extraneous activities around the performer, and tend to try to establish competence in one shot. As noted earlier in the discussion of general performance measures in organizations, measurement is not a major activity in most organizations, and measurement that involves human interaction in systems is sometimes de-emphasized.

In HRD measurement efforts, the tendency is to gather data as close to the training event as possible, with strong reliance on subjective participant reaction sheets. While such data are useful, they are often taken as a spot analysis of a given course session and are rarely studied for any cumulative effect. These reaction sheets are generally completed at the end of a session. Trainers and course managers will look carefully at such reaction sheets to spot potential problems in the actual delivery of the session. The trainer can then correct any delivery errors prior to the next session. This is incremental learning on the part of the course manager and trainer, but both people assume that the basic nature of the course design will remain the same.

At the same time, the course manager may look at cumulative comments and reactions from participants to spot trends that may impact the core design of activities within the course. When this happens, the design may be changed on the fly, if the change can be done quickly and easily by the facilitators, or a designer may re-develop an activity or rethink an instructional strategy.

The measures used in this first level of evaluation are few and simple. Each participant may fill out a questionnaire about the course experience and may rate the course and its effectiveness on some arbitrary scale. Usually, there is a tendency toward 1–5 scales, which allow a participant the luxury of remaining neutral by rating course elements as "3." Sometimes the rating scale will not allow a middle rating so that participants are forced to favor or reject a particular question on the reaction sheet. The totals and averages from an individual questionnaire will usually be combined with the totals and averages from a full session in order to provide the instructor with a statistical portrait for the session. Measurement of these results can be very elaborate if session data are combined into course historical records. It is possible to run more sophisticated statistical tests to compare sessions, or to compare courses, based on cumulative historical score data. Generally, two types of interpretations are used from such data analysis. First, course managers want to know how one set of delivery circumstances might differ from another. If, for instance, a given instructor in a warehouse with folding chairs delivers one series of sessions, the extent to which environment might affect reactions might be the basis for providing more comfortable learning surroundings. So, in measurement, the differences between session ratings are important.

Second, course managers want to know if the course itself is improving over time. There is an expectation that as sessions are conducted, there will be a cause-effect relationship that can be tracked to show that the course is receiving quantitatively higher results on the reaction questionnaire.

In both instances, the emphasis is on actual results, and not on the underlying core dynamics of the learning support system. The focus is on very few variables and on continuous improvement of scores over time. Any need for radical changes in the course strategy, indicated from reaction questionnaires, is generally a sign of poor design to begin with. The first level of course evaluation tends to focus on incremental changes that might be needed to fine-tune the course and its delivery. The measures are snapshots in time, and any ability to compare one group with another group or one set of session data with another set is often obscured by significant differences in audience, location, or delivery circumstances. These are linear measures, depending heavily on central tendency and statistical deviation from the central tendency. While the learning system itself may operate in nonlinear ways, the tools for measurement and decision-making are decidedly linear. The course, to be successful in this view, must reach stasis or as close as possible to it.

A second type of testing that sometimes occurs in training is the "pre-post" test, intended to measure before and after training performance. The comparison of results then indicates the difference in learning attributable to the session. This form of testing is almost always used with formal training events since trainers recognize the near-impossibility of claiming credit for changes due to informal and incidental learning. In the usual pre-post test scenario, a pretest is administered at session start or before, and a posttest is administered at session end. Most often, such tests, like the reaction questionnaires used at the first level of evaluation, use questions that depend on recall and recognition in order to establish numerical results. Sometimes, particularly if the test is to be used for formal certification purposes, the test instrument will be checked for validity and reliability and will be administered only to audiences and under circumstances that will reduce bias. In other instances, especially general corporate leadership and management training, and public generic courses, such testing will be overlooked. If used, these pre-post tests may not be subjected to validity and reliability testing and will be referred to as "assessment" to avoid the connotation of formality. Such assessments may have been constructed as a part of the course machinery but may not have been validated and are not used for certification. In fact, results may not be available, on an individual basis, to management above the course manager.

Such assessments rely on quantitative analysis rather than qualitative analysis, and the focus is again on scores and averages. This may be the case whether the test is norm-referenced or criterion-referenced. Where performance against an objective is the focus of criterion-referenced tests, that performance is often measured at the cognitive level, using recall questions in the form of multiple choice. In technical courses, it is sometimes possible to test all of the job-related performance requirements in a class setting, but it is rare. In leadership and management courses, it becomes more difficult to reproduce the situations that call for exercise of leadership or management behaviors, and so pre-post testing is almost always confined to cognitive and not practical test questions. The resulting data, of course, are presented as scores and averages, again relying on an underlying certainty in the system that allows one answer to be right and the others totally wrong. The effect of analysis of such data is linear. The measures are taken only once (pre and post), and there is little evidence to demonstrate any dynamic integration of learning into the dynamic systems that are being represented in the classroom or in the computer.

Other forms of traditional evaluation of training rely on measures that are more distant from the formal learning event but still depend to a large extent on the existence of such an event. A training course is considered to be a change event, and management expects some impact as the learning is transferred back to the organizational situation. As the effect of learning becomes more remote from the actual learning event itself, measurement follows this pattern, relying on qualitative data more heavily than on quantitative data. Most often, however, the qualitative data are not fully analyzed. Training course managers will often report cumulative summaries of impressions from comments and responses. At this point in measuring the effect of learning, quantitative measures are largely set aside because it is just at this point that measurement becomes problematic in most organizations.

There is, in all of these organizational performance measurement efforts, a trade-off between what can be justified as worthy of investment and what cannot. In most instances, training and human performance technology specialists find it difficult to justify the cost and investment in evaluation, beyond the relatively simple measures collected close to the event. That is, reaction questionnaires and pre-post tests are not expensive to develop and, since most of the data is quantitative, fairly cheap to analyze and store.

At the point at which the performance consultant may be asked to go back out into a population that has been through formal training at some earlier point, the costs begin to mount. Measurement of actual impact of a training course on the performance of the organization relies on the degree to which learning from the classroom is carried over into the actual performance situation. Kirkpatrick [5] provides three of the considerations at this point in an evaluation system:

1. The operating system must actually provide opportunities for performance.
2. No one can predict when some learned performance may actually occur.
3. The learner may: accept the learning completely, and use it; reject the learned behavior and return to prior patterns; decide that it is politically unwise to adopt new behavior; or find that situational circumstances do not support the new learning.

All of these things suggest the complexity of measurement of learning from a formal course, as it is applied outside of the course setting. Most solutions involve questionnaires, using multiple choice and short answer, which are designed to be completed by course participants, as well as by other stakeholders such as the learner's supervisor. Added to this may be interviews conducted by trainers or performance consultants who know both the work situations of the learners and the course content.

As with the other two forms of metrics involved with training, the results tend to rely on traditional scoring and averaging of quantitative results, with brief summaries of qualitative data. The weakness in this measurement approach is its cost and time but also its persistent conformity. It is a clockwork measurement philosophy, designed to measure the extent to which a performance gap has been closed by a single formal training course. At the same time, we recognize the complexity of the organizational situation and the multiple ways in which the formal learning support may be subverted or influenced as it moves back into that situation. Measurement, here, understands and accepts bias, and attempts to make some accommodation to preclude external influences in determining the actual impact of a given formal training event. Yet it is clearly evident to all that, after some months have passed, the influence of a training course is difficult to distinguish from other constant influences on the operating system.Where we try to impose linear measurement practices in a nonlinear system, we feel frustrated, and it is often this frustration that influences performance consultants away from dependence on such transfer of learning studies.

In Kirkpatrick's highest level of evaluation and measurement of training, the focus is on the effect of training on the business itself. Did it reduce scrap, error rates, turnover, or hard feelings? Did it improve customer satisfaction scores? Did it improve employee satisfaction scores? Did it improve quality or productivity in delivery of goods or services? Are the processes better than they were? The reliance on gap analysis is obvious at this level. Evidence of learning at this fourth level is evidence of change in the organization, and that change is measured in relation to the way things were before the training event. As with the measures of transfer, however, the distance between the learning event and the point of measurement may offer many opportunities for other influences in the system. These business measures, furthermore, are generally linear measures, useful in the short term but not reflective of the variability in a nonlinear dynamical system. They provide spot measures only and do not reveal the nature of the attractor that influences the whole system.

As Phillips [6] considered the problem of measurement of learning impact, he expanded the concept to incorporate organizational measures more completely into the design and development phases for formal training and applied a traditional financial measurement practice, return on investment (ROI), to training activity. He argues that this ratio "provides a sound basis for calculating the efficient utilization of the financial resources allocated to HRD activities." The ROI formula, as modified for this application, is shown in Figure 13-5.

In this calculation, what may have been previously considered soft measures, such as listening skills, are probed for exactness and definition. By increasing the range of such definition, Phillips is able to present a more holistic portrait of the influence of a training event on a system. Program benefits include the hard to measure as well as the easy to measure and therefore include values for some benefits that might otherwise not be included in a value equation for training.

What is equally clear from a consideration of the ROI approach to calculating the value of training to an organization's performance is that it can be labor-intensive and provides a static picture of the system. While it organizes the idea that Kirkpatrick had concerning the need to measure the impact of training on organizational systems, it leaves us with a portrait of how things were in the system. There are two major advantages in applying Phillips' approach. First, he places strong emphasis on measuring system activity prior to the training event itself. While this may call for an unusual investment of time and effort, the ability to carry those measures through the design, delivery, and post-evaluation process are highly valuable. Second, by focusing on soft as well as hard metrics, the approach is a precursor to the valuation of control parameters that must be a part of measurement in nonlinear dynamical systems. Here, Phillips offers a key process for defining variables and parameters for measurement of change at the core level of system behavior. While the calculation of ROI itself may contribute little to an understanding of system dynamics, the preparatory work outlined in the ROI methodology is basic to a clear understanding of integral dynamics in organizational systems.

The approach to training and OD measurement is incomplete on several fronts. First, we have failed to develop ways to measure dynamic system behavior, as influenced by our interventions. Second, we have failed to measure soft results. Third, we have not integrated qualitative results with quantitative results and have been satisfied to think of them and report them separately. Finally, we have relied

$$ROI = \frac{\text{Net program benefits}}{\text{Program costs}}$$

Figure 13-5. Phillips' ROI formula.

on central tendency and variation from a standard to establish the viability of an intervention. Our focus tends to be on the immediate and narrow results we can quantify in short-term system performance, and not on development of a clear understanding of how dynamical systems may operate over the longer term. We have focused on how we can help people learn, and not on how we may need to help them unlearn. We have emphasized change in people behavior exclusively from changes in other agents in the system. Our measurement processes are, in many cases, erratic, static, and ill-suited to the needs of chaotic systems and the support of change in those systems.

METRICS IN NONLINEAR DYNAMICAL SYSTEMS

Getting the Whole Picture

Imagine that twenty-five years ago, you had an 8mm audio-free home movie camera, and you captured your son's sixth birthday party. Now imagine yourself twenty-five years later, viewing that silent film. The sights, sounds, smells, and tastes of that birthday party compared with what you see on that strip of film are worlds apart. From the film, only one sense is stimulated—vision. Your memory adds a certain richness but, after twenty-five years, cannot recapture the dialogue, the nuances of children's voices, the background noises of parents and neighbors. Memory does even less well with the smells and tastes of the occasion.

The movement you perceive is a highly contrived illusion. The camera lens is small and cannot capture a panorama. There is illusion of movement, but it is localized to whatever is in front of the lens. What is equally important is that the little camera is only capturing a fraction of the real action and is depending upon your eyes and brain to interpolate approximately half of what is really happening. At best, you are seeing thirty frames per second, which is to say thirty still images per second. Your eye is not good enough to detect the actual frame transition, and your brain is willing to build the other thirty seconds worth of action during every minute's worth of video. It simply trusts that nothing much happened in the intervening seconds and builds a logical bridge for you, from one still picture to the next. As you sit and watch, you see motion.

What you are viewing on screen is highly comparable to the types and forms and methods of measurement through which organizations are controlled, managed, and directed. The measuring lens is usually small. The metrics of an organization are generally viewed from a high level, and not in detail. Such metrics are, consequently, gathered at as high a level as possible, without granularity or detail.

Measurement intervals, unlike the relatively steady thirty frames per second of the movie camera, vary within an organization, depending on the perceived velocity of what is being measured. Some processes may be measured every second if a change in the process could happen quickly and have serious consequences on a product or service. For example, a call detail report taken from a telephone switch is highly detailed since the switch knows every call transaction and it knows a number of characteristics about the call. If the organization using such data were a call center, such measurements might contribute to critical short-term decisions regarding call routing and line availability.

At the other extreme, some variables in the system are measured only yearly, including, in many cases, human performance and employee satisfaction. The current belief is that the momentum of human change in the organization does not warrant more frequent data points. This, of course, refers to documented reviews of human performance and not undocumented, informal reviews that take place hourly and daily. Generally, the role of the supervisor includes oversight and constant granular measurement of human performance. Generally, such informal measures are subjective, within some framework of policies and procedures. Such measures, carried out on a daily basis but rarely documented, then become the collective background against which the individual human performer is measured, formally, on a yearly or semi-yearly basis. Such metrics have been widely accepted as a way to ensure compliance and to identify needs for human development, including training and education.

Further, given the metrics now widely prized in organizations, most have to do with financial performance. This narrow focus through the lens means that many activities throughout the system, which may seriously impact the behavior of the system, go unnoticed. Just as only one sense is dominated by the playback of the silent 8mm film, so one sense dominates the review of most organizational behavior. The rest is left to interpolation and imagination. What is worse, executives often believe that if the company is productive and its financial measures are high, then it follows logically that employees are satisfied, customers are satisfied, suppliers are satisfied, and the infrastructure of capital equipment and networks is well-integrated with the human side of the enterprise. What actually occurs off-camera or in the unheard dialogues portrayed on the silent screen might belie such logical extrapolations. Yet, few organizations provide integrated metrics that demonstrate to shareholders, job candidates, or business analysts that there is a holistic approach to measures and their interpretation.

There is also a difficulty in measurement introduced by Werner Heisenberg, one of the pioneers of quantum theory. Heisenberg observed that, in measuring particles, the observer can measure either the position of the particle at a given instant or the momentum of the particle. To measure both at the same time is not possible. This "uncertainty principle" is important when organizational behavior is studied as a nonlinear dynamical process. The elements of the organization, regardless of how those elements are described—persons, machines, network nodes, leaders, teams— are not static. They have independent activity as subsystems operating in the environment of what is described as the overall organizational system. The position of such elements may be described in different variables, including physical location or position, funding or budget status, headcount, or other characteristics of the element. Momentum in such organizational systems may be described in variables including asset turnover, staff turnover, production cycle time, or returns on money invested. Momentum may also be described, though it rarely is, as a measure of the rate of change in the various elements in the organization, which would correspond to a form of velocity measure. How fast, in other words, are the changes in the elements of the organization?

Nonlinear Mathematics and Learning

We have already reviewed, earlier in the book, the basic nature of nonlinear equations. My purpose here is not to turn us all into mathematicians but to illustrate some of the things we need to think about as we incorporate different forms of metrics into the development of chaotic system capability. The growth in popularity of nonlinear mathematics is due, in no small part, to the role of the computer, which can calculate more variables and input data, and extend the calculations out to more iterations, than was reasonably possible before the machines. The availability of machines for calculation has allowed mathematicians and others to explore beyond linear equations and beyond the restrictions of averaged data points. The ability to use nonlinear data and equations has provided the means through which we can examine and understand the complexity of the systems in which we are a part.

It is through the use of nonlinear equations that we can define the small system changes that often result in major outcomes in system behavior and we can trace the behavior of a system to find the underlying order in it. As Capra [7] notes:

> In nonlinear systems . . . small changes may have dramatic effects because they may be amplified repeatedly by self-reinforcing feedback. Such nonlinear feedback processes are the basis of the instabilities and the sudden emergence of new forms of order that are so characteristic of self-organization.

These characteristics of nonlinear equations are important in the study of systems in which development of system agents may constitute the force that is responsible for system changes. Such mathematics, in other words, may help us unravel the actual impact of change in organizational systems. The bifurcation diagram produced and discussed earlier in the book is an example of a nonlinear equation, which considers the behavior of variables in a system, over a number of iterations of system activity. That equation is represented here:

$$x_{n+1} = k \times x_n \times (1 - x_n)$$

This formula, called the logistic equation, is often portrayed to demonstrate a simple view of how chaos can develop out of iterated system behavior [8]. In the formula, x is a variable that describes one characteristic of a system. In population studies, for example, it might represent the number of members in the population. The letter "k" is often used in such formulas to represent some constant factor. A constant can be set at any value and represents an accepted behavior in the system. In the population study, it is used to represent a given rate of growth of the population. The letter "n" indicates the number of the iteration and therefore suggests the passage of time, as measures are taken. The calculation $(1 - x_n)$ acts to control the growth as shown in the equation.

In English, this equation might be explained as follows. The number of members in the population will vary depending on the effect of the rate of growth that is determined by the environment. That is, the status of the population system is dependent on the growth factor that is a function of the environment. The value of this information lies in the iterated picture it gives us of dynamic system behavior over time. Moreover, it gives us the ability to see what the population will do, if the effects of the environment "k" are changed. In fact, as we saw with the bifurcation diagram, at certain rates of growth, over one hundred or so iterations, the effect is to take the system into technically chaotic behavior.

Beyond the mathematical representation of formulas and their numbers, however, lies the capability to represent system activity in some topological form. As we have discussed, the strange attractor operates in phase space and may have a very complex path when mapped to a graph. The ability to solve nonlinear equations through many iterations has led to the equally useful ability to diagram these paths and to see, qualitatively, what the dynamics of the system look like. The key lies in an understanding of the variables in the system and an ability to measure those variables so that they can be plotted in phase space. The plot requires that all coordinates that describe the point be used to describe the point of the system in its phase space.

So, if we want to consider organizational system variables in this light, we would need a list of variables that describe the activity of the system. We would then get the value of each variable, and we would need enough values, or measures, to plot out the system behavior on a graph of its phase space. All of the values taken at a single point in time would represent a point on the plot. The number of variables that are used to describe its behavior accurately would determine the nature of the phase space in which such a system operates. Earlier, I showed a graphic representation of phase space (Figure 5-4, phase space, x,y,z dimensions) that described three dimensions, with an x plot, a y plot, and a z plot. More descriptors are possible, and the true nature of system behavior may require any number of values in order to establish its position in phase space.

The outcome of plotting many such points in phase space, from a dynamic system, is a topology that may be contorted and complex. The representation of multiple variables and the possibility that those variables may have wide ranges of possible values leads to a system portrait that reflects such change behavior. The key for us is that it does lead to a picture of changes in the system, as it is impacted by multiple variables and as those variables are considered together. It is a whole picture, and not a piecemeal approach to understanding the dynamics of the system. The phase portrait shown earlier (Figure 5-10, Lorenz attractor, as generated from sample program) represents a weather system but might as well represent any other kind of system with variables under the influence of some environmental constants. Where convection and density of the fluid in the atmosphere affect temperature and fluid motion, we could just as easily be considering organizational variables and constants.

The caution, of course, is that, as with any existing experimental methodology, the outcomes and findings will depend completely on the starting values and the accuracy with which changes were tracked. To try to model or simulate the behavior of a business, for instance, based on a set of initial conditions requires that the initial conditions be carefully, and not casually, measured. The need to integrate various equations representing activity of different variables adds complexity to the measurement process.

Priesmeyer [2] describes the application of nonlinear mathematics to organizational concerns. In applying this thinking to production and manufacturing, he puts forward the idea that:

> Chaos theory can be used to identify specific sources of instability or stabilizing effects by relating changes in input or changes in the production process to measures of subsequent output.

Using an image of a phase plane, a Cartesian coordinate system, similar to the one in Figure 13-6, Priesmeyer associates the horizontal axis with production volume and quality with the vertical axis.

If we were tracking production data and quality data using actual measurement points over time, the plot might go logically from lower left quadrant to upper right quadrant. We would expect that as production volume increases, quality would increase over time. What are tracked on the phase plane, however, are not time-based data points, but change data as measurements are taken periodically. It is the difference in behavior of the system from one point to the next and the calculation of multiple points that is of interest, when describing the phase portrait of a nonlinear dynamical system. If we find that the change measures maintain a point around the 0,0 midpoint on this graph, then the behavior of the system is steady and has a low sensi-

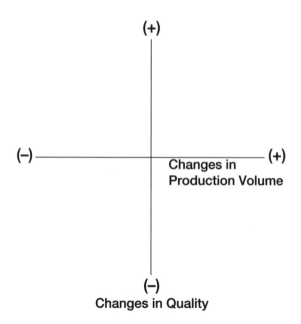

Figure 13-6. Production phase plane.

tivity to changes in conditions that might affect volume and quality. On the other hand, if we find a widely scattered set of points over the four quadrants, we would have a performance system that is highly sensitive and reacting to one or more changes in characteristics that affect the relationship between volume and quality. By connecting the dots of the measurement points plotted on such a graph, we will see the basin of attraction for the system represented in three dimensions, the x coordinate, the y coordinate, and time, represented by the distance between the dots.

In interpreting the graphical representation of the trajectory of the system in its phase space, the relative positioning of the basin of attraction in the four quadrants is a key to system behavior. For example, a set of changes that tends to be in Quadrant 1 (upper right) suggests a general relationship of high changes in production volume and high change in quality (Figure 13-7). By portraying the activity of the system in this way, the dynamic of the system behavior is reflected as the variability of the changes that have taken place in the relationships between production volume and quality, and not the actual metrics selected by the organization to represent either volume or quality.

To apply continuous improvement thinking to this view of a system might not produce the degree of change necessary to modify the behavior of the overall system. Incremental change might not be enough to keep pace with a chaotic system. That is, the attractor might change little. While the outward metrics may be different, unless attention is directed toward changing the *rate and degree of change,* there may be little impact in the system. The difference in viewpoints can have a major difference as we address organizational change. As Priesmeyer notes, inter-

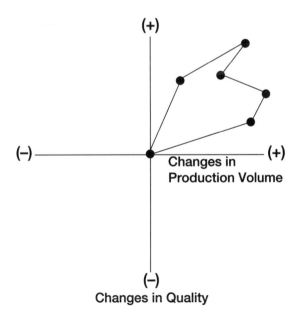

Figure 13-7. Production/quality basin.

ventions in such a system can be tracked using the phase portrait. Changes in system behavior because of an intervention in, say, a production characteristic will be immediately noted in the phase portrait of system behavioral changes. Statistically, it might take much longer to establish a number of meaningful observations to determine that the intervention has had the desired effect. Priesmeyer supports the value of this form of behavioral analysis by noting that "every process and any intervention in the production process are deterministically related to final production measures. To the extent that we can discover association between our activities and the finished products we gain a better control over the process."

In other studies, reported and summarized by Guastello [9], we can see a further elaboration of the value of topology as we consider the behavior of chaotic systems. In particular, some of the work has to do with organizational change and with education and training processes. Much of the work reported here relies on catastrophe models, which emerge from the definition of control parameters in a system. The data from the control parameters are change data and provide the basis for constructing models of nonlinear systems behavior. A control parameter, as Guastello explains,

> denotes an independent variable that has a particular function in the change process. In research, the investigator would identify one or more psychological measurements that would correspond to a particular function.

This independent variable might be affected by one or more research variables that would impact the status of the control parameter.

The topologies that are described include cuspoids, such as a fold, a cusp, a swallowtail, or a butterfly pattern. Each geometric pattern describes the trace of a system's behavior in phase space. A simple cusp is diagrammed in Figure 13-8.

The cusp will emerge as the description of system behavior when there is some form of transitional behavior between two stable states. It responds to two control parameters, asymmetry and bifurcation. The change from one state to another is

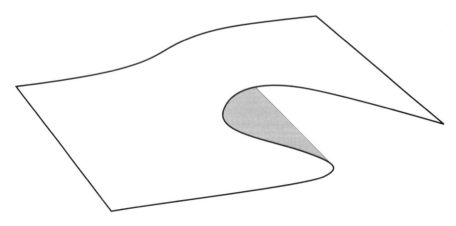

Figure 13-8. Simple cusp catastrophe model.

smooth, so long as the bifurcation parameter is small. In the figure, the change from one state of behavior to the other comes along the curve on the lower side of the diagram. This "cusp" represents a set of points at which the parameters of the system have changed enough so that the overall behavior of the system has changed. Mathematically, the challenge is to identify the values of the parameters that direct the change.

Besides this so-called cuspoid group of models, there is a second group of umbilic models including "wave crest," "hair," and "mushroom." These models form a set of basic classifications that are used to describe the activities of the system. The research that is ongoing in the application of chaos theory in the behavioral sciences and in organizational learning and behavior in particular relies on the interpretation of system behavior in relationship to these basic models and their underlying mathematics.

Guastello, for instance, relates an experiment with a group of students enrolled in introductory psychology. Performance measures included four exams, plus extra credit for student participation. Values that were a part of the calculations included standard deviations on the exam results and the number of exam points a student might be expected to get through random guessing on the exam. Two variables contributed to the "a" parameter in the equation: number of semesters of college in the study population and the completion of a statistics course prior to the introduction to psychology course. The second, "b," parameter consisted of gender differences. Since different versions of the course were available, course version was used as a "d" parameter. The findings suggested that the system behavior resembled the butterfly model, with significant influence from the version of the course. Gender difference was found to have strong potential for initiating bifurcation of results. This approach provided more detailed information about the behavior of the course and its outcomes for students than would have been available from traditional statistical measures alone.

In another instance, there is similar research on the evaluation of a training course. The results of the course were traditionally measured by a standardized test, based, in this instance, on supervisory practice. The study was conducted with data available over a five-year period, from a total of 136 students. In this research, investigators tested both cusp and butterfly models for their ability to reflect system behavior. In this case, the "a" control variable was the number of semesters of college experience; the "b" control was extrinsic motivation of students; "c" was made up of achievement, affiliation, and power motivation, derived through separate measures; and "d" considered a training group versus a control group. Researchers concluded that a nonlinear dynamical process was involved, as motivation and learning were integrated. They also demonstrated, among other things, that motivation to achieve was a factor that strongly influenced bifurcation in the system [9].

The mathematics that underlie this research are made up of a combination of traditional statistics, such as ANOVA, along with the data that contribute to the development of quadratic equations to describe system performance graphically. While researchers have made considerable headway in transferring mathematical need for precision into the realm of human systems, there is considerable work to be done before this is an easy exercise. The studies that have been conducted so far are largely constructed as carefully organized experiments. There are, as yet, no easy plug-in formulas for general use in organizational or human resource development work. Development of such easily accessible tools is in the future of systems performance improvement. The results to date, even though narrowly confined to experimental circumstances, are encouraging because they bring to light the confirmation of the approaches. Experiments confirm the value of application of calculus and other mathematical tools to understand the business side of an organization's operations, as well as the people side. The advantages that appear to lie in the future of this application of mathematics to system behavior include:

1. A clear distinction between the impression of chaotic behavior (classical chaos) and a technically chaotic system that will yield to measurement of its chaotic activity.
2. More insight into the ways in which system parameters affect the system behavior.
3. Increased possibility that, once identified, agents can manipulate control parameters and significant system variables in the system, in order to take deliberate advantage of chaos in the system.

The ultimate value of these forms of nonlinear measures is undeniable. We get data in a consolidated form that we have not been able to examine before. We begin to understand the operation of so-called soft measures [10], which, in most instances, can be quantified and are less soft than many believe. Directly to our purposes in learning and the support of learning, we establish ways to measure the effects of interventions on the variables in the system. The chief value of higher-level metrics, for the support of learning in a chaotic system, is the ability to view the qualitative effects of changes in the dynamics of the system. Learning and interventions constitute ways by which initial conditions are changed. Learning acts on system behavior, but we have not had clear ways to determine just how it might be impacting the system. Moreover, an attention to variables and their integration will help in the design activity itself. Design success is predicated on understanding not only the content but the environment into which the learning support or performance support mechanism will be introduced. The design process, long criticized for its clumsiness, yields to a closer analysis of the variables associated with design in any given set of circumstances [11].

The use of nonlinear measurements and integral calculus may seem a bit far-fetched, given the difficulties we now encounter in obtaining more familiar and traditional data on system behavior, learning, and system change. Yet, while current measurement tools are useful, they are unable to account for much that is happening in the system and are unable to provide us with the portrait we need of activity in a nonlinear dynamical system. The next step in measuring performance will take us to a means of measuring performance of all of the agents in the system, in such a way that we can see the dynamic paths followed by the system as it responds to change. Here, the role of the learner is to understand the ways in which a change in behavior can be used in the system to change the system. The role of the learning facilitator is to understand the ways in which interventions may affect the dynamics of the ever-moving system. Both of these roles can be enhanced through the use of appropriate nonlinear metrics.

There are important implications of these mathematical approaches to chaotic systems for the practitioners of OD, HRD, and HPT. Most significantly, where these roles have become involved in the use of traditional business measures, whether balanced scorecard or other forms, the toolkit must be expanded. Measurement skills for system behavior must now focus not only on superficial measures of system history but must incorporate pictures of system change characteristics. The integration of data means the use of mathematical tools that are unfamiliar to most people who are grounded in traditional business or educational math and statistics. The role of geometry increases. The need for integral calculus is evident. If we are to maximize the performance and energy of nonlinear dynamical systems, then these are the additional tools we will need for metrics and measurement, to go along with calculations of profit and loss, revenue and costs, costs and benefits, and ROI or other ratio-based expressions of performance.

REFERENCES

1. Stacey, R. D., *The Chaos Frontier: Creative Strategic Control for Business,* London: Butterworth Heinemann, 1991, pp. 181, 183, 202, 212.
2. Priesmeyer, H. R., *Organizations and Chaos: Defining the Methods of Nonlinear Management,* Westport, Conn.: Quorum Books, 1992, pp. 3, 135, 136, 153.
3. Shrock, S. A. and W. C. C. Coscarelli, *Criterion-Referenced Test Development: Technical and Legal Guidelines for Corporate Training,* New York: Addison-Wesley Publishing Company Inc., 1989.
4. Mager, R. F., *Measuring Instructional Results.* 2nd ed., Belmont, Calif.: David S. Lake Publishers, 1984.
5. Kirkpatrick, D. L., *Evaluating Training Programs,* San Francisco: Berrett-Koehler, 1994, pp. 52, 63ff.
6. Phillips, J. J., *Handbook of Training Evaluation and Measurement Methods,* 2nd ed, Houston: Gulf Publishing Company, 1991, p. 77.
7. Capra, F., *The Web of Life: A New Scientific Understanding of Living Systems,* New York: Doubleday, 1996, p. 124.
8. Pritchard, J., *The Chaos Cookbook,* 2nd ed., Oxford: Butterworth-Heinemann, 1996.
9. Guastello, S. J., *Chaos, Catastrophe, and Human Affairs,* Mahwah, N.J.: Lawrence Erlbaum Associates, 1995, pp. 34,158–159, 162–163, 263, 311.
10. Phillips, J. J., *Accountability in Human Resource Management,* Houston: Gulf Publishing Company, 1996.
11. Broadbent, B., "The training formula," *Training & Development,* October 1998, pp. 41–43.

Chapter 14

Chaotic Performance

A FREE SYSTEM

As the new order is secured in chaotic organizational systems, performance enhancement will replace current concepts of performance management and consulting. Self-organizing systems leave little to manage. They are self-managing. The focus, instead, is on ensuring that energy is maintained to the attractor for the system and that it is not overcome with bureaucracy and nuclear management. The focus is on the underlying pattern and not the details of the system's day-to-day trace. We will be interested in sustaining energy in systems that are diverse and volatile. Because many such systems will be virtual, the enhancers will help ensure high levels of interaction among the nodes or agents of the networks. Where these networks may have far-flung nodes with tentative connections, the enhancer will have the challenge of sustaining a balance between this tentative nature of the chaotic system and its tendency to stabilize. The role of performance enhancement is, therefore, a part of the makeup of the strange attractor, influencing the basic pattern underlying the chaotic system.

The successful support of a chaotic system lies in a minimalist and open approach. Such a system does not require a nuclear skeleton in order to succeed. The performance of such a system will depend, instead, on its ability to trade energies with other such systems and to connect with overall systems in such a way that the connected systems can succeed. The organization is not boundaryless since the attractive force is in place. It is not closely bounded because a chaotic system, by definition, is dynamic, allowing wide behavior scales and swings in the values of its parameters.

Success in a chaotic system may not be the same as success in more traditional systems that display periodic or quasiperiodic behavior. Success is not built on a fixed standard. The standards for performance in a chaotic organizational system lie in its ability to change, not in its ability to maintain consistency and predictability. The predictability lies in an understanding of the attractor, but because it is a strange attractor, its shape and influences will be complex.

If external controllers (managers or performance consultants) change the basic nature of the strange attractor, then it is possible that the system could become random or, at the other end of the scale, overly tight and hierarchical. Rarely will managers take a system toward irrational randomness; the opposite tendency is most often observable. We know how to create rigid and nuclear organizational structures and tend to fall back to that position in times of crisis. We choose, when faced with uncertainty, to take what we can carry with us and retreat to the cave, where the walls are solid, our backs are protected, and we only have to defend one opening to the outside world.

It is this natural fear of uncertainty that leaders and performance consultants must overcome. They must overcome it in their own nature before they can support and lead organizations that are capable of sustained uncertainty. To overcontrol the strange attractor underneath a chaotic organization is to retreat to the cave and eliminate the complexity of the attractive force. We are then left with an attractor that is more stable and more predictable. In the cave, we can hold our own, but we cannot explore new territories. Survival is not enough, and maintenance of stable systems is not enough. Nor is it enough to venture occasionally into the wilderness with a foraging party. The occasional emphasis on R&D or on new organizational ideas or new services is not enough. Organizations are willing enough to take conservative risks but are rarely brave enough to support truly chaotic activity. It is, however, such bravery that is needed if the full potential of chaotic organizational systems is to be realized.

The cave lets us pretend that there is a place where we can exist and avoid change, but we cannot remain in the cave. Regardless of the type of organizational system with which we work, resistance to change is not an option. The alternative for change leaders is to use change to the advantage of the system. This does not mean using change as a vehicle for moving from one cave to the next. It means that change leaders and organizational managers will become performance enhancers. They will be able to assess the basic nature of chaotic systems, identify the parameters and variables, and use tools and interventions that sustain chaos. They will enhance performance to a point at which it goes beyond creative tension and beyond superficial order.

The roles of managers and organizational change leaders should now focus on:

1. *Understanding the complexity of the networks that exist and interact.* Leaders should develop new measures that comprehend chaotic system behavior. In particular, they should understand the nature of the attractive force in the organization and explore the extent to which the shape of the attractor can be measured and understood. This will lead to greater understanding of the dynamics of the system and to greater understanding of the variables and parameters that are influencing the operation of the system. Take nothing for granted in a chaotic system. What seems minor may have significant impact on the activity of the system, and may drain energies.

2. *Investigating new technologies, both electronic and biological, as they integrate with the humans and their social system.* It is time to give up the homocentric view of the organization. We can now see that non-human agents will be as important as the human agents to the success of the enterprise. As we transfer intellective skill from humans to machines, we go beyond the simple engineering of the past. We once transferred our human physical capabilities to levers and pulleys and mechanical parts. We then transferred our routine cognitive tasks to computers. Now we are transferring decision-making and more advanced intellectual capabilities to computing machines. We will next use cloned organic instruments to do those things that machine-based computers cannot. These technologies will redefine systems and redefine learning activity and behavior across the nodes in the system.

3. *Connecting with external environments and co-evolving systems.* We are at a point where we know how to develop a rich supply chain in an organization. We need to extend that capability so that we can establish supply chains that understand their nature to be chaotic, not stable. Often, the nature of the supply chain itself will generate instability that can be used by an alert system. The supply chain may consist of a number of variables, and those variables may alter themselves or be altered in many ways. There is the potential for high degrees of freedom in the chain. This freedom, however, is not guaranteed. It is possible for one or more agents to over-control the system. For example, a manufacturing organization that over-defines its acceptance criteria for parts may restrict the creativity in the part-supplying link. This may stifle innovative input from that supplier, which may be alternatively realized through the supplier's relationship with another manufacturer. A control point for this system lies in the rules established by the manufacturing engineers and purchasing groups. These groups can either sustain freedom, creativity, and energy in the system or push it toward stability and entropy.

4. *Allowing chaotic behavior and encouraging it.* Only in this way will an organization maximize its energy and reach beyond survival through evolution. We will need to support chaotic behavior with chaotic learning. Chaotic learning will support all agents in the system and will help those agents behave in chaotic ways. The desired behavior is exploratory and creative. Chaotic learning avoids strict patterns and rules for behavior. It springs from a recognition of multiple possible futures for the system. Chaotic learning is the exploration of these multiple possible futures in a highly volatile what-if atmosphere.

5. *Unlearning.* Develop unlearning capabilities throughout the web. While this may at first glance seem to be simple, it is not so simple in practice. We are often influenced not only by our intrapersonal reflections on what has worked for us in the past, but by the echoes of tradition and history, which bounce through the network from agent to agent. Such echoes may serve to reinforce traditional ways of thinking and doing and therefore block our individual and collective ability to stand back and reassess what we know and what we want to know. Concepts, models, theories, and constructs are all good things to have, but many of us have learned them too well. Once memorized, these architectures become settled into our long-term memories, and we lose some of the circumstantial validation for the models. In these models lies safety and security, and what passes for efficiency. It is more efficient to follow history and the models we have learned and used than to reconstitute those models and their basic functionality. That might mean that we would have to rethink the models themselves, and there is little time in most organizational or personal schedules for that. Yet, mold-breaking and unlearning can serve to open the way for chaotic behavior that could have advantages as we redesign our organizations toward the fitness landscape.

SECURING THE NEW ORDER

My purpose in this book has been to explore some of the connotations of nonlinear dynamical systems theory and to suggest some ways in which this theory may apply to learning and efforts to support learning. In achieving this end, I have reviewed the basic nature of systems as we understand them today, the concepts of chaos that are the basis for our thinking, and some of the things that we know about learners and ways to help them learn. Here, I want to pull together some key messages that I have assembled across the foregoing ocean of prose.

1. We have research and thinking that is taking chaos theory and nonlinear dynamical systems theory into practical applications. The physical sciences have led the way in clarifying ways to view the order that underlies apparently random system events. Organizational studies have followed, with some initial experimentation to see if the approaches that work in the physical world can be applied in the world of networked organizations. Evidence is strong that organizational analysis can benefit from efforts to discover the order underlying what we have assumed is random activity.

2. We see the realization of quantum theory outside of science and its implications for ways in which humans and organizations operate. The idea that variance is not only acceptable but to be expected is an important facet in helping us to give up traditional views of rightness and wrongness. Our sense of stability relies, now, on our understanding that there may be multiple futures, depending on the set of facts with which we begin. Quantum theory has helped us to open systems on the basis that they may have no predestined future. It is this nonlinear view that suggests changes in the ways in which we measure system performance, and changes in the way we support futures that may be uncertain. What we are trying to reconcile is the point and purpose of acquiring knowledge in such fast-changing and radically morphing systems.

3. Organization development theory has moved well beyond the idea of a stable state. Presented as a defining architecture for organizational change, the nature of OD has always tended to support theories of change. This means that it is well-positioned to take advantage of chaotic methods and tools.

4. Organization development, in practice, has not always achieved the openness of OD theory. At the level of practice, in fact, OD change efforts often try to substitute one form of stability for another. In many circumstances, this is caused by the attitudes and approaches used at the outset of the change initiative. If the focus is on redrawing organizational charts in much the same way that they were drawn before, we will get small changes. If the focus is on analyzing details of process flow and redrawing process flow diagrams for the system to follow, small changes will result. So, while OD theory might suggest that many things are possible in change efforts, the reality is rarely so open or experimental. The intent, all too often, is simply to fix a new, highly defined process in place.

5. Learning theories accommodate open and virtual organizations, and open approaches to learning. As theorists accept the role of dialectics in shaping learning and subsequent behavior, they have proposed the inclusion of dialectical thinking in learning theories. Furthermore, cognitive and humanistic theories clearly recognize the role of learner control. For learners, learning is quantum. It may take many forms in order to meet many purposes, and there may not be clear cause-effect routes that can be traced from learning to performance. As participants in organizational networks, humans prepare themselves to participate and contribute in several ways and to develop learning strategies that go well beyond formal, fixed scholastic models.

6. Learners still tend to seek stability, often forming their learning strategies on existing school models. This idea, of course, introduces a paradox between learning theory and learning practice. While learning theory says that people learn in many ways in many times and pick learning topics selectively, learning practice suggests otherwise. In fact, much learning does go on outside of formal settings or structures, but learners tend to look for stability not uncertainty. What we learn, we believe, should have value, and that value is often time-based. How long facts and process knowledge will last we cannot say, and this is uncomfortable. What we carry forward from our formal educational experience is a sense that there are right and wrong answers, if we could only learn them. As learners, we want to invest our time and energy in learning things that will help us individually or help our organizations. Yet, for open and virtual organizational webs, such learning may be too fixed and factual to be of use tomorrow or the next day. Learners must adopt different attitudes and strategies for learning in complex or chaotic systems.

7. Learning support models remain locked in ISD tradition. The development of learning support in a straight-line fashion does not work particularly well, but we have failed to develop a nonlinear process. Our learning support activity, therefore, is often criticized because it is complicated, doesn't deliver on time, or delivers low-quality learning support products or services. Efforts to change this have generally focused on eliminating steps in the process in order to simplify or expedite product delivery. Such an approach, however, suggests logically that the missing steps probably aren't worth having in the process to begin with. In fact, an ISD-based process will satisfy needs neither of a complex adaptive system nor of a chaotic system. Learning support development processes must match the volatility of the system network and must produce products and services that will complement that volatility.

8. Learning support remains largely dedicated to a school model, especially the local classroom. The local classroom is one that is inhabited, physically, by a teacher and students and that relies solely on resources within the four walls of the classroom. It is this traditional model toward which most learning support design tends. There are some widely held views on how such products should be assembled, what they should contain, and how it should be presented. While such guidelines may be helpful, they also tend to structure the thinking of designers. In this regard, designers may depend more than they should on

formulas for design, rather than deriving the design and the design process from the system itself. Formulaic design, while it appears to offer advantages of efficiency, may not represent accurately the dynamics of the supported system. In particular, any design that assumes that an open or virtual system can be supported through traditional classroom delivery should be revisited.

9. Organizational life, we have noted, is homocentric. This view of organizations influences the ways in which organizations are organized, as well as the ways in which organizational learning is supported and carried out. Therefore, if we see humans as the only piece of the organization with any intelligence, we will miss the incremental knowledge and even the basic forms of intelligence that are beginning to appear in other system agents. If we overlook this nascent intellect, we will misdirect system organization efforts to ignore these alternative agents. We will not have a whole system unless non-human agents are included in organizational development and learning support.

10. With the realization that we operate in complex adaptive systems (CAS) and chaotic systems comes the reality that learning and learning support must be oriented to the strange attractor. Where we have treated superficial processes and procedures and factual information, we are now challenged to deal with underlying parameters that we may not be as familiar with. We now must look for the order that underlies the organizational system. It is no longer good enough to write off instability as something that is wrong and that must be overcome. It is no longer enough to begin our learning or learning support projects with the assumption that we are learning things that will be secure over time or in all circumstances. We simply cannot assume the continuity of facts or circumstances. We must now focus on variables and ranges of potential behavior as topics to be addressed in learning. We will learn to learn and to develop learning support in an environment of instability, and not in an atmosphere of certainty.

Taken as a whole, these ideas form what I believe is a basis for revisiting the ways in which learning and learning support occur in chaotic systems. The new order is constituted not only of our new activities in open and virtual systems, but also in our ways of learning. The realization of the new order, evident on both local and global scales, is evident to us every day. Along with this new order in systems thinking comes the need to establish a new order in learning.

Changes in learning and the support of learning are needed in order to match systems that are much more sensitive and volatile and complex than once believed. Ours is not a role calling for management to existing norms, or training or educating to existing norms. We have a role, instead, to lead change in the ways in which we relate to agents in systems, and changes in the ways in which learning is integrated into complex systems.

We are not simply seeking compliance with known facts or processes or models. We are seeking revolution in the analysis, design, delivery, and evaluation of change interventions. The new order is defined as change, and to secure it, we must work to ensure that learning and organizational interventions complement the volatile networks within which we organize.

CONCLUSION

Whether we are managing in a time of change, or a time of uncertainty, or a time of revolution, or a time of chaos, we are leading organizations that have an increasing need to interoperate, exchange information, and make changes to adjust to their situations. Leading organizations has never been easy, but it was easier when direction and control were revered and a parent-child relationship between leader and subordinates was understood. We are coming to an end of the time when this understanding of organization is sufficient or warranted.

We have a stronger sense now than before that things are more chaotic. Beginning with this sense of classical chaos, we are beginning to come to terms with change and uncertainty in organizational behavior. To do this, we must (1) understand the nature of chaotic organizations; and (2) understand the nature of learning in chaotic organizations. It is only through learning that chaotic organizations can understand how they function chaotically. This understanding will yield a comprehension of the attractive forces at work and of the variables and parameters that influence the behavior of those attractive forces. The essence of a chaotic organization lies as much in the nature of the strange attractor as in its actual events and histories. For those concerned with learning in chaos, then, the first search should be directed toward the organization's system.

With our understanding of the chaotic operation of the system, we can understand the nature of learning and learning support. Both must be attuned to the chaotic behavior of the system and must complement it. Learning cannot be overly concentrated on the here and now since a dynamic system does not tolerate the here and now. What is here and now is merely history in the making. Today's point in phase space will not be the same point tomorrow. When we go home from work or school and come back the next morning, things have changed. We know this instinctively and experience it in every organizational setting. It is not toward stable knowledge that an agent's attention should be directed, but toward ways to capture and use unstable knowledge. The learner should be focused on capability in the larger sense of comprehending the integration of a role in a mix of overlapping subsystems.

Equally, learning support should not be planned, executed, or evaluated as if it were a stable force. If it truly reflects learning in a chaotic system, it too will be chaotic. It will not only support organizational change; it will *be* organizational change. The challenge is to make this happen in such a way that learning, regardless of whether it is formal or informal, is made as effective as possible at any given point in phase space. The system will not stop and wait for learners to catch up, nor for learning tools to be put in place. Learning and performance support that is attuned to filling gaps is already historical and therefore out of place in a chaotic system. Learning support must reflect the nature of the chaotic system that it is designed to support and must be an integral part of that system. It is a parameter to be measured in understanding the whole system.

Once we understand that organizational learning is far more complex than simply integrating traditional learning into stable organizational systems, then it becomes more clear that new approaches to leadership and performance consulting are necessary. The idea of the performance consultant role has been derived from the past history of business consulting and attempts to integrate the complete organizational presence, including structure, human resources, politics, and symbols. Neither that role nor other leadership roles as currently defined are adequate to build or support chaotic organizations. Again, the natural tendency that underlies more management missions is to restore order and maintain control. Drivers for this can be identified in stock markets, which reward order and control and predictability, and stakeholders internal to the organization who depend on predictable salaries and bonuses. The reward systems are a predominant factor in nuclear leadership, and the performance consultants dance to the same tune. The nature of the performance consulting role (or performance technology) is to satisfy the needs of the system, as those needs are defined through a stable interpretation of the system. That is, given a set of standards and expectations, the performance consultant can test the system for conformity and compliance and can recommend ways in which the system can be made to comply with standards. That interpretation of the role, all too common today, is a further drag on system energies and a nail in the coffin of creativity. Such roles, along with traditional leadership and management roles, should be dismissed in a chaotic organization. These roles conflict with self-generation and introduce entropy. They slow the system in their efforts to control it. Such roles make changes in the direction of stability and standardization, which are contrary to the elemental nature of the strange attractor. In traditional roles, leaders do not have the time or want to spend the effort to understand that attractive force and what it means for the variables in the system. In fact, they are highly selective about the variables they choose to change and rarely understand the holistic impact on the system of the changes they do make.

Finally, then, the success of organizations depends on leaders who are willing to question their stability and to encourage instability and uncertainty. The success of learning in chaotic organizations depends on learners who are willing to understand more than facts and local applications. The success of learning support in chaotic organizations depends on the flexibility of the support and its focus beyond the human agents to include other agents. It depends on learning support that makes informal learning highly successful. It depends on learning that is widely available and not geographically restricted. This, in turn, will ensure that learning is complementary to the chaotic systems it supports and is a part of. Learning in chaos is not a simple matter, but its mastery will take us beyond our current static and stable learning strategies and toward strategies and methods that are much more fluid, dynamic, and energetic. Such learning will help us adopt new forms of organization, such as open and virtual organization, and will support chaotic systems as they maintain coherence, attraction, and order in the apparent disorder of their operating environments.

Index